19-50
nett

THE LAW OF THE COUNTRYSIDE
THE RIGHTS OF THE PUBLIC

by

Tim Bonyhady

PROFESSIONAL BOOKS
MILTON PARK ESTATE, ABINGDON.

Published in 1987 by
Professional Books Limited
Milton Park Estate, Abingdon, Oxon.

Typeset by Fleetlines Southend-on-Sea
Printed and bound in Great Britain by
Mackays of Chatham Ltd, Chatham, Kent

ISBN

0 86205 2564 Hardback
0 86205 2572 Paperback

PROFESSIONAL BOOKS 1987

To Kevin Gray and Paul Finn

TABLE OF CONTENTS

TABLE OF STATUTES

TABLE OF CASES

ABBREVIATIONS

Bl. Comm.	William Blackstone, *Commentaries on the Laws of England*, Oxford, Clarendon Press, 1765, 4 vols
Bracton	*Bracton on the Laws and Customs of England*, (translated, with revisions and notes, by Samuel E. Thorne), Cambridge, Massachusetts, Belknap Press, 1968–77, 4 vols
Buckland	W. W. Buckland, *A Text-book of Roman Law from Augustus to Justinian*, 3rd ed. (Peter Stein), Cambridge, Cambridge University Press, 1963
Clayden & Trevelyan	Paul Clayden & John Trevelyan, *Rights of Way: a Guide to the Law and Practice*, Commons, Open Spaces and Footpaths Preservation Society/Ramblers' Association, 1983
Co. Litt.	*Coke upon Littleton*, 18th ed. (with notes by F. Hargrave & C. Butler), London, Clarke, 1823, 2 vols
D.A.R.T., *Green Lanes*	Dartington Amenity Research Trust, *Green Lanes: a Report to the Countryside Commission*, 1979
D.A.R.T., *Rights of Way*	Dartington Amenity Research Trust, *Modification of Rights of Way: a Report for the Countryside Commission*, 1977
Dower	John Dower, *National Parks in England and Wales*, (Cmnd. 6628, 1945)
Gosling	Ministry of Housing and Local Government, *Report of the Footpaths Committee*, London, H.M.S.O., 1968
Hale	Sir Matthew Hale, *De Jure Maris*, in Francis Hargrave (ed.), *A Collection of Tracts relative to the Law of England from Manuscripts*, London, 1787
Hall	Robert Gream Hall, *The Rights of the Crown and the Privileges of the Subject in the Seashores of the Realm*, London, 1830
Halsbury	*Halsbury's Laws of England*, 4th ed.
Harris and Ryan	Bryan Harris & Gerard Ryan, *An Outline of the Law relating to Common Land*, London, Sweet & Maxwell, 1967

Hobhouse	Ministry of Town and Country Planning, *Footpaths and Access to the Countryside: Report of the Special Committee (England and Wales)*, (Chairman: Sir Arthur Hobhouse), Cmd. 7207, 1947
Holdsworth	Sir W. S. Holdsworth, *A History of English Law*, London, Methuen, 1903–52, 16 vols, latest editions as in 61 L.Q.R. 346 (1945); also vol 1, 7th ed., 1965; vol. 13, 1952; vol. 14, 1964; vol, 15, 1965; vol. 16, 1966
Megarry & Wade	Sir Robert Megarry & H. W. R. Wade, *The Law of Real Property*, 5th ed., London, Stevens, 1984
Moore, *Fisheries*	Stuart A. & Hubert Stuart Moore, *The History and Law of Fisheries*, London, Steven & Haynes, 1903
Moore, *Foreshore*	Stuart A. Moore, *A History of the Foreshore and the Law relating thereto*, London, Steven & Haynes, 1888
North	P. M. North, *The Modern Law of Liability for Animals*, London, Butterworth, 1972
Pratt and Mackenzie	*Pratt and Mackenzie's Law of Highways*, 21st ed., London, Butterworths, 1967
Smith	J. C. Smith, *The Law of Theft*, 5th ed., London, Butterworths, 1984
S.S.	Selden Society
Telling & Foster	A. E. Telling & Sheila E. Foster, *The Public Right of Navigation*, Severn-Trent Water Authority, 1977, 2 vols.
Thomas, *Institutes*	J. A. C. Thomas, *The Institutes of Justinian: Text, Translation and Commentary*, Cape Town, Juta, 1975
Thomas, *Textbook*	J. A. C. Thomas, *Textbook of Roman Law*, Amsterdam, North-Holland, 1976
Vaines	*Crossley Vaines' Personal Property*, 5th ed., London, Butterworths, 1973
Wade	H. W. R. Wade, *Administrative Law*, 5th ed., Oxford, Clarendon Press, 1982
Webb	Sidney & Beatrice Webb, *The Story of the King's Highway*, London, Longmans, Green, 1913
Wellbeloved	Robert Wellbeloved, *A Treatise on the Law relating to Highways*, London, Brooke, 1829
Williams, *Liability*	Glanville Williams, *Liability for Animals*, Cambridge, Cambridge University Press, 1939
Woolwych, *Waters*	Humphrey W. Woolwych, *A Treatise on the Law of Waters and of Sewers*, London, Saunders & Benny, 1830

Woolwych, *Ways*   Humphrey W. Woolwych, *A Treatise on the Law of Ways*, London, Saunders & Benny, 1829

ACKNOWLEDGEMENTS

This book began as a Ph.D. thesis submitted to the University of Cambridge in 1985. While working on the thesis, I was fortunate to have been supported first by Shell Australia, which awarded me a scholarship to go to Cambridge, and then by the Faculty of Law of McGill University, Montreal, which gave me a Boulton Fellowship to complete my dissertation. I was also fortunate to have the guidance of, in effect, four supervisors: Kevin Gray and David Williams in Cambridge, and Michael Bridge and William Foster in Montreal.

In revising the thesis, I have received great assistance and encouragement from Ross Cranston, now of Queen Mary's College, London, and Paul Finn and Sam Stoljar at the Australian National University, Canberra.

As ever, Claire Young has been wonderful.

Tim Bonyhady
Australian National University, Canberra
June 1987

INTRODUCTION

When considering their rights as individuals, people ordinarily think of their "fundamental freedoms" or civil liberties – freedom of expression, freedom of religion and so on. They rarely consider questions of land law or issues involving the environment. Yet all members of the public, whether or not they are landholders, have certain rights to enjoy the countryside. This book examines the evolution and current state of these rights.

The book begins by asking why members of the public today have only limited rights in the countryside. It shows that in medieval England members of the public enjoyed many more rights; that for a variety or reasons, these rights were significantly reduced by the courts until about the end of the nineteenth century; that since then, in order both to expand and to legalize the public's opportunities for recreation in the countryside, Parliament has slowly increased the public's rights.

The greater part of the book provides a detailed account of the law governing public access to and taking from the countryside. It defines the public's rights of access and taking, such as the right of passage on footpaths and bridleways, the right to ramble over certain common land, and the right to navigate and to fish over the foreshore. In addition, it examines the law governing unlawful access and taking in order to indicate the consequences for members of the public of acting beyond the bounds of their enforceable rights. In particular it shows that the public enjoys a number of *de facto* rights in the countryside because Parliament and the courts have refused to assist landowners seeking to prevent certain interferences with their property.

This book is, then, intended to serve three purposes. It seeks to explain the development of an area of law generally ignored by historians. It seeks to provide lawyers with a detailed statement of current law, much of which has otherwise gone unexamined. At the same time it is intended for any member of the public – whether rambler, fisherman, treasure hunter or landowner – who wishes to find out about those rights which everyone has in the countryside.

PART ONE

THE INDIVIDUAL AND THE COUNTRYSIDE

It may seem strange that in England, the land where above all others the personal and political rights of the simplest freeman have been saved whole through all changes of princes and dynasties, the law should find so little room for public and unstinted rights of using the very elements. Even the air is not free . . .[1]

In *The Land Laws* (1883), one of a remarkable series of books concerned with "The English Citizen: his Rights and Responsibilities", Sir Frederick Pollock alerted his audience to the very limited rights which members of the public enjoy in the countryside. To Pollock, one of the great writers on English law, this question of public rights was of considerable personal importance. Pollock was a keen climber and rambler, a believer in the nexus between a healthy body and healthy mind, and a member of both the Commons and Footpaths Preservation Society and the Sunday Tramps, one of the earliest walking clubs set up around London.[2] The issue of public rights was also highly topical at the time Pollock wrote because of increasing conflict between the urban population and rural landowners over public enjoyment of the countryside. While landowners, particularly in the Peak District, attempted to exclude the public from their land, organizations such as the Commons and Footpaths Preservation Society sought to preserve common land as public open spaces and protect public rights of way as an avenue for recreational access to the countryside. For these urban campaigners, the problem was that public rights in the countryside were few and frequently vulnerable in practice as well as at law. It is this parsimonious stance of the common law that Pollock sought to explain: why had the common law been so ungenerous when giving members of the public rights in the countryside?

Pollock's answer was that the common law did not recognize extensive public rights because, so far as England was concerned, "history tells us that the conception of rights common to all the public is a modern one".[3] He recognized that rights common to all citizens had been part of Roman law, but suggested that the concept of such rights had been lost with the decline and fall of the Empire, and that "far into the Middle Ages law was for many purposes not general, or territorial, but personal".[4] Even in medieval England, "a man's rights were still for the most part his rights, not simply as an Englishman, but as a member of some particular class and community".[5] In this period, there was also no need for public rights because Englishmen, as members of their local community, had substantial customary rights of access and taking over certain pieces of land in their neighbourhood such as village greens. They also had rights of common which allowed them to graze animals, cut turf, gather wood and fish on land owned by the lord of the manor. Together these rights provided for the medieval Englishmen's "wants both of use and of recreation. People did not then travel for their pleasure, or make recreation a study. The legal theory which denied the possibility of public rights over land was [therefore] only the formal expression of the dispositions and habits of society."[6]

Pollock also explained that, perhaps surprisingly, the state of the common law was no cause for dismay as, in practice, members of the public had access to almost all unenclosed, uncultivated land in England. Landowners had no reason to exclude the public and would have found it difficult to do so, since "Against a trespasser not in pursuit of game the only remedy is a civil action, and no jury would give substantial damages, nor any judge give costs, against a trespasser on a wild moor or down who had neither molested the owner, disputed his title, nor injured his property."[7] Members of the public therefore enjoyed large *de facto* rights in the countryside because in many respects their recreation, while strictly unlawful, could not be the subject of effective actions in court. These *de facto* rights were, in Pollock's view, "an example of a principle that runs through the whole administration of law, and in English law is very conspicuous". Just as "for many things of great importance, including all the modern developments of the British Constitution, we are content to rely on understandings rather than positive law", so

It is impossible so to limit the rights of owners that they cannot sometimes be harshly and vexatiously used. But it is possible to have things so ordered that the extreme use of a man's legal rights which would be intolerable to his neighbours shall also give to himself so much trouble as will deter most men from attempting it. This is accomplished in England partly by an active public opinion, partly by the wide discretion entrusted to judges and juries.[8]

Finally, Pollock noted that Parliament had recently begun to legislate in relation to public rights, enacting statutes which dedicated certain areas of land to public use. Pollock recognized that if the public's *de facto* rights proved inadequate, the day might come "when express law has to take the place of these informal understandings". He acknowledged that "It is useless to deprecate changes of this kind in the face of need". However, he hoped that such change would not occur. He thought there would "always be a sort of people, often the best sort, who regret the old easy-going ways".[9]

A century later, with vastly increased pressure on the countryside as a recreation ground, Pollock's account of the public's rights in the countryside remains broadly accurate. At common law there are still only few public rights in the countryside; these are ameliorated by the public's *de facto* rights; they are also supplemented by a number of express rights which have gradually been conferred by Parliament. Pollock's explanation of how the law has evolved appears, however, largely incorrect. Far from having had very limited public rights in the countryside, as Pollock suggested, medieval Englishmen enjoyed substantial public rights which the courts have significantly cut down over the following centuries. Largely because of this judicial reduction of their rights, members of the public have been forced to rely on *de facto* rights which in fact have also been cut down (though principally by Parliament). The rights which Parliament has expressly conferred over the last century are simply some compensation for what the public has otherwise lost.

To trace this evolution (or decline), one must begin with Roman law which forms the basis of the rights in the countryside which members of the public enjoy at common law. While in earlier periods the Romans employed a relatively simple classification of public rights,[10] according to the classical Roman law of Justinian's *Institutes* (553) there were three different categories of property which were subject to public rights. Air, running water, the sea and the seashore were regarded as incapable of ownership but open to public use.[11] Highways, rivers, river banks and harbours were owned by the

State but were also open to public use.[12] Fish, wild animals and birds (regardless of whether they were on someone else's land),[13] inanimate objects such as pebbles from the seashore,[14] and things abandoned by their owner,[15] were treated as ownerless until someone reduced them into possession.

This Roman law appears to have come to England during one of two periods. Some variant of it may have been transplanted while England was a Roman province between the first and fourth centuries. However, if it did so, its influence probably soon faded following the departure of the legions and the Germanic invasions of the fifth and sixth centuries.[16] More likely, this Roman law was adopted in about the twelfth century when a centralized legal system emerged in England. Although this system developed largely without reference to Roman law – hence the distinctiveness of the common law[17] – a number of areas of English land law were based primarily on Roman principles,[18] which contemporaneously were being revived as a subject of study on the continent.

The Roman basis of the public's rights in the countryside is clearest in Henry de Bracton's famous treatise *On the Laws and Customs of England*, which was probably completed about 1256-7. Although this treatise has sometimes been characterized as a bastardization of Roman learning (rather than an accurate statement of English law),[19] it now seems clear that Bracton "was a trained jurist with the principles and distinctions of Roman jurisprudence firmly in mind, using them throughout his work, wherever they could be used to rationalize and reduce to order the results reached in the English courts."[20] This modern appreciation of Bracton clearly holds in relation to the countryside, where Bracton described the public as having substantial rights, much as under Roman law,[21] but also recognized the significance of the rights of the English Crown. Thus, he followed Justinian's *Institutes* in stating that the sea and seashore were of common use[22] but he omitted the passage from the *Institutes* which described the seashore as owned by no-one[23] – a passage which clearly would have been inconsistent with the English doctrine that all land has an "owner".[24] Equally, he recognized that the Crown's "revenue" prerogatives over wild animals, royal fish, treasure trove and wreck meant that members of the public could not acquire ownership of these things by taking possession of them.[25]

Bracton's account of the public's rights consequently appears as a broadly accurate – if sometimes speculative – statement of the law at the time he was writing. The only respect in which he clearly exaggerated the public's rights was in describing the public right of fishing as extending over all perennial waters,[26] when there was probably no such right in relation to non-tidal waters and most tidal waters.[27] Bracton understated the public's rights in describing all wild animals as the property of the Crown.[28] In fact, in the thirteenth century members of the public were entitled to ownership of wild animals they captured so long as they were outside the "privileged" areas of forests, chases, parks and free warrens.[29]

From this substantial base, the courts over the following six hundred years greatly reduced the public's rights of access to and taking from the countryside. This judicial reduction of public rights to a certain extent parallels the well-known story of the Inclosure Acts, passed mainly between 1760 and 1845, which extinguished rights of common and converted common land into freehold. It also parallels the decisions by the courts that the poor did not have a general right of gleaning[30] and that local inhabitants could not have customary rights of taking in their neighbourhood.[31] In all four cases landowners benefited from the changes in the law. However, there are significant differences between the Parliamentary attack on rights of common on the one hand and the judicial decisions against public rights and local customary rights on the other. While inclosure was greeted grudgingly if not with hostility by the great bulk of the population,[32] it now appears that the legislation did not involve a ruthless expropriation of the property rights of the poor, as was once accepted.[33] Rather the Acts in general resulted in considerable respect for the property rights of the commoners and the payment of fair compensation.[34] By way of contrast, the judiciary effectively engaged in expropriation of public rights and customary rights of taking by denying their existence. In doing so, the courts failed to apply the laws of property equally to rich and poor.[35]

The judicial reduction of rights of access to the countryside is clearest in relation to areas abutting water. First, in *Ball* v. *Herbert* (1789),[36] the King's Bench Division held unanimously that there was no general public right to use river banks for purposes connected with navigation. Then in *Blundell* v. *Catterall* (1821),[37] the court by majority took a very narrow view of the public's rights over the foreshore – that is the area technically defined as bordered by the mean high and low water marks.[38] The majority rejected the plaintiff's claims that there was a public right of way over all the foreshore when dry;

that members of the public had a right to bathe in the sea; and that in order to exercise that right members of the public were entitled to cross the foreshore to reach the sea and could also remain on the foreshore for a reasonable time. Instead, they suggested that the public's rights over the foreshore might be restricted to a right of navigation and, prima facie, a right to fish.

Beginning in the eighteenth century, the courts also took a very narrow view of the circumstances in which footpaths, bridleways and carriageways could be created.[39] Whereas these public rights of way were, as a matter of fact, frequently a result of long unchallenged use by members of the public, the courts held that to exist as a matter of law the right of way must have been "dedicated" to the public by the relevant landowner. In many cases, this emphasis on the landowner as the source of the public's rights made it difficult, if not impossible, to establish rights of way. Regardless of the form of ownership of the land, there was no fixed period of public use of a path after which existence of a right of way was necessarily presumed. Over the great tracts of rural England subject to "family settlements", many judges held that no rights of way could be created as each landholder during the settlement was only a limited owner and hence lacked capacity to dedicate rights to the public.[40]

The judicial reduction in rights of access even extended, though with a distinctive twist, to the public's right to hunt wild animals across different parcels of land without committing trespass. This issue had some general significance, but principally arose in relation to hunts which began lawfully on land under one ownership and then went on to adjoining properties in pursuit of their quarry. Until the eighteenth century hunting on horses with hounds was mainly the preserve of royalty and the aristocracy,[41] and the courts favoured them in their conflicts with other landowners by holding that "hot pursuit" on to adjoining land did not involve trespass.[42] However, by the early nineteenth century even modest squires, rich tenant farmers, and city and country town lawyers, merchants and shopkeepers were turning to foxhunting.[43] This new popularity increased the damage caused by the hunts, and in the resulting conflicts between landowners of more or less equal status (or even between non-landowners and landowners), the courts switched their allegiance. "The sport of foxhunting", Lord Coleridge declared, "must be carried on in subordination to the ordinary rights of property."[44]

These developments in relation to the public's rights of access were paralleled in relation to rights of taking. Most significantly – though quite predictably in an era of draconian game laws – Lord Holt in *Sutton* v. *Moody* (1697)[45] reduced the public's right by holding that generally, if a trespasser killed a wild animal, the relevant landowner rather than the trespasser was entitled to his "bag". Trespassers could keep the fruits of their labours only if they killed the animal having followed it from one piece of land to another – an exception clearly designed to benefit hunts.[46] In addition, in a series of cases commencing in the 1860s, the courts held that a public right of fishing could not exist in non-tidal waters. Even where members of the public had fished in non-tidal rivers without challenge for generations, they were held to have no right to do so: their fishing was said to depend simply on the tolerance of landowners.[47]

In reaching these decisions, judges adopted a variety of different approaches to the authorities in favour of public rights. In part they simply ignored these authorities.[48] In other cases, they considered but rejected them either as *dicta*[49] or, in the case of Bracton, as unrepresentative of English law.[50] Elsewhere they interpreted cases which were at least ambiguous, if not in favour of public rights, as supporting private rights.[51] Finally, when confronted by a relative absence of authority, they interpreted this absence as meaning that the alleged public rights did not exist rather than that the activities in question had never previously been challenged because they had always been regarded as lawful.[52]

The reasons why judges manipulated the law in these ways are complex, but rarely appear to be fully articulated in individual judgments. Of the cases decided prior to the mid-nineteenth century, only *Blundell* v. *Catterall* produced lengthy judgments containing detailed reasons for decision. That the judges went to this effort in this case was partly a consequence of the importance of the issues in question. However, it was also a response to the dissenting judgment of Best J. – the one dissent in all reported cases concerning public rights. Confronted with the very cogent arguments advanced by Best J. in favour of the disputed public rights, the majority judges clearly felt compelled to justify their conclusions at length.

One explanation of the courts' decisions in favour of landowners, which is not discussed in any of the cases, is quite apolitical. Just as it has been argued that legal systems, simply on grounds of intellectual convenience, have a tendency to agglomerate rights, privileges and powers in a thing in a single individual,[53] so it may be that convenience led English courts to assume that the owner of the soil was entitled to exclusive enjoyment of all things on, under or attached to it. This explanation of the courts' decisions is supported by the fact that some of the decisions in favour of landowners[54] predate the rise of possessive individualism, the philosophy that might be thought to have given rise to them.[55]

The decisions reached by the courts may also be partly explained by the judges' belief, shared by Pollock, that public rights were unnecessary because members of the public could generally rely on the tolerance of landowners while intolerant landowners would find no effective sanction in the courts. This attitude was most clearly expressed in *Blundell* v. *Catterall*. All three majority judges emphasized that where the Crown retained ownership of the foreshore, it could be expected to allow members of the public to use the foreshore so long as "no mischief or injury" was likely to occur.[56] Abbott C.J. also asked whether private owners of the foreshore would "be allowed to bring any action against any person who may drive his carriage along these parts of the seashore, whereby not the smallest injury is done to the owner". His answer was that "The law has provided suitable checks to frivolous and vexatious suits; and, in general, experience shows that the owners of the shore do not trouble themselves or others for such matters."[57] By way of contrast, Best J. in his dissenting judgment rejected the contention that the public did not need rights because "lords of the manor will find it in their interest to indulge the public with the privilege of going on or over the sands of the sea, and that judges and juries will check the vexatious exercise of the right to exclude them." He considered that "free access to the sea is a privilege too important to Englishmen to be left dependent on the interest or caprice of any description of persons."[58]

A further explanation of the decisions lies in the obvious problems involved in recognizing unrestricted public rights in a period when Parliament enacted relatively little regulatory legislation and hence could not be expected to create administrative mechanisms to control the exercise of these rights. This issue clearly arose to some extent in relation to alleged rights of access. Thus in *Blundell* v. *Catterall* Bayley J. argued against a public right to bathe so that landowners would be able to ensure that bathing took place with decency[59] (whereas Best J.

felt that it was better to rely on "disinterested and responsible" magistrates to punish indecency rather than "interested and irresponsible" landowners).[60] This issue arose in even starker form in relation to alleged rights of taking in renewable resources. Partly because of the risk of over-exploitation, if not destruction of the resources, the courts refused to recognize customary (and hence local public) rights.[61]

By way of contrast, private property and exclusive rights were, according to classical economics, a means of ensuring efficient use of resources. This viewpoint was highly influential from the eighteenth century, underlying for example Blackstone's writing on property,[62] and may well have formed the basis of much of the common law's preference for private property at the expense of public or, for that matter, local customary rights.[63] Even Best J., in his dissenting judgment in *Blundell* v. *Catterall* invoked classical economics when arguing that:

> The principle of exclusive appropriation must not be carried beyond things capable of improvement by the industry of man. If it be extended so far as to touch the right of walking over these barren sands, it will take from the people what is essential to their welfare, whilst it will give to individuals only the hateful privilege of vexing their neighbours.[64]

In reply Abbott C.J. argued that while the foreshore was for the moment "in general, of little value to its owner", he "did not know how that little is to be protected, and much less how it is ever to be increased, if such a general [public] right be established."[65]

Finally, it seems clear that some of the decisions were at least partly a result of judicial bias in favour of the landed classes.[66] Not surprisingly, direct proof of such bias is difficult to find. It appears, however, in relatively obvious form in *Ball* v. *Herbert* where one of Lord Kenyon's principal reasons for rejecting a public right to tow on river banks "was the extreme inconvenience to which individuals having lands adjoining the public rivers would be subject"[67] – a factor more important to the judge than that the right, if recognized, "would be highly convenient to the persons using the navigations".[68]

In the second half of the nineteenth century, there were some signs that this judicial bias against the public might be changing. Possibly because they carefully selected the courts in which to proceed, and therefore had the advantage of the "enlightened views"[69] of such Liberal Judges as Lord Romilly,

Lord Hatherley, and Sir George Jessel, the Commons Preservation Society won a series of cases in the 1860s and 1870s in
which they prevented lords of the manor from inclosing
common land.[70] In deciding these cases, the courts did not lay
down any new principle, but clearly dealt with the issues in a
very different spirit to that of earlier judges.[71] The Society's
victories also came by invoking the private rights of individual
commoners rather than any public rights. However, it was
generally recognized that the object of the cases was to
preserve the commons as public open spaces – a result which
was achieved in relation to several commons in and around
London including Berkhamsted, Hampstead Heath and
Epping Forest.[72]

The hopes generated in the "open spaces movement", as a
result of the litigation over common land, were re-inforced by a
series of cases in which the courts went to considerable lengths
to avoid previous authority and uphold local customary rights
of taking.[73] Most significantly, in *Goodman* v. *Mayor of
Saltash* (1882)[74] – a "splendid effort of equitable imagination in
furtherance of justice"[75] – the House of Lords implied from
long use that a local corporation held fishing rights on trust for
the inhabitants of the area. In the leading judgment, Lord
Selbourne emphasized that if there was "open and uninterrupted enjoyment from time immemorial under a claim of
right", the court should find a legal origin for the practice if
reasonably possible.[76] However, later judges (including Sir
George Jessel) generally either construed these cases very
narrowly[77] or chose not apply them.[78] As a result, the devices
used to support customary rights of taking were quickly
reduced to mere theoretical significance, just as the hopes of a
new judicial attitude to public rights were soon disappointed.

The greatest defeat for the Commons Preservation Society
came in *Attorney-General* v. *Antrobus* (1905),[79] which concerned public access to Stonehenge. In 1901 Sir Edmund
Antrobus, who owned the land embracing the monument, had
erected a barbed-wire fence around it and begun to charge an
admission fee of a shilling. Antrobus erected the fence with the
support of the Society of Antiquaries in order allegedly to
protect the stones from a newly established military camp on
Salisbury Plain. He justified the entrance charge as a means of
recouping his outlay on the fence and enabling him to employ
two custodians. However, there was no evidence of the camp
causing damage to Stonehenge, while if care of the stones was
Antrobus' only object, he could have brought Stonehenge

within the protection of the Ancient Monuments Act 1882, which would have allowed it to be protected from injury and open to the public free of charge. In fact, it seems that Antrobus enclosed Stonehenge "as a means of extorting money for its purchase from the public".[80] When the Government refused to pay a prohibitive sum for the monument, Antrobus' agent "suggested that the owner might be persuaded to sell the stones to some American millionaire, who would ship them across the Atlantic".[81]

Because of the entrance fee, many members of the public were prevented from visiting Stonehenge. Moreover, as noted in an editorial in *The Times:*

> if it is within SIR EDMUND'S power to enclose Stonehenge with an open fence and to charge a shilling for the right of entry, it is equally within his power to enclose it with a high park paling or a brick wall, to charge a guinea for admission, or to exclude the public altogether. Thus the most complete and impressive specimen of megalithic work in the British Isles . . . may be altogether closed to the nation, which has had free access to it from time immemorial.[82]

The noted archaeologist Flinders Petrie, and George Shaw-Lefevre and Sir John Brunner of the Commons Preservation Society consequently brought an action for removal of the fences. However, Farwell J. dismissed the action as one which "ought never to have been brought".[83] The judge clearly considered that, in seeking to have Stonehenge declared a public place subject to a public right of access, the plaintiffs were attempting to confiscate private property without paying compensation.[84] He also was manifestly unconcerned by the exclusion from the monument of the great bulk of the public, whom he felt only constituted a threat to it.[85] As a result, he refused to imply that Antrobus held the land subject to a trust in favour of the public. He suggested that at common law members of the public could not obtain a right to wander at large around open spaces such as Stonehenge. Finally, he held that five roads leading to the monument were not public rights of way. He reached this conclusion partly on the basis that the public's use of the paths had always depended on the tolerance of the landowners even though it dated from time immemorial. He also suggested that public rights of way to points of interest (such as Stonehenge) could only be established by express dedication. In the absence of such dedication, a public right of way could not be "a beautiful walk leading to a cliff or a place on the seashore."[86]

A lack of judicial sympathy for public rights is also clear in a series of cases decided around the turn of the century which raised the question of the correctness of *Blundell* v. *Catterall* and its apparent restriction of public rights over the foreshore to navigation and fishing.[87] In the United States, the courts, "quick to sense the undemocratic character of the English rule",[88] had rejected it, holding that there is a public right of passage over the foreshore when dry as well as a right to bathe in the sea.[89] By way of contrast, the Chancery Division confirmed the earlier decision with gusto, reserving particular praise for the judgment of Holroyd J. "as one of the finest examples we have of the way in which the judgment of an English judge ought to be expressed, and the reasons for it given."[90]

The courts also held against public rights through their interpretation of evidence of long use by the public – whether in cases concerning access such as *Antrobus* or in relation to alleged rights of taking. Instead of making the eminently plausible assumption that such use had taken place under claim of right, and hence looking for a lawful origin of the right as suggested by *Goodman* v. *Mayor of Saltash*, they construed the use as based on the tolerance of the landowner. In then refusing to infer any rights from such use, the courts repeatedly admonished the public claimants on the basis that

> nothing worse can happen in a free country than to force people to be churlish about their rights for fear that their indulgence may be abused, and to drive them to prevent the enjoyment of things which, although they are matters of private property, naturally give pleasure to many others beside the owners, under the fear that their good nature may be misunderstood.[91]

Over the last eighty years, the judicial reduction of public rights in the countryside appears to have come to an end, and some slight judicial sympathy for public rights has emerged so far as access to the countryside is concerned. In rejecting *Antrobus*, the courts have held that rights of way may lead to points of interest and that such paths may be created by recreational use.[92] In rare cases, judges have shown some enthusiasm for implying dedication of a path from long, uninterrupted use.[93] Most recently in *R.* v. *Doncaster Metropolitan Borough Council* (1986),[94] McCullough J. held, again contrary to *Antrobus*, that a public right of recreation, and hence a public right to ramble, can be created at common law.

The relative stability of the law in this century can be

explained in at least three ways. One factor undoubtedly is that the weight of authority in favour of the relatively few public rights which survive is too strong to be overriden lightly. Another possibility, for those seeking continuing economic rationality in the law, is that the public rights of access which survive are justifiable in economic terms, while if the public right of fishing leads to over-exploitation of the resource, the solution arguably lies in government management rather than the traditional judicial response of privatization.[95] Alternatively (or additionally) the new judicial tolerance of public rights may be a result of the changed function of these rights as objects of recreation rather than as a means of subsistence and the large and respectable body of public opinion which since the 1860s has increasingly favoured the protection, if not the expansion, of these rights.[96] Judicial sympathy for this point of view was expressed most clearly in *Jones* v. *Bates* (1938),[97] where Scott L.J. stated:

> In these days, when motor buses, motor cars and motor cycles transport so many into the countryside both for business and for pleasure, and when practically all agricultural workers, and indeed most of the rural population, have their bicycles, long footpaths, which 50 years ago meant so much for ease of communication, are infinitely less frequented, and it becomes easier and easier for real public rights of way to disappear, just because they become unprovable. Yet the rambler – sometimes called the "hiker" – needs the footpath more than ever. The movement represented by the ramblers' societies is of national importance, and to the real lover of the country, who knows that to see it properly he must go on foot, but who is driven off all main roads and a good many others by the din and bustle of motor traffic, the footpath is everything. In short, it is of real public moment that no genuine public footpath should be lost, without statutory action to close it.

If the public's common law rights in the countryside are therefore no longer being reduced, the same cannot be said of *de facto* rights which, as recognized by Pollock, have traditionally ameliorated the public's declining bundle of actual rights in the countryside. *De facto* rights exist where public recreation is strictly wrongful but "dispunishable" in practice. In other words, the conduct, though tortious, is not open to an effective civil action and does not involve the commission of a crime.

The existence of significant *de facto* public rights in the countryside is paradoxically a result of the common law in certain respects being overly generous to landowners. A number of other legal systems recognize that members of the public have what the great Dutch jurist, Hugo Grotius, termed a right of "innocent use" of the countryside, which allows conduct which is of advantage to the public and involves no detriment to landowners.[98] Thus, all members of the public in Sweden and Norway have a right of access on foot to uncultivated land so long as they do no damage; they also have certain rights to pick wild flowers and berries.[99] However, at common law English landowners are theoretically entitled to exclusive occupation and enjoyment of their land. Consequently, any invasion of land without permission or right is a trespass, even if no damage results. Any taking of sand, soil, wild plants or wild animals is also tortious even if the landowner suffers no more than trivial harm.

If landowners could assert these rights effectively, they could greatly reduce public recreation in the countryside. However, the courts have generally awarded only nominal damages of one or two pounds and have refused to award costs where landowners bring actions in relation to trivial infringements of their rights. They have also refused to grant injunctions to landowners seeking to restrain members of the public from enjoying harmless recreation in the countryside.[100] In reaching these decisions judges have emphasized the oppressive nature of the litigation. They have also advised landowners that the refusal of an effective remedy is in fact also in their interest since "The existing security of the tenure of land in this country is largely maintained by the fact that the owners of the land behave reasonably in its enjoyment."[101]

At the same time, many forms of tortious enjoyment of land have not been treated as crimes where the infringements by the public have been considered to be relatively minor. Thus, at common law simple trespass to land is not an offence, while the taking of wild animals and things "savouring of the realty", such as the soil itself and plants, did not constitute the old offence of larceny.[102] Under statute bare trespass is, in general, still not a crime.

Since the fourteenth century, however, Parliament has enacted legislation which has steadily reduced the public's *de facto* rights by criminalizing an increasing range of acts in the countryside (while in significant respects exempting the activities of hunts from the new offences).[103] Most of this legislation has sought to protect the property of landowners by bringing the exceptions to larceny within the criminal law.[104] However, a number of Acts have sought to conserve plants and wildlife and to prevent cruelty to animals.[105] Together these statutes have almost destroyed the public's *de facto* rights of taking. Only few things – such as foxes and the fruit, flowers and foliage of some wild plants – can now be taken without committing an offence.

This legislative contraction of the public's *de facto* rights has in some instances been compounded by judicial interpretation of the statutes. The generally accepted view of the legislation has been that some *de facto* rights survive, so that, for example, "not every walking over another man's land for recreation" constitutes an offence under the malicious damage legislation. On this view, "actual, positive damage" rather than "imaginary damage" is necessary.[106] However, in some cases the courts have interpreted the criminal legislation expansively precisely because, as they have acknowledged, to hold otherwise would "leave a large number of acts of trifling damage remediless".[107] Most notably, in *Gayford* v. *Chouler* (1898)[108] – a clear case of "imaginary damage" – the Queen's Bench Division upheld a conviction of malicious damage where the accused had simply walked across a field through thick long grass and asserted he would do so as often as he liked.

Quite recently *de facto* rights have also come under threat as a result of a series of cases concerning the granting of injunctions to prevent simple trespasses. In these cases, which have arisen out of disputes between adjoining landowners over building operations, the courts have suggested that they should always issue injunctions when simple trespasses occur since "if the injunction is refused the result will be no more nor less than a licence to continue the tort of trespass in return for nominal payment."[109] If this approach were extended to the countryside, as suggested by a recent building case,[110] it would spell the end of *de facto* rights. But the better view is that the building cases are at most authoritative within their own context and that the courts may continue to refuse injunctions to landowners who wish to prevent harmless rural recreation.[111]

While Parliament and the courts preserve the public's *de facto* rights, they encourage landowners to accept the principle of innocent use and hence tolerate public recreation on their land, as currently happens in much of the countryside. Thus, in many parts of the uplands, private landowners make no attempt to prevent public access to uncultivated land. Where the Crown owns the foreshore and retains possession of this land, it allows public access (as predicted by the majority in

Blundell v. *Catterall*). Where the Crown grants leases of the foreshore to local authorities, it ordinarily makes a reservation in the leases ensuring that members of the public can resort to these parts of the foreshore on foot for private recreational purposes.[112]

De facto rights are, however, inherently a partial and unreliable substitute for public rights of access and taking. The problem is that these "rights" are no more than a result of Parliament and the courts denying landowners an effective remedy for trivial wrongs. Consequently English landowners are free to use self-help measures to exclude the public[113] (unlike in Norway, for example, where there are restrictions on the circumstances in which landowners may fence uncultivated land). Apart from erecting fences, English landowners and their employees – notably gamekeepers – may warn off and then use reasonable force to expel intransigent trespassers. Through these means, members of the public, especially over the last 100 years, have been and continue to be excluded from large parts of rural England.

Within this context, organizations concerned with promoting and protecting public enjoyment of the countryside have, not surprisingly, turned to Parliament for greater public rights. The first attempts to obtain such legislation were made in the 1860s, and since then Parliament has slowly replaced the courts as the main forum for debate over public rights of access to the countryside. The issue of public rights of taking has arisen only once, in the late 1880s, in response to the series of cases which held that public rights of fishing could not exist in non-tidal waters. These cases conflicted with the understanding of many members of the public "that the public right exists not only in the tidal, but also in the navigable parts of all rivers, and that the riparian owners are merely usurping and encroaching when they seek to exclude the public from the modest enjoyments of angling wherever they can scull a boat".[114] On the basis that this understanding represented the law, the Corporation of Nottingham unsuccessfully promoted a Bill which sought to declare that navigable rivers were subject to a public right of fishing (except where a private right of fishing could be shown to have already existed in the reign of Henry II).[115]

The campaign for increased public rights of access to the countryside has been led by the Commons and Footpaths Preservation Society (now the Open Spaces Society) and, more recently, by the Ramblers' Association. Since the 1870s, these advocates of the public cause have had a number of successes.

However, parliamentary reform of the law has rarely come easily or quickly because of opposition from landowners and a lack of interest from government, which has led the proponents of the legislation to rely frequently on private member's bills. The measures which have been enacted have, moreover, generally been compromises between the conflicting interest groups which, from the viewpoint of members of the public, means that they have tended to be at least partly ineffectual, if not adverse to their interests.

In its early stages, the campaign for legislation granting public rights focussed on open spaces in and immediately around English cities, which could serve as recreation grounds for the rapidly expanding middle class.[116] The campaign only gradually extended further into the countryside. As noted by Avner Offer, "The Tories, as landowners, were in possession and the Liberals mounted the challenge."[117] A succession of important Liberal parliamentarians including George Shaw-Lefevre, Henry Fawcett, Charles Dilke and James Bryce formed organizations such as the Commons Preservation Society and for almost half a century led the struggle for public rights. These groups had their greatest parliamentary successes with the enactment of legislation which effectively prevented the inclosure of all common land. They also succeeded in pushing through Parliament a series of statutes creating rights of access over certain commons.[118] However, they failed in their efforts to obtain legislation which would have facilitated the creation of public rights of way by implied dedication and given the public a right to ramble over all "open country".

In the period leading up to World War II, the open spaces movement succeeded in persuading Parliament to enact three statutes governing rights of access. While involving substantial concessions to landowners, two of these Acts significantly expanded public rights. First, in 1925 the Law of Property Act created a public right to ramble over all common land in urban districts (rather than all common land as originally proposed).[119] Then in 1932, almost fifty years after the introduction of the first Footpaths Bill, Parliament enacted a rather cumbersome Rights of Way Act which facilitated proof of creation of public rights of way by implied dedication.[120] However, the Access to Mountains Act 1939 was a complete failure, never being implemented. During its passage through Parliament the Bill changed from one creating a general right of access to all uncultivated mountain and moorland, to one which only provided expensive, cumbersome machinery for obtaining limited access to specified areas. Most controversially, the Act adversely affected the position of ramblers by providing that they not only became trespassers but also committed a summary offence if they breached any of 15 specified conditions – as by failing to shut a gate – while on land covered by an access order.[121]

At the end of the war, the Attlee Labour government instituted two major inquiries into public recreation in the countryside. Both called for much greater public rights, including a general right of access to all uncultivated land.[122] However, under pressure from landowners, the government failed to implement these recommendations in the National Parks and Access to the Countryside Act 1949. Far from being "a people's charter for the open air",[123] as the Government claimed, the Act was based on the premise that *de facto* rights of access were generally sufficient. Like the impotent Access to Mountains Act 1939, the 1949 Act merely established a procedure for creating public rights of access over "open country". In almost forty years, this procedure has led to public rights being established over only about 100,000 acres or just over 0.3% of the total area of England and Wales.[124] The Act also made only inadequate provision for the establishment of long-distance routes by empowering the National Parks Commission to suggest routes for the paths but leaving implementation of the proposals to local authorities. As a result the Pennine Way took twenty-one years to establish; the Pembroke Coast path, seventeen years.[125]

Since the failure of the 1949 Act, there has been almost no legislation increasing public rights in the countryside. The main statutes concerning the countryside – the Commons Registration Act 1965, the Countryside Act 1968, and the Wildlife and Countryside Act 1981 – have at most provided some protection for existing public rights. In the case of the Commons Registration Act the many weaknesses of the registration system established under the Act have, if anything, reduced the area of land which may one day be subject to public rights of access.[126] Only the Dartmoor Commons Act 1985 – a product of more than eight years of negotiation – has expanded public rights by creating a general right to ramble and to ride on horseback over the 100,000 acres of common land on Dartmoor.

The result of these developments is that public enjoyment of the countryside still depends on a fragile combination of rights and the tolerance of landowners encouraged by the lack of an effective legal remedy for many trivial wrongs. The public's rights at common law are clearly only few, though as shown by this book there is authority for them being significantly greater than is generally thought. The statutory rights of access equally cover only a small area and will continue to do so even if Parliament finally creates a universal right of access to common land as recommended by the Royal Commission on Common Land as long ago as 1958 and proposed most recently by the Common Land Forum in 1986.[127] *De facto* rights are therefore likely to remain critical as a means of ameliorating the public's lack of express rights. Consequently, it is essential not only that simple trespass remain outside the ambit of the criminal law but also that judges continue to refuse effective civil remedies to landowners who wish to use the courts as a means of preventing the public from enjoying peaceful, harmless recreation in the countryside.

NOTES TO PART ONE

1. Frederick Pollock, *The Land Laws*, Macmillan, 1883, p. 15.
2. See Lord Eversley, *Commons, Forests and Footpaths*, London, Cassell, 1910, p. 329; Frederick Pollock, *For my Grandson*, London, John Murray, 1933, chap. 6; A. W. B. Simpson (ed.), *Biographical Dictionary of the Common Law*, London, Butterworths, 1984, p. 422.
3. Pollock, p. 16.
4. *Ibid*.
5. *Ibid*., p. 17.
6. *Ibid*., pp. 17-18.
7. *Ibid*., p. 14.
8. *Ibid*., p. 15.
9. *Ibid*.
10. The classification *res communes* – embracing things incapable of ownership but open to public use – was a late development in Roman law, dating probably from the third century. See Buckland, p. 183, note 9.
11. 2 Justinian, *Institutes*, tit. 1, ss. 1, 5 (*res communes*). Note that in practice the Romans sometimes allowed exclusive appropriation of the sea and the seashore (as they also did of fishing rights). See Patrick Deveney, 'Title, Jus Publicum, and the Public Trust: an Historical Analysis', (1976) 1 Sea Grant L.J. 13, esp. pp. 21-36.
12. *Ibid*., tit. 2, s. 4 (*res publicae*).
13. Gaius, *Institutes*, II, 66-7; 2 Justinian, *Institutes*, tit. 1, s. 12 (*res nullius*).
14. 2 Justinian, *Institutes*, tit. 1, s. 18.
15. *Ibid*., tit. 1, s. 47.
16. See David A. Thomas, "Origins of the Common Law, Part 1: The

Disappearance of Roman Law from Dark Age Britain", (1984) Brigham Young University Law Review 563-98.

17. See, for example, R. C. van Caenegem, *The Birth of the English Common Law*, Cambridge, Cambridge University Press, 1973, pp. 90-2.

18. Most notably, the law of accretion and the law of easements. See Paul Jackson, "Alluvio and the Common Law", (1983) 99 L.Q.R. 412-31; Paul Jackson, *The Law of Easements and Profits*, London, Butterworths, 1978, pp. 4-5.

19. For an account of Bracton's fluctuating reputation, see D. E. C. Yale, " 'Of No Mean Authority': Some Later Uses of Bracton" in Morris S. Arnold, Thomas A. Green, Sally A. Scully & Stephen D. White (eds), *On the Laws and Customs of England*, Chapel Hill, University of North Carolina Press, 1981, pp. 383-96, esp. pp. 394-6.

20. Samuel E. Thorne, "Translator's Introduction" in Bracton, vol. 1, p. xxxiii.

21. *Ibid.*, vol. 2, pp. 39-41.

22. *Ibid.*, vol. 2, p. 40.

23. 2 Justinian, *Institutes*, tit. 1, s. 5.

24. On this passage in Bracton, see Hall, pp. 161-2, 166. Compare Moore, *Foreshore*, p. 33. See also T. E. Scrutton, "Roman Law in Bracton", (1885) 1 L.Q.R. 425, 431; Paul Vinogradoff, "The Roman Elements in Bracton's Treatise", (1923) 32 Yale L.J. 751, 756; John L. Barton, *Roman Law in England*, (Ius Romanum Medii Aevi, Pars V, 1971, 13a). p. 15, esp. n. 28. Compare Deveney, *op. cit.,* pp. 36-38.

25. Bracton, vol. 2, pp. 41, 58, 338-40, 167, discussed by Scrutton, *op. cit.,* p. 425.

26. *Ibid.*, vol. 2, p. 40.

27. See Moore, *Foreshore*, appendix II; Moore, *Fisheries*.

28. Bracton, vol. 2, p. 167. At vol. 2, p. 42 Bracton also stated that fish were the property of the King, but it seems clear from pp. 40, 58, 167, 339 that this statement should be read as restricted to royal fish. See also Fleta, Bk. I, chaps 43-4, Bk. III, chap. I. Compare Deveney, *op. cit.,* p. 39, n.168.

29. See G. J. Turner, *Select Pleas of the Forest*, S.S. 13, 1899, p. cxxiii; Charles Petit-Dutaillis, *Studies and Notes Supplementary to Stubbs' Constitutional History*, Manchester, Manchester University Press, 1914, vol. 2, pp. 155-6.

30. *Steel* v. *Houghton* (1788) 1 H. Bl. 51; 126 E.R. 32.

31. Most notably, in *Gateward's Case* (1607) 6 Co. Rep 59b; 77 E.R. 344. See Kenelm Edward Digby, *An Introduction to the History of the Law of Real Property*, 5th ed., Oxford, Clarendon Press, 1897, p. 184, n.1; Holdsworth, vol. 3, p. 171; E. P. Thompson, "The Grid of Inheritance: A Comment", in Jack Goody, Joan Thirsk & E. P. Thompson (eds), *Family and Inheritance: Rural Society in Western Europe 1200-1800*, Cambridge, Cambridge University Press, 1976, pp. 340-41.

32. J. A. Yelling, *Common Field and Enclosure in England 1450-1850*, London, Macmillan, 1977, p. 214.

33. See J. L. & B. Hammond, *The Village Labourer 1760-1832*, London, Longmans, Green, 1911.

34. See, particularly, G. E. Mingay, "Introduction" to E. C. K. Gonner, *Common Land and Enclosure*, 2nd ed., London, Cassell, 1966: J. D. Chambers & G. E. Mingay *The Agricultural Revolution 1750-1880*,

London, Batsford, 1966, chap. 4. Compare E. P. Thompson, *The Making of the English Working Class*, London, Gollancz, 1980, pp. 237-8.

35. Compare P. S. Atiyah, *The Rise and Fall of Freedom of Contract*, Oxford, Clarendon Press, 1979, p. 15.
36. (1789) 3 T.R. 253; 100 E.R. 564.
37. (1821) 5 B. & Ald. 268; 106 E.R. 1190.
38. *Blundell* v. *Catterall* (1821) 5 B. & Ald. 268; 106 E.R. 1190; *Scratton* v. *Brown* (1825) 4 B. & C. 495; 107 E.R. 1140, 1144; *Attorney-General* v. *Chambers* (1854) 4 De G.M. & G. 206; 43 E.R. 486.
39. See further, below pp. 29-30.
40. See Eversley, *op. cit.*, pp. 299-302; *Jones* v. *Bates* [1938] 2 All E.R. 237, 244 *per* Scott L.J.
41. Raymond Carr, "Country Sports" in G. E. Mingay (ed.), *The Victorian Countryside*, London, Routledge & Kegan Paul, 1981, p. 477.
42. *Grundy* v. *Feltham* (1786) 1 T.R. 334; 99 E.R. 1125, discussed by David C. Itzkowitz, *Peculiar Privilege: a Social History of English Foxhunting 1753–1885*, Hassocks, Harvester Press, 1977, p. 68.
43. Raymond Carr, *English Fox Hunting: a History*, London, Weidenfeld & Nicholson, 1976, esp. pp. 44-5.
44. *Paul* v. *Summerhayes* (1878) 4 Q.B.D. 9, 10. See also *Earl of Essex* v. *Capel* (1809) in Chitty, *A Treatise on the Game Laws and on the Fisheries*, vol. 2, pp. 1381-3.
45. (1697) 3 Salk. 290; 91 E.R. 831.
46. This exception was doubted in *Blades* v. *Higgs* (1865) 11 H.L.C. 621, 639-40; 11 E.R. 1474, 1482 *per* Lord Chelmsford, discussed below, p. 225.
47. See below, pp. 241-3.
48. For example, in *Sutton* v. *Moody* (1697) 3 Salk. 290; 91 E.R. 831.
49. *Ball* v. *Herbert* (1789) 3 T.R. 253; 100 E.R. 560; in relation to *Young* v. —————— (1698) 1 Ld. Raym. 725; 91 E.R. 1384. See also, the gleaning case, *Steel* v. *Houghton* (1788) 1 H. Bl. 51; 126 E.R. 32, where the authorities dismissed as dicta include Hale and Blackstone.
50. See *Ball* v. *Herbert* (1789) 3 T.R. 253, 263; 100 E.R. 560, 565 *per* Buller J.; *Blundell* v. *Catterall* (1821) 5 B. & Ald. 268, 290-2, 308-10, 312; 106 E.R. 1190, 1198-9, 1204-5, 1206.
51. Most notably in the cases concerning public rights of fishing in non-tidal waters. See, especially, *Murphy* v. *Ryan* (1868) I.R. 2 C.L. 143; *Smith* v. *Andrews* [1891] 2 Ch. 678.
52. Most notably, in *Blundell* v. *Catterall* (1821) 5 B. & Ald. 268; 106 E.R. 190; *Howe* v. *Stawell* (1833) Alc. & Nap. 349, 355. See Hall, pp. 158-9; H. Gallienne Lemmon, *Public Rights in the Seashore*, London, Pitman, 1934, p. 175. For a later example of this approach, see *Lord Fitzhardinge* v. *Purcell* [1908] 2 Ch. 139, 165, 167. Compare the approach adopted in the Scottish case, *Hope* v. *Bennewith* (1904) 12 S.L.T. 243, 246.
53. See Charles Donahue Jr., "The Future of the Concept of Property predicted from its Past", in J. Roland Pennock & John W. Chapman (eds), *Property*, Nomos 22, New York, New York University Press, 1982, pp. 28-68, esp. pp. 44-5.
54. Most notably, *Sutton* v. *Moody* (1697) 3 Salk. 290; 91 E.R. 831.
55. See Donahue, *op. cit.*, p. 34, and C. B. Macpherson, *The Political Theory of Possessive Individualism*, Oxford, Clarendon Press, 1962.

56. 5 B. & Ald. 268, 300, 314; 106 E.R. 1190, 1202, 1204, 1207.
57. 5 B. & Ald. 268, 316; 106 E.R. 1190, 1207.
58. 5 B. & Ald. 268, 275; 106 E.R. 1190, 1193.
59. (1821) 5 B. & Ald. 268, 306, 310; 106 E.R. 1190, 1204, 1205.
60. (1821) 5 B. & Ald. 268, 288; 106 E.R. 1190, 1197.
61. See below, p. 104, n.91.
62. See Herbert Hovenkamp, "The Economics of Legal History", (1983) 67 Minnesota L.R. 645, 663-6.
63. See Carol Rose, "The Comedy of the Commons: Custom, Commerce and Inherently Public Property", (1986) 53 U. Chicago L.R. 711-12.
64. 5 B. & Ald. 268, 287; 106 E.R. 1190, 1197.
65. 5 B. & Ald. 268, 313; 106 E.R. 1190, 1206.
66. Atiyah, *op. cit.*, pp. 97-8.
67. (1789) 3 T.R. 253, 262; 100 E.R. 560, 565.
68. (1789) 3 T.R. 253, 261; 100 E.R. 560, 564.
69. Eversley, *op. cit.*, p. 31.
70. See below, p. 154, note 70.
71. See Pollock, *op. cit.*, pp. 186-7.
72. See, generally, Eversley, *op. cit.*, chaps 4 to 15.
73. See, particularly, *Willingale* v. *Maitland* (1866) L.R. 3 Eq. 103; *Goodman* v. *Mayor of Saltash* (1882) 7 App. Cas. 633. Judicial unhappiness with the old authorities is clearest in *Warrick* v. *Queen's College, Oxford* (1871) L.R. 6. Ch. 716, 723-5 *per* Lord Hatherley L.C.; *Goodman* v. *Mayor of Saltash* (1882) 7 App. Cas. 633, 669 *per* Lord Fitzgerald.
74. (1882) 7 App. Cas. 633.
75. *Harris* v. *Earl of Chesterfield* [1911] A.C. 623, 633 *per* Lord Ashbourne.
76. (1882) 7 App. Cas. 633, 639-40.
77. See, especially, Jessel M.R.'s judgment in *Chilton* v. *Corporation of London* (1878) 7 Ch.D. 735, which rendered insignificant *Willingale* v. *Maitland*. For another contentious judgment of Jessel M.R. in which he refused to recognize customary rights, see *Hammerton* v. *Honey* (1876) 24 W.R. 603, criticized by Eversley, *op. cit.*, p. 285.
78. *Goodman* v. *Mayor of Saltash* was not followed in *Attorney-General* v. *Antrobus* [1905] 2 Ch. 188, esp. 198-9; *Lord Fitzhardinge* v. *Purcell* [1908] 2 Ch.139, 165; *Harris* v. *Earl of Chesterfield* [1911] 2 A.C. 623. Compare *In re the Company or Fraternity of Faversham* (1887) 36 Ch.D. 329; *Haigh* v. *West* [1893] 2 Q.B. 19.
79. [1905] 2 Ch. 188. The main account of the background to the litigation is in Lord Eversley, *Commons, Forests and Footpaths*, pp. 302-11.
80. Eversley, p. 304.
81. *Ibid.*
82. *The Times*, 20 April 1905, p. 7.
83. [1905] 2 Ch. 188, 208.
84. For this argument, see (1905) 21 T.L.R. 471, 473.
85. See especially, [1905] 2 Ch. 188, 209, and Eversley, p. 307.
86. *Eyre* v. *New Forest Highway Board* (1892) 56 J.P. 517, 518 *per* Wills J., quoted in *Attorney-General* v. *Antrobus* [1905] 2 Ch. 188, 208.
87. *Llandudno U.D.C.* v. *Woods* [1899] 2 Ch. 705; *Brinckman* v. *Matley* [1904] 2 Ch. 313; *Fitzhardinge* v. *Purcell* [1908] 2 Ch. 139.
88. "Water and Watercourses – Right of Public Passage along Great Lakes Beaches", (1933) 31 Michigan L.R. 1134, 1138-9.
89. See, for example, John Norton Pomeroy, *A Treatise on the Law of*

Water Rights, rev. ed, St. Paul, Minn., West, 1893, sect. 222.
90. *Brinckman* v. *Matley* [1904] 2 Ch. 313, 323 *per* Vaughan Williams L.J.
91. *Blount* v. *Layard* [1891] 2 Ch. 688n., 69ln., quoted with approval in *Simpson* v. *Attorney-General* [1904] A.C. 476, 493 *per* Lord Macnaghten; *Attorney-General* v. *Antrobus* [1905] 2 Ch. 188, 200 *per* Farwell J.; *Folkestone Corporation* v. *Brockman* [1914] A.C. 338, 369 *per* Lord Atkinson; *Attorney-General* v. *Sewell* (1919) 88 L.J. K.B. 425, 430 *per* Swinfen Eady M.R. See also *Shearburn* v. *Chertsey R.D.C.* (1914) 78 J.P. 289, 291.
92. See below, p. 31.
93. See *Attorney-General and Newton Abbot R.D.C.* v. *Dyer* [1947] Ch. 67, 86, quoted below, p. 34.
94. *The Times*, 11 October 1986, CO/1455/85 (transcript). See below, pp. 127-8.
95. See Rose, *op. cit.*, esp. p. 774.
96. See Avner Offer, *Property and Politics 1870-1914; Landownership, Law, Ideology and Urban Development in England*, Cambridge, Cambridge University Press, 1981 pp. 338-40; John Ranlett, "Checking Nature's Desecration: Late-Victorian Environmental Organization", *Victorian Studies*, winter 1983, pp. 197-222.
97. [1938] 2 All E.R. 237, 249.
98. Hugo Grotius, *De Jure Belli ac Pacis Libri Tres*, Oxford, Clarendon Press, 1925, vol. 2, p. 196.
99. See John E. Cribbet, "Some Reflections on the Law of Land – a View from Scandinavia", (1962) 67 Northwestern U.L.R. 277, 290-1; Judith Mary Cullington, "The Public Use of Private Land for Recreation", M.A. thesis, Geography Department, University of Waterloo, Waterloo, Ontario, 1980, pp. 29-31. For the similar position in Finland, see Simo Zitting, "Modes of Land Use" in Jaako Uotila (ed.), *The Finnish Legal System*, Helsinki, Union of Finnish Lawyers, 1961, p. 164.
100. See below, p. 164-8.
101. *Behrens* v. *Richards* [1905] 2 Ch. 614, 622 *per* Buckley J. See further, below, pp. 167-8.
102. See Jerome Hall, *Theft, Law and Society*, 2nd ed., Indianapolis, Bobbs-Merrill, 1952, chapter 3.
103. See below, p. 216 and Malicious Damage to Property Act 1820, s. 6; Malicious Injuries to Property Act 1827, s. 24; Malicious Injuries to Property Act 1861, s. 52, discussed by Hammond, *op. cit.*, pp. 199-200; Game Act 1831, s. 35; Protection of Animals Act 1911, s. 15(a), discussed below, p. 229.
104. See, particularly, the various larceny statutes and the Theft Act 1968, discussed below, pp. 181-2, 193, 200-2; the Malicious Injuries to Property Acts and the Criminal Damage Act 1971, discussed below, pp. 202-4; and the Game and Fishing Acts, discussed below, pp. 217, 230-1, 258.
105. See, below, pp. 204-5, 226, 228-30, 231-33, 257-8.
106. *Butler* v. *Turley* (1827) 2 C. & P. 585, 589; 172 E.R. 266, 268, approved in *Gardner* v. *Mansbridge* (1887) 19 Q.B.D. 217, 221.
107. *Hamilton* v. *Bone* (1888) 4 T.L.R. 450.
108. [1898] 1 Q.B. 316.
109. *Woollerton and Wilson* v. *Costain Ltd* [1970] 1 W.L.R. 411, 413 *per* Stamp J.
110. *Patel* v. *W. H. Smith (Eziot) Ltd*, [1987] W.L.R. 853.

111. See below, pp. 168-9.
112. See *Alfred F. Beckett Ltd* v. *Lyons* [1967] Ch. 449, 465; *Report of the Crown Estate Commissioners for the year ended March 31, 1966*, pp. 11-12; *Report of the Crown Estate Commissioners for the year ended March 31, 1967*, p. 19. For the older form of such leases, see Geoffrey Marston, *The Marginal Seabed: United Kingdom Legal Practice*, Oxford, Clarendon Press, 1981, p. 27.
113. See below, pp. 162-4.
114. "Fishing in Non-tidal Waters", (1888) 52 J.P. 305, 306. See also "Rights of Boating in Rivers", (1890) 54 J.P. 177, 178.
115. See P. Edward Dove, *Public Rights in Navigable Rivers*, London, Cox, 1887.
116. H. L. Malchow, "Public Gardens and Social Action in Late Victorian London", *Victorian Studies*, autumn 1985, 98, 100.
117. See, especially, Offer, *op. cit.*, pp. 338-40.
118. See below, pp. 139-41.
119. See below, pp. 134-7.
120. See below, pp. 30-1
121. See below, pp. 146-7.
122. See below, p. 147.
123. See Gordon E. Cherry, *Environmental Planning 1939-1969, volume II: National Parks and Recreation in the Countryside*, London, H.M.S.O, 1975, p. 105.
124. See below, p. 150.
125. Ann & Malcolm MacEwen, *National Parks: Conservation or Cosmetics?*, London, George Allen & Unwin, 1982, pp. 141-5.
126. See below, pp. 141-5.
127. See below, pp. 133-4.

PART TWO

ACCESS TO THE COUNTRYSIDE

At common law, landowners are generally entitled to exclusive possession of their land. As stated by Lord Camden in *Entick* v. *Carrington* (1765),[1]

> Our law holds the property of every man so sacred that no man can set foot upon his neighbour's close without his leave. If he does, he is a trespasser, though he does no damage at all; if he will tread upon his neighbour's ground, he must justify it by law.

Nevertheless, there are three different bases on which members of the public may lawfully have access to the countryside. Moreover, even where access is unlawful, members of the public may have a *de facto* right to enjoy the countryside.

Of the public's rights of access, probably the most significant, and in legal terms certainly the most complex, is the right of passage which primarily involves a right to pass and repass on some defined route. This right is most clearly established on land – on the 120,000 miles of highway variously designated as footpaths, bridleways, byways and "roads used as public paths". However, it also exists over many non-tidal rivers and a few canals.

In certain parts of the countryside, there is also a public right to ramble – a right to wander at large on land and to navigate at will over water. At common law, this right has traditionally been recognized in relation to almost all tidal waters and some non-tidal waters, and can now it seems also be established over land. Under statute, this right has been created over a relatively small area of common land and "open country".

Even without these rights, public access to the countryside may still be lawful as a result of permission granted by the relevant landowners. Such permission or licence is sometimes given expressly, However, there are many parts of the countryside where such licence can probably be implied from the fact that landowners have allowed long unchallenged public access over their land.

Otherwise public access is unlawful, which may result in members of the public facing actions for damages or injunctions or even prosecutions if they commit trespass. Yet the lack of a right of access may be of no consequence to members of the public where they are not physically excluded from the land in question. So long as they do no damage, they may be able to go on to the land with impunity because in many instances neither the civil nor the criminal law provides landowners with an effective remedy.

NOTES TO PART TWO

1 (1765) 2 Wils. 275, 291; 95 E.R. 807, 817.

Chapter 1

RIGHTS OF PASSAGE

On footpaths, bridleways and carriageways as well as over certain non-tidal waters, members of the public have rights of passage. On all these "highways" the fundamental nature of the public's rights is the same – in all four cases members of the public have a right to pass and repass over a defined route. However, even at common law there were some differences between the law governing rights of way over land and water, and these differences have been increased by two largely discrete bodies of legislation; statutes have also created significant differences in the law governing footpaths and bridleways on the one hand and carriageways on the other.

For members of the public, the most important issue in relation to all their rights of passage is the exact nature of these rights and the manner in which they can be created and extinguished. However, of almost equal significance is the law governing such matters as the recording, signposting and maintenance of public rights of way and interference with public ways. These matters are strictly not part of the public's "rights". However, they are integral to the public's enjoyment of rights of way and hence are also discussed below. Where there is no provision for such matters, or if local authorities fail to carry out their duties and if infringements by landowners go unpunished, the rights of members of the public can become useless in practice; the law governing the creation and nature of the public's rights is reduced to a matter of only theoretical interest.

I. THE CREATION OF PUBLIC RIGHTS OF WAY

In Roman law there were a number of types of land and water which were always the subject of public rights of access. Thus, the foreshore was open to all,[1] there was a public right to use the banks of rivers as an incident to navigation,[2] and a public right of navigation on perennial waterways.[3] The existence of all these rights was recognized by Bracton.[4] In two cases in the late seventeenth and early eighteenth centuries, courts affirmed the public right to tow on river banks.[5] However, in the late eighteenth and in the nineteenth century, the courts ruled against the existence of these general public rights. In *Ball* v. *Herbert* (1789),[6] the Court of King's Bench held that there is no general right of towing on the banks of rivers. In *Blundell* v. *Catterall* (1821),[7] the same court held that there is no general right of way over the foreshore when dry. The courts also accepted that the public's general right of navigation is restricted to tidal waters (where it is in fact a right to navigate at will rather than a right of passage); they held that over non-tidal waters there is no such general right even if the waters are perennial.[8]

Over certain non-tidal rivers it is possible that members of the public may have a right of passage as a matter of common law (rather than as a result of some process recognized at common law or by or under statute). Thus, in *Williams* v. *Wilcox* (1838)[9] Lord Denman C.J. regarded it is as "clear that the channels of public navigable rivers" – whether above or below the tide – "were always highways". He stated that if the public right of navigation in such waters existed by permission of the Crown, "the permission supposed must be coeval with the monarchy". However, Lord Denman did not provide any guidance as to how these public navigable rivers were to be identified. Because obvious forms of proof, such as immemorial use or the mere fact of navigation, may independently be modes of establishing the creation of rights of passage, it is probably irrelevant whether the rivers are regarded as having always been subject to public rights.

Disregarding *Williams* v. *Wilcox,* it is clear that public rights of way over both land and water exist only where created either by some process recognized at common law or by or under statute. Strictly speaking, all public ways must have their origin in one of these two sources, but there is something of an intermediate category of public rights of way which are the subject of "declaratory" Acts. These statutes may leave the common law right intact, in which case the right has two foundations with its ultimate source at common law. Alternatively, these statutes may extinguish the common law right, in which case the legislation becomes the sole source of the public right.

(A) CREATION AT COMMON LAW

The common law governing the creation of public rights of way may be of medieval origin[10] but the earliest reported cases concerning this topic date only from the 1730s.[11] Almost all the reported litigation since then has concerned the dedication of highways, and the rules governing the creation of such ways have become relatively settled. It has also been established that public rights of navigation may be created by dedication,[12] presumably under the same rules as highways.[13] However, it remains unclear whether public rights of way over land or water may be established by immemorial use; it is also unclear whether the mere fact of public use of a non-tidal river (without it being immemorial) may result in the creation of a public right of passage.

(1) Dedication

As the term suggests, the key to "dedication" is that the owner of the soil gives the public a right of passage over his soil.[14] Sometimes – especially as part of establishing housing estates – landowners expressly dedicate rights of passage to the public. More usually, public rights of passage are created by "implied dedication" in which use of the way by the public is treated as evidence of dedication. In these cases, the consent of the landowner to the creation of the public right is "often a pure legal fiction".[15] As explained by Robert Wellbeloved in the first general text on highway law, "that which is, in point of fact, acquired by adverse possession, is considered by law as emanating from the bounty and free will of the proprietor; although it may be entirely without his consent, and opposed to his wishes".[16]

Because of its basis in legal fiction, implied dedication could be considered as a form of taking without compensation and hence as unfair to landowners.[17] Yet it may also be regarded as an undue restriction on the creation of rights of passage – especially when compared with Scottish law where the creation of a right of way does not depend on a fictional consent from the relevant landowners but on use as of right.[18] Whereas 40 years' use results in Scotland in the creation of a public right of passage,[19] in England there is no set period of use at common law after which a right of passage is even presumptively created. Hence, even if members of the public have used a path or waterway as of right for generations, this use will not result in the creation of a public right if the courts do not infer a

dedication from the fact of use. Such findings against dedication are most likely where the persons in possession of the land
have not owned it in fee simple and hence were incapable of
dedicating a public right of passage. In Scotland such capacity
is irrelevant because the creation of a right of passage depends
on use rather than on an implied grant.[20]

As a result of analogous impediments to the creation of
private rights of way (and other easements as well as profits à
prendre), the Real Property Commissioners recommended in
1829 that 60 years' use as of right should be conclusive evidence
of the existence of an easement while 20 years' use should
constitute presumptive evidence of such a right.[21] These
recommendations were broadly adopted in the Prescription
Act 1832. In relation to public rights of passage, however, the
first attempt to achieve statutory reform of the law occurred
only in 1888 when George Shaw-Lefevre, President of the
Commons Preservation Society, introduced a Footpaths and
Roadside Wastes Bill into the House of Commons. This Bill,
which failed to obtain a second reading in 1888, 1889 and 1892,
provided that "The use as of right by the public of a footpath
for twenty years shall be conclusive proof that such footpath
was legally dedicated to the public as a right of way."[22]

In 1906 private members introduced the first Public Rights of
Way Bill which also adopted the principle of use as the basis of
public rights of passage. Over the next 25 years, this Bill came
before the House of Commons on 11 occasions and four times
obtained a second reading but was not enacted – as much it
seems because of lack of parliamentary time as opposition from
landowners.[23] Finally in 1932, the centenary of the Prescription
Act 1832, the Rights of Way Bill was passed. Following
amendments made in 1949, the rules for "statutory dedication"
created by the 1932 Act were incorporated in the Highways
Act 1959, and are now found in sections 31 to 33 of the
Highways Act 1980.

Notwithstanding this context in the highways legislation,
which is concerned primarily with carriageways, bridleways
and footpaths, not only public rights of way over land but also
public rights of navigation can almost certainly be established
by statutory dedication. From 1906 until 1910, the Rights of
Way Bills applied to "any way upon or over any land or
water",[24] a formulation which clearly covered public rights of
navigation. In 1911 the Bill was changed so that its key
provision applied to ways "upon or over any land", but then,
as in the 1980 Act, "land" was defined as including "land

covered with water"[25] – an expression described by the Law
Commission as encompassing "lakes, rivers and foreshore".[26]

As with the Prescription Act 1832, the method of dedication
laid down in the Highways Act is an alternative to rather than a
replacement of the rules developed at common law.[27] Nevertheless, statutory dedication incorporates certain of the common law rules. Because of this overlap and in order to highlight
differences between the two methods of dedication, the main
requirements of common law and statutory dedication are
discussed together below.

(a) Use as of right

Both at common law and under section 31(1) of the Highways
Act 1980, the public's use of the way must have been "as of
right" in order to form the basis of implied dedication. As
explained by Tomlin J. in *Hue* v. *Whiteley* (1929),[28] members
of the public must have "believe[d] themselves to be exercising
a public right to pass from one highway to another". Their use
of the way must not have been secret, by force or under
licence.[29]

(b) Purpose of use

Both at common law and under the Highways Act, the motive
of members of the public in using a way appears irrelevant in
determining whether the way has been dedicated.[30] Thus,
there is no special difficulty in establishing dedication of a
thoroughfare which has been used primarily or even exclusively for recreational purposes.[31] The courts appear equally
willing to find dedication of a cul-de-sac used for recreation, at
least if the way leads to some beauty spot such as a waterfall or
ravine.[32]

(c) Use without interruption

By interrupting public use with the intention of stopping public
enjoyment of a way,[33] the relevant landowner can prevent the
creation of public rights both at common law and under the
Highways Act. Such interruption has this effect at common law
because it indicates that the landowner has no intention to
dedicate the way to the public.[34] Under the Highways Act, the
landowner's action has this effect because the statutory
presumption of dedication operates only if there has been
public use for the stipulated period "without interruption".[35]

(d) Length of use

At common law, use is simply evidence of implied dedication. There is no fixed period during which public use must continue in order to constitute evidence that a landowner intends to dedicate a public right of passage. Hence, as noted by Chambre J. in *Woodyer* v. *Hadden* (1813), "if the act of dedication be unequivocal, it may take place immediately".[36] Use for a period as short as 18 months has been held sufficient to justify an inference of dedication.[37] But equally, there is no set period of use which automatically creates a presumption of dedication. Even if there is no contradictory evidence, tribunals of fact need not infer dedication from long and uninterrupted use.[38]

Dedication under the Highways Act requires at least 20 years' use as of right.[39] Where there has been such use of the way, the requirements for statutory dedication have in practice supplanted the common law rules. Section 31(1) provides that

> where a way . . . has been actually enjoyed by the public as of right and without interruption for a full period of twenty years, the way is to be deemed to have been dedicated as a highway unless there is sufficient evidence that there was no intention during that period to dedicate it.

As explained by Denning L.J. in *Fairey* v. *Southampton C.C.* (1956), this provision "reverses the burden of proof: for whereas previously the legal burden of proving dedication was on the public who asserted the right, now after 20 years' use the legal burden is on the landowner to refute it".[40] Where the statutory presumption operates, the affirmant of the public right need not discharge the "artificial onus" of establishing that "somebody or other had in fact dedicated . . . which [at common law] was often fatal to his success". By removing these difficulties of proof, section 31 largely assimilates the English legal position to "the more sensible one obtaining north of the Tweed".[41]

(e) Intention to dedicate

Both at common law and under the Highways Act, the intention of the relevant landowner is critical to proof of the creation of a public right of passage by implied dedication. However, as indicated in the preceding section, the onus of proving such intention is on the affirmant of the public right only at common law. Where 20 years' use as of right has been established, section 31(1) of the 1980 Act places landowners under the onus of bringing "sufficient evidence that there was no intention during that period to dedicate it".

Probably because the concept of dedication has its basis in legal fiction, the requirement of an "intention" to dedicate is itself misleading. Rather than depending simply on the state of mind of the landowners, the "intention" which the courts look for to establish or to disprove dedication is the intention of the landowner as communicated to the public. As stated by Littledale J. in *Barraclough* v. *Johnson* (1838),[44] the landowner's intention "is not decided by what he says. A man may say that he does not mean to dedicate a way to the public, and yet, if he allowed them to pass every day for a length of time, his declaration alone would not be regarded". Even if the landowner's intention that there should not be a public right of passage is communicated to certain users of the way, this may be insufficient to prevent an inference of dedication if the members of the public who have generally asserted the right are unaware of the landowner's intention.[43]

Because of this emphasis on communication of the landowner's intention, there logically should be a strict rule that where a landowner has taken no steps to disabuse members of the public of their belief that a right of way has been dedicated, the courts must infer dedication. Judges have sometimes adopted this view. Thus in *R.* v. *Lloyd* (1808),[44] Lord Ellenborough stated:

> If the owner of the soil throws open a passage, and neither marks by any visible distinction, that he means to preserve all his rights over it, nor excludes persons from passing through it by positive prohibition, he shall be presumed to have dedicated it to the public.

Yet the weight of judicial opinion, in the wake of the House of Lords' decision in *Mann* v. *Brodie* (1885),[45] favours the proposition that where a landowner apparently acquiesces in the public use, the courts simply may infer dedication.

Especially in cases concerning the countryside, the courts have been reluctant to infer an intention to dedicate from a landowner's failure to disturb the public in their use of a way. In several cases, the main issue has been the manner in which the courts should construe the benevolence of landowners in allowing the public to pass across their land. As observed by the Court of Appeal in *Attorney-General and Newton Abbot R.D.C.* v. *Dyer* (1946),[46] "there is no rule or principle which requires . . . [a court] to attribute the user to tolerance if it is possible so to do". Nevertheless, following a dictum of Bowen

L. J. in *Blount* v. *Layard* (1888),[47] judges have frequently argued that dedication should not be inferred from use which has its basis in the charity of landowners since the creation of public rights in this manner might force "landowners to be churlish about their rights for fear that their indulgence may be abused". The logical difficulty with this argument is that, if applied consistently, it would mean that rights of passage could never be created by implied dedication since dedication by definition involves a landowner in making a gift to, and hence in being charitable towards, the public. In terms of public policy, one may also prefer the opinion of the Court of Appeal in the *Dyer* case. Adopting the view of Justice Cardozo that "property like other social institutions has a social function to fulfil",[48] Evershed J. stated that where public use of a footpath has its origin in "the toleration and neighbourliness" of previous landholders, "it may be no bad thing that the good nature of earlier generations should have a permanent memorial".[49]

Possibly the clearest instance of the difficulties which may arise from inferring dedication from the benevolence of landowners is provided by the decision of the Californian Supreme Court in *Gion* v. *City of Santa Cruz* (1970).[50] In that case, the court held that an implied dedication of a "permanent recreational easement" should be inferred from extended use by the public of private beaches and of the access routes to them. In response to this decision, many owners of beaches, who had previously left their property open for public recreation, installed barbed wire fences and hired private security guards in order to display opposition to public use of their land.[51]

Superficially, this chain of events appears to support the general reluctance of English judges to infer dedication from the charity of landowners. The creation of the public right in the *Gion* case was, as Bowen L.J. might have predicted, contrary to the public interest because it resulted in a net reduction in the beach area to which the public had access. Yet the actions of Californian landowners can in large measure be attributed to the Supreme Court's suggestion that a landowner who wished to manifest an intention not to dedicate would have to do more than erecting notices and in fact would have to make "significant" efforts to exclude the public.[52]

In England, by contrast, there is a range of simple means by which a landowner may allow public access over his land while preventing this access from resulting in rights of passage. Since the early nineteenth century, it has been settled at common law that a landowner may indicate that he has no intention of dedicating a public right of passage by preventing the public from using the path for one day a year,[53] by placing a bar across the path[54] or by erecting and maintaining a notice board declaring the path to be private.[55] The latter means of manifesting an intention not to dedicate a highway is affirmed by the Highways Act 1980,[56] which also provides that if the notice is

> torn down or defaced, a notice given by the owner of the land to the appropriate council that the way is not dedicated as a highway is, in the absence of proof of a contrary intention, sufficient evidence to negative the intention of the owner of the land to dedicate the way as a highway.[57]

Under section 31(6), a landowner may similarly demonstrate his intention not to dedicate by lodging with the authority maps, appropriate statements and statutory declarations indicating the paths over his land which he admits to be highways.

In view of the ease with which a landowner may consequently prevent members of the public from acquiring rights of passage, it seems appropriate for the courts to infer that a landowner intends to dedicate unless for example he has erected a notice or otherwise interfered with public use of the way. If the courts readily infer an intention to dedicate in this situation, landowners who do not wish to allow the public to acquire rights over their land will not be forced to exclude the public from their land: they may prevent the creation of public rights simply by erecting barriers or notices or by lodging maps with the appropriate authority.

(f) Capacity to dedicate

(i) LAND UNDER TENANCY

Because dedication results in the creation of a right in perpetuity and "a man cannot dedicate that which is not his own",[58] at common law only the owner in fee simple of land can dedicate a right of passage to the public. Generally public use of a path against a lessee is not even evidence of dedication because the landlord may have been powerless to prevent this use and should not therefore be treated as having acquiesced in it.[59] However, if the land has been in the occupation of a series of lessees, the freeholder's assent may be assumed on the basis that at the termination of each lease he had a fresh opportunity

to interfere with the public's use of the way.[60] Moreover, even
if the land has been under lease during the whole period of
public use, dedication may be inferred as having occurred at
some time before the commencement of the lease provided
that the evidence of use extends as far back as living memory.[61]

Under the 1980 Act, freeholders have two means which they
lack at common law of preventing the creation of public rights
of passage.[62] Where land is in the possession of a tenant for a
term of years or from year to year, the reversioner may erect
and maintain a notice inconsistent with dedication.[63] Where
land is in the possession of a tenant for life or *pur autre vie,* the
reversioner may bring actions for trespass or seek injunctions
to stop the public using the way.[64] But because freeholders
have these powers, the fact that a tenant was in possession of
the land is not a barrier to the creation of a right of way.[65]

(ii) LAND OWNED BY STATUTORY CORPORATIONS OR PUBLIC
TRUSTEES

At common law, the requirement that a landowner have
capacity to dedicate applies to persons and corporations in
possession of land for public and statutory purposes. Under the
Highways Act 1980, this requirement has been preserved in
relation to statutory dedication.[66] Hence, relative to other
landowners, statutory corporations and public trustees are in a
privileged position under the Act because they will not be
deemed to have dedicated public rights of passage if they lack
capacity to do so.

As laid down by Parke J. in *R.* v. *Inhabitants of Leake*
(1833),[67] the test of capacity in this context turns on whether
dedication of a right of way is compatible with the purposes for
which the corporation or trustees hold the land. According to
Viscount Simonds in *British Transport Commission* v. *Westmorland C.C.* (1957),[68] the rationale of this test is that "it
would be improper that commissioners or other persons having
acquired land for a particular statutory purpose should
preclude themselves from using it for that purpose". Where,
however, the existence of a right of way is consistent with the
statutory purpose, there is "no impropriety in such secondary
use".

At least superficially, many of the reported cases concerning
dedication by statutory corporations and public trustees appear
to be irreconcilable. Thus, railway undertakers have been held
both capable and incapable of dedicating a bridge over a
railway affording an accommodation crossing;[69] they have

equally been held capable of dedicating a footpath crossing a line on the level,[70] and a footpath running along a railway track[71] but not a footpath over land which may come to be used as a railway.[72]

The differences between these decisions may be explained on the basis that the issue of compatibility is one of fact[73] and therefore lower courts and juries have considerable discretion as to their findings. But these differences may also be attributable to a shift in judicial attitudes. Almost all the reported cases in which dedication has been found to be *ultra vires* occurred around the turn of the present century.[74] Since then the courts have, without exception, found that dedication was within the powers of the trustees or relevant corporation.

In so far as principles emerge from the decided cases, the only clear instance of incompatibility is where the existence of a public right of passage would result in a substantial increase in the cost of maintaining the statutory work.[75] Otherwise, the landowner must suffer much more than inconvenience before dedication will be held to be incompatible with the purpose for which the undertaker holds the land.[76] The fact that there has been long public use of a path is, in itself, evidence that the creation of a public right is compatible with the landowner's statutory function or public duty.[77] On this basis, it seems that statutory corporations and public trustees generally have capacity to dedicate public rights of passage.

(g) Acceptance by the public

The rule that creation of a public right of passage depends on both the landowner dedicating and the public accepting the right of way was developed in litigation in the early nineteenth century when the inhabitants of a parish were generally bound to repair all highways in their area.[78] In this period, there was concern over landowners deliberately opening rights of way to the public in order to avoid the expense of maintaining them.[79] To overcome this problem, Bayley J. in *R*. v. *Inhabitants of St Benedict, Cambridge* (1821)[80] argued that liability to repair should result from "some act of acquiescence or adoption of the parish" as well as public use. Then in *R*. v. *Mellor* (1830)[81] Littledale J. linked adoption by the public or parish with the creation of public rights. He stated, "A road becomes public by reason of a dedication of the right of passage to the public by the owner of the soil, and of an acceptance of the right by the public or the parish. In this case, the facts stated do not furnish any ground for presuming an adoption by the public; that being so, the township . . . would not be bound to repair . . .".[82]

In *R.* v. *Inhabitants of Leake* (1833)[83] the Court of King's Bench rejected the novel requirement that the parish's liability to repair should depend on adoption. In the Highway Act 1835 Parliament intervened and severed the connection between the parish's liability and the creation of public highways by providing that parishes would become liable to repair newly created roads only if certain conditions were satisfied including that the roads were made in a substantial manner to the satisfaction of the surveyor of the parish.[84] Nevertheless, the *Mellor* case became established authority for the proposition that dedication of a public right of passage is effective only if the dedication is accepted by the public. This proposition is, however, without practical significance since acceptance by the public is established by the use by the public which also constitutes the evidence of dedication by the landowner.[85]

(2) Immemorial use

At common law a party may claim a private right of way by prescription if he can show that he and his predecessors have used the way since "time immemorial" – that is, the year 1189, the arbitrary limit of legal memory.[86] There is considerable judicial support for the proposition that public rights of way over both land[87] and water[88] can also be established by prescription. In at least one reported case, concerning navigation on the River Trent, a public right was established on this basis.[89] However, recognition of immemorial use as a basis for the creation of public rights of way would be inconsistent with the many cases concerning rights to take profits à prendre in which the courts have held that the public as such is incapable of acquiring rights by prescription.[90] This proposition has been stated in such general terms that it appears to apply to all rights and is therefore at odds with the judicial authority in favour of acquisition of public rights of passage by prescription. This conflict can be resolved only by rejecting the dicta in the right of way cases as ill-considered or by narrowing the rule against prescription so that it applies only to public rights of taking, if not only to rights to take profits.

In terms of both policy and principle, there appears to be no good reason why immemorial use should not bring about the creation of public rights of passage. By analogy with the law relating to the acquisition of local rights by the inhabitants of particular districts, the main rationale of the decisions against the public acquiring rights of taking by prescription is probably that the creation of such rights would lead to the destruction of the resource[91] – an argument which manifestly does not apply to rights of passage. The theoretical basis of these decisions is that only defined groups of persons can prescribe for rights because prescription in all cases presupposes a grant and, as a matter of principle, a grant cannot be made to the public at large.[92] This rule is hardly convincing in relation to public rights of passage since such rights can be dedicated to the public which – as the courts have occasionally admitted – is in effect identical to a grant to the public.[93]

The acceptance of immemorial use as a basis of public rights of passage would be of considerable theoretical importance. It would involve recognizing that a grant can be made to the public or that use, of itself, can be the basis of a public right. In practical terms, however, such acceptance of immemorial use is likely to be of little or no significance – and hence may never become the subject of litigation – since rather than satisfying the onerous requirement of showing use back to 1189, the affirmant of a public right of passage may simply show much shorter use from which dedication may be implied.

(3) Substantial use

In *De Jure Maris,* which provides the source of much of the common law concerning public rights of navigation, Hale did not present a developed theory of how public rights of navigation were created in non-tidal waters. However, he recognized that only some such waters were subject to public rights of navigation, stating that

> There be some streams or rivers, that are private . . . in use, as little streams and rivers that are not a common passage for the king's people. Again, there be other rivers, as well fresh as salt, that are of common or publick use for carriage of boats and lighters. And these, whether they are fresh or salt, whether they flow and reflow or not, are *prima facie publici juris,* common highways for man or goods or both from one inland town to another.[94]

In *Attorney-General* v. *Simpson* (1901) Farwell J. interpreted this passage as meaning that "common use" turns non-tidal rivers into "common highways". He stated:

> the question whether a non-tidal river is navigable or not depends, not on the question of possibility of navigation, but on the proof of the fact of navigation. If the fact be proved, then the channel of the river is the King's highway, and as such is open to the free passage of all the subjects of the Crown.[95]

By "the fact of navigation", Farwell J. is unlikely to have meant isolated public use of a river. Rather he probably meant "use for a substantial period of time on a substantial scale openly carried on".[96] Consequently, even if Farwell J.'s views on the creation of public rights of navigation are correct – and they are open to attack on the same basis as "immemorial use" discussed above[97] – proof of the fact of navigation is again unlikely to provide an easier means of establishing the existence of public rights than does dedication.

(B) DECLARATORY ACTS

In relation to certain highways and rivers, an assortment of local Acts has confirmed the existence of public rights of passage which had previously been created at common law. So long as these statutes remain in force, the existence of the common law rights is of little or no practical significance – the various Acts provide ready proof of the public rights, so making it unnecessary to consider establishing their existence at common law. In the event of these statutes being repealed, however, the relation between the common law and statutory rights becomes critically important. Only if the common law basis of a public right coexists with or is modified by the legislation will the public right continue to exist after the relevant Act is repealed. If the common law right either merges with or is superseded by the legislation, the public right will be extinguished on repeal of the Act.

(1) The range of legislation

(a) Highways

The only declaratory Acts in relation to the existence of highways appear to be turnpike and inclosure Acts, which in the present context are both of minor significance. From 1663 until about 1700, turnpike Acts at least implicitly recognized that certain roads were public highways as part of empowering trustees to impose tolls in order to finance the maintenance and repair of these roads.[98] These Acts were passed for limited periods – usually 21 years – and, although generally extended, they had all either expired or been repealed by the late nineteenth century. In making awards under inclosure Acts in the eighteenth and nineteenth centuries, inclosure commissioners generally made substantial changes to road networks – sweeping away the existing patterns and creating simpler ones.[99] However, in exercising their various road-making powers, the commissioners sometimes set out roads which followed the line of existing highways. As determined in *R*. v. *Inhabitants of Cricklade* (1850),[100] such action by the commissioners did not involve the creation of new public ways (possibly even where the old roads were narrowed in some parts or diverted in others). Rather, in setting out these roads in their awards, the commissioners were confirming the existence of the rights created at common law.

(b) Rivers

There is no list of the statutes which confirm the existence of common law rights of navigation, but it is clear that many English rivers – including a number of the most important – are the subject of such legislation. In some cases, the relevant Acts contain provisions which are strictly "declaratory" in the sense that they provide an exact restatement of the right which had been created at common law. Alternatively, they confirm that a public right exists but change some of its incidents, most significantly by making exercise of the right subject to payment of a toll. All these Acts appear to be "perpetual" measures which either remain in force or have been repealed by Statute Law Revision Acts,[101] which do not change the law but simply justify omission of the repealed matter from the official volumes of the revised statutes.[102]

The earliest of the declaratory statutes was enacted in 1430 in relation to the River Severn. As part of providing a remedy for travellers on the Severn against the depredations of "Welshmen and other persons", the Act affirmed that the "liege people of the King may have and enjoy their free passage in the said river with floates and drags, and all manner of merchandises and other goods and chattels, at their will without disturbance of any".[103]

From the sixteenth century, various Acts which authorized either the construction of artificial "cuts" or the "improvement" of existing unnavigable rivers also included provisions declaratory of public rights of navigation on other stretches of these waterways. Thus, the River Lee Act 1571 both authorized the making of cuts to bring the River Lee to the north side of London and provided that "all the Queen's subjects their boats and vessels shall have free passage through the said river, as well the new cut as the old river . . . as in other common rivers and waters they may lawfully do".[104]

Since at least the eighteenth century, various Acts have also included declaratory provisions in relation to stretches of river

which were made the subject of statutory works having
previously been navigable at common law. Generally in this
situation, the legislation not only confirms the public right but
also makes its exercise subject to a toll. In such statutes, the
public's right is described in much the same terms as are the
public rights of navigation created by legislation in relation to
canals.[105] Members of the public are typically given "free
liberty" to use the waterway on payment of the authorized
tolls.[106]

(2) The effect of the legislation on the common law rights

The Acts which confirm the existence of public rights of way do
not expressly indicate whether they affect the common law
basis of these rights, and there is almost no direct judicial
authority on this issue.[107] However, cases which have considered legislation which has more or less confirmed private
rights created by custom, charter, prescription or franchise
indicate that such legislation may act in any one of three
ways.[108] It may leave the old right standing and place a new
right beside it.[109] Alternatively, it may modify the common law
right.[110] Or it may extinguish the common law right, in which
case the right can continue only "by virtue of the statute,
without any power of revival or reverter back to its original
nature".[111] The greater the differences between the statutory
and the common law right, the more likely it is that the
common law right will have been extinguished as repugnant to
the statute.[112] But even where the statute simply restates the
pre-existing right, statute may have replaced the common law
as the "root of the title" of the public's right.[113]

Because the courts are slow to disturb public rights of
way,[114] they may be inclined to find that a declaratory statute
does not constitute the sole source of a public way. They may
therefore find that statutes which are strictly declaratory of
public rights have simply affirmed the existence and provided
ready proof of these rights. Statutes which make the exercise of
public rights of navigation subject to the payment of a toll may
be held to have simply modified the common law basis of these
rights. This view appears to have been adopted – without
analysis – by Littledale J. in *R.* v. *Winter* (1828)[115] which
concerned a turnpike road. The judge stated that "If the road
. . . had become a public highway before the Act of Parliament
passed, the making it a turnpike road merely during the
continuance of the Act of Parliament would not prevent its
continuing a public highway [when the Act expired]."

(C) CREATION BY OR UNDER STATUTE

Although occasionally described as a form of "dedication",[116] the creation of public rights of way by or under statute is quite unlike the creation of such rights at common law. Rather than depending on the assumed benevolence of landowners and inferences from public use, the creation of public rights of way under statute usually results from the exercise of powers clearly granted by Parliament which, as a last resort, frequently include powers of compulsory purchase of land. The main point of interest in relation to the statutory creation of public ways is consequently not whether a public right has come into existence in a particular case,[117] but the range and operation of the different types of legislation which have authorized the creation of public rights of way.

(1) Local and private Acts

Until the nineteenth century, the statutory creation of rights of way occurred primarily under local or private Acts (which sometimes were modified by or incorporated provisions from general public legislation). These local private Acts fell broadly into two categories. Turnpike, river improvement and canal Acts empowered undertakers to create public rights of way in return for the right to impose tolls. Inclosure Acts authorized the creation of public ways as part of a general reorganization of the road network.

(a) Turnpike Acts

Parliament first gave turnpike trustees a limited power to change the road network in the early 1700s when a number of turnpike Acts authorized trustees to acquire land to widen roads.[118] From the early 1740s, this power was consistently included in new turnpike Acts. From the late 1750s, most turnpike Acts empowered trustees to divert parts of their roads and to build completely new sections, while the General Turnpike Act 1822 conferred this power on all turnpike trusts.[119] As determined in *R. v. Inhabitants of Lordsmere* (1850),[120] the public had a right of passage over all these new stretches of turnpike road regardless of whether the Acts expressly provided that these roads should be "public" or "common" highways. Patterson J. considered it "manifest that in all Turnpike Acts all persons are to have a right to use the road as a highway, paying toll".[121]

(b) Inclosure Acts

Until the end of the eighteenth century, the power of inclosure commissioners to set out new public rights of way depended on the terms of private Acts which authorized the inclosure of particular areas. Each of these Acts appears to have included some form of provision empowering the commissioners to set out such "public and private highways" as they thought "convenient or necessary".[122] On the basis that a " 'highway' is *the genus* of all public ways",[123] it consequently seems that the commissioners were always entitled to create footpaths and bridleways as well as carriageways.[124]

The main difference between the powers of the various commissioners to create highways related to the width of the ways which they set out. While some inclosure Acts specified a minimum width (generally 60 feet) only in relation to carriageways,[125] many Acts specified the same minimum width for all types of highway.[126] The latter approach was adopted in the Inclosure (Consolidation) Act 1801 which set out model clauses which were incorporated in almost all local inclosure Acts after 1801.[127] Section 8 of the 1801 Act provided that all "highways", including footpaths and bridleways,[128] set out by the local inclosure commissioners,

> shall be, and remain thirty feet wide at the least, and so as the same shall be set out in such directions as shall, upon the whole, appear to . . . them most commodious to the public. . . .

This provision of a minimum width was abandoned in the General Inclosure Act 1845 which, unlike the 1801 Act, did not require the passing of a local Act before particular areas could be inclosed. The 1845 Act provided for the appointment of "valuers" whose primary function was to divide, set out and allot the land which was to be enclosed,[129] but who also were given a power to create rights of way which was unrestricted by any stipulation as to the minimum width of the new ways.[130]

(c) River improvement and canal Acts

Between the mid-sixteenth and the mid-nineteenth centuries, Parliament enacted a succession of private and local Acts which empowered undertakers either to make navigable existing rivers which were impassable or to construct canals.[131] The great majority of the river improvement Acts were passed between 1660 and 1720; the canal Acts date primarily from the period 1760 to 1830.[132] Probably all these Acts created public rights of navigation, but generally these rights have been extinguished by subsequent legislation.

In every canal Act and most of the river improvement Acts there appear to have been provisions which expressly created public rights of navigation. A small number of the river improvement Acts did not contain such provisions,[133] but this does not necessarily indicate that these statutes conferred no rights on members of the public. Rather it appears likely that these Acts impliedly created public rights of navigation, just as turnpike Acts authorizing the construction of new roads have been held to have created public rights of way even where the relevant legislation did not expressly declare these roads to be public highways.[134]

The river improvement and canal Acts generally made exercise of the public right of navigation subject to payment of tolls, but they occasionally left it free – at least in circumstances which then occurred infrequently, such as where a vessel carried no goods[135] or did not pass through any locks.[136] The Acts also usually imposed no express restrictions on the purpose for which the right could be exercised, although in some cases they limited the right to the carriage of goods.[137] Possibly because a small number of these Acts expressly gave members of the public a right to use pleasure boats,[138] it has been suggested that the public right of navigation on these waterways generally did not extend to these boats.[139] However, those statutes which did not limit navigation to the carriage of goods appear to have clearly allowed pleasure boating as part of giving all persons "free liberty" to navigate on the waterways "with boats or vessels".[140] The few statutory provisions which expressly conferred a right to use pleasure boats can be regarded as having been enacted *pro majore cautela*.[141]

Partly as a result of the decline in the use of inland waterways by commercial transport, Parliament over the last 150 years has extinguished the public right of navigation on most statutory navigations, including all such waterways owned or managed by the British Waterways Board.[142] Public rights of navigation created by river improvement and canal Acts survive in relation to a few waterways such as the upper Avon Navigation,[143] which are owned and managed by undertakers other than the British Waterways Board. They also survive in relation to those waterways where the undertaker has been dissolved under the Companies Acts or has disappeared without trace and the Act establishing the navigation has not been repealed.[144] Even if the undertaker conveyed the navigation to another party, the public right survives, but there is no-one in this situation who can either impose tolls or, for that matter, is under a duty to maintain the navigation.[145]

(2) Public General Acts

Since the late nineteenth century, public Acts have entrusted a range of authorities with general powers to create public rights of way over land.[146] Most of these powers have related to the creation of carriageways. However, since the enactment of the National Parks and Access to the Countryside Act 1949, local authorities have also been empowered to create footpaths, bridleways and "long-distance routes" by agreement or order; the Secretary of State has also been empowered to create such highways by order.

(a) Creation of paths by agreement

Under what is now section 25 of the Highways Act 1980, "a local authority may enter into an agreement with any person having the necessary power in that behalf for the dedication by that person of a footpath or bridleway over land in their area". The one significant difference between such agreements and express dedication at common law is that it may be a condition of dedication under section 25 that the landowners receive payment.[147]

(b) Creation of paths by order

Under section 26 of the Highways Act 1980, both local authorities[148] and the Secretary of State for the Environment[149] may make orders creating footpaths and bridleways (and hence also sections of long-distance routes). Before making such an order an authority or the Secretary of State need not have sought and failed to create the path by agreement. Instead they must simply have decided that there is a need for the path and that it is expedient the path be created having regard to

> (a) the extent to which the path or way would add to the convenience or enjoyment of a substantial section of the public, or to the convenience of persons resident in the area; and
> (b) the effect which the creation of the path or way would have on the rights of persons interested in the land, account being taken of the provisions as to compensation . . .[150]

If an order made by an authority is unopposed, it takes effect without any further approval; opposed orders require the confirmation of the Secretary of State.[151] In respect of all orders, compensation may be obtained by any person with an interest in the land over which the path was created.[152] The amount paid to such persons is equal to any depreciation in the value of their interest in the land or to any damage which they have suffered as a result of disturbance in their enjoyment of the land.[153]

(c) Long-distance routes

Under the National Parks and Countryside Act 1949, the Countryside Commission (formerly the National Parks Commission) may recommend to the Secretary of State that long-distance routes be established so that members of the public may make extensive journeys on foot or horseback (and probably now, also bicycle)[154] without for the most part travelling along roads used mainly by vehicles.[155] The creation of these routes may (and generally does) involve a combination of existing and new paths,[156] but the Act makes no specific provision as to how the new paths are to be created. Ministerial approval of a route has no effect of itself, and the Commission has no powers of its own to create paths. The result is an unsatisfactory, byzantine process whereby the Commission works through local authorities who must also be convinced of the need for making a path, and whose orders – if opposed – must again be approved by the Minister.[157] Only once, in 1984, has the Minister intervened and exercised his power under section 26 of the Highways Act 1980 to make a compulsory path creation order where the local authority had declined to do so.[152]

II. THE RIGHTS OF MEMBERS OF THE PUBLIC

The rights of members of the public on rights of way can only be determined by reference to two discrete bodies of law. These rights are, of course, a product of the creation of public ways which, by definition, involves members of the public being entitled to use these ways for certain activities (while conduct falling outside this permitted sphere remains a trespass against the relevant landowner). The public's rights are, however, also delimited by the various torts and offences – especially public nuisance and wilful obstruction of the highway[159] – which may be committed by persons using public ways independently of whether their conduct is lawful vis-a-vis the owner of the soil.

The extent to which these two bodies of law are consistent is unclear.[160] However, at least in relation to highways, public nuisance and the statutory offence of wrongful obstruction in practice provide the main controls on public conduct. Actions in trespass can be brought only by the owner of the surface[161] who at common law is *prima facie* the adjoining landowner.[162] These landowners could be expected to bring actions at least in respect of conduct which interferes with their enjoyment of their property (if not also conduct which impedes members of the public exercising their right of way). However, under statute the surface of all highways maintainable at public expense – that is nearly all footpaths and bridleways and the great majority of carriageways – is owned by the relevant highway authority[163] and it appears to be their policy not to bring actions for trespass against persons whose conduct falls outside the rights of members of the public.

(A) THE RIGHT OF PASSAGE

As the term "public right of way" suggests, members of the public have a clearly established right to use such ways for passing and repassing. This right is, however, subject to at least one and possibly two major limitations (apart from the statutory rules of the road and the various byelaws which govern the use of certain waterways). The first limitation affects the mode of use of the right of way – that is, whether, for example, a highway can be used only on foot or also on horseback or by vehicular traffic. The second limitation concerns the purpose for which the way is used – whether the right of passage extends only to commercial, recreational and other "legitimate" purposes or whether the public can lawfully go back and forth for any purpose whatsoever.

(1) Limitations on the mode of passage

The primary limitation on rights of passage is their restriction to particular forms of use. At common law, there are three categories of highway – footpaths, bridleways and cartways – each of which is subject to different types of use. At first these classifications served primarily to delimit the burden to which the owners of the soil of the highway were subject, but since at least the nineteenth century they have primarily been important for preventing conflicts between different types of use. To a significant extent they still fulfil this role, although they have been supplemented by statutory powers. In relation to waterways, the public right of passage at common law is limited simply by a concept of reasonable use, but various authorities have also been given statutory powers to limit use to particular types of vessel.

(a) Highways

The development of the common law's division of public rights of way into footpaths, bridleways and carriageways is to some extent obscure. Far from recognizing any such division of highways, Roman law treated public rights of way as open to all forms of traffic.[164] Bracton does not discuss this point. However, by the fourteenth century some distinction appears to have been drawn between ways for foot passengers, horsemen and carriages.[165] An Act passed in 1532–3 contains the earliest categorization of rights of way. The Act, which provided for "where a man killing a thief shall not forfeit his goods", applied to robberies and murders "in or nigh any common highway carteway horseway or footway".[166]

The exact content of the three categories of right of way was first discussed by Coke in the first part of his *Institutes* (Coke on Littleton) published in 1628. In considering private rights – that is the right of a tenant at will to re-enter his land and harvest corn he had planted after the termination of his tenancy – Coke with some modifications adopted the Roman classification of private ways into footpaths *(iter)*, bridleways *(actus)* and cartways *(via)*. However, Coke at least to some extent applied this classification to public ways, in considering the King's highway as a form of *via*.[167] In the main restatement of Coke's ideas on rights of way, William Hawkins in the *Pleas of the Crown* (1716) accepted that Coke's three categories applied to both private and public rights of way.[168] The application of these categories to public rights of way has since gone unchallenged, even though in the nineteenth century these categories were largely rejected in relation to easements (notwithstanding their development in this context).

Until the decline of cattle droving in the mid-nineteenth century, the main difficulty with Coke's classification of public rights of way was probably his failure to recognize driftways as a distinct category of public right of way. The source of this problem was Coke's reliance on Roman law with its three categories of right of way when English law might have been better served by a fourfold classification – footpaths, bridleways, driftways and carriageways. Coke tinkered with the Roman categories – attributing new meanings to *iter, actus* and *via*[169] – but he did not break the Roman mould. Instead, having labelled his second category a "foot way and horse way", he also described it as including a "drift way".[170] Emphasis on the latter part of this definition might have resulted in the second of Coke's categories being identified as a driftway rather than as a bridleway. By focusing, however, on the first part of Coke's definition, most later commentators and now Parliament and the courts have reduced the right to drive animals to an optional extra to the rights to walk and ride on a bridleway.[171] The resulting uncertain content of bridleways has been matched in relation to carriageways. As determined by Mansfield C.J. in *Ballard* v. *Dyson* (1808), there is only a "presumption" that a public highway is "for cattle as well as carriages".[172]

Since the mid-nineteenth century, further problems with Coke's classification of rights of way have arisen in relation to new forms of transport. In *Case* v. *Midland Railway Co.* (1859)[173] and *R.* v. *Mathias* (1861),[174] which were respectively concerned with a steamboat on a canal and a pram on a footpath, the courts accepted that a right of passage once acquired will extend to more modern forms of traffic reasonably similar to those for which the highway was originally dedicated. The only proviso is that these new forms of traffic neither significantly increase the burden on the owner of the soil nor substantially inconvenience persons exercising the right of passage in the manner originally contemplated.

In view of these rules, it is perhaps surprising that there has been no litigation over the right of drivers of motor vehicles to use carriageways. Such vehicles increase significantly the burden of the soil (especially in the case of lorries) and substantially inconvenience persons exercising their right of passage on foot or horseback or, for that matter, in carts. Nevertheless, it has generally been assumed that motor vehicles may be driven on cartways. In *Hubbard* v. *Pitt* (1974)[175] – the only reported case to contain any discussion of this issue – Forbes J. commented "the only changes time legitimates in relation to highway law are changes in the modes of user for passage. Where, for instance, it was once permissible to pass with a horse and cart, it may now be legal to use a lorry."

The main litigation over the use of new forms of transport arose in the late nineteenth century in relation to bicycles. Because it involves use of a vehicle, the riding of a bicycle is hardly analogous to passage on foot. Consequently, it is clear that cyclists have no right to ride on footpaths. But it is uncertain whether they have a right at common law to ride on bridleways. In terms of burden on the soil and inconvenience to other path-users, the riding of a bicycle is much more like riding a horse than driving a car; on this basis, cyclists may have a right at common law to use bridleways. However, it has generally been assumed that the courts will classify bicycles as "carriages" in this context, because they are a mechanical form of transport;[176] hence the enactment of section 30(1) of the Countryside Act 1968 which provides that members of the public may ride bicycles on bridleways so long as in doing so they give way to pedestrians and persons on horseback. Provision of a similar right to cycle on footpaths was not accepted by Parliament.[177] It consequently remains a trespass to cycle on footpaths, while it is an offence under the Highway Act 1835 (as amended in 1888)[178] not only to ride[179] but probably even to wheel a bicycle on a roadside footpath.[180]

So far as recreation in the countryside is concerned, the main significance of Coke's classification lies in its separation of different classes of potentially conflicting use. The existence of such conflict between cattle droving and carriage driving was an important factor in the Court of Common Pleas' decision in *Ballard* v. *Dyson*[181] that a right to drive cattle did not necessarily exist over a private carriageway. The possibility that cyclists would endanger or at least disturb pedestrians was central to Parliament's decision in 1968 not to give cyclists a right to ride on footpaths.[182] The most important example of such conflict is, however, that between users of motor vehicles and all other classes of user of rights of way. As noted by the Dartington Amenity Research Trust in 1979:

> the speed of motor vehicles and the smooth, hard surfaces they require make most roads unpleasant and dangerous for slower traffic. At the same time interest in walking, riding, cycling and driving for pleasure rather than necessity have increased considerably over the last twenty years.[183]

Within this context, the crucial aspect of footpaths and bridleways is that motor vehicles may not be used on them.

Debate over limitations on the use of motor vehicles has been greatest in relation to rights of way which are carriageways but which are used primarily as footpaths or bridleways rather than by cars. As discussed further below,[184] the National Parks and Access to the Countryside Act 1949 provided unsatisfactorily for the recording of such carriageways when it created the category of "roads used as public paths" – generally referred to as RUPPs – as part of its survey of public rights of way used for recreational non-motoring purposes.[185] Because of difficulties with the definition of a RUPP, Parliament first in 1968 and then again in 1981 has created procedures for reclassifying these roads as either footpaths, bridleways or byways open to all traffic.[186] However, for non-motoring users of RUPPs, the reclassification holds no advantages. If a RUPP is reclassified as a byway, the new classification confirms the right of members of the public to use motor vehicles on the way. If a RUPP is reclassified as a bridleway, it becomes open to destruction by ploughing.

The solution to this problem lies in the considerable range of statutory powers to limit the use of public rights of passage, although, as evidenced by the decade long controversy over banning motorcycles and cars from the Berkshire Ridgeway, there are considerable practical difficulties in persuading the authorities to exercise these powers. Under the Road Traffic Regulation Act 1984, county councils may make traffic regulation orders by which the use of a road by any class of traffic may be prohibited, restricted or regulated[187] so as to prevent traffic of a kind which "is unsuitable having regard to the existing character of the road"[188] or to preserve "the character of the road in a case where it is specially suitable for use by persons on horseback or on foot".[189] In relation to such places as National Parks, Areas of Outstanding Natural Beauty and long-distance routes, the Minister of Transport acting on the advice of the Countryside Commission may make such orders for "the purpose of conserving or enhancing the natural beauty of the area, or of affording better opportunities for the public to enjoy the amenities of the area, or recreation or the study of nature in the area".[190] Finally, under the Town and Country Planning Act 1971, the Secretary of State for the Environment may, on application by the relevant local planning authority, extinguish the right of vehicles to use a highway where the authority by resolution has adopted a proposal for improving the amenity of their area.[191]

(b) Non-tidal rivers

The restriction at common law of the public right of navigation to reasonable forms of use[192] means that exercise of the right must, as stated by Lord Wilberforce, be consistent with "the capacity and quality of the river".[193] If parts of a river are suitable only for small craft, use of them by a large vessel is unreasonable if it unduly restricts or prevents the exercise by other navigators of the public right.[194] This does not mean, however, that there can be a public right of navigation restricted specifically to any class of vessel. Rather the public right of navigation thus limited is a full right for all craft to pass in the waters concerned. To state otherwise is "to confuse its extent with its description".[195]

Under a number of public Acts, various authorities are empowered to limit the public right of navigation over non-tidal waters to particular types of vessels as part of more general powers to regulate boating. Under the Countryside Act 1968, statutory water undertakers can exercise this power in relation to any waterways owned or managed by them in order to achieve a range of purposes including "that persons resorting to the waterway . . . behave themselves as to avoid undue interference with the enjoyment of the waterway . . . by other persons".[196] Under the Water Resources Act 1963, water authorities can exercise this power in relation to certain rivers in the interests of water navigation, land drainage or fisheries[197] (rather than because of conflicts between classes of navigators such as the users of canoes and power boats). More specifically, the Anglian Water Authority is empowered by its private Act of 1977 to make byelaws prescribing classes of vessels which may not enter waterways in respect of which the Authority is for the time being the navigation authority.[198]

(2) Limitations on the purpose of passage

Apart from a dictum in *Rouse* v. *Bardin* (1790), in which Wilson J. stated that members of the public have a right to use public highways "for all purposes",[199] the reasons for which members of the public can lawfully exercise their right of passage were not discussed by the courts or text-writers until the mid-nineteenth century. Since then, in a series of cases beginning with *R.* v. *Pratt* (1855),[200] the courts have held that the public right extends only to "legitimate" purposes, so that a person on a highway for other purposes commits trespass, notwithstanding that he is in fact passing along the way. This line of authority appears to have never been expressly doubted in England: it was affirmed as recently as 1975 by Lord Denning in *Hubbard* v. *Pitt*.[201] Nevertheless, the better view appears to be that the various decisions can be supported, if at all, on the basis that the *acts* (rather than the intentions) of the members of the public made them trespassers.[202] As suggested by observations of the House of Lords in the Scottish case

Wills' Trustees v. *Cairngorm Canoeing and Sailing School Ltd* (1976),[203] the various rules laid down as to purpose are incorrect, since it is inappropriate for the courts to examine the intentions of persons exercising their right of passage.

In seeking to limit the public's right of passage to certain purposes, the courts – especially the Court of Appeal in *Harrison* v. *Duke of Rutland* (1892)[204] – have invoked a fictional "self-interested" landowner. In dedicating the way to the public, such a landowner simply wishes to prevent uses of the way which interfere with his enjoyment of his property, but is unconcerned about interferences with other landowners or users of the way. On this basis, a person does not commit trespass if he passes along a highway with the intention of doing something unlawful as against someone other than the owner of the soil of the highway.[205] However, if he intends to interfere with how the owner of the soil of the highway uses his adjacent land, he commits trespass regardless of whether such interference is unlawful in itself.[206]

The three most important cases dealing with such trespasses against self-interested landowners are *R.* v. *Pratt, Harrison* v. *Duke of Rutland* and *Hickman* v. *Maisey* (1900).[207] In *Pratt* the defendant was held to have committed trespass to the highway by being there in search of game.[208] In the *Rutland* case, Harrison trespassed by using the highway to interfere with the defendant's right of shooting by preventing grouse from flying towards the butts occupied by the shooters. In *Hickman* v. *Maisey* the defendant was held to have trespassed when for an hour and a half he went back and forth on the highway, watching and taking notes of the trial of race-horses on the plaintiff's land.

In holding that the members of the public on the highways were trespassers, the courts in these three cases were influenced by what they clearly regarded as the impropriety of the conduct in question. Yet in *Pratt* they could have reached this conclusion on the basis that the defendant had fired a gun on the highway, so that his conduct fell outside the bounds of permissible acts of the public. In the *Rutland* case, where Harrison had disturbed the grouse by waving his handkerchief and opening and shutting his umbrella, this view could possibly also have been adopted, and Harrison's conduct could in any event have been regarded as a private nuisance if this tort can be committed on highways.[209] In *Hickman* v. *Maisey* the issue was really one of theft of information, and this is an interest which the courts have not upheld so far as looking over land is concerned.[210] Rather the courts have held that if a landowner wishes to prevent someone from being able to see his land, he should build the necessary fences.[211]

The courts should arguably have considered these cases in this way since, according to both Lords Hailsham and Wilberforce in the *Cairngorm* case,[212] the public right of passage is not restricted to particular purposes. Lord Hailsham noted that he found the argument to the contrary "most unattractive".[213] Lord Wilberforce stated "once a public right of passage is established, there is no warrant for making any distinction, or even for making any enquiry, as to the purpose for which the right is exercised."[214] He clearly considered it impractical to delimit the public right by reference to purpose, remarking "One cannot stop a canoe, any more than one can stop a pedestrian on a highway, and ask him what is the nature of his use."[215]

These statements are clearly inconsistent with the approach taken by the Court of Appeal in cases such as *Harrison* v. *Duke of Rutland*. Theoretically, one could distinguish the *Cairngorm* case on the basis that it was a Scottish decision, but there is nothing in the relevant passages of Lords Hailsham's and Wilberforce's judgments to suggest that the judges were expressing a principle limited to Scottish law. More significantly, it could be argued that the question of "illegitimate" use of ways was not before the House of Lords, which was directly concerned only with upholding the right of members of the public to use rights of way for recreational rather than simply for commercial purposes. Yet this does not undermine the force of the two judges' remarks. The better view consequently appears to be that the acts rather than the intentions of members of the public should determine whether they trespass on the highway.

(B) PUBLIC RIGHTS OTHER THAN PASSAGE

From the fourteenth until the late nineteenth century, the courts repeatedly held that over highways "The owner of the soil has right to all above and under ground, except only the right of passage, for the King and his people."[216] In so defining rights in highways, the courts' primary concern was to emphasize the property rights of the owners of the soil (and hence to make clear that the Crown had no interest in the soil of highways and that members of the public had no rights to take their profits). The courts were not concerned with whether the public could use highways for purposes other than passage which did not involve taking. Consequently, it is not surprising that in *Harrison* v. *Duke of Rutland* (1892) Lord Esher rejected the proposition that members of the public have only a right of passage on highways, and stated:

> Highways are, no doubt, dedicated *prima facie* for the purpose of passage; but things are done upon them by everybody which are recognized as being rightly done, and as constituting a reasonable and usual mode of using a highway as such. If a person on a highway does not transgress such reasonable and usual mode of using it, I do not think that he will be a trespasser.[217]

In subsequent cases the courts have accepted that the rights of members of the public on highways and rivers extend beyond mere passage, but have been unable to agree as to how these rights should be defined.

Apart from the great divergence of views expressed by the courts,[218] the main difficulty in determining the scope of the public's rights is that these rights may be delimited by actions for trespass, public nuisance and wilful obstruction of the highway. While wilful obstruction appears to be a statutory version of highway nuisance,[219] it is far from certain whether trespass and nuisance have the same ambits in this context. There consequently may be some acts which are trespasses but not nuisances (or *vice versa*). Nevertheless, if the various decisions are divided between those which take a narrow and those which take a broad view of the public's rights, there are many similarities between the trespass and nuisance cases in each of these categories.[220] According to the narrow view, the rights of members of the public extend only to things incidental to passage. On the broader view, the public is entitled to make reasonable use of public ways.

If members of the public are only entitled to do things which are incidental to passage, the extension of the public's rights is quite slight. A pedestrian may stop to tie his shoelaces; a milkman may deliver milk on his rounds; a motorist may load goods or repair a minor breakdown.[221] However, as noted by Glidewell L.J. in *Hirst* v. *Chief Constable of West Yorkshire* (1986),[222] two friends who meet in the street, not having seen each other for some time, would not be entitled to "stop to discuss their holidays for a quarter-of-an-hour or twenty minutes" since "what they are discussing has nothing to do with passing or re-passing in the street". Moreover, even those activities which are incidental to passage will have to be conducted in a reasonable fashion in order to be lawful.[223]

The great difficulty with this line of authority is that it results in an unnecessarily restricted view of the public's rights, according to which members of the public may be wrongdoers even where their acts are otherwise lawful, injure no-one or cause only trivial damage. As stated by Collins L.J. in *Hickman* v. *Maisey* (1900), the better view consequently appears to be that

> The right of the public to pass and repass on a highway is subject to all those reasonable extensions which may from time to time be recognised as necessary to its exercise in accordance with the enlarged notions of people in a country becoming more populous and highly civilized, but they must be such as are not inconsistent with the maintenance of the paramount idea that the right of the public is that of passage.[224]

On this approach, members of the public are entitled to use public rights of way for activities which have no relation to passage, so long as the relevant conduct is otherwise lawful and reasonable[225] – a matter which should be judged against all the circumstances of the case, including the length of time the activity continued, the place where it occurred, whether it in fact caused an obstruction, and the purpose for which it was done.[226]

At one extreme, the adoption of this test may lead to a very broad view being taken of the public's rights. Thus in *Culkin* v. *McFie & Sons Ltd* (1939)[227] – a personal injuries action in which the court clearly did not want to hold that the plaintiff was a trespasser because this would have precluded him from obtaining relief[228] – the court held that a child who chased his ball on to the street

> was not a trespasser upon the highway, and that he was, in all the circumstances, making a reasonable use of it. To hold otherwise would be to turn into a trespasser any child who chased his ball into the roadway or ran across the roadway in play.[229]

At the other extreme, the test of reasonable use may result in a very narrow construction of the public's rights, as in *Nagy* v. *Weston* (1964)[230] where a lorry driver who parked his vehicle by the roadside for five minutes was held to have acted unlawfully. It should, however, allow members of the public to use public rights of way in the countryside for many activities unconnected with passage – not only for sketching (as suggested by A. L. Smith L.J. in *Hickman* v. *Maisey*[231]) but also, for example, for bird-watching, picnics[232] and even fishing in waters where there is a public right of fishing.[233]

(C) THE EXTENT OF THE PUBLIC'S RIGHTS

Apart from any special enactment, the extent of the space subject to public rights of passage is a question of fact. However, if a highway is bounded by fences, the public right of passage *prima facie* extends to the whole space between the fences.[234] In relation to rivers there may also be a presumption that the public's right extends from bank to bank,[235] although it clearly is possible for the public's right to be confined to a particular channel or part of the river.[236]

III. INTERFERENCES WITH RIGHTS OF WAY

Because of the importance which the law attaches to unimpeded passage, interferences with rights of way are generally unlawful. Thus, at common law it is a public nuisance for occupiers or members of the public to obstruct or render dangerous a highway[237] or public right of navigation;[238] under statute it is an offence wilfully to obstruct a highway[239] and there are several offences dealing with particular forms of obstruction.[240] However, in certain situations legislation authorizes interferences with highways by farmers which may significantly impede public access to the countryside.[241] Moreover, even where interference with public rights of way is unlawful, there are considerable practical problems with enforcement of the law.

(A) LAWFUL INTERFERENCES

To the detriment of members of the public, occupiers of land have a broad right to plough both footpaths and bridleways, and have at least a limited right to keep potentially dangerous domesticated animals in fields crossed by rights of way. These interferences with the public's rights of passage have been justified on grounds of agricultural necessity. However, in relation to the keeping of dangerous domesticated animals, it is uncertain whether the farmers' agricultural advantage should be allowed to jeopardize public safety and to interfere with public enjoyment of the countryside. Even if a right to plough public paths is essential to farmers, which frequently may not be the case, there appears to be no good reason why they should not be under a duty to indicate the line of the path as soon as they have finished ploughing.

(1) The ploughing of footpaths and bridleways

Over the last 120 years the law has taken an increasingly sympathetic attitude towards the ploughing by occupiers of public rights of way which cross their land. Whereas it was accepted until the mid-nineteenth century that the ploughing of a public path was in all circumstances a public nuisance,[242] the Court of Queen's Bench held in *Mercer* v. *Woodgate* (1869)[243] that there could be dedication subject to a right to plough. While statute initially made it an offence to destroy the surface of highways,[244] and hence to plough rights of way,[245] the Defence of the Realm Regulations 1939 and 1940 empowered the Minister of Agriculture to authorize the ploughing of rights of way[246] and the National Parks and Access to the Countryside Act 1949 established a general right to plough footpaths and bridleways for agricultural purposes.[247]

The conferment of this general right to plough was contrary to the report of the Hobhouse Committee which in 1947 had simply recommended the continuation of a procedure of authorization of ploughing in certain situations.[248] The new right was, however, consistent with the post-war policy of encouraging British agriculture. With the increasing use of large agricultural equipment, the principle that occupiers should have a general right to plough footpaths for agricultural purposes has gone largely unchallenged. Instead, debate has centred on both the nature and enforcement of the occupier's obligation to reinstate the path following ploughing. This obligation is not only vaguely formulated but also widely ignored by occupiers. A recent report published by the Countryside Commission showed that 59% of paths in arable fields in the areas studied had been affected by ploughing and other acts of cultivation.[249]

Because of the enactment of a statutory right to plough, the common law rules about ploughing rights of way now have only residual significance. Apart from carriageways, which generally have hard surfaces and hence cannot be ploughed, the common law applies only to those footpaths and bridleways which follow the headlands or sides of a field or enclosure[250] or which the landowner ploughs for reasons other than agricultural advantage.[251] If an occupier ploughs a highway in these situations it is both a public nuisance and an offence unless the highway was dedicated subject to a right to plough.[252] The onus of establishing such limited dedication is probably on the occupier who must show that ploughing of the path is coeval with the public's use of it.[253]

The statutory provisions concerned with the ploughing of footpaths and bridleways are currently found in the Highways Act 1980 as amended by the Wildlife and Countryside Act 1981.[254] Under this legislation, an occupier has an almost blanket right to plough a footpath or bridleway which crosses agricultural land or land which he is bringing into use for agriculture. The only restriction on the occupier is that it must be "in accordance with the rules of good husbandry to plough the land, and . . . convenient, in so ploughing the land, to plough the path or way together with the rest of the land".[255] The requirement under the 1980 Act that the occupier give the relevant highway authority seven days' notice of his intention to plough[256] was repealed in 1981 on the ground that it was unenforceable.[257]

Having ploughed a footpath or bridleway in exercise of the statutory right, an occupier is under a duty to make good the surface of the path and failure to do so constitutes an offence.[258] The occupier is not required to return the path to its condition prior to ploughing. Rather he must make the surface of the path "reasonably convenient for the exercise of the public right of way".[259] This vague requirement probably involves not only making the route clear to people not familiar with it but also making the surface suitable for the expected use of the path.[260] However, the only reported decision concerning the duty to restore is unsatisfactory. In *Woodcock* v. *Philip Solari Farms Ltd* (1967)[261] justices held that this duty had been fulfilled by an occupier who had delineated the direction of the path simply by walking along it. On appeal, Lord Parker refused to hold that the justices were wrong even though he recognized that "it might be the true position that the path was not left reasonably convenient for the exercise of the public right-of-way".[262]

The main point of contention between farmers and ramblers concerns the period which farmers are given in order to "make good" the path. From the point of view of members of the public, it is most important that the whereabouts of the path should be made clear immediately. If the land is fit to plough, farmers should be able to run a tractor wheel along the right of way after ploughing, and hence should be under a duty at the end of a day's ploughing to show the line of the paths which they have ploughed.[263] Instead, the legislation has consistently been lax in this respect. The 1949 Act simply required restoration to be "as soon as may be".[264] Even the 1981 Act provides that under ordinary conditions the occupier has two weeks for restoration. In exceptional weather conditions he need only restore the path as soon as is practicable.[265] Moreover, an occupier who feels unable to restore the path within the ordinary two week period, may obtain an order diverting the path for up to three months if he can show such order is "in the interests of good farming".[266]

(2) The keeping of dangerous domesticated animals

At common law occupiers are free to keep domesticated animals of all species (however dangerous) in fields crossed by public rights of way, and they are largely exempt from liability for injuries inflicted by these animals on members of the public using public paths. This freedom of occupiers has been curtailed by Parliament since the early 1970s[267] but the restrictions and liabilities imposed by statute have hardly been onerous. The one specific prohibition on the keeping of domesticated animals, which relates to bulls, in fact involves a relaxation of restrictions which were previously imposed by byelaws in most counties. The one general restraint, which can apply to animals of any species, is simply a result of the new statutory duty of all employers and self-employed persons to conduct their undertakings in such a way that those who are not in their employment should not be exposed to risks to their health and safety. The extension of liability for animals straying on to public rights of way rests primarily on the application of ordinary principles of negligence.

(a) Bulls

Because of their capacity and propensity to inflict injury, bulls have been the focus of debate over excluding dangerous domesticated animals from fields crossed by public rights of way. For members of the public wishing to exercise their right of passage, the problem is not only the possibility of actual injury but also the fear inspired by the presence of a bull in such a field. As noted by the Hobhouse Committee in 1947, "allowing a bull to roam at will in a field through which a right of way passes is tantamount to the creation of a complete barrier to public progress".[268] For farmers the problem is one of economic loss from their land use being curtailed. A prohibition on bulls would leave farmers free to graze herds of cows and heifers in fields crossed by public paths. However, it would stop the form of livestock production known as the "single suckler herd system", whereby the bull must run with the herd for much of the year in order to ensure a good crop of calves. To prevent farmers from raising livestock in this manner allegedly could "in some cases seriously prejudice production and the viability of the farm".[269]

Since World War II, three official inquiries have recommended that there should be a broad prohibition on the keeping of bulls in fields with public paths.[270] However, because of the strength of the farming lobby, four separate attempts to legislate on this matter failed between 1949 and 1978.[271] Consequently, the Government initially encouraged local councils to adopt a model byelaw prohibiting the keeping of adult bulls in such fields (but not open hill country);[272] by 1970 all except two county councils in England and Wales had byelaws more or less to this effect.[273] Thereafter, however, farmers campaigned successfully for an easing of the restrictions on keeping bulls. By 1980 fourteen counties had byelaws allowing bulls to run in fields crossed by public rights of way so long as the bulls were accompanied by cows or heifers.[274]

As part of the Wildlife and Countryside Act 1981, the Conservative Government secured the passage of a provision on the keeping of bulls. This provision broadly conforms to the wishes of farming interests by significantly increasing the situations in which bulls can be kept lawfully. However, the new section was justified in Parliament largely in terms of the need for uniformity – an ideal rejected by the Government elsewhere in the Act.[275] Subject to two broad exceptions, occupiers are prohibited from keeping bulls on land crossed by public rights of way. The first situation in which bulls may be kept is where they do not exceed the age of ten months. The second is where the bull is not of a "recognized dairy breed" and is at large in any field or enclosure together with cows or heifers.[276] Because of the difficulties for members of the public – the natural complainants – in determining whether a bull falls within these exceptions, the general prohibition on keeping bulls in fields crossed by rights of way appears largely unenforceable in practice. Moreover, whilst as yet there have been "no recorded incidents of members of the public being injured by previously banned bulls in fields crossed by public rights of way, th' users of those rights of way continue to believe that the running of any bull in such a field puts them at risk and deters them from using the way. The publication by the Government's own advisers on health and safety at work of detailed guidance to those obliged to work with bulls on how best to avoid injury only serves to reinforce that view."[277]

(b) Animals of any species

Legislation against occupational hazards has traditionally been concerned simply with the safety of workers rather than that of the general public.[278] However, following a recommendation by the Robens Committee,[279] section 3(1) of the Health and Safety at Work Act 1974 imposes a duty on all employers and self-employed persons to conduct their undertakings in such a way as to ensure, so far as is reasonably practicable, that persons not in their employment who may be affected thereby are not exposed to risks to their health and safety. In Committee in the House of Commons, the Solicitor-General suggested that the phrase "persons not in their employment" might be construed by the courts as covering only sub-contractors.[280] However, in a number of cases the duty under section 3(1) has been held to apply to people other than sub-contractors (such as people placed in factories by the Manpower Services Commission).[281] Most likely, the statute extends at least to persons directly affected by the way in which an undertaking is conducted, including members of the public who are endangered or injured by domesticated animals kept in a field crossed by a public path.

From the point of view of members of the public using public paths, the great weakness of section 3(1) is that it does not prohibit the keeping of particular types of animals in specific situations. Consequently, prosecutions for breach of the statutory duty, which is an offence under the Act,[282] will generally depend on questions of fact more difficult than the determination of the age or breed of bulls under the Wildlife and Countryside Act. The one considerable advantage of section 3(1) of the 1974 Act is that it potentially covers all species of animal.

When a member of the public exercising his right of passage is either endangered or injured by a domesticated animal, the crucial test under section 3(1) is whether it would have been "reasonably practicable" for the occupier to conduct his undertaking in such a way that the health and safety of members of the public would not have been put at risk. Cases decided under the old Factory Acts indicate that what is "reasonably practicable" involves a "computation . . . in which the quantum of risk is placed on one scale, and the sacrifice involved in the measures necessary for averting the risk (whether in money, time or trouble) is placed in the other".[283] Because the burden of proof is cast by statute on the defendant,[284] the occupier must establish that the risk was "insignificant in relation to the sacrifice".[285] He would therefore probably need to show that the capacity and propensity of the animal to inflict injury was slight and that he would have suffered considerable economic loss had he not kept the animal in the field crossed by the public path or that erecting extra fences would have involved costs disproportionate to the risk.

(c) Liability for injury

At common law there were two heads of liability for injuries by domesticated animals to members of the public on rights of way. However, such liability was in practice extremely difficult to establish. Under the so-called *scienter* principle, liability depended essentially on moral culpability.[286] The plaintiff had to show that the animal's owner or keeper knew that the particular animal which inflicted the injury had a vicious propensity. Alternatively, liability could be established in negligence, although as affirmed by the House of Lords in *Searle* v. *Wallbank* (1946),[287] an occupier was under no duty to fence off his land from the highway and was under no liability if his domesticated animals strayed on to the highway and injured a member of the public there.

Under section 2 of the Animals Act 1971, a claim for damages can be brought which, while replacing the old *scienter* principle,[288] is not significantly different in either form or effect from the old common law action. Under section 2, liability depends on whether an animal belongs to a "dangerous species" within the meaning of the Act. If an animal is a member of a dangerous species, then under section 2(1) its keeper is as a general rule absolutely liable for any injury it inflicts. But if a species or sub-species is commonly domesticated in the United Kingdom, then the species is not classified as dangerous regardless of how dangerous it is in fact.[289] Under section 2(2) the keeper of an animal belonging to such a domesticated species is liable for injury it inflicts only if the plaintiff can establish that:

> (a) the damage is of a kind which the animal, unless restrained, was likely to cause or which, if caused by the animal, was likely to be severe; and (b) the likelihood of the damage or of its being severe was due to characteristics of the animal which are not normally found in animals of the same species or are not normally so found except at particular times or in particular circumstances; and (c) those characteristics were known to that keeper or were at any time known to a person who at that time had charge of the animal as that keeper's servant . . .

These conditions are difficult to establish since if a domesticated animal belongs to a species which is not generally dangerous, the damage it causes will probably have been unlikely and hence outside paragraph (a); if a domesticated animal belongs to a species which frequently is dangerous, the injuries may not have been due to characteristics of the animal which are abnormal in its species and hence paragraph (b) may not be satisfied.[290]

In view of these difficulties in satisfying section 2(2), a member of the public, injured by a domesticated animal while on a public right of way, is more likely to recover damages from the owner of the animal if he brings his action in negligence. As a result of the most far-reaching change effected by the 1971 Act, the rule in *Searle* v. *Wallbank* has been abolished,[291] and liability for animals straying on to a highway is now no different from other liability in negligence.[292] The duty of care owed by farmers in tort is probably the same as that under section 3(1) of the Health and Safety at Work Act 1974, although, unlike under section 3(1), the onus is on the injured party to establish that the farmer was negligent.[293]

B. UNLAWFUL INTERFERENCES

In their capacity as highway authorities, county councils have the primary responsibility for ensuring that public highways are not interfered with. This responsibility is expressed in the councils' broad statutory duty "to assert and protect the rights of the public to the use and enjoyment of highways."[294] It is also expressed in the more specific duties of councils, which include prevention, as far as possible, of the stopping up or obstruction of highways,[295] and prosecution of occupiers who wrongfully plough public paths or fail to reinstate them after ploughing.[296] To enable councils to fulfil these duties, they have been given a wide range of powers to obtain the removal of obstructions,[297] prosecute offenders for committing either public nuisance or statutory offences, as well as obtain injunctions to restrain the continuance of public nuisances.[298]

Because many councils do not fulfil their duties to protect footpaths, bridleways and unmetalled carriageways, the critical issue in this context so far as members of the public are concerned is the scope of their remedies when faced by obstructions. Depending on the circumstances, members of the public may be entitled to deviate around the obstruction or to remove it. If they have suffered particular damage, they may be able to recover their loss and obtain an injunction to restrain continuance of the nuisance. Regardless of whether they have suffered particular damage, they may prosecute the wrongdoer and, with the permission of the Attorney-General or the relevant local council, seek an injunction by way of a relator action. Finally, they may be able to obtain a mandamus requiring the council to fulfil its statutory duty.

The range of remedies available to members of the public is consequently considerable. However, each of these remedies is either available in only limited circumstances or is the subject of significant practical problems. With the exception of actions for recovery of loss in cases of particular damage, none of these remedies is as satisfactory for path-users as highway authorities fulfilling their statutory duties to protect the public's rights and to prevent the obstruction of highways.

(1) The right to deviate

In certain situations, which are far from clear, a member of the public exercising his right of passage on a right of way over land (but not water)[299] is entitled to go on to the adjoining land if the highway is impassable. He may then travel so far as is necessary on the adjoining land, doing as little damage as possible, before resuming his passage on the highway.[300] Although lacking the permission of the relevant landowner, this use of the adjoining land is lawful – most likely because the member of the public has a right to deviate or alternatively because he may justify his trespass on the basis of necessity.[301]

According to Holdsworth,[302] the right to deviate should be restricted to the situation discussed in *Henn's Case* (1633).[303] On this view, the right to deviate would be insignificant as it would exist only where a landowner, who had inclosed his land on each side of a highway, fails to fulfil the duty to repair the highway which he incurred by reason of the inclosure. Such a construction of the right to deviate is, however, inconsistent with a considerable body of dicta in cases decided in the seventeenth, eighteenth and nineteenth centuries.[304] Holdsworth's rationale for confining the right in this way is also not convincing. He regarded it as "obvious that, at the present day, a general right to deviate is unnecessary",[305] whereas the extent of interferences with public rights of way suggests that members of the public continue to need a right to deviate which is much broader than that in *Henn's Case*.

A more acceptable, albeit still narrow, construction of the

right to deviate confines the right to the case where members of the public cannot continue on the highway because of the wrongdoing of the owners of the adjoining land. The rationale of this approach is that the adjoining landowner should be subject to members of the public going over his land only where he is responsible for the condition of the highway. On this view, the right to deviate extends only to the situation where the owner of the adjoining land has not fulfilled his duty to repair the highway[306] or has obstructed the way;[307] there is no right to deviate where, for example, the highway is obstructed due to natural causes[308] or where the landowner has exercised his right to plough the way.[309]

Alternatively, members of the public may have a right to deviate where the adjoining landowner is not responsible for the condition of the path. This right may either be limited to those cases where the highway is "founderous and out of repair"[310] or may extend to all situations where the highway is either founderous or obstructed.[311] Both rules can be justified on the basis that highways "are for the public service, and if the usual tract is impassable, it is for the general good that people should be entitled to pass in another line".[312]

(2) The right to abate nuisances

In certain circumstances where a public right of way is obstructed, members of the public have a right to abate the nuisance. This right of self-help – which is an alternative to seeking damages[313] – has been recognized by the courts because

> injuries . . . which obstruct or annoy such things as are of daily convenience and use, require an immediate remedy; and cannot wait for the slow progress of the ordinary forms of justice.[314]

In the case of public rights of way, abatement is particularly important because members of the public may have no other remedy against the person who created the obstruction. However, it is a remedy which members of the public should invoke with caution since, if their actions in abating the nuisance fall outside the scope of the right, they will be open to civil and possibly criminal sanctions.[315]

Until the early nineteenth century, it was accepted that members of the public were entitled to abate any nuisance – regardless of whether it in fact impeded their way – and in doing so they were not restricted to the minimum force which was necessary.[316] However, as part of the general judicial antipathy towards self-help remedies, which developed during the course of the nineteenth century and still prevails,[317] the courts have curtailed this wide right of abatement. The right to abate is now clearly limited to the situation where the rights of passage could not otherwise be exercised with reasonable convenience,[318] and is possibly restricted to where passage would otherwise be altogether impeded.[319] A member of the public abating a nuisance is also required to exercise reasonable care so that he does as little damage as possible to the obstruction.[320]

Subject to these two conditions, a member of the public is probably entitled to abate any nuisance which he encounters on a public right of way. However, in *Mayor of Colchester* v. *Brooke* (1845)[321] and *Dimes* v. *Petley* (1850)[322] the courts suggested that a person could abate such a nuisance only if it caused him special injury. If "special injury" were interpreted in this context in the same way as it is in actions for damages for public nuisance,[323] a member of the public exercising his right of passage for recreation would be unable to abate a nuisance. But in *Campbell Davys* v. *Lloyd* (1901) Collins L.J. recognized that "there may, in the case of positive nuisance, be a right to abate where there is no cause of action, there being insufficient special damage".[324] Moreover, in the *Colchester* case, Denman C.J.'s example of particular inconvenience giving rise to a right of abatement was "a gate across a highway which prevents a traveller from passing".[325] If this example is correct, as has generally been accepted,[326] the requirement of special injury in relation to abatement is just a restatement of the condition that a person can abate only those nuisances which either totally obstruct or at least significantly impede his passage on public ways.

(3) Civil actions

With the consent of the Attorney-General, any member of the public can seek an injunction to restrain the continuance of a public nuisance. However, a member of the public may seek an injunction without the assistance of the Attorney-General and he can also recover damages for his loss so long as he has suffered some "special" or "particular" loss over and above that suffered by the general public. It is unclear whether such loss need be different in kind or only different in degree from that suffered by the public at large.[327] Reflecting this uncertainty over principle, there is conflicting authority as to whether damages can be recovered by persons who, without being able to establish any financial loss, suffer substantially more inconvenience and delay than that suffered by the general public.[328] However, it is clear that a member of the public can recover if the nuisance has caused him personal injury,[329] or has resulted in loss of custom to his business,[330] or, as in the case of a carrier, has caused loss of time resulting in trouble and expense.[331] A member of the public cannot recover if he has simply "suffered an inconvenience common to all who happened to pass that way".[332]

This restriction on the circumstances in which members of the public can bring actions for the infringement of their rights has been justfied primarily on the basis that there otherwise might be a multiplicity of actions which might clog the legal system and result in substantial administrative costs.[333] Yet this approach also "carries with it the unfortunate consequence, not that aggrieved parties will not collect trivial sums, but that injuring parties will not pay substantial ones"[334] for the total harm they have caused. Where members of the public cannot proceed in respect of a public nuisance, it consequently is particularly important that redress be obtained for the community by the Attorney-General or the relevant local authority[335] who, in bringing legal actions, are not fettered by the requirement of establishing particular damage.

(4) Criminal actions

Members of the public have a right to bring private prosecutions in respect of all criminal offences, unless this right has been specifically removed by statute. In relation to public rights of way, members of the public retain this right of prosecution in relation to both public nuisances[336] and the statutory offence of wilfully obstructing a highway.[337] However, because of the opposition of landowning interests,[338] members of the public have been barred from bringing prosecutions under section 134 of the Highways Act against farmers who plough paths wrongfully or fail to reinstate them after ploughing.[339] Only local authorities may bring prosecutions under this section and few authorities are prepared to act against these "anti-social" practices.[340]

Insofar as the right of private prosecution subsists, it is theoretically "a valuable constitutional safeguard against inertia or partiality on the part of authority",[341] and since 1983 the Ramblers' Association has successfully launched a series of prosecutions for obstruction of public rights of way. However, members of the public wishing to exercise this right are in practice subject to three constraints.[342] First, any prosecution they institute is subject to the control of the Director of Public Prosecutions who may take over the prosecution and enter a *nolle prosequi*. Secondly, and more significantly,

> Legal aid is not available to institute criminal proceedings. If the prosecution succeeds the prosecutor may be awarded costs but these will be taxed so that he may not recover the entire cost of the prosecution. If the defendant is acquitted costs may be awarded against the prosecutor who then has to bear his own costs and those of the defendant. Such costs are sufficient to deter most would-be prosecutors.[343]

Finally, the prosecutor must have the legal knowledge necessary to institute proceedings and the resources to investigate and produce the evidence to support the allegation.[344]

(5) Enforcement of the duties of local authorities to protect highways

Where a council fails to fulfil its statutory duties to protect highways, a member of the public may be able to compel it to do so by obtaining a writ of mandamus from the courts. However, to obtain such relief, the member of the public must first satisfy the rules concerned with standing. Even if he does so there are considerable limits on the type of relief which the courts are willing to grant.

Until 1978 a member of the public who had not suffered special damage was almost certainly unable to obtain a writ of mandamus from the courts compelling a recalcitrant authority to fulfil its duties to protect highways. He would have been held to lack standing to bring the action on the basis either that his legal rights had not been infringed or that he did not have a sufficient interest in the matter.[345] However, as a result of the new rules of court which came into effect in January 1978[346] and the decision of the House of Lords in *R. v. Inland Revenue Commissioners* (1981),[347] it seems that the old requirements of standing have to a significant extent been replaced by a test which looks to the legal duty to be performed. The courts may still dismiss an application for judicial review on the ground that the applicant is a mere "busybody", just as an applicant who is not a busybody may still lack standing.[348] However, where an applicant can establish a strong enough case on the merits, he will not be prevented from obtaining redress by the fact that his interest in the matter is no greater than that of other members of the public.[349]

If a member of the public has standing, he may be unable to obtain an order compelling the council to institute legal proceedings. The House of Lords took this view of the scope of mandamus in *R*. v. *Southampton Port Commissioners* (1870)[350] and, if this decision is still good law,[351] a member of the public could not compel a highway authority to fulfil its duty of prosecuting occupiers who plough paths wrongfully or fail to reinstate them after ploughing.[352] A member of the public is probably also unable to obtain an order simply requiring the council to protect the public's rights and prevent obstructions of highways, as the courts are unwilling to make such imprecise, prospective orders.[353] Equally, he may be unable to obtain an order requiring the council to remove an obstruction in a particular way, as the courts are unwilling to specify what has to be done.[354] However, there appears to be no reason why the courts should not grant an order requiring a council to obtain the removal of certain existing obstructions without specifying the way in which the council should fulfil its duty.

IV. THE RECORDING OF RIGHTS OF WAY

The recording of rights of way is one of the matters for which there is legal provision only in relation to public rights of way over land. However, recently there have been calls for a survey of public rights of navigation because (as previously in relation to rights of way over land) there is great uncertainty as to which rivers are subject to public rights of navigation.[355] If such a survey of public rights of navigation takes place, it can only be hoped that it is conducted more efficiently than the survey of public paths or else it may well result in a reduction in the public's rights, contrary to the rationale of the survey.

Although the first attempts to secure a survey of public rights of way over land – and thereby conclusively establish the existence of such rights – were made in the late nineteenth century,[356] legislation providing for a general survey of rights of way over land was enacted only in 1949. Under the National Parks and Access to the Countryside Act, county councils were required to compile maps and accompanying statements of footpaths and bridleways as well as a third category of way, termed "roads used as public paths".[357] The maps and statements were to pass through three stages – draft, provisional and definitive.[358] At the first two stages, there was provision for objection and amendment but inclusion of a path in a definitive map was to be "conclusive evidence" of the existence of that path. Omission of a path was not to affect its status.[359] Reviews of definitive maps were to be conducted every five years in order primarily to take account of changes in the network of rights of way which had taken place in that period.[360]

Despite this sensible framework, the survey scheme had many defects and it was also poorly implemented. County boroughs were given a choice as to whether they conducted surveys.[361] Most of them did not do so.[362] The survey, therefore, resulted in incomplete coverage of England and Wales until the Wildlife and Countryside Act 1981 extended the survey to all areas apart from the administrative district of the former London County Council.[363] While some councils claimed every possible path in their area, others thought no claims were necessary because all local people knew the landowners and could cross their land anyway.[364] Numerous county councils failed to complete their surveys within the period originally anticipated by Government, and the production of definitive maps for counties was in fact only completed in May 1982 with the publication of the map for North Bedfordshire.[365] Where begun by authorities, the quinquennial comprehensive review proved unworkable because of the number of objections[366] and consequently it was replaced in 1981 by a process of continuous review.[367] This new process has "caused work to be started on updating the definitive map where no prospect of so doing was in sight before."[368] However, as ever with the survey, progress so far has been slow reflecting the very limited resources applied to this task by local authorities, the Department of the Environment and the Welsh Office.

While these and other problems have significantly undermined the objects of the survey, the scheme's greatest flaw has been its failure to constitute the basis of what the Hobhouse Committee in 1947 termed "an authoritative record of rights of way".[369] The 1949 Act did not satisfactorily achieve this aim and amendments to the legislation, prompted by errors in the original surveys, have resulted in further departures from the principle of "definitiveness". These changes fall broadly into three categories. The "conclusive" effect of the definitive maps has been diminished. The extent to which these maps can be revised has progressively been increased. Lastly, the category of "roads used as public paths" has been abandoned, and a scheme of reclassification instituted for all paths initially classified in this way.

(A) THE "CONCLUSIVE" EFFECT OF DEFINITIVE MAPS

In providing that definitive maps and statements were "conclusive evidence" of their contents,[370] Parliament had two choices in the 1949 Act. The characterization of a path – as a footpath, bridleway or road used as a public path – could have been made an absolute statement of the public's rights. Thus where a path was shown as a bridleway, the map would have conclusively established that the public had rights on foot and horseback (and now bicycle) over the path but had no vehicular rights. Alternatively, the characterization of a path could have been made a minimum statement, so that where a path was shown as a bridleway the map would not have prejudiced the question whether the public had any vehicular rights. While only the former approach was properly consistent with the object of establishing a conclusive record of public rights of way, it would – unlike the latter – have led to the extinguishment of public rights when a bridleway was wrongly classified as a footpath or a cartway was wrongly classified as a footpath or bridleway.

Probably as a result of poor drafting, section 32 of the 1949 Act arbitrarily appeared to fail to ascribe the same form of conclusive effect to all categories of right of way shown in the definitive maps. Section 32(4)(b) included a proviso which made clear that bridleways and roads used as public paths were minimum statements of the public's rights. However, section 32(4)(a) did not contain a similar proviso in relation to footpaths. Consequently it appeared to provide that where a footpath was shown on a definitive map, the map conclusively established that where a definitive map showed a footpath, the public's only right was on foot, and this interpretation of section 32(4)(a) was adopted by a majority of the House of Lords in *Suffolk C.C.* v. *Mason* (1979).[371]

In consultations prior to the enactment of the Wildlife and Countryside Act 1981, the Government took the view that the majority ruling in the *Mason* case should be extended to bridleways so that the definitive map would be "truly definitive" and "could be read in the knowledge that it reflected no more and no less than the rights which exist on each path shown".[372] However, because of the many mistakes made when definitive maps were prepared, the Government was persuaded by interested parties – especially the organizations representing horseriders, motor-cyclists and motorists – to retreat from this proposal. As introduced in the House of Lords, the Wildlife and Countryside Bill contained a compromise clause which would have given local authorities seven years in which to correct their maps before footpaths and bridleways shown therein became absolute statements of the public's rights.[373] In Committee, the Government abandoned even this provision and, according to a Department of the Environment consultation paper, "undermine[d] the value of the map"[374] by providing contrary to *Mason* that both footpaths and bridleways represent minimum statements of the public's rights.[375]

(B) THE REVISION OF DEFINITIVE MAPS

Under the 1949 Act, the object of the quinquennial review was to take account of "a limited range of events intervening between the original preparation of the map and the subsequent revision".[376] These events were expected generally to be actual changes in the right of way network during the relevant period. Thus authorities were empowered to alter their maps where a right of way had been created either by dedication or statute or where new legislation had stopped up, diverted, widened or changed the status of a right of way.[377] But section 33(2)(e) of the Act also empowered authorities to alter their maps where there was new evidence "such that, if the authority were then preparing a draft map . . . they would be required . . . to show on the map, as a highway of a particular description, a way not so shown on the definitive map". This power of alteration was possibly intended simply to allow for the addition to the map of paths which had previously been omitted, but it could be interpreted as extending to both the upgrading and downgrading of paths.[378] While the power to upgrade paths on the basis of new evidence was at least consistent with the classification of paths in the maps being minimum statements of the public's rights, the power to downgrade was clearly inconsistent with the principle that the maps should be definitive.

In order to make the maps properly authoritative, the power to review should have been reduced by removing the power to downgrade if not also that to upgrade paths. Instead the power to review the maps has been expanded because, as exemplified by *Morgan* v. *Hertfordshire C.C.* (1965),[379] the mapping procedures have proved far from foolproof. *Morgan* concerned a definitive map which, as a result of a misunderstanding by

county council officers, showed a bridleway on a strip of land
where there had been no public right of way and which was in
fact studded with trees and impassable. Under the original
legislation the one unsatisfactory remedy open to the landowner was to seek an order stopping up the bridleway on the
basis that it was "not needed for public use".[380] Consequently,
Parliament in the Countryside Act 1968 provided that in the
periodical reviews of definitive maps, authorities could delete
rights of way which were shown not to exist and, in the event
that they could not have done so already, could regrade those
paths which had been wrongly classified.[381] The one limitation
on this power was that in deciding to change the maps,
authorities were restricted to evidence which the relevant
landowners could not reasonably have been expected to
produce before.

In establishing the new procedure for continuous review, the
Wildlife and Countryside Act 1981 further extended the power
of review by removing the restriction on the evidence which
authorities can consider in deciding whether to exercise their
powers to delete or regrade rights of way.[382] The Government
justified the removal of the evidentiary restriction on the basis
that it penalized only landowners and the legislation should be
evenhanded in its treatment of both landowners and path-
users.[383] This view was disputed by Labour Peers who argued
that it was proper for the survey legislation to favour path-users
because their interest in particular paths – unlike that of
landowners – is inherently diffused and they will not necessarily hear through local advertisements that the status of a path
is being reviewed.[384] If it is accepted, however, that the review
provisions should impose the same evidentiary restrictions on
landowners and path-users, it would have been better had the
1981 Act adhered more closely to the original goal of a
conclusive map by strictly limiting the new evidence which
could be brought on behalf of all parties in cases of review. The
failure of the Act to do so may seriously prejudice the rights of
members of the public since, as noted by Lord Denning,
definitive maps were "based on evidence then available,
including, no doubt, the evidence of the oldest inhabitants then
living. Such evidence might [now] have been lost or forgotten
. . . So it would be very unfair to reopen everything".[385]

As it is, the only possible barrier to authorities exercising
their power to review is section 56 of the 1981 Act which, as
discussed previously, provides that the inclusion of a path in a
definitive map is "conclusive evidence" that, for example, a

footpath or bridleway existed at the date when the map was compiled. As a result of the principle, "once a highway, always a highway", the inclusion of a path in a definitive map is also conclusive evidence that the path still exists (unless it has been extinguished by statute). Such conclusive evidence would, on a literal interpretation of the Act, prevent any path from being deleted or downgraded as part of a review since the authorities can, for example, delete a path only if the evidence shows "that there is no public right of way over land shown in the map and statement as a highway of any description".[386] This result would, however, be inconsistent with the clear intention of Parliament that authorities should, as part of their continuous review, be able to delete or downgrade paths. Consequently, it seems that the authorities' power to review should be read as unfettered by the "conclusive evidence" stipulation in section 56. On this view, the 1981 Act is not the basis of a definitive record of rights of way since authorities are free to alter their maps if the evidence, apart from that contained in the maps and statements, shows that there is no right of way or that a right of way shown on a map has been wrongly classified.

(C) THE RECLASSIFICATION OF "ROADS USED AS PUBLIC PATHS"

In providing that the definitive maps should include not only footpaths and bridleways but also "roads used as public paths" (RUPPs), the 1949 Act sought to extend the survey of rights of way to unmetalled highways such as the Berkshire Ridgeway over which there was a vehicular right of passage but which were primarily used by pedestrians and equestrians.[387] Like footpaths and bridleways, such "green lanes" were (and are) used mainly for recreational purposes and they also were in danger of being lost if their existence was not recorded. The legal definition of such roads was difficult, however, because it turned not only on the nature of the public's rights of passage but also on the current use of these paths. Perhaps this category of way should simply have been defined as "carriageways used primarily by pedestrians and/or equestrians". Instead, a "road used as a public path" was defined with "outstanding obscurity"[388] as "a highway, other than a public path" – that is other than a footpath or bridleway – "used by the public mainly for the purposes for which footpaths and bridleways are so used".[389] In response to this definition many county councils either classified rights of way wrongly as

RUPPs or ignored this category of way altogether.[390]

Because of the confusion surrounding roads used as public paths, the Gosling Committee on footpaths recommended in 1968 that this category of way should be abandoned.[391] The third schedule of the Countryside Act 1968 largely followed this recommendation in providing for a "special review" in which RUPPs were to be reclassified as footpaths, bridleways or a new category of way termed "byways open to all traffic".[392] The review provisions were, however, so badly conceived that they created more uncertainty and inconsistencies than they resolved.[393]

The 1968 Act was firstly unclear as to the nature of the authorities' power to reclassify those RUPPs over which no vehicular rights were in fact shown to exist. Had the reclassification power not been bound by the "conclusive evidence" provision in section 32 of the 1949 Act, the authorities would have been free to consider whether the public actually had only a right on foot over these ways. As determined, however, by the Court of Appeal in 1975,[394] the authorities were bound to treat the maps as conclusively establishing that rights on foot and horseback existed over the former RUPPs. The court consequently determined that, contrary to first appearances and common practice, authorities had no power to reclassify RUPPs as footpaths, except where the status of the path could be changed under the general powers of review discussed in the previous sub-section.

In relation to RUPPs over which a vehicular right was shown to exist, the 1968 Act clearly empowered authorities either to downgrade these roads to bridleways or to maintain the vehicular rights by classifying these roads as byways open to all traffic. The Act failed, however, to state clearly the considerations which authorities were to weigh in making this choice. One of the two main tests was suitably for vehicular traffic but it was unclear whether this meant "some or all traffic. Almost any lane can be traversed by a skilled rider on a good trail bike but few roads used as public paths are suitable for ordinary private cars".[395] The other main criterion – whether restriction of vehicular rights would cause "undue hardship" – was equally unsatisfactory since, for example, if a lane was used only occasionally for recreational trail riding, it was "hard to decide whether closing the lane to vehicles causes 'undue hardship' in any one case yet, taken together, a series of such reclassifications may well unduly restrict trail riders' activities".[396]

Notwithstanding these problems, the Government in preparing the Wildlife and Countryside Act proposed initially not to amend the tests for reclassifying roads used as public paths.[397] Only after widespread criticism did it recognize that "the differing interpretations placed on the tests and consequent inconsistencies in their application" necessitated amendment.[398] Rather than attempting to reformulate the policy considerations on which the RUPPs should be downgraded, the Government decided to leave restriction of their use to traffic regulation orders (and thereby favoured motorists and motorcyclists by at least significantly postponing curtailment of their vehicular rights). The new basis for reclassifying roads used as public paths depends largely on existing rights of passage over these roads. If vehicular rights are shown to exist, a RUPP must be reclassified as a byway open to all traffic.[399] If vehicular rights are not established, and "public bridleway rights have not been shown not to exist", a RUPP must be reclassified as a bridleway.[400] There is also provision for reclassification of RUPPs as footpaths,[401] but it is unclear whether such reclassification can ever take place because the Act provides that depiction of a path as a RUPP on a definitive map is conclusive evidence of the existence of a bridleway.[402]

V. THE SIGNPOSTING OF RIGHTS OF WAY

In relation to footpaths, bridleways and byways but not waterways, Parliament has enacted legislation which to some extent seeks to make known the whereabouts and exact route of the public's rights of way. The provision for such matters in relation to rights of way over land can partly be seen as a supplement to the survey of these ways: if members of the public, especially those not resident in a particular district, are to be able to locate and follow rights of way, they should be able to have ready access to the information contained in the definitive maps, rights of way should be signposted and in some cases also waymarked. However, the provision for such matters in relation only to public ways over land is, of course, also a result of the nature of these ways: that otherwise there may be little or no indication of the existence and route of a footpath or bridleway whereas waterways are an obvious feature of the landscape.

Under current legislation, no provisions ensure that the information resulting from the survey of rights of way is available to path-users (although this object has largely been achieved by non-statutory means). Local authorities are under certain duties in relation to signposting and they probably also are empowered to waymark rights of way. The particular form of these provisions reflects a middle course drawn by successive Governments between the demands of amenity groups on the one hand, who clearly are in favour of such measures, and landowners and local authorities on the other. Even though waymarking has been shown to benefit landowners since it reduces accidental trespass,[403] many landowners remain opposed to any measure which may lead to increased use of paths over their land. A number of local authorities have also resisted any increase in their obligations in relation to rights of way.

Under the Wildlife and Countryside Act 1981, as under the 1949 Act, local authorities are under a duty to keep a copy of the relevant survey map availabe for inspection in the area to which the map relates.[404] If the authority considers it practicable, it must keep a copy of the relevant map in each parish. Otherwise it must keep a copy at one or more places in each county district.[405] This provision was designed to allow members of the public to participate in the compilation and review of the maps. It was not intended to assist members of the public to discover the whereabouts of rights of way and then use them and it does not achieve this goal. Government has also refused to impose a duty on local authorities to sell copies of their definitive maps. Nevertheless, the legitimate interest of path-users in having easy access to the information contained in the definitive map has been secured in two ways. Most significantly, as a result of representations from amenity organizations and pressure from the Ministry of Housing and Local Government, the Ordnance Survey agreed in 1958 to incorporate in its maps details of rights of way taken from the definitive maps of local authorities.[406] The Survey's Pathfinder sheets on a 1:25,000 scale show rights of way and from 1990 should be available for all England and Wales. In addition, a few authorities sell copies of their maps, though many appear not to have followed a Department of the Environment circular, issued in 1983, instructing authorities that if they do not already sell their maps, they should "make copies available for purchase if there is sufficient demand".[407]

At common law the erection of a signpost may constitute a trespass to and an obstruction of the highway, and local authorities therefore need statutory authorization before they can signpost rights of way. In 1773 highway authorities were for the first time empowered to erect signposts at the intersection of highways,[408] including the intersection of a footpath with a carriageway or even the intersection of two footpaths, but most authorities prior to World War II simply erected signposts at the intersection of carriageways.[409] In 1947 the Hobhouse Committee consequently recommended that rights of way should be signposted "in all cases where it appears that such action is required for the convenience of the public".[410] After this matter was addressed more specifically by the Gosling Committee,[411] Parliament enacted section 27 of the Countryside Act 1968 which placed authorities under certain limited duties to signpost rights of way and extended the authorities' powers to erect signposts.

As a preliminary step to fulfilling their duties or exercising their powers in relation to signposting, highway authorities are required by section 27(1) to consult "with the owner or occupier of the land concerned".[412] A highway authority is the owner of the surface of all those rights of way which it is required to maintain[413] – that is, nearly all footpaths and bridleways and most carriageways. Section 27(1) could therefore be read as requiring a highway authority to consult in the great majority of cases with itself but this interpretation would to a large extent render this provision otiose. Consequently it seems that the authority must consult with the owner of the subsoil but, even if he disagrees with the erection of a signpost, the authority can still erect the sign because the section does not require the authority to obtain the landowner's consent.[414]

In order "to keep down the number of signposts in the countryside . . . [and] to preserve the nice look of . . . parishes",[415] the primary duty of highway authorities to erect signposts under the 1968 Act is subject to an exception where the relevant parish council or chairman of a parish meeting agrees with the authority that no signposts are needed.[416] Otherwise authorities are required by section 27(2) to erect and maintain a signpost at every point where a footpath, bridleway or byway[417] leaves a metalled road. Such a signpost must indicate whether the right of way is a footpath, bridleway or byway.[418] Where the authority considers it "convenient and appropriate", the signpost should also indicate the destination of the path and the distance thereto.[419] Although the Government intended that authorities should comply with this duty within four to five years of the passing of the 1968 Act,[420] it chose not to place authorities under a time limit[421] and many authorities have even now carried out little or no signposting.[422] Because of the expense of making individual signs, those authorities which have erected signposts have generally chosen not to specify the places to which particular paths lead.[423]

Highway authorities are also required by section 27(4) to erect such signposts as may in their opinion "be required to assist persons unfamiliar with the locality to follow the course of a footpath, bridleway or byway". The element of discretion in section 27(4) means, however, that this provision adds little or nothing to the general power of highway authorities under section 27(1). Both sub-sections provide a basis on which authorities may waymark paths by erecting cairns or painting arrows since any references in section 27 to signposts "include references to other signs or notices serving the same purpose" while references to the erection of a signpost "include references to positioning any such other sign or notice".[424] In practice neither subsection is of much importance because of the reluctance of authorities to work voluntarily on footpaths, bridleways and byways. Most waymarking has been done by volunteers from user groups and local authorities,[425] for whom the most important statutory provision is section 27(5) which provides that "with the consent of the highway authority, any other person may erect and maintain signposts along a footpath, bridleway or byway".

VI. THE MAINTENANCE OF RIGHTS OF WAY

In order for members of the public to be able to use rights of way with ease (or, at least, without danger), there need be someone under a duty to maintain the way at an appropriate standard. At common law, the rules governing maintenance of highways are to this effect, and even under current legislation there is someone obliged to maintain almost all footpaths and bridleways and most carriageways. However, as a general rule no-one is under a duty at common law to maintain rivers subject to public rights of navigation, and Parliament has imposed such duties on only a piecemeal basis. Consequently, there are many waterways for which there is currently no navigation authority at all or which are under the control of the British Waterways Board but which are classified as "remainder waterways" which means that the Board is under no obligation to maintain them.

(A) HIGHWAYS

(1) The incidence of the duty to maintain highways

Since medieval times there have been two major types of change in the law governing the incidence of the duty to maintain highways. The first has concerned the identity of the public entity entrusted with the duty of maintaining highways. The second has concerned the scope of the public duty – that is, the extent to which the public rather than private invididuals should be responsible for highway maintenance, and whether in fact there need be someone responsible for the maintenance of every highway.

As analyzed by Sidney and Beatrice Webb, "the characteristic medieval assumption of local administration" was "that the common services needed for social life were to be performed, not by any specialized organs for the community, but by being shared by all the citizens, serving compulsorily without pay".[426] In the case of highways, this meant that the public duty was cast at common law on the inhabitants of the manor[427] and then by legislation of 1555 on the inhabitants of the parish.[428] However, concurrent duties of maintenance were gradually imposed[429] – first on the parish highway surveyors, then on turnpike trusts and then on highway boards, the forerunners of the current highway authorities. By the late nineteenth century, the parishioners' duty was in practice "wholly superseded by a modern device of a specialised organ of administration, alimented by compulsory taxation, and having, as its express object, the satisfying of the increasing needs of a progressive society".[430] In 1959 this development was finally recognized by Parliament, when it abolished the duty of local inhabitants to maintain highways within their area.[431]

Until 1836 someone was under a duty to maintain every highway. *Prima facie* this duty fell on the inhabitants of the relevant parish who were liable to repair both old and new highways.[432] The duty of the parish could, however, be displaced by a liability falling on individuals either under statute; by reason of tenure of particular land;[433] as a result of inclosure of the land adjacent to the highway, if the public had previously deviated over that land when the highway was impassable;[434] or by reason of injury to the way under statutory authorization, in which case the body responsible was (and is) required to restore and thereafter maintain the highway, unless the statute contained some contrary provision.[435]

As a result of the Highway Act 1835, it became possible for carriageways (but not footpaths or bridleways)[436] to be created without anyone being responsible for their repair. The relevant provisions were enacted primarily in response to the development of building estates following the Napoleonic Wars.[437] It had become common for builders to dedicate ways across their estates irrespective of public needs "and thereby cast on the parish or its successors in obligation the cost of the repairs which enured almost exclusively to the advantage of themselves and their tenants or purchasers".[438] Section 23 of the Act of 1835 consequently provided that a parish would come under a duty to repair a new road only if two justices of the peace certified that it had been made at the expense of the applicant in a substantial manner and of the width required by the Act. The section further provided that, even if these conditions were satisfied, the parish could avoid liability if a vestry meeting of the parish found that the road was "not . . . of sufficient utility to justify its being kept in repair at the expense of the said parish" and the justices agreed in this finding.

The changes effected by the 1835 Act are still broadly in force in relation to carriageways. As a result, if a carriageway was created prior to 20 March 1836,[439] there is someone liable to repair it, and *prima facie* such liability falls on the highway authority. If a carriageway was created on or after that date, there may not be anyone liable to repair it. In any litigation the onus may be on the authority to show that it is not liable,[440] but it can do so by establishing that the procedure set out in section 23 of the 1835 Act (or its modern equivalent) has not been complied with. Furthermore, the authority may be discharged of its duty to maintain a carriageway if a magistrates' court, on application by the authority, accepts that the road is unnecessary for public use and therefore ought not to be maintained at public expense.[441]

So far as footpaths and bridleways are concerned, the crucial date is 1949 not 1836. Partly because many highway authorities contended (wrongly) that they were not under a duty to maintain such paths as a result of section 23 of the 1835 Act, the Hobhouse Committee recommended that highway authorities be expressly made liable to repair all footpaths and bridleways.[442] This proposal was implemented in the 1949 Act so far as all footpaths and bridleways then existing were concerned.[443] However, contarary to the recommendations of the Hobhouse Committe,[444] the Act did not abolish the liability of private individuals to repair footpaths and bridleways,[445] and hence there are some such paths established prior to 1949 for which there is now dual liability.

In relation to footpaths and bridleways created after 15 December 1949, liability to repair depends on the manner in which the path is created. If created by a creation agreement or order or by a diversion order, a path is maintainable by the relevant highway authority.[446] However, if created by dedication and if nothing further has been done, the path will not be publicly maintainable.

(2) The nature of the duty to maintain highways

The two main issues in relation to the nature of the duty to maintain highways concern the kind of activities which fall within the scope of "maintenance" and the standard at which the way must be maintained. With the exception of private liability to maintain highways under statute – in which case the nature of the liability depends upon the terms of the relevant Act[447] – the law governing these two issues appears to be the same regardless of whether the liability to maintain is public or private.

(a) The meaning of "maintenance" and "repair"

In the Highways Act 1980 both public authorities and private individuals are described as being under a duty "to maintain"[448] highways and, as provided by the definition section of the Act, "maintenance includes repair, and 'maintain' and 'maintainable' are to be construed accordingly".[449] Both MacKenna J., who took a wide view of the meaning of "repair" in *Worcester C.C.* v. *Newman* (1975),[450] and Lord Denning M.R., who took a narrow view of the term in *Haydon* v. *Kent C.C.* (1978),[451] have suggested that "repair" and "maintenance" may be synonymous in this context. However, the weight of authority supports the view – which is consistent with a literal interpretation of the Act – that "maintenance" is wider in scope than "repair".[452]

In the *Worcester* case the Court of Appeal by majority held that "the mere removal of an obstruction . . . [was not] in itself a repair".[453] Lawton L.J. reached this conclusion by focusing on the causes of the conditions which repair could remedy. He stated that repair "connotes the restoration to a sound or unimpaired condition that which has become unsound or impaired by neglect or use".[454] Cairns L.J. – whose views were adopted by Lord Denning in the *Kent* case[455] – stated simply that "a highway can only be said to be out of repair if the surface of it is defective or disturbed in some way. Not every defect in the surface would constitute being out of repair".[456] In practice there is likely to be little difference between these approaches as impairments arising through use will necessarily affect only the surface; impairments arising through neglect will probably also affect only the surface (once neglect of obstructions, such as barbed wire, is excluded).

In the *Kent* case, the Court of Appeal, again by majority, held that "maintenance" extends beyond repair to all acts necessary for keeping a highway "in a state which enables it to serve the purpose for which it eixists".[457] The stopping of encroachments and removal of obstructions are therefore part of the duty to maintain,[458] which in this respect overlaps with the duty of highway authorities to prevent as far as possible the stopping up or obstruction of highways.[459]

(b) The standard of the duty

Until the early nineteenth century it was generally accepted that the duty to maintain a highway did not extend to placing it "in better condition than it has been time out of mind".[460] Hence, a parish might not be in breach of its duty even where a highway was so muddy and narrow that people could hardly pass along it.[461] However, in the mid-nineteenth century this view was rejected by the courts which instead required parishes to put highways "in such repair so as to be reasonably passable for the ordinary traffic of the neighbourhood at all seasons of the year".[462] The immediate importance of the new test was that it operated so as to increase the obligation of parishes which were required to maintain roads in a condition suitable for traffic as it grew progressively heavier.[463] The current importance of this test lies in its flexibility. As stated by Erle J. in *R.* v. *Henley Inhabitants* (1847), if a highway "is little used, then little repair is necessary; but if much used, then proportionately more".[464]

(3) The enforcement of the duty to maintain highways

At common law the primary means by which a member of the public could secure compliance with the duty to maintain highways was indictment on the basis that a public nuisance had been committed. Both parishioners and persons privately liable could be indicted, and when highway authorities were placed under a duty to maintain public rights of way it became possible to indict them also.[465] However, in 1959 this right to enforce the repair of highways was abolished,[466] because such proceedings were "a very rare occurrence and . . . virtually obsolete".[467]

There is some authority that the courts will not grant a mandamus or mandatory injunction to enforce the duty to maintain highways.[468] However, the two main cases in this context no longer appear persuasive. Thus, in *R. v. Trustees of the Oxford and Witney Turnpike Roads* (1840),[469] Lord Denman C.J. refused mandamus on the basis that indictment was a more suitable remedy. In *Attorney-General v. Staffordshire C.C.* (1904)[470] Joyce J. partly justified his decision not to grant a mandatory injunction on the basis that "the court will not superintend works of building or of repair". However, this rationale is at most applicable to works requiring continuous supervision over a long period of time;[471] it does not apply to definite works of a limited nature.[472] Consequently, so long as the applicant for relief can satisfy the rules as to standing and there is no other adequate remedy,[473] there appears to be no reason why the courts should not grant either mandamus or a mandatory injunction in relation to particular works of maintenance of highways (just as they are willing to do so in relation to waterways).[474]

The principal way in which a member of the public can, however, enforce the duty to maintain is under section 56 of the Highways Act 1980.[475] Under this provision, a complainant may serve a notice on the person alleged to be liable to maintain the highway ("the respondent") requiring the respondent to state whether he admits that the way is a highway and that he is liable to maintain it.[476] If the respondent either fails to answer the notice or admits the matters contained in it,[477] the complainant may apply to the County Court for an order requiring the respondent to put the highway "in proper repair within such reasonable period as may be specified in the order". If the respondent does not act within the specified period, the court may authorize the complainant to put the highway in proper repair,[478] in which case the complainant can recover his expenses from the respondent summarily as a civil debt.[479]

The main limitation on this procedure is that it is restricted to where a highway is out of "repair", in the sense discussed above,[480] rather than where it has not been maintained. As a result, the procedure can be invoked where the surface of a highway is defective through use or neglect. It may even be used where vegetation obstructs a highway because of neglect to maintain the surface (rather than because the vegetation was deliberately planted there).[481] However, it may not be invoked against obstructions, such as barbed wire, which do not affect the surface and which result from positive acts.[482]

As a matter of practice, a further limitation on this procedure may be that the courts have a discretion under section 56 to deprive a successful complainant of costs if "he is no more than a member of the public, and the public themselves have not benefited adequately out of the bringing of the proceedings".[483]

(B) WATERWAYS

(1) The incidence of the duty to maintain waterways

At common law, there is no general duty on parishioners or any other class of persons to keep waterways navigable,[484] although it appears that such a duty could arise in specific instances by prescription.[485] By legislation, the Commissioners of Sewers and then the statutory undertakers of river improvements and canals were empowered to maintain waterways[486] but it was only in the 1840s that Parliament began to require statutory undertakers to maintain waterways in order to prevent railway companies from buying up canals and then failing to maintain them in order to get rid of competition. Until 1873 such duties were imposed in the private Acts which authorized the amalgamation of the railway and canal companies.[487] Then Parliament enacted general legislation, section 17 of the Regulation of Railways Act 1873, requiring railway companies to maintain canals which they either owned or managed.

When most of Britain's inland transport was nationalized in 1947, the greater part of the inland waterway network was vested in the British Transport Commission. Because the Commission was a railway company for the purposes of the 1873 Act,[488] it was required by section 17 to maintain not just those canals which had formerly been owned by railway companies but all the canals it had taken over.[489] In 1962 this duty was extended to all inland waterways (rather than simply canals) comprised in the undertaking of the British Waterways Board,[490] which had taken over waterways of the British Transport Commission.[491] However, the Board's liability to maintain the waterways was suspended in fundamental respects until the end of 1968.[492] By then the Transport Act 1968 had provided that section 17 of the Act of 1873 would no longer apply to waterways in the undertaking of the Board.[493] Instead, the Board was required to maintain only those waterways classified as "commercial" or "cruising" as opposed to the "remainder" waterways.[494]

(2) The nature of the statutory duty to maintain waterways

The nature of the statutory duty to maintain waterways turns simply on the terms of the relevant legislation. In the case of the "independent" statutory undertakers, this duty, if any, is likely to be found only in the relevant local Acts and not in section 17 of the Regulation of Railways Act 1873, since section 17 applies only to railway companies and all such companies were nationalized in 1947. In the case of the British Waterways Board, the duties are defined by the Transport Act 1968 which requires the Board to maintain "commercial" waterways[495] "in a suitable condition for use by commercial freight-carrying vessels"[496] and "cruising" waterways[497] "in a suitable condition for use by cruising craft, that is to say, vessels constructed or adopted for the carriage of passengers and driven by mechanical power".[498]

(3) Enforcement of the duty to maintain waterways

In the event of an independent undertaker or the British Waterways Board failing to fulfil its duty to maintain, a member of the public may have four remedies. One of these remedies, indictment, appears to be available in all cases of breach of this duty, but has the disadvantage that it simply results in punishment of the breach. Of the other three remedies, both injunctions and mandamus are discretionary and the statutory remedy under the Transport Act 1968 is quite narrow in scope. However, they have the advantage that they may result in actual enforcement of the duty to maintain.

As determined in *Lane* v. *Newdigate* (1804),[499] the courts may enforce a duty to repair by granting an injunction. Because he was uncertain whether an injunction could be granted in positive terms, Lord Eldon in the *Newdigate* case granted a prohibitory injunction restraining the defendants from keeping the banks of a canal and locks out of repair. However, if a court were to grant such relief now, it would issue a mandatory injunction requiring the undertaker to keep the waterway in repair.[500]

As determined in *R.* v. *Bristol Dock Co.* (1841),[501] the courts may also enforce a duty to repair by issuing a mandamus against the undertaker. In that case the dock company, which had been under a duty to make, complete and maintain a new channel of a river, had completed the channel but part of the bank had then fallen out of repair. In granting a mandamus requiring the company to repair and maintain the banks, Denman C.J. stated "Those who obtain an Act of Parliament for executing great public works are bound to fulfil all the duties thereby thrown upon them, and may be called upon by this Court so to do."[502]

So far as the waterways of the British Waterways Board are concerned, the existence of a specific means of enforcing the duty of maintenance under section 106 of the Transport Act 1968 may result in the courts refusing to grant an injunction or mandamus against the Board, at least where the special remedy applies. Section 106 provides that where there has been "a serious and persistent failure" by the Board to carry out their maintenance duties, the High Court on application from any person may require the Board to remedy that failure.[503] If the Board's breach of duty falls within this section, it provides the obvious remedy for members of the public. However, it is subject to the qualification that, even though such "enforcement proceedings" are in progress, the Minister may in certain circumstances reclassify the waterway (presumably into the "remainder" category) and hence absolve the Board from its duty.[504]

VII. THE DIVERSION AND STOPPING UP OF RIGHTS OF WAY

In theory the diversion and stopping up of public rights of way may be authorized at either common law or under statute. However, in practice the mechanisms by which such changes may occur at common law are now insignificant, and the common law has in fact become something of a bastion for the protection of public rights. In its place, legislation has emerged as the primary means by which public rights can lawfully be either relocated or extinguished.

(A) COMMON LAW

At common law public rights of way can be diverted or stopped up only by natural causes, where the way is no longer traversible,[505] or through the writ of *ad quod damnum*,[506] which has fallen into disuse. Beyond these two situations, it is generally correct to say "once a highway, always a highway".[507] Neither disuse by members of the public[508] nor unchallenged obstruction of a right of way by landowners[509] can extinguish the public's rights, regardless of the length of time for which they continue. As a matter of law, members of the public are also deemed incapable of releasing their rights.[510]

Consequently, the common law is generally protective of public rights of passage. In particular, the courts have been reluctant to presume lawful closure of a public right of way in the absence of express evidence.[511] At most, the courts may presume that a right of way was lawfully closed where the way in question has long been disused and another way was created for members of the public.[512] However, even in this situation there is strong authority that the courts will hold that the old highway still exists.[513]

B. LEGISLATION

There are two ways in which Parliament may divert or extinguish public rights of way. It may enact legislation which of itself either expressly or implicitly[514] has this effect – a result which is more often a feature of local rather than general Acts. Alternatively, it may enact legislation which authorizes either the courts or some arm of government, generally a Minister of the Crown, to make these decisions in particular circumstances.

(1) Highways

Since the sixteenth century, Parliament has created a variety of procedures whereby highways may be diverted or closed.[515] Until the eighteenth century these procedures were only established on a local basis. However, under the Highway Act 1773 justices of the peace throughout England were empowered to divert and stop up highways;[516] section 8 of the Inclosure (Consolidation) Act 1801 made general provision for these powers to be given to all inclosure commissioners.[517]

Under current legislation, magistrates, local authorities and Ministers are empowered to divert and close highways permanently[518] under at least 13 different public Acts – two of which, the Highways Act 1980 and the Town and Country Planning Act 1971, establish a number of different procedures under which such changes can be made. The various powers apply in express terms only to individual highways. However, local authorities can in practice exercise their powers so as to effect large-scale changes in the network of footpaths and bridleways, as is the case with the "rationalisation" schemes currently being carried out in two counties, Nottinghamshire and West Sussex.[519]

Under almost all the legislation relating to the diversion and extinguishment of public highways, there is some provision for public notice followed by consideration of objections. In the case of decisions made by magistrates' courts, there must be public notice of an application to the court[520] and users of the highway then have a right to be heard and to make objections at the hearing.[521] In the case of decisions by local authorities, the relevant authority makes an order which is the subject of various notices.[522] If there are no objections to the order, it may be confirmed by the authority.[523] If there are objections, confirmation is left to the Secretary of State who generally appoints an inspector to hold a public inquiry.[524] Only under the Defence Acts of 1842[525] and 1860[526] – which relate to paths on or near military lands – is there power to close public rights of way without anyone being given an opportunity to object.

The legislation is much more diverse in the extent of the discretions which it entrusts to the various decision-making bodies. In relation to conflicts between private landowners and members of the public, the legislation tends to include quite detailed statements of the factors which must be considered before a highway can be diverted or stopped up.[527] Where the power is exercised in the interests of a government department or statutory undertaker, the discretion tends to be quite broad.[528] In extreme cases, such as the power of the Secretary of State of the Environment to extinguish highways over land vested in urban development[529] or new town development corporations,[530] the discretion appears unfettered.[531]

The legislation is equally diverse in terms of the type of interests which benefit from exercise of the various powers. Orders diverting highways may, of course, be to the advantage of members of the public. Generally, however, it is a matter of the extent of the detriment suffered by path-users and whether the beneficiaries of the change are private landowners or some arm of government.

(a) Diversions in the public interest
Under section 119 of the Highways Act 1980, a council may make an order diverting a footpath or bridleway in their area if it considers that such a change would be "expedient" in the

interests of the public.[532] There are no limitations on this test of "expediency", so the council can make the route of a path more direct, more commodious or, for that matter, more scenic. The council also need not obtain the consent of the relevant landowers. Subject to the payment of compensation,[533] it consequently can divert a path to a route which is less advantageous to the relevant landowners or even divert a path from land in one ownership to land in different ownership.

Such a decision to divert a public path cannot be made, however, in complete disregard of the relevant landowners. Firstly, the council in making such an order is under a duty "to have due regard to the needs of agriculture and forestry".[534] Secondly, under section 119(6) of the Act, the authority confirming the order must be satisfied *inter alia* that, taking into account the provisions as to compensation, the order is expedient having regard to the effect which . . .

> (b) the coming into operation of the order would have as respects other land served by the existing public right of way; and
> (c) any new public right of way created by the order would have as respects the land over which the right is so created and any land held with it . . .

(b) Diversions in the interests of both the public and landowners
On application by a local authority,[535] a magistrates' court may under section 116 of the Highways Act divert a highway if this would make it "nearer or more commodious to the public".[536] While superficially straightforward, the test of nearness is in fact only clear where the diversion does not change the end-points of a path and the relevant section of the path is not crossed by any other highways. Then, if the new route is more direct, the test will be satisfied. However, if the diversion is not of this type, it will bring the path nearer to some places and further from others: in this situation it is unclear whether the test can ever be satisfied.[537] As interpreted by Woolf J. in *Gravesham B.C.* v. *Wilson* (1983), "commodious" has "a flavour of utility" as well as "convenience, roominess and spaciousness".[538] Consequently, it seems that a highway will, for example, be more commodious if it is a carriageway open to all traffic rather than a footpath open only to foot passengers.[539]

In the context of the Highway Act 1773, which was the first general legislation to authorize diversion on these grounds,[540] the test of "nearer or more commodious" was clearly intended to allow diversions which would be in the public interest by making a highway a more efficient means of travelling between two points.[541] However, in view of the current recreational importance of highways – especially footpaths and bridleways – this rationale is now outdated, and the tests for diversion consequently appear too narrow. Thus, it is unlikely that a footpath could be diverted in order to make it follow a more scenic route, since such a change probably would not result in a highway which was "more commodious" within the meaning of the Act. Moreover, even within their present limited scope, the grounds for diversion are open to criticism on the basis that they do not necessarily represent a test of the public interest. The problem is that it is a sufficient ground for diversion that the new route is "nearer", yet the shorter route may not benefit members of the public if it is less commodious than the old highway.[542]

Finally, a diversion may occur under section 116 only if "the written consent of every person having a legal interest in the land over which the highway is to be diverted is produced to and deposited with the court".[543] As a result, the court's power of diversion is in practice limited to diversions which benefit both landowners and (hopefully) members of the public. Also, because the courts do not have power to compensate a landowner for a diversion which is contrary to his interests,[544] section 116 is likely to be used only where the changes relate to land within single ownership so that the one landowner obtains both the benefit and the burden of the change.

(c) Closure in the interest of landowners where no significant public detriment

Under the Highways Act 1980 both magistrates' courts and county councils may stop up public highways where, at least in theory, no significant public detriment will result from the closure.[545] As noted as early as 1829 by Robert Wellbeloved, such a closure is "in almost every instance . . . an absolute gift, without consideration, to an individual out of the possessions of the public".[546] If one accepts the theory of creation of public rights of way at common law by dedication – which involves a similar gift to the public – it can be argued that it is appropriate for the public to make reciprocal gifts of unnecessary paths to landowners. However, as noted previously, implied dedication is in many respects a fiction, and it is really use which creates the public right of way. Furthermore, where a highway is created under statute, the landowner is usually compensated on the basis that the path decreases the value of his land. Since the closure of a path increases the value of the landowner's' interest, the current legislation may well be misfounded. Instead landowners should have to pay for the benefit they receive.[547]

Under the powers of both magistrates' courts and the councils, the decision to make an extinguishment order depends upon the need for the path. In the case of magistrates' courts, the sole test is that the path is "unnecessary"[548] – which encompasses the needs of both members of the public and landowners. In the case of the councils' power, the initial test is that the path "is not needed for public use"[549] – but the needs of adjoining landowners represent one of a number of factors which the confirming authority must consider.[550]

On a literal reading of the provisions, orders could be made in both cases only if there were no need for a path. However, in *R. v. Secretary of State for the Environment, Ex parte Stewart* (1980)[551] Phillips J. suggested that an order may also be made if there is only "minimal public need". Closure is most straightforward and likely where a path has fallen into disuse.[552] However, mere evidence of use is not sufficient to determine the question of need, and a highway which is in use may nevertheless be found to be unnecessary,[553] as where alternative routes are available.[554]

In relation to orders made by councils, the relevant authority may confirm an order only if

> satisfied that it is expedient so to do having regard to the extent (if any) to which it appears to him . . . that the path or way would, apart from the order, be likely to be used by the public, and having regard to the effect which the extinguishment of the right of way would have as respects land served by the path or way . . .[555]

As interpreted by Phillips J. in the *Stewart* case,[556] this test offers little protection to members of the public over and above that already contained in the requirement that the path be unnecessary for public use. As with the council's initial decision, so an order may be confirmed even if "the path was, or was going to be, used to something more than a minimal extent".[557]

A more significant fetter on councils and confirming authorities is that in reaching their decisions they must disregard "any temporary circumstances preventing or diminishing the use of a path or way by the public".[558] According to Phillips J. in the *Stewart* case, even if an obstruction appears to be permanent in nature, it can still be regarded as a "temporary circumstance" if it is a public nuisance which can be abated or otherwise removed by legal steps.[559] In any event, Phillips J. stated that it could only rarely be "right to make an order stopping up a highway on the ground that as a result of an unlawful obstruction or as a result of doubt as to the line of the highway it was dificult to use it".[560] Any decision to the contrary "would be an encouragement to those who improperly obstruct highways".[561]

(d) Diversions and closures in the interest of landowners and to the detriment of the public

Under both the Highways Act 1980 and the Town and Country Planning Act 1971, changes can be made to the highway network which are intended to benefit landowners and are to the clear detriment of members of the public. In the case of the Highways Act, the relevant provision is in one respect very broad: the change need simply be expedient in the interests of the landower. However, this power is restricted to diversions and there are also some safeguards of the interests of members of the public. By way of contrast, the relevant provisions of the planning legislation apply only where planning permission has been granted under the Act. However, there then is not only a power to divert highways but also a power of closure (which, as discussed above, involves a conveyance to the landowner without consideration).[562] Furthermore, there are no safeguards of the public interest. It consequently is not surprising that, where possible, landowners prefer to invoke the provisions of the planning rather than the highways legislation.[563]

(i) THE HIGHWAYS LEGISLATION

Under section 119 of the Highways Act 1980, a council may on its own initiative make an order diverting a footpath or bridleway in their area if they consider that such a change would be expedient "in the interests of the owner, lessee or occupier of land crossed by the path or way".[564] The original version of this power – which was enacted in 1949 and referred to "securing the efficient use of the land"[565] – was directed principally at promoting agriculture, and most diversions under this power are likely to be done with this object. However, the "interests" of the landowner is clearly a very broad concept which includes the privacy and even the safety of the occupiers. Thus, in *Roberton* v. *Secretary of State for the Environment* (1976),[566] which was in fact decided under the original narrower legislation, a footpath which ran across the Chequers Estate was diverted because of the possibility that continued use of the path by the public might facilitate attempts to assassinate the Prime Minister.

In re-routing the path, the council need not obtain the consent of the owner of the land made subject to the new right of way. Consequently, subject to the payment of compensation,[567] the council is not restricted to keeping the path within land under single ownership. However, in the interest of members of the public, there are certain restrictions on the council's choice of a new route for the path. The council cannot alter the path's point of termination if that point is not on a highway[568] – hence, if the path is a cul-de-sac leading to a mountain top or edge of a bluff, a diversion order cannot alter the end-point of the path. If the path terminates on a highway, the council can only alter its point of termination "to another point which is on the same highway, or a highway connected with it, and which is substantially as convenient to the public".[569]

The public interst in the use of footpaths and bridleways is further protected by the requirement that diversion orders can only be confirmed by the relevant authority if it is satisfied on five counts.[570] Most significantly, the authority cannot confirm the order unless it is satisfied that the path will not be substantially less convenient to the public in consequence of the diversion and that it is expedient to confirm the order having regard to the effect which "the diversion would have on public enjoyment of the path or way as a whole".[571]

(ii) THE PLANNING LEGISLATION

Under the Town and Country Planning Act 1971, the effect of a proposed development on a public highway is a material consideration in determining applications for planning permission. However, the grant of planning permission cannot of itself result in the diversion or extinguishment of a public right of way. Such changes in the highway network may be made only through a second legal process which can take place either under the Highways Act, as discussed above,[572] or more usually under the planning legislation itself. Under Part 10 of the 1971 Act the Secretary of State directly[573] or the local authority, with the confirmation of the Secretary of State in the case of opposed orders,[574] may "authorise the stopping up or diversion of any highway if he is satisfied that it is necessary to do so in order to enable development to be carried out in accordance with planning permission".

The problem with this two level process is that at the first stage, where public rights are not directly affected, the issue of the diversion or stopping up of public paths may receive inadequate consideration – especially as there is no requirement that authorities publicize that an application has been made to develop land over which a highway runs.[575] At the second stage, when the diversion or closure of public paths is directly in issue, the matter has in practice generally been decided, notwithstanding the discretion of the Secretary of State or the council. If the development which has been approved is inconsistent with the existence of the highway, it will be necessary to approve the diversion or closure so that the development can proceed lawfully.[576]

(e) Diversion and closures for public purposes

Under numerous Acts, Ministers of the Crown (and in one case, magistrates' courts) are empowered to divert and extinguish public rights of way in order to achieve certain public purposes. In at least four cases, exercise of these powers is fettered so that they should not result in any significant detriment to path-users. However, in the remaining cases the public purpose may override the interests of path-users so that a path can be extinguished even where it would otherwise be considered to be needed by the public.

The powers which are fettered in the interests of path-users fall into two categories. In relation to land which local authorities hold for planning purposes or have acquired by compulsory purchase, the Secretary of State can extinguish a path over such land only if he is satisfied that an alternative path has been or will be provided or that an alternative way is not required.[577] In relation to defence lands, the power of magistrates and the Secretary of State to divert or extinguish paths can only be exercised if the old path will be replaced by another which is convenient to the public.[578]

The powers which allow the public interest to be overridden are quite diverse. The Minister of Transport may stop up or divert any highway if he is satisfied that it is necessary to do so in order to secure the safe and efficient use of land for civil aviation purposes.[579] If a highway either is or will be used for defence purposes, it may be stopped up or diverted by the Minister of Transport if he is satisfied that such a measure is necessary "for the land to be so used efficiently without danger to the public".[580] Where new roads are being constructed or existing roads improved under the Town and Country Planning

Act and another highway crosses or enters the route of the new
highway, the Secretary of State may authorize the closure or
diversion of the other highway if satisfied that it is expedient to
make the order in the interests of the safety of users of the new
highway or to facilitate the movement of traffic along that
highway.[581] As part of authorizing water companies and
authorities to carry out various works, the Secretary of State
may stop up and divert public paths.[582] Finally, the Secretary
of State may extinguish any highway over land which is vested
in or acquired by urban development[583] or new town development corporations[584] or their associated highway authorities.

(2) Waterways

The question of extinguishment of public rights of navigation
by statute has arisen largely, if not exclusively, in relation to
waterways where the public right had previously been created
under river improvement or canal Acts. Until 1968, private
Acts were the only type of legislation which extinguished the
public rights over these waterways. However, since then the
Minister of Transport has been empowered to extinguish
public rights of navigation over canals not comprised in the
undertaking of the British Waterways Board. The public's
rights over all of the Board's "artificial" waterways have also
been extinguished.

(a) The position prior to 1968

Until 1968 there were at least two procedures whereby
statutory undertakers could be relieved of their duties to
maintain waterways, but neither procedure directly affected
the public's rights. Thus, a canal company established under a
private Act could be wound up under the ordinary companies
legislation, but the winding-up did not affect the public's rights
in the navigation.[585] Equally, the Board of Trade could
authorize the abandonment of a canal under section 45 of the
Railway and Canal Traffic Act 1888.[586] As part of such
authorization, the Board could relieve the proprietors of the
canal from all obligations, but the Board had no power to
interfere directly with the public's rights.

(b) Extinguishment under the Transport Act 1968 of public rights over "independent" canals

Because section 45 of the Railway and Canal Traffic Act 1888
was defective in several respects[587] (including its failure to
provide for the extinguishment of the public's rights), Parlia-

ment repealed this provision in 1968[588] and replaced it with section 112 of the Transport Act 1968. Under the new provision, which applies to any canal which is not comprised in the undertaking of the British Waterways Board, the Minister may extinguish any public right of navigation conferred by a local Act[589] and may also extinguish any duties to maintain the canal.[590] In making such an order, the Minister has an unfettered discretion (unlike the Board of Trade which could only authorize abandonment on specific grounds, such as, that the canal was "unnecessary for the purposes of the public navigation").[591] The Minister is required to hold a public inquiry only if the canal was "used to a significant extent for the purpose of navigation at the time when notice of the proposed order was published" and an objection has been made to the order by an organization representing a substantial number of persons who used the canal at the time of the order.[592]

(c) Extinguishment by the Transport Act 1968 of public rights over "artificial" waterways of the British Waterways Board
By section 105(5), (6) of the Transport Act 1968, public rights of navigation which had been conferred by local Acts were extinguished in relation to those waterways then owned or subsequently acquired by the British Waterways Board.[593] The most unusual aspect of this extinguishment of public rights of navigation was that on the whole it was not linked to the closure of the relevant waterways; members of the public have in fact remained able to navigate these waterways under licence. For this reason, it has been asserted that the extinguishment of the public's rights was of no consequence.[594] However, the extinguishment of the public rights of navigation has deprived members of the public of a number of remedies in respect of waterways which are obstructed or out of repair. In particular, where the public right has been extinguished, members of the public probably lack standing to obtain an injunction or mandamus to enforce the Board's duties to maintain the "commercial" and "cruising" waterways. Even if they suffer what would otherwise be classified as "particular damage",[595] they are probably unable to recover their loss since public nuisance appears to apply to only those waterways which are subject to public rights of navigation.

NOTES TO CHAPTER 1

1. Justinian, *Institutes*, 2.1.1; Buckland, p. 183.
2. Justinian, *Institutes*, 2.1.4; Buckland, p. 185.
3. See *Wills' Trustees* v. *Cairngorm Canoeing and Sailing School Ltd* 1976 S.L.T. 162, 200 *per* Lord Hailsham.
4. Bracton, vol. 2, p. 40.
5. *Young* v. _____ (1698) 1 Ld. Raym. 725; 91 E.R. 1384; *R.* v. *Cluworth Inhabitants* (1704) 6 Mod. 163; 87 E.R. 920. Compare *Pierce* v. *Lord Fauconberg* (1757) 1 Burr. 292; 97 E.R. 320 where the claim for a public right to tow was made in relation to a particular place, suggesting that it was accepted that there was no general right.
6. 3 T.R. 253; 100 E.R. 560. See also *Winch* v. *Thames Conservators* (1872) L.R. 7 C.P. 458, 471. Compare *Attorney-General* v. *Tomline* (1879) 12 Ch. D. 214, 232-3 *per* Fry J.
7. 5 B. & Ald. 268; 106 E.R. 1190. See also *Llandudno U.D.C.* v. *Woods* [1899] 2 Ch. 705; *Brinckman* v. *Matley* [1904] 2 Ch. 313; *Lord Fitzhardinge* v. *Purcell* [1908] 2 Ch. 139, 165-6; *Alfred F. Beckett Ltd.* v. *Lyons* [1967] Ch. 449.
8. See, for example, *Lyon* v. *Fishmongers' Co.* (1876) 1 App. Cas. 662, 682 *per* Lord Selbourne.
9. 8 Ad. & E. 314; 112 E.R. 857.
10. See Holdsworth, vol. 10, p. 302.
11. See *R.* v. *Hudson* (1732) 2 Str. 909; 93 E.R. 935; *Lade* v. *Shepherd* (1735) 2 Str. 1004; 93 E.R. 997.
12. *Caldwell* v. *McLaren* (1884) 9 App. Cas. 393, 405; *Simpson* v. *Attorney-General* [1904] A.C. 476. See also *Frost* v. *Richardson* (1910) 103 L.T. 22.
13. In the Scottish case, *Wills' Trustees* v. *Cairngorm Canoeing and School Ltd* 1976 S.L.T. 162, the House of Lords held that different rules may in part apply to the creation of public rights of way over land and over water. However, the issue in question – the need for public termini – is not part of the rules governing the creation of public rights of way at common law.
14. See *Eyre* v. *New Forest Highway Board* (1892) 56 J.P. 517 *per* Wills J.
15. *Jones* v. *Bates* [1938] 2 All E.R. 237, 244 *per* Scott L.J. See also *Mann* v. *Brodie* (1885) 10 App. Cas. 378, 391 *per* Lord Watson; *Eyre* v. *New Forest Highway Board* (1892) 56 J.P. 517 *per* Wills J. Compare *Folkestone Corporation* v. *Brockman* [1914] A.C. 338, 354 *per* Lord Kinnear.
16. Wellbeloved, pp. 41–2.
17. See *Gloucestershire C.C.* v. *Farrow* [1985] 1 All E.R. 878, 882 *per* Fox L.J.
18. *Mann* v. *Brodie* (1885) 10 App. Cas. 378, 390-1 *per* Lord Watson.
19. In relation to public rights of way over land but not public rights of navigation, this period has been reduced to 20 years by the Prescription and Limitation (Scotland) Act 1973, s. 3(3). See *Wills' Trustees* v. *Cairngorm Canoeing and Sailing School Ltd* 1976 S.L.T. 162, 214 *per* Lord Fraser.
20. *Kinross C.C.* v. *Archibald* (1899) 7 S.L.T. 305, 306 *per* Lord Kincairney. Compare *Edinburgh Magistrates* v. *North British Railway Co.* (1904) 6 F. 620.

21. *The First Report to His Majesty by the Commissioners appointed to inquire into the Law of England respecting Real Property,* 1829, pp. 51–2.
22. Footpaths and Roadside Wastes Bill 1888, cl. 6.
23. See Sir Lawrence Chubb, "The Rights of Way Act, 1932: its History and Meaning", *Journal of the Commons, Open Spaces and Footpaths Preservation Society,* vol. 2, no. 8, October 1932, p. 245.
24. Public Rights of Way Bill 1906, cl. 2.
25. Public Rights of Way Bill 1911, clauses 2, 5; Highways Act 1980, ss. 31(11), 329(1).
26. The Law Commission and Scottish Law Commission, *Interpretation Bill,* Cmnd. 7235, 1978, para. 12, in relation to the definition of "land", as including "land covered with water", adopted in the Interpretation Act 1978, sched. 1. See also *Trafford* v. *Ashby* (1969) 21 P. & C.R. 293, a case under the Commons Registration Act 1965, in which Megarry J. stated that as " 'land' includes 'land covered with water' . . . it is capable of applying to a subject-matter such as the River Wye". Note that by reference to section 328(1) of the 1980 Act, the general definition section, it could be argued that statutory dedication applies only to ways over land, because section 328(1) defines "highway" as excluding waterways. However, on this approach, it is difficult to see what meaning could be attributed to "land covered with water". The definition in section 328(1) does not apply "where the context otherwise requires", and section 31 appears to be one such case, since there was no such definition section in the 1932 Act and the consolidation of the Act with the general highways legislation should not be held to have changed the scope of statutory dedication.
27. Highways Act 1980, s. 31(9); *Jones* v. *Bates* [1938] 2 All E.R. 237, 251 *per* Farwell J.; *Attorney-General and Newton Abbot R.D.C.* v. *Dyer* [1947] Ch. 67; *Fairey* v. *Southampton C.C.* [1956] 2 Q.B. 439, 462 *per* Birkett L.J. Compare *Jones* v. *Bates* [1938] 2 All E.R. 237, 247 *per* Scott L.J.
28. [1929] 1 Ch. 440, 445, quoted with approval in *Jones* v. *Bates* [1938] 2 All E.R. 237, 241 *per* Slesser L.J., 245 *per* Scott L.J.; *Attorney-General and Newton Abbot R.D.C.* v. *Dyer* [1947] Ch. 67, 85; *Lewis* v. *Thomas* [1950] 1 K.B. 438, 442 *per* Evershed M.R.
29. *Merstham Manor Ltd* v. *Coulson and Purley U.D.C.* [1937] 2 K.B. 77, 82–4 *per* Hilbery J.; *Jones* v. *Bates* [1938] 2 All E.R. 237, 245 *per* Scott L.J.
30. See *Miles* v. *Rose* (1814) 5 Taunt. 705; 128 E.R. 868; *Mildred* v. *Weaver* (1862) 3 F. & F. 30; 176 E.R. 15; *Hue* v. *Whiteley* [1929] 1 Ch. 440, 445.
31. *Hue* v. *Whiteley* [1929] 1 Ch. 440, 445.
32. See, for example, *Moser* v. *Ambleside U.D.C.* (1925) 23 L.G.R. 533, 540; *Williams-Ellis* v. *Cobb* [1935] 1 K.B. 310, 319–22, 329; *Roberts* v. *Webster* (1968) 66 L.G.R. 298.
33. *Attorney-General* v. *Hemingway* (1916) 81 J.P. 112; *Lewis* v. *Thomas* [1950] 1 K.B. 438, 444 *per* Lord Evershed M.R., 447 *per* Cohen L.J.; *Owen* v. *Buckinghamshire C.C.* (1957) 121 J.P. 516.
34. See *Poole* v. *Huskinson* 11 M. & W. 827, 830; 152 E.R. 1039, 1041 *per* Parke B.
35. Highways Act 1980, s. 31(1). See especially *Lewis* v. *Thomas* [1950] 1 K.B. 438.
36. 5 Taunt. 125, 137; 128 E.R. 634, 639. See also *Guest* v. *Goldsborough &*

Co. Ltd (1886) 12 V.L.R. 804, 807 *per* Higinbotham C.J.

37. *North London Railway Co.* v. *Vestry of St Mary, Islington* (1872) 27 L.T. 672. See also, *Rowley* v. *Tottenham U.D.C.* [1914] A.C. 95 (3 years' use); *R.* v. *Petrie* (1855) 4 B. & El. 737; 119 E.R. 272 (7 years' use).

38. *Folkestone Corporation* v. *Brockman* [1914] A.C. 338; *Williams-Ellis* v. *Cobb* [1935] 1 K.B. 310.

39. Highways Act 1980, s. 31(1).

40. [1956] 2 Q.B. 439, 459.

41. *Jones* v. *Bates* [1938] 2 All E.R. 237, 244–5 *per* Scott L.J.

42. 8 Ad. & El. 99, 105; 112 E.R. 773, 775.

43. See *R.* v. *Broke* (1859) 1 F. & F. 514, 515; 175 E.R. 832 *per* Pollock C.B.; *Fairey* v. *Southampton C.C.* [1956] 2 Q.B. 439, 457–8 *per* Denning L.J.

44. 1 Camp. 261, 262; 170 E.R. 950, 951.

45. (1885) 10 App. Cas. 378, esp. at 386 *per* Lord Blackburn, followed in *Folkestone Corporation* v. *Brockman* [1914] A.C. 338, 352 *per* Lord Kinnear, 362–3 *per* Lord Atkinson; *Williams-Ellis* v. *Cobb* [1935] 1 K.B. 310, 331 *per* Talbot J.

46. [1947] Ch. 67, 85. Compare *Fenwick* v. *Huntingdon R.D.C.* (1928) 92 J.P. 41, 43 *per* Romer J., "If the user is consistent with the use of the path by sufferance, then I must not presume dedication . . .".

47. *Blount* v. *Layard* (1888) [1891] 2 Ch. 681n, 691n.

48. Benjamin Nathan Cardozo, *The Nature of the Judicial Process*, New Haven, Yale University Press, 1922, p. 87.

49. *Attorney-General and Newton Abbot R.D.C.* v. *Dyer* [1947] Ch. 67, 85, 86.

50. 465 P. 2d 50 (1970).

51. See Michael A. O'Flaherty, "This Land is my Land: the Doctrine of Implied Dedication and its Application to California Beaches", (1970–1) 44 Southern California L.R. 1092, 1094–6.

52. 465 P. 2d 50, 57–8. See also O'Flaherty, *op. cit.*, pp. 1115–6.

53. *British Museum Trustees* v. *Finnis* (1833) 5 C. & P. 460; 172 E.R. 1053. See, further, Alec Samuels, "Annual Closure of a Way", (1986) Conveyancer 161–4.

54. *Roberts* v. *Kerr* (1808) 1 Camp. 262; 170 E.R. 951.

55. *Poole* v. *Huskinson* (1843) 11 M. & W. 827; 152 E.R. 1039; *Healey* v. *Batley Corporation* (1875) 19 Eq. 375, 388 *per* Bacon V.-C.

56. Highways Act 1980, s. 31(3), discussed in *R.* v. *Secretary of State for the Environment, Ex parte Blake* [1984] J.P.L. 101, 103–4.

57. Highways Act 1980, s. 31(5).

58. *Farquhar* v. *Newbury R.D.C.* [1909] 1 Ch. 12, 19 *per* Farwell L.J.

59. *Baxter* v. *Taylor* (1832) 4 B. & Ad. 72, 75; 110 E.R. 382, 384 *per* Patteson J.; *Eyre* v. *New Forest Highway Board* (1892) 56 J.P. 517 *per* Wills J.; *Farquhar* v. *Newbury R.D.C.* [1909] 1 Ch. 12, 18 *per* Farwell L.J.

60. *R.* v. *Barr* (1814) 4 Camp. 16; 171 E.R. 6. See also *Attorney-General* v. *Simpson* [1904] A.C. 476, 507 *per* Lord Davey.

61. *Winterbottom* v. *Lord Derby* (1867) L.R. 2 Ex. 316, 317–8 *per* Mellor J.; *Williams-Ellis* v. *Cobb* [1935] 1 K.B. 310.

62. See *Attorney-General and Newton Abbot R.D.C.* v. *Dyer* [1947] Ch. 67, 87; *Fairey* v. *Southampton C.C.* [1956] 2 Q.B. 439, 452 *per* Stable J.

63. Highways Act 1980, s. 31(4).

64. *Ibid.*, s. 33.
65. *Fairey* v. *Southampton C.C.* [1956] 2 Q.B. 439, 459 *per* Denning L.J. It is no longer even necessary, as under the Rights of Way Act 1932, s. 1(1), (2), that 40 years' use be shown where during the first 20 years there was no-one in possession of the land capable of dedicating the way. As a result of section 58(1) of the National Parks and Access to the Countryside Act 1949, 20 years' use is now sufficient in this situation.
66. Highways Act 1980, s. 31(8). See *British Transport Commission* v. *Westmorland C.C.* [1958] A.C. 126, 146 *per* Viscount Simonds.
67. 5 B. & Ad. 469, 478; 110 E.R. 863, 867.
68. [1958] A.C. 126, 142.
69. See respectively *British Transport Commission* v. *Westmorland C.C.* [1958] A.C. 126; *Taff Vale Railway Co.* v. *Pontypridd U.D.C.* (1905) 69 J.P. 351.
70. *Attorney-General* v. *London and South Western Railway Co.* (1905) 69 J.P. 110.
71. *Arnold* v. *Morgan* [1911] 2 K.B. 314.
72. *Great Central Railway Co.* v. *Balby-with-Hexthorpe U.D.C.* [1912] 2 Ch. 110.
73. *Arnold* v. *Morgan* [1911] 2 K.B. 314, 324 *per* Hamilton J.
74. See, for example, *Great Western Railway Co.* v. *Solihull R.D.C.* (1902) 66 J.P. 772; *Taff Vale Railway Co.* v. *Pontypridd U.D.C.* (1905) 69 J.P. 351; *Lancashire and Yorkshire Railway Co.* v. *Davenport* (1906) 70 J.P. 129; *Great Central Railway Co.* v. *Balby-with-Hexthorpe U.D.C.* [1912] 2 Ch. 110.
75. *Great Western Railway Co.* v. *Solihull R.D.C.* (1902) 66 J.P. 772. See also *Conservators of the Thames* v. *Kent* [1918] 2 K.B. 273, 294 *per* Scrutton J.
76. *Arnold* v. *Morgan* [1911] 2 K.B. 314, 324 *per* Hamilton J.; *British Railways Board* v. *Chestnut U.D.C.* (1970) 216 E.G. 1275, 1276 *per* Megarry J.
77. See *R.* v. *Inhabitants of Leake* (1833) 5 B. & Ad. 469, 481; 110 E.R. 863, 868 *per* Parke J.; *British Railways Board* v. *Carmarthenshire C.C.* (1968) 206 E.G. 979.
78. See below, p. 82.
79. See Wellbeloved, p. 63.
80. 4 B. & Ald. 447, 450; 106 E.R. 1001, 1002.
81. 1 B. & Ad. 32; 109 E.R. 699.
82. 1 B. & Ad. 32, 37; 109 E.R. 699, 701. See also at 1 B. & Ad. 32, 38; 109 E.R. 699, 701 *per* Parke J.
83. 5 B. & Ad. 469; 110 E.R. 863.
84. Highway Act 1835, s. 23.
85. See *Cubitt* v. *Maxse* (1873) L.R. 8 C.P. 704, 715 *per* Brett J.
86. For an account of the evolution of this rule, see Holdsworth, vol. 3, p. 8; vol. 7, pp. 343–5.
87. *Mann* v. *Brodie* (1885) 10 App. Cas. 378, 385 *per* Lord Blackburn; *Williams-Ellis* v. *Cobb* [1935] 1 K.B. 310, 330 *per* Talbot J.; *Fairey* v. *Southampton C.C.* [1956] 2 All E.R. 439, 456 *per* Denning L.J. Compare *Cubitt* v. *Maxse* (1873) L.R. 8 C.P. 704, 714–15 *per* Brett J.; *Eyre* v. *New Forest Highway Board* (1892) 56 J.P. 517 *per* Wills J.; *Jones* v. *Bates* [1938] 2 All E.R. 237, 244 *per* Scott L.J., all of which describe dedication as the sole means of creating public rights of way at common law.

88. *Caldwell* v. *McLaren* (1884) 9 App. Cas. 392, 405.
89. *Mayor of Nottingham* v. *Lambert* (1738) Willes 111, 114; 125 E.R. 1083, 1085.
90. See *Hargreaves* v. *Diddams* (1875) L.R. 10 Q.B. 582, 586 *per* Quain J.; *Neill* v. *Duke of Devonshire* (1882) 8 App. Cas. 135, 154 *per* Lord Selbourne L.C.; *Smith* v. *Andrews* [1891] 2 Ch. 678, 700 *per* North J.; *Attorney-General* v. *Antrobus* [1905] 2 Ch. 188, 198 *per* Farwell J. See also *Alfred F. Beckett Ltd* v. *Lyons* [1967] Ch. 449, 479 *per* Winn L.J.
91. See, for example, *Race* v. *Ward* (1855) 4 El. & Bl. 702, 705; 119 E.R. 259, 260 *per* Lord Campbell C.J.; *Le Strange* v. *Rowe* (1866) 4 F. & F. 1048, 1051; 176 E.R. 903, 905 *per* Erle C.J.; *Lord Rivers* v. *Adams* (1877) 3 Ex. D. 361, 364 *per* Kelly C.B. The further rationale against prescription by the public – that the public cannot release its rights – is clearly irrelevant in this context since members of the public also cannot release their rights over rights of way created by other means.
92. This principle is an extrapolation from the rule that "there could not be a valid grant unto so fluctuating a body and a body as incapable of succession" as local inhabitants. See *Lord Rivers* v. *Adams* (1877) 3 Ex. D. 361, 364–5 *per* Kelly C.B. Compare *R.* v. *Doncaster Metropolitan Borough Council; ex parte Braim* (1986), CO/1455/85, where McCullough J. described public rights of recreation as being created by "grant".
93. *Taff Vale Railway Co.* v. *Pontypridd U.D.C.* (1905) 69 J.P. 351, 353 *per* Buckley J.: "Dedication . . . operates by way of grant". See also *Folkestone Corporation* v. *Brockman* [1914] A.C. 338, 352, 354 *per* Lord Kinnear.
94. Hale, pp. 8–9.
95. [1901] 2 Ch. 671, 687.
96. *Wills' Trustees* v. *Cairngorm Canoeing and Sailing School Ltd* 1976 S.L.T. 162, 203 *per* Lord Hailsham. Note that in *Rawson* v. *Peters* (1972) 116 S.J. 884 Lord Denning apparently stated (although he was not reported on this point) that a public right of navigation could be acquired by "long use". See Halsbury, vol. 49, para. 911, note 7.
97. See above, pp. 38–9.
98. See Webb, p. 118; William Albert, *The Turnpike Road System in England 1663–1840,* Cambridge, Cambridge University Press, 1972, p. 45.
99. See Christopher Taylor, *Roads and Tracks of Britain,* London, Dent, 1979, p. 172.
100. 14 Q.B. 735, 740–1; 117 E.R. 283, 285–6.
101. Both the River Severn Act 1430 (9 Hen. 6, c. 5) and the River Lee Act 1571 (13 Eliz. 1, c. 18) were repealed by the Statute Law Revision Act 1948.
102. See *Craies on Statute Law,* 7th ed., London, Sweet & Maxwell, 1971, p. 359.
103. 9 Hen. 6, c. 5.
104. 13 Eliz. 1, c. 18, s. 9. See also the River Trent Act 1698, 10 Wil. 3, c. 26, s. 13, in relation to the Trent from Gainsborough to Wilden Ferry (Shardlow). This statute is c. 20 in the common printed editions.
105. See below, p. 45.
106. See, for example, Parrett Navigation Act 1836, s. 136, discussed in *Parrett Navigation Co.* v. *Robins* (1842) 10 M. & W. 593; 152 E.R. 608.

107. See, however, the dictum of Littledale J. in *R.* v. *Winter,* quoted below, p. 42.
108. See *Mayor of Manchester* v. *Lyons* (1882) 22 Ch. D. 287, 310 *per* Bowen L.J., quoted with approval in *Taylor* v. *New Windsor Corporation* [1898] 1 Q.B. 186, 194–5 *per* Smith L.J.
109. See *Bishopsgate Motor Finance Co. Ltd.* v. *Transport Brakes Ltd* [1949] 1 K.B. 322, 329.
110. *Duke of Bedford* v. *Emmett* (1820) 3 B. & Ald. 366; 106 E.R. 696; *Stevens* v. *Chown* [1901] 1 Ch. 894; *Hailsham Cattle Market Co.* v. *Tolman* [1915] 1 Ch. 360, 367.
111. *New Windsor Corporation* v. *Taylor* [1899] A.C. 41, 45 *per* Earl of Halsbury L.C. See also *Abergavenny Improvement Commissioners* v. *Straker* (1889) 42 Ch. D. 83, 89.
112. See *Mayor of Manchester* v. *Lyons* (1882) 22 Ch. D. 287, esp. at pp. 305–6 *per* Jessel M.R.; 310 *per* Bowen L.J.
113. See *New Windsor Corporation* v. *Taylor* [1899] A.C. 41, 45 *per* Earl of Halsbury L.C.
114. *Logan* v. *Burton* (1826) 5 B. & C. 513, 524; 108 E.R. 191, 195 *per* Littledale J.; *Attorney-General* v. *Shonleigh Nominees* [1972] 1 W.L.R. 577, 584.
115. 8 B. & C. 785, 793; 108 E.R. 1234, 1237–8.
116. *Stourbridge Canal Co.* v. *Wheeley* (1831) 2 B. & Ad. 792, 796; 109 E.R. 1336, 1338 *per* Tenterden C.J.
117. The only significant issue in relation to whether there has in fact been statutory creation of a public right of way concerns the possible need for the way to be completed in its entirety in order for it to become subject to a public right of passage. See *Cubitt* v. *Maxse* (1873) L.R. 8 C.P. 704; *R.* v. *French* (1879) 4 Q.B.D. 507; *Reynolds* v. *Barnes* [1909] 2 Ch. 361, 364–5.
118. See Eric Pawson, *Transport and Economy: the Turnpike Roads of Eighteenth Century Britain,* London, Academic Press, 1977, pp. 84, 97–99.
119. 3 Geo. 4, c. 126, ss. 84–106.
120. 15 Q.B. 689; 117 E.R. 620.
121. 15 Q.B. 689, 699; 117 E.R. 620, 623-4. See also *R.* v. *French* (1879) 4 Q.B.D. 507, 512, 513 *per* Bramwell L.J.
122. See, for example, 8 Geo. 3, c. 16 (Millington Inclosure Act) and 8 Geo. 3, c. 16 (Winfrith Newburgh Inclosure Act).
123. *R.* v. *Saintiff* (1704) 6 Mod. 255; 87 E.R. 1002 *per* Holt C.J.
124. See *R.* v. *Aldborough* (1853) 17 J.P. 648, 649 *per* Crompton J.
125. For example, Lemington Prior Inclosure Act 1768, 8 Geo. 3, c. 14.
126. For example, Bridlington Inclosure Act 1768, 8 Geo. 3, c. 17. For the practice in laying out highways in this period, see Michael Turner, *English Parliamentary Enclosure: its Historical Geography and Economic History,* Folkestone, Dawson/Archon Books, 1980, p. 18.
127. W.E. Tate, *A Domesday of English Inclosure Acts and Awards,* Reading, University of Reading, 1978, p. 30.
128. See *Logan* v. *Burton* (1826) 5 B. & C. 513, 525; 108 E.R. 191, 196 *per* Bayley J.
129. 8 & 9 Vict., c. 118, s. 33.
130. *Ibid.,* s. 62.
131. For an account of earlier, illegal attempts at river improvement by the

Commissioners of Sewers and under Letters Patent, see Frank A. Sharman, "River Improvement Law in the Early Seventeenth Century", (1982) 3 Journal of Legal History 222–45.
132. See T.S. Willan, *River Navigation in England 1600–1750*, Oxford, Oxford University Press, 1936; Charles Hadfield, *The Canal Age*, Newton Abbot, David & Charles, 1981.
133. See, for example, Aire and Calder Navigation Act, 10 Wil. 3, c. 25 (1698); Derwent Navigation Act, 1 Anne, c. 4 (1702); River Weaver Navigation Act, 7 Geo. 1, c. 10 (1720).
134. See above, pp. 43–4.
135. 23 Geo. 3, c. 47, discussed in *Proprietors of the Leeds and Liverpool Canal* v. *Hustler* (1823) 1 B. & C. 424; 107 E.R. 157.
136. Stourbridge Canal Act, 16 Geo. 3, c. 28, discussed in *Stourbridge Canal Co.* v. *Wheeley* (1831) 2 B. & Ad. 792; 109 E.R. 1336.
137. H.L. Deb., 5th series, vol. 296, cols 1038–45, 8 October 1968, Viscount St Davids.
138. *Ibid.*
139. H.L. Deb., 5th series, vol. 295, cols 754–7, 22 July 1968, Lord Hailsham; H.C. Deb., 5th series, vol. 770, col. 971, 21 October 1968, Stephen Swingler.
140. See, for example, Ashby-de-la-Zouch Canal Act, 34 Geo. 3, c. 93, discussed in *Case* v. *Midland Railway Co.* (1859) 27 Beav. 247; 54 E.R. 96.
141. See *Stourbridge Canal Co.* v. *Wheeley* (1831) 2 B. & Ad. 792, 796–7; 109 E.R. 1336, 1338.
142. Transport Act 1968, s. 105(5)(a). See below, p. 99.
143. See Upper Avon Navigation Act 1972, s. 9.
144. *In re Bradford Navigation Co.* (1870) L.R. 5 Ch. App. 600. For examples of rivers made navigable under statute for which no navigation authority now exists, see Telling & Foster, vol. 2.
145. *In re Woking U.D.C. (Basingstoke Canal) Act 1911* [1914] 1 Ch. 300.
146. See, for example, Public Health Act 1875, s. 154; Local Government Act 1894, s. 8(1)(g); Development and Road Improvement Funds Act 1909; New Towns Act 1981, s. 11.
147. Highways Act 1980, s. 25(4).
148. *Ibid.*, s. 26(1).
149. *Ibid.*, s. 26(2).
150. *Ibid.*, s. 26(1).
151. *Ibid.*, s. 26(1), (2).
152. *Ibid.*, s. 28(1), (4), (5).
153. *Ibid.*, s. 28(1).
154. See Countryside Act 1968, s. 30(1).
155. National Parks and Access to the Countryside Act 1949, s. 51(1).
156. *Ibid.*, s. 51(2)(b).
157. W. Brunsdon Yapp, *Long-Distance Routes*, Countryside Commission, 1975, p. 38.
158. The County of Cornwall (Pine Haven-Port Quinn) Public Path Creation Order 1984, discussed by Alec Samuels, "Public Path Creation Order", [1984] J.P.L. 90–1. Under section 105(1)(b) of the National Parks and Access to the Countryside Act 1949, the Minister had a default power where any authority failed to give effect to approved proposals relating to a long-distance route. This power was never used and was repealed by the Local Government Act 1974, sched. 8. See Yapp, pp. 36, 43.

159. Highways Act 1980, s. 137.
160. See below, p. 56.
161. *Cox* v. *Glue* (1848) 5 C.B. 533; 136 E.R. 987.
162. See *Lord* v. *Sydney Commissioners* (1859) 12 Moo. P.C. 473; 14 E.R. 991; *Harrison* v. *Duke of Rutland* [1893] 1 Q.B. 142, 155.
163. Highways Act 1980, s. 263(1). See *Coverdale* v. *Charlton* (1878) 4 Q.B.D. 104; *Wandsworth Board of Works* v. *United Telephone Co.* (1884) 13 Q.B.D. 904; *Mayor of Tunbridge Wells* v. *Baird* [1896] A.C. 434; *Foley's Charity Trustees* v. *Dudley Corporation* [1910] 1 K.B. 317; *Tithe Redemption Commission* v. *Runcorn U.D.C.* [1954] 1 Ch. 383.
164. See Raymond Chevallier, *Roman Roads,* Berkeley, University of California Press, 1976, pp. 65–6.
165. See C.T. Flower (ed.), *Public Works in Mediaeval Law,* S.S. 32, 1915, vol. 1, pp. 184–5; S.S. 40, 1923, vol. 2, pp. 45, 65, 79–80, 98, 102, 141, 230, 233, 321.
166. 24 Hen. 8, c. 5.
167. Co. Litt., 56a.
168. 1 *Pleas of the Crown,* ch. 76, preamble.
169. For the rather uncertain meaning of these terms in Roman law, see Buckland, p. 262; Thomas, *Textbook,* p. 196; Alan Watson, *The Law of Property in the Later Roman Republic,* Oxford, Clarendon Press, 1968, pp. 183, 187, n. 6; Alan Watson, *Rome of the XII Tables: Persons and Property,* Princeton, Princeton University Press, 1975, p. 161, n. 21.
170. Co. Litt., 56a.
171. Highways Act 1980, s. 329(1); *Suffolk C.C.* v. *Mason* [1979] A.C. 705, 710 *per* Lord Diplock; 727 *per* Lord Fraser of Tullybelton.
172. 1 Taunt. 279, 283; 127 E.R. 841, 842.
173. 27 Beav. 247; 54 E.R. 96.
174. 2 F. & F. 570; 175 E.R. 1191.
175. [1976] Q.B. 142, 155. For this issue in relation to private rights of way, see *Lock* v. *Abercester Ltd* [1939] Ch. 861, 864.
176. For judicial classifications of bicycles as "carriages" in other contexts, see *Taylor* v. *Goodwin* (1879) 4 Q.B.D. 228; *Ellis* v. *Nott-Bower* (1896) 60 J.P. 760; *Cannon* v. *Earl of Abingdon* [1900] 2 Q.B. 66; *Corkery* v. *Carpenter* [1950] 2 All E.R. 745. Compare *Williams* v. *Ellis* (1880) 5 Q.B.D. 175. The decision in *Taylor* v. *Goodwin* – that an offence of furious driving of "carriages" applied to bicycles – should be seen in its late nineteenth century context when bicycles were seen as a novel and dangerous form of traffic.
177. H.L. Deb., 5th series, vol. 292, cols 111–5, 13 May 1968; H.C. Deb., 5th series, vol. 762, cols 1120–34, 9 April 1968.
178. Highway Act 1835, s. 72; Local Government Act 1888, s. 85(1).
179. See *Brotherton* v. *Tittensor* (1896) 60 J.P. 49–50; *R.* v. *Pratt* (1867) L.R. 3 Q.B. 64. See also *Rodgers* v. *Ministry of Transport* (1952) 1 T.L.R. 625, 627 *per* Lord Goddard C.J.
180. Wheeling a bicycle on a roadside footpath is an offence if such wheeling is judged to be "driving" within the Highway Act 1835, s. 72 (as amended). In *R.* v. *MacDonagh* [1974] Q.B. 448, the Divisional Court disapproved of an artificial use of the word "drive". Yet it can be argued that since "the Highway Act 1835 creates an offence specifically designed to protect the rights of the pedestrian to free passage of the footway, the term, 'drive', in section 72 should be given a broader interpretation than in other traffic offences". See Richard Macrory,

"Cycle Lore", (1979) 129 New L.J. 602.
181. 1 Taunt. 279; 127 E.R. 841.
182. H.L. Deb., 5th series, vol. 292, cols 111–25, 13 May 1968; H.C. Deb., 5th series, vol. 762, cols 1120–34, 9 April 1968.
183. D.A.R.T., *Green Lanes*, p. 1.
184. See below, pp. 76–7.
185. National Parks and Access to the Countryside Act 1949, s. 27(6).
186. Countryside Act 1968, s. 31, sched. 3; Wildlife and Countryside Act 1981, s. 54(3).
187. Road Traffic Regulation Act 1984, s. 2.
188. *Ibid.*, s. 1(1)(d).
189. *Ibid.*, s. 1(1)(e).
190. *Ibid.*, s. 22(2).
191. Town and Country Planning Act 1971, s. 212.
192. *Original Hartlepool Collieries Co.* v. *Gibb* (1877) 5 Ch. D. 713.
193. *Wills' Trustees* v. *Cairngorm Canoeing and Sailing School Ltd* 1976 S.L.T. 162, 191.
194. Telling & Foster, vol. 1, p. 55 (para. 10.02).
195. *Wills' Trustees* v. *Cairngorm Canoeing and Sailing School Ltd* 1976 S.L.T. 162, 191 *per* Lord Wilberforce.
196. Countryside Act 1968. s. 22(6).
197. Water Resources Act 1963, s. 79(3), (4).
198. Anglian Water Authority Act 1977, ss. 7, 10, 18(1)(c)(ii).
199. (1790) 1 H. Bl. 351; 126 E.R. 206.
200. (1855) 4 El. & Bl. 860, 868; 119 E.R. 319.
201. [1976] Q.B. 142, 175. See also *Allen* v. *Flood* [1898] A.C. 1, 20 *per* Hawkins J.; *Lord Fitzhardinge* v. *Purcell* [1908] 2 Ch. 130, 167–8 *per* Parker J.; *Randall* v. *Tarrant* [1955] 1 All E.R. 600, 603 *per* Evershed M.R.
202. See *Barker* v. *R.* (1983) 57 A.L.J.R. 426, 441 *per* Dawson J.
203. 1976 S.L.T. 162.
204. [1893] 1 Q.B. 142.
205. *Harrison* v. *Duke of Rutland* [1893] 1 Q.B. 142, 147 *per* Lord Esher M.R.
206. *R.* v. *Pratt* (1855) 4 El. & Bl. 860, 868; 119 E.R. 319, 322 *per* Crompton J.; *Harrison* v. *Duke of Rutland* [1893] 1 Q.B. 142, 158 *per* Kay L.J.
207. [1900] 1 Q.B. 752.
208. See also *Mayhew* v. *Wardley* (1863) 8 L.T. 504.
209. There is conflicting authority as to this issue. In *Southport Corporation* v. *Esso Petroleum Co. Ltd* [1953] 3 W.L.R. 773, 776 and *Halsey* v. *Esso Petroleum Co. Ltd* [1961] 2 All E.R. 145, 158, Devlin J. and Veale J. respectively stated that private nuisance could be committed by someone on a highway. Notwithstanding the remarks of Veale J., this view was rejected in *Southport Corporation* v. *Esso Petroleum Co. Ltd* [1954] 2 Q.B. 182, 195 *per* Lord Denning M.R.; [1956] A.C. 218, 242 *per* Lord Radcliffe.
210. See Brian Neill, "The Protection of Privacy", (1962) 25 M.L.R. 393, 394–6.
211. See *Victoria Park Racing and Recreation Grounds Ltd* v. *Taylor* (1937) 58 C.L.R. 479, esp. at 494 *per* Latham C.J.
212. 1976 S.L.T. 162.
213. *Ibid.*, p. 203.
214. *Ibid.*, p. 191.

215. *Ibid.*
216. *Goodtitle dem. Chester* v. *Alker* (1754) 1 Burr. 133, 146; 97 E. R. 231, 238. See also *Lade* v. *Shepherd* (1735) 2 Strange 1004; 93 E.R. 997; *Dovaston* v. *Payne* (1795) 2 H. Bl. 526; 126 E.R. 684; *Vestry of St Mary, Newington* v. *Jacobs* (1871) L.R. 7 Q.B. 47; *Orr Ewing* v. *Colquhoun* (1877) 2 App. Cas. 839; *Ex parte Lewis* (1888) 21 Q.B.D. 191, 197 *per* Wills J.
217. [1893] 1 Q.B. 142, 146–7.
218. See especially Hazel Carty, "The Legality of Peaceful Picketing on the Highway", [1984] P.L. 600–17.
219. *Ibid.*, p. 605.
220. Compare Peter Wallington, "Injunctions and the 'Right to Demonstrate' ", [1976] Cambridge L.J. 82, esp. at p. 108.
221. See *Iveagh* v. *Martin* [1961] 1 Q.B. 232, 273 *per* Paull J.; *Pitcher* v. *Lockett* (1966) 64 L.G.R. 477, esp. 479; *Dymond* v. *Pearce* [1972] 1 Q.B. 496, 502 *per* Sachs L.J.; *Hubbard* v. *Pitt* [1976] Q.B. 142, 149–50 *per* Forbes J; *Waite* v. *Taylor* (1985) 149 J.P. 551.
222. (1987) 151 Local Government Review 130, 133.
223. *Hubbard* v. *Pitt* [1976] Q.B. 142, 150 *per* Forbes J.
224. [1900] 1 Q.B. 752, 757–8.
225. *Original Hartlepool Collieries Co.* v. *Gibb* (1877) 5 Ch. D. 713, 721 *per* Jessel M.R.; *Lowdens* v. *Keaveney* [1903] 2 I.R. 82; *Cooper* v. *Metropolitian Police Commissioner* (1985) 82 Cr. App. R. 238, esp. 242 *per* Tudor Evans J.; *Hirst* v. *Chief Constable of West Yorkshire* (1987) 151 Local Government Review 130–4.
226. See *Nagy* v. *Weston* [1965] 1 W.L.R. 280, 284 *per* Lord Parker C.J., especially as applied in *Hirst* v. *Chief Constable of West Yorkshire.*
227. [1939] 3 All E.R. 613.
228. See also in this respect, *Harrold* v. *Watney* [1898] 2 Q.B. 320, 322 *per* A.L. Smith L.J.; *Farrugia* v. *Great Western Railway Co.* [1947] 2 All E.R. 565, 566–7 *per* Lord Greene M.R.
229. [1939] 3 All E.R. 613, 620–1 *per* Croom-Johnson J. Under what is now Highways Act 1980, s. 161(3), it is an offence for a person to play football or any other game on a highway to the annoyance of a user of the highway. See *Woolley* v. *Corbishley* (1860) 24 J.P. 773; *Pappin* v. *Maynard* (1863) 9 L.T. 327.
230. [1965] 1 W.L.R. 280. See also *Scarfe* v. *Wood* (1969) 113 S.J. 143; *Nelmes* v. *Rhys Howells Transport Ltd* [1977] Crim. L.R. 227.
231. [1900] 1 Q.B. 752, 756. Compare *Harrison* v. *Duke of Rutland* [1893] 1 Q.B. 142, 156 *per* Kay L.J.
232. By analogy with *Rodgers* v. *Ministry of Transport* [1952] 1 T.L.R. 625.
233. See below, pp. 254–5.
234. See, for example, *R.* v. *Wright* (1832) 3 B. & Ad. 681, 683; 110 E.R. 248, 249 *per* Lord Tenterden C.J.; *Elwood* v. *Bullock* (1844) 6 Q.B. 383, 409; 115 E.R. 147, 156 *per* Lord Denman C.J.; *R.* v. *United Kingdom Electric Telegraph Co.* (1862) 3 F. & F. 73; 176 E.R. 33; *Harvey* v. *Truro R.D.C.* [1903] 2 Ch. 638, 643 *per* Joyce J.
235. *Williams* v. *Wilcox* (1838) 8 Ad. & El. 314, 329–30; 112 E.R. 857, 862 *per* Lord Denman C.J. It is possible that Lord Denman was considering only tidal rivers but the rationale he gave for his views applies equally to non-tidal rivers.
236. See *Orr Ewing* v. *Colquhoun* (1877) 2 App. Cas. 839, 843 *per* Lord Hatherley.

237. *Trevett* v. *Lee* [1955] 1 W.L.R. 113, 117 *per* Lord Evershed M.R.; *Dymond* v. *Pearce* [1972] 1 Q.B. 496, 501 *per* Sachs L.J. See also *Jacobs* v. *London C.C.* [1950] A.C. 361, 375 *per* Lord Simonds.
238. Hale, *De Jure Maris*, p. 9; *Williams* v. *Wilcox* (1838) 8 Ad. & El. 314, 334; 112 E.R. 857, 864 *per* Lord Denman C.J.; *Attorney-General* v. *Earl of Lonsdale* (1868) L.R. 7 Eq. 377, 389 *per* Malins V.-C.
239. Highways Act 1980, s. 137.
240. *Ibid.,* ss. 138, 139(1), 141(1), 148.
241. For a discussion of the legislation authorizing such bodies as statutory undertakers and local authorities to interfere with public rights of way as part of carrying out public works, see Pratt and Mackenzie, chapter 8; Halsbury, vol. 21, paras 479–700.
242. *Griesly's Case* (1669) 1 Vent. 4; 86 E.R. 4; Wellbeloved, p. 443.
243. (1869) L.R. 5 Q.B. 26. Affirmed in *Arnold* v. *Blaker* (1871) L.R. 6 Q.B. 433.
244. Highway Act 1835, s. 72.
245. See *Brackenborough* v. *Thoresby* (1869) 33 J.P. 84 *per* Mellor J.; *Dennis and Son Ltd* v. *Good* (1918) 88 L.J.K.B. 338; *Owen* v. *Buckinghamshire C.C.* (1957) 121 J.P. 556, 557 *per* Goddard C.J.
246. Hobhouse, para. 100.
247. National Parks and Access to the Countryside Act 1949, s. 56.
248. Hobhouse, para. 80.
249. Countryside Commission, *Ploughing Footpaths and Bridleways*, 1985.
250. Highways Act 1980, s. 134(2).
251. *Ibid.,* s. 134(1).
252. Wildlife and Countryside Act 1981, s. 61(5), creating new Highways Act 1980, s. 134(5A).
253. *Mercer* v. *Woodgate* (1869) L.R. 5 Q.B. 26; *Harrison* v. *Danby* (1870) 34 J.P. 759.
254. Highways Act 1980, ss. 134, 135; Wildlife and Countryside Act 1981, s. 61.
255. Highways Act 1980, s. 134(1).
256. *Ibid.,* s. 134(3).
257. Wildlife and Countryside Act 1981, s. 61(2). See H. L. Deb., 5th series, vol. 418, col. 629, 16 March 1981, Earl of Avon and Lord Melchett.
258. Highways Act 1980, s. 134(5).
259. *Ibid.,* s. 134(4).
260. See Pratt and Mackenzie, p. 675; Clayden & Trevelyan, p. 103. For the standard at which highways should be maintained, see below, pp. 84–5.
261. (1967) 203 E.G. 133.
262. *Ibid.*
263. H.L. Deb., 5th series, vol. 418, col. 629, 16 March 1981, Lord Melchett; H.C. Deb., 6th series, vol. 4, col. 573, 27 April 1981, Mr Michael Spicer, stating the view of the National Rights of Way Committee.
264. National Parks and Access to the Countryside Act 1949, s. 56(3).
265. Highways Act 1980, s. 134 (4).
266. *Ibid.,* s. 135.
267. The Highway Act 1864, s. 25 made it an offence for the keeper of horses, cattle, sheep, goats or swine to allow these animals to stray or lie on or at the side of a highway. However, this offence – now found in the Highways Act 1980, s. 155(1) – "does not apply in relation to a part of a highway passing over any common, waste or unenclosed ground".

Therefore, it presumably does not apply to a footpath running through a field which for the purposes of the section would be "unenclosed ground". See *Bothamley* v. *Danby* (1871) 24 L.T. 656.

268. Hobhouse, para. 83.
269. Gosling, para. 58. See also, Advisory Council for Agriculture and Horticulture in England and Wales, *Report on Bulls and Public Foot-paths,* March 1975, paras 44–5.
270. Hobhouse, para. 83; Gosling, para. 60, which would have restricted the prohibition to bulls aged over 12 months; Advisory Council for Agriculture and Horticulture in England and Wales, paras 61–9, 73–5, which would have restricted the prohibition to the lowlands.
271. H.L. Deb., 5th series, vol. 417, col. 836, 19 February 1981, Earl of Avon. See H.L. Deb., 5th series, vol. 164, cols 928, 962 in relation to the National Parks and Access to the Countryside Bill 1949; Countryside Bill 1968, cl. 23; Bulls and Public Paths Bill 1973, cl. 1; Countryside Bill 1978, cl. 111 and, as revised by Standing Committee B, clauses 7 and 8.
272. Ministry of Town and Country Planning, Circular no. 91, 30 June 1950.
273. H.C. Deb., 5th series, vol. 854, col. 1193, 10 April 1973, David Clark.
274. H.L. Deb., 5th series, vol. 415, col. 988, 16 December 1980, Lord Bellwin.
275. H.L. Deb., 5th series, vol. 415, col. 1094, 16 December 1980, Earl of Avon. Compare the Government's endorsement of regional bans on Sunday wildfowling, below p. 226.
276. Wildlife and Countryside Act 1981, s. 59.
277. Countryside Commission, *Rights of Way Legislation: 1st Monitoring Report,* 1985, pp. 33–4.
278. Charles D. Drake & Frank B. Wright, *Law of Health and Safety at Work: the New Approach,* London, Sweet & Maxwell, 1983, p. 85.
279. *Safety and Health at Work, Report of the Committee 1970–72, Chairman Lord Robens,* Cmnd. 5034, 1972, chapter 10.
280. See Alison Broadhurst, *The Health and Safety at Work Act in Practice,* London, Heyden, 1979, p. 15.
281. *Carmichael* v. *Rosehall Engineering Works Ltd* 1984 S.L.T. 40. See also *Aitchison* v. *Howard Doris Ltd* 1979 S.L.T. (Notes) 22; *R.* v. *Mara* [1987] 1 All E.R. 478.
282. Health and Safety at Work Act 1974, s. 33.
283. *Edwards* v. *National Coal Board* [1949] 1 K.B. 704, 712 *per* Asquith L.J.
284. Health and Safety at Work Act 1974, s. 40.
285. *Edwards* v. *National Coal Board* [1949] 1 K.B. 704, 712 *per* Asquith L.J. See also *Marshall* v. *Gotham* [1954] A.C. 360.
286. Williams, *Liability,* p. 273.
287. [1947] A.C. 341.
288. Animals Act 1971, s. 1(1)(a).
289. *Ibid.,* s. 6(2)(a).
290. See, however, *Wallace* v. *Newton* [1982] 1 W.L.R. 375 in which the plaintiff recovered for injuries caused by a horse which was unpredictable and unreliable in behavior.
291. Animals Act 1971, s. 9(1).
292. North, p. 152.
293. The only reported negligence action concerning injury by a domesticated animal to a member of the public on a right of way is *Fitzgerald* v.

E.D. and A.D. Cooke Bourne (Farms) Ltd [1964] 1 Q.B. 249. In this decision, the Court of Appeal took the view that members of the public must assume the risk of sustaining injury from such animals. Even at the time of the *Fitzgerald* case, this decision was strongly criticized. See A. L. Goodhart, "Owner's Liability for Injury caused by Animals", (1964) 80 L.Q.R. 34–40. Since the passing of the 1971 Act, it is unlikely that a court would adopt the same approach.

294. Highways Act 1980, s. 130(1), discussed in *R.* v. *Lancashire C.C., Ex parte Guyer* [1980] 1 W.L.R. 1024.

295. Highways Act 1980, s. 130(3).

296. *Ibid.*, s. 134(6). Highway authorities are also under a duty to remove obstructions attributable to natural causes which occur without warning and need to be quickly removed. See what is now Highways Act 1980, s. 150(1), as interpreted in *Worcestershire C.C.* v. *Newman* [1974] 1 W.L.R. 938, 945.

297. A council may directly abate a nuisance. See *Bagshaw* v. *Buxton Local Board of Health* (1875) 1 Ch. D. 220; *Reynolds* v. *Presteign D.C.* [1896] 1 Q.B. 604; *Louth D.C.* v. *West* (1896) 65 L.J.Q.B. 535; *Harris* v. *Northamptonshire C.C.* (1897) 13 T.L.R. 440. Alternatively, a council may invoke a variety of statutory procedures under which the authority gives notice to the wrongdoer that he should remove the obstruction; if he fails to do so, the authority can remove the obstruction itself and recover reasonable expenses incurred in doing so from the person concerned. See Highways Act 1980, ss. 143, 149, 154, 164.

298. Under Local Government Act 1972, s. 222, discussed by Stephen Tromans, "Crime Prevention the Civil Way", [1986] C.L.J. 374–7.

299. *Ball* v. *Herbert* (1798) 3 T.R. 253, 263; 100 E.R. 560, 565; *Williams* v. *Wilcox* (1838) 8 Ad. & El. 314, 330; 112 E.R. 857, 862 *per* Denman C.J.

300. *Henn's Case* (1633) W. Jones 296, 297; 82 E.R. 157; *Dawes* v. *Hawkins* (1860) 8 C.B. (N.S.) 848, 856; 141 E.R. 1399, 1403. See also *Lawson* v. *Weston* (1850) 1 Legge 666, 670 (N.S.W.).

301. See *Pollock's Law of Torts*, 15th ed., London, Stevens, 1951, p. 296; Glanville Williams, "The Defence of Necessity", (1953) 6 Current Legal Problems 216, 217.

302. Holdsworth, vol. 10, p. 307, relying in part on *Arnold* v. *Holbrook* (1873) L.R. 8 Q.B. 96, 100–1 *per* Blackburn J.

303. W. Jones 296; 82 E.R. 157.

304. See the authorities cited below in notes 306–12.

305. Holdsworth, vol. 10, p. 307.

306. See *Henn's Case* (1633) W. Jones 296; 82 E.R. 157; *Absor* v. *French* (1678) 2 Show. K.B. 28; 89 E.R. 772.

307. *Absor* v. *French* (1678) 2 Show. K.B. 28; 89 E.R. 772; *Dawes* v. *Hawkins* (1860) 8 C.B. (N.S.) 848, 859; 141 E.R. 1399, 1404 *per* Byles J.; *R.* v. *Oldreve* (1868) 32 J.P. Jo. 271 *per* Willes J.; *Neill* v. *Byrne* (1878) 2 L.R. Ir. 287, 289; *Smith* v. *Wilson* [1903] 2 I.R. 45, 62–3.

308. *R.* v. *Oldreve* (1868) 32 J.P. Jo. 271 *per* Willes J.

309. *Arnold* v. *Holbrook* (1873) L.R. 8 Q.B. 96.

310. *R.* v. *Stoughton* (1670) 2 Wms. Saund. 160, 161 n.12; 85 E.R. 908, 909: *Young* v. ─────── (1698) 1 Ld. Raym. 725; 91 E.R. 1384; *Absor* v. *French* (1678) 2 Show. K.B. 28; 89 E.R. 772; *Ball* v. *Herbert* (1798) 3 T.R. 253, 263; 100 E.R. 560, 565; *Steel* v. *Prickett* (1819) 2 Stark. 463, 469; 171 E.R. 706, 708; *Eyre* v. *New Forest Highway Board* (1892) 56 J.P. 517, 518 *per* Wills J.; *The Calgarth* [1927] P. 93, 107.

311. *Taylor* v. *Whitehead* (1781) 2 Dougl. 745, 749; 99 E.R. 475, 477 *per* Lord Mansfield; *Bullard* v. *Harrison* (1815) 4 M. & S. 387, 392–3; 105 E.R. 877, 879 *per* Lord Ellenborough C.J. See also *Lawson* v. *Weston* (1850) 1 Legge 666, 670; *Walker* v. *Peel Shire Council* (1908) 8 S.R. N.S.W. 608, 610.

312. *Taylor* v. *Whitehead* (1781) 2 Dougl. 745, 749; 99 E.R. 475, 477 *per* Lord Mansfield. See also *Campbell* v. *Race* 54 Am. Dec. 728, 730 *per* Bigelow J. (1851).

313. *Baten's Case* (1610) 9 Co. Rep. 53b; 77 E.R. 810.

314. 3 Bl. Comm. 6.

315. *Wyatt* v. *Great Western Railway Co.* (1865) 6 B. & S. 709, 720; 122 E.R. 1356, 1360 *per* Blackburn J.

316. *James* v. *Hayward* (1630) Cro. Car. 184; 79 E.R. 761; *Lodie* v. *Arnold* (1697) 2 Salk. 458; 91 E.R. 396. See also Woolrych, *Ways*, p. 52.

317. See *Earl of Lonsdale* v. *Nelson* (1823) 2 B. & C. 302; 107 E.R. 396; *Lagan Navigation Co.* v. *Lambeg Bleaching, Dyeing and Finishing Co.* [1927] A.C. 226, esp. at 244–5 *per* Lord Atkinson. Compare *R.* v. *Chief Constable of Devon and Cornwall; ex parte Central Electricity Generating Board* [1982] Q.B. 458, esp. at 470 *per* Denning M.R.

318. *Dimes* v. *Petley* (1850) 15 Q.B. 276, 283; 117 E.R. 462, 465 *per* Lord Campbell C.J. See also *Alexander* v. *Sydney Corporation* (1861) 2 Legge 1451, 1452 *per* Wise J.

319. *Bateman* v. *Bluck* (1852) 18 Q.B. 870, 876; 118 E.R. 329, 331 *per* Lord Campbell C.J., doubted by R.A. Buckley, *The Law of Nuisance,* London, Butterworths, 1981, p. 146. In *Arnold* v. *Holbrook* (1873) L.R. 8 Q.B. 96, 100, Cockburn C.J. stated, "A private individual can abate a nuisance when necessary to exercise a right".

320. *Wyatt* v. *Great Western Railway Co.* (1865) 6 B. & S. 709, 720; 122 E.R. 1356, 1360 *per* Blackburn J. See also *Greenslade* v. *Halliday* (1830) 6 Bing. 379; 130 E.R. 1326; *Lagan Navigation Co.* v. *Lambeg Bleaching, Dyeing and Finishing Co.* [1927] A.C. 226, 245 *per* Lord Atkinson.

321. (1845) 7 Q.B. 339, 377; 115 E.R. 518, 532 *per* Lord Denman C.J.

322. (1850) 15 Q.B. 276, 283; 117 E.R. 462, 465 *per* Lord Campbell C.J., applied in *Arnold* v. *Holbrook* (1873) L.R. 8 Q.B. 96, 101 *per* Blackburn and Mellor JJ. See also *Bagshaw* v. *Buxton Local Board of Health* (1875) 1 Ch. D. 220, 224 *per* Jessel M.R.

323. See below, pp. 68–9.

324. [1901] 2 Ch. 518, 525.

325. (1845) 7 Q.B. 339, 377; 115 E.R. 518, 532 *per* Denman C.J.

326. See *Clerk and Lindsell on Torts,* 15th ed., London, Sweet & Maxwell, 1982, p. 308; John G. Fleming, *The Law of Torts,* 6th ed., Sydney, Law Book Co., 1983, p. 415; Halsbury, vol. 21, para. 436.

327. The test of damage different in kind is supported by G. H. L. Fridman, "The Definition of Particular Damage in Nuisance", (1951–3) 2 University of Western Australia L.R. 490–503; William L. Prosser, "Private Action for Public Nuisance", (1966) 52 Virginia L.R. 997–1027. The test of damage different only in degree is endorsed by Fleming, pp. 381–2.

328. Authorities in favour of recovery in this situation are *Vanderpant* v. *Mayfair Hotel* [1930] 1 Ch. 138, 154; *Walsh* v. *Ervin* [1952] V.L.R. 361. Compare *Hubert* v. *Groves* (1794) 1 Esp. 148; 170 E.R. 308; *Winterbottom* v. *Lord Derby* (1867) L.R. 2 Ex. 316.

329. For example, *Almeroth* v. *W.E. Chivers & Sons* [1948] 1 All E.R. 53.

330. For example, *Iveson* v. *Moore* (1699) 1 Ld. Raym. 486; 91 E.R. 1224; *Benjamin* v. *Storr* (1874) L.R. 9 C.P. 400.
331. For example, *Rose* v. *Miles* (1815) 4 M. & S. 101; 105 E.R. 773.
332. *Winterbottom* v. *Lord Derby* (1867) L.R. 2 Ex. 316, 322 *per* Kelly C.B.
333. Co. Litt., 56a.
334. Richard A. Epstein, "Nuisance Law: Corrective Justice and its Utilitarian Constraints", (1979) 8 Journal of Legal Studies 49, 100.
335. Under Local Government Act 1972, s. 222.
336. See *Hubert* v. *Groves* (1794) 1 Esp. 148; 179 E.R. 308.
337. Highways Act 1980, s. 137. In relation to a number of the more specific offences of obstructing highways, the right of private prosecution may be exercised only with the consent of the Attorney-General. See Highways Act 1980, s. 312, schedule 22.
338. See H.L. Deb., 5th series, vol. 418, col. 628, 16 March 1981.
339. Highways Act 1980, s. 134(6).
340. Countryside Review Committee, *Leisure and the Countryside: a Discussion Paper,* London, H.M.S.O., 1977, para. 111. See also K.W. Lidstone, Russel Hogg & Frank Sutcliffe, *Prosecutions by Private Individuals and Non-Police Agencies,* Royal Commission on Criminal Procedure, Research Study No. 10, London, H.M.S.O., 1980, p. 93, n. 1.
341. *Gouriet* v. *Union of Post Office Workers* [1978] A.C. 435, 477 *per* Lord Wilberforce. See also at p. 498 *per* Lord Diplock.
342. See *Royal Commission on Criminal Procedure: Report,* Cmnd. 8092, 1981, para. 7.48, drawing on the conclusion of Lidstone, Hogg & Sutcliffe in the research study referred to above in note 340.
343. Lidstone, Hogg & Sutcliffe, *op. cit.,* p. 111.
344. *Ibid.*
345. See S.M. Thio, *"Locus Standi* in relation to Mandamus", [1966] P.L. 133–47; Wade, pp. 585–6, 642–3; P.P. Craig, *Administrative Law,* London, Sweet & Maxwell, 1983, pp. 423–5.
346. S.I. 1977 No. 1955, Order 53, r. 3(5). See now, Supreme Court Act 1981, s. 31(3).
347. *R.* v. *Inland Revenue Commissioners, Ex parte National Federation of Self-Employed and Small Businesses Ltd* [1982] A.C. 617.
348. Peter Cane, "Standing, Legality and the Limits of Public Law", [1981] P.L. 322-39, esp. at p. 335.
349. See Wade, pp. 588–91; and, also, R.J.F. Gordon, *Judicial Review: Law and Procedure,* London, Sweet & Maxwell, 1985, ch. 4.
350. (1870) L.R. 4 H.L. 449, esp. at p. 499 *per* Lord Chelmsford, discussed in *R.* v. *Surrey C.C., Ex parte Send Parish Council* [1979] J.P.L. 613, 615–6 *per* Geoffrey Lane L.J. See also *Elwood* v. *Belfast Corporation* (1923) 57 Ir. L.T. 138.
351. See, however, *R.* v. *Metropolitan Police Commissioner, Ex parte Blackburn* [1968] 2 Q.B. 118, in which the *Southampton Port* case was mentioned in argument but ignored in the judgments of the Court of Appeal.
352. Highways Act 1980, s. 134(6).
353. See *R.* v. *Lancashire C.C., Ex parte Guyer* [1980] 1 W.L.R. 1024, 1034 *per* Stephenson L.J.
354. *Attorney-General* v. *Staffordshire C.C.* [1905] 1 Ch. 336, 343 *per* Joyce J.
355. See Telling & Foster, paras 7.02–03; Sheila E. Foster, "Inland

Waterways: Legal Aspects of Public Access and Enjoyment", [1985] J.P.L. 440, 459–60; A.E. Telling & Rosemary Smith, *The Public Right of Navigation*, London, Sports Council, 1985; *Time for Change? Managing the Public Right of Navigation*, London, Sports Council, 1985.

356. The basic requirements of such a survey were set out in the Footpaths Preservation Bill 1892.
357. National Parks and Access to the Countryside Act 1949, s. 27.
358. *Ibid.*, ss. 27–32.
359. See *Andover* v. *Mundy* [1955] J.P.L. 518.
360. National Parks and Access to the Countryside Act 1949, ss. 33, 34.
361. National Parks and Access to the Countryside Act 1949, s. 35.
362. "The 'Survey Provisions' ", *Journal of the Commons, Open Spaces and Footpaths Preservation Society*, vol. 12, no. 6, October 1966, p. 151.
363. Wildlife and Countryside Act 1981, s. 58.
364. D.A.R.T. *Green Lanes*, para. 2.19.
365. Clayden & Trevelyan, p. 29.
366. Department of the Environment, *Wildlife and Countryside Bill Consultation Paper No. 2. Review of Definitive Maps of Public Rights of Way: Revision of Procedures*, 1979, para. 4.
367. Wildlife and Countryside Act 1981, s. 53. See, further, J.J. Pearlman, "Definitive Map Amendment Orders under the Wildlife and Countryside Act 1981", [1986] J.P.L. 176–83.
368. Countryside Commission, *Rights of Way Legislation: 1st Monitoring Report*, 1985, p. 39.
369. Hobhouse, para. 21.
370. National Parks and Access to the Countryside Act 1949, s. 32(4).
371. [1979] A.C. 705, over-ruling *Attorney-General* v. *Honeywill* [1972] 1 W.L.R. 1506.
372. H.L. Deb., 5th series, vol. 417, col. 792, 19 February 1981, Lord Bellwin speaking of the Government's ambition that the definitive maps should represent absolute statements of the public's right over ways shown on the maps.
373. Wildlife and Countryside Bill 1980, cl. 42.
374. Department of Environment, *Wildlife and Countryside Bill Consultation Paper on the Revision of Procedures for (1) the Review of Definitive Maps of Public Rights of Way and (2) Public Path Orders*, para. 17.
375. Wildlife and Countryside Act 1981, s. 56(1).
376. *R.* v. *Secretary of State for the Environment, Ex parte Hood* [1975] Q.B. 891, 905 *per* Sir John Pennycuick.
377. National Parks and Access to the Countryside Act 1949, s. 33(2) (a)–(d).
378. See *Suffolk C.C.* v. *Mason* [1979] A.C. 705, 714 *per* Lord Diplock.
379. (1965) 63 L.G.R. 456.
380. National Parks and Access to the Countryside Act 1949, s. 43(1).
381. Countryside Act 1968, Third Schedule. See *R.* v. *Secretary of State for the Environment, Ex parte Hood* [1975] Q.B. 891, 898 *per* Lord Denning M.R.; *Suffolk C.C.* v. *Mason* [1978] 1 W.L.R. 716, 720 *per* Lord Denning M.R.; 723 *per* Geoffrey Lane L.J.
382. Wildlife and Countryside Act 1981, s. 53(3) (c)(ii), (iii).
383. H.L. Deb., 5th series, vol. 417, cols 633–4, 17 February 1981, Lord Bellwin; H.C. Deb., 6th series, vol. 9, col. 1299, 30 July 1981, Mr. Monro.

384. H.L. Deb., 5th series, vol. 417, col. 635, 17 February 1981; vol. 418, cols 561–2, 16 March 1981, Lord Melchett.
385. R. v. Secretary of State for the Environment, Ex parte Hood [1975] Q.B. 891, 899–900.
386. Wildlife and Countryside Act 1981, s. 53(3)(c)(iii).
387. Ministry of Town and Country Planning, Circular 91, 30 June 1950, para. 6.
388. R. v. Secretary of State for the Environment, Ex parte Hood [1975] Q.B. 891, 904 per Sir John Pennycuick.
389. National Parks and Access to the Countryside Act 1949, s. 27(6).
390. R.N. Hutchins, "Bridleways and Roads used as Public Paths", (1951) 115 J.P. 713–14; D.A.R.T., Green Lanes, para. 2.19.
391. Gosling, para. 58.
392. The 1968 Act did not, however, repeal section 27(2) of the 1949 Act which provided for the recording of rights of way as "roads used as public paths". Nor did the 1968 Act provide for the initial classification of public rights of way as "byways open to all traffic".
393. D.A.R.T., Green Lanes, para. 2.21.
394. R. v. Secretary of State for the Environment, Ex parte Hood [1975] Q.B. 891.
395. D.A.R.T., Green Lanes, para. 2.23.
396. Ibid. See also R. v. Secretary of State for the Environment, Ex parte Stewart (1979) 77 L.G.R. 431.
397. Department of the Environment, Wildlife and Countryside Bill Consultation Paper No. 2. Review of Definitive Maps of Public Rights of Way, 1979, para. 19.
398. Department of the Environment, Wildlife and Countryside Bill Consultation Paper on the Revision of Procedures for (1) the Review of Definitive Maps of Public Rights of Way and (2) Public Path Orders, paras 10–11.
399. Wildlife and Countryside Act 1981, s. 54(3)(a).
400. Ibid., s. 54(3)(b).
401. Ibid., s. 54(3)(c).
402. Ibid., s. 56(1)(d). See above, p. 76.
404. D.A.R.T., Rights of Way, para. 5.37.
404. National Parks and Access to the Countryside Act 1949, s. 38(2); amended by Countryside Act 1968, sched. 3; now Wildlife and Countryside Act 1981, s. 57(5).
405. Wildlife and Countryside Act 1981, s. 57(5).
406. Ordnance Survey Review Committee 1979. Ordnance Survey Evidence, vol. 1, p. 12; Clayden & Trevelyan, p. 64.
407. Department of the Environment, Circular no. 1/83, para. 69. See, also, Countryside Commission, Rights of Way Legislation: 1st Monitoring Report, 1985, p. 20.
408. Highway Act 1773, s. 26; re-enacted as Highway Act 1835, s. 24.
409. Hobhouse, para. 85.
410. Ibid., para. 86.
411. Gosling, paras 51–6.
412. This requirement also forms part of the duties of highway authorities under section 27(2) and (4) of the Countryside Act since these subsections refer back to section 27(1).
413. Highways Act 1980, s. 263(1).

414. Compare Countryside Act 1968, s. 27(3) which specifically requires not only consultation with but also the agreement of a parish council or chairman of a parish meeting before a signpost is not erected.
415. H.L. Deb., 5th series, vol. 292, col. 552, 20 May 1968, Lord Kennet.
416. Countryside Act 1968, s. 27(3).
417. The application of section 27 was extended to byways by the Wildlife and Countryside Act 1981, s. 65.
418. Countryside Act 1968, s. 27(2)(a).
419. Countryside Act 1968, s. 27(2)(b).
420. H.L. Deb., 5th series, vol. 417, col. 872, 19 February 1981, Earl of Avon.
421. Clayden & Trevelyan, p. 122.
422. D.A.R.T., *Rights of Way*, para. 3.19; H.L. Deb., 5th series, vol. 417, col. 872, 19 February 1981, Earl of Avon.
423. Department of the Environment, *Report of the National Parks Policies Review Committee*, London, H.M.S.O., 1974, para. 16.20.
424. Countryside Act 1968, s. 27(7). For a full discussion of the application of this provision to waymarking, see Countryside Commission, *Waymarking for Footpath and Bridleway*, London, H.M.S.O., 1974.
425. Clayden & Trevelyan, p. 121.
426. Webb, p. 2.
427. *Ibid.*, p. 5.
428. 2 & 3 P. & Mary, c. 8. For the administration of this system, see J.S. Gardner, "The Justices of the Peace and the Repair and Maintenance of Bridges and Highways in Denbighshire in the Seventeenth Century", (1985) Cambrian L.R. 52, 64–76.
429. See, for example, *R. v. St George, Hanover Square, Inhabitants* (1812) 3 Camp. 222; 170 E.R. 1361.
430. Webb, p. 2.
431. Highways Act 1959, s. 38(1).
432. See, for example, *Austin's Case* (1672) 1 Vent. 189; 86 E.R. 128; *R. v. Sheffield Inhabitants* (1787) 2 T.R. 106, 111; 100 E.R. 58, 61.
433. See *R. v. Hatfield Inhabitants* (1820) 4 B. & Ald. 75; 106 E.R. 866; *R. v. Skinner* (1805) 5 Esp. 219; 170 E.R. 791.
434. *Henn's Case* (1633) W. Jo. 296; 82 E.R. 157; *Duncomb's Case* (1634) Cro. Car. 366; 79 E.R. 919.
435. See *Hertfordshire C.C. v. Great Eastern Railway Co.* [1909] 2 K.B. 403.
436. See Hobhouse, para. 60; *Robinson v. Richmond (Surrey) B.C.* [1955] 1 Q.B. 401.
437. See *Cababé v. Walton-upon-Thames D.C.* [1913] 1 K.B. 481, 489 *per* Farwell L.J.
438. *Ibid.*, p. 494 *per* Hamilton L.J.
439. See Highway Act 1835, s. 119, discussed in Halsbury, vol. 21, para. 176, n. 11.
440. *Attorney-General v. Watford R.C.* [1912] 1 Ch. 417, 433 *per* Parker J. Compare *Cababé v. Walton-upon-Thames D.C.* [1913] 1 K.B. 481, 493 *per* Hamilton L.J.
441. Highways Act 1980, s. 47.
442. Hobhouse, paras 65, 66.
443. National Parks and Access to the Countryside Act 1949, s. 47(1), replaced by Highways Act 1959, s. 38(2), and now Highways Act 1980, s. 36(1).
444. Hobhouse, para. 68.

445. National Parks and Access to the Countryside Act 1949, s. 49.
446. Highways Act 1980, s. 36(2)(d).
447. See *Sharpness New Docks and Gloucester and Birmingham Navigation Co.* v. *Attorney-General* [1915] A.C. 654; *Attorney-General* v. *Great Northern Railway Co.* [1916] 2 A.C. 356; *Manchester Corporation* v. *Audenshaw U.C. and Denton U.C.* [1928] Ch. 763, 780.
448. Highways Act 1980, ss. 41, 45.
449. *Ibid.*, s. 329(1).
450. [1975] 1 W.L.R. 901, 905.
451. [1978] Q.B. 343, 356, 359–60.
452. *Worcester C.C.* v. *Newman* [1975] 1 W.L.R. 901, 911–13 *per* Lawton L.J.; *Haydon* v. *Kent C.C.* [1978] Q.B. 343, 361–2 *per* Goff L.J.; 364 *per* Shaw L.J.
453. [1975] 1 W.L.R. 901, 910 *per* Cairns L.J. See also at 912 *per* Lawton L.J.
454. *Ibid.*, p. 912.
455. [1978] Q.B. 343, 357.
456. [1975] 1 W.L.R. 901, 911.
457. [1978] Q.B. 343, 364 *per* Shaw L.J. See also at 361–2 *per* Goff L.J. This view was followed in *Bartlett* v. *Department of Transport* (1984) 83 L.G.R. 579, 590 by Boreham J. who, however, expressed a preference for the view of Denning M.R. that maintenance and repair are synonymous.
458. *Worcester C.C.* v. *Newman* [1975] 1 W.L.R. 901, 911 *per* Lawton L.J.; *Haydon* v. *Kent C.C.* [1978] Q.B. 343, 364 *per* Shaw L.J.
459. Highways Act 1980, s. 130(3), discussed above at p. 65.
460. See *R.* v. *Cluworth Inhabitants* (1704) 1 Salk. 359; 91 E.R. 313; 6 Mod. 163; 87 E.R. 920; Woolrych, p. 87; Webb, p. 58.
461. *R.* v. *Stretford Inhabitants* (1705) 2 Ld. Raym. 1169; 92 E.R. 273.
462. *R.* v. *High Halden Inhabitants* (1859) 1 F. & F. 677, 678; 175 E.R. 903, 904 *per* Blackburn J.
463. See Webb, esp. chapter 5.
464. (1847) 2 Cox C.C. 334, 335.
465. See *Halsbury's Laws of England*, 3rd ed., vol. 19, p. 139.
466. Highways Act 1959, s. 59(1).
467. *Report of the Committee on Consolidation of Highway Law*, Cmnd. 630, 1959, para. 35.
468. See *Attorney-General* v. *Colchester Corporation* [1955] 2 Q.B. 207, 216 *per* Lord Goddard C.J.
469. 12 Ad. & El. 427; 113 E.R. 873.
470. [1905] 1 Ch. 336, 342.
471. See *Gravesham B.C.* v. *British Railways Board* [1978] 1 Ch. 379, 404–5 *per* Slade J.
472. See *Kennard* v. *Cory Brothers* [1922] 2 Ch. 1.
473. See Wade, pp. 624, 643–4.
474. See below, pp. 88–9.
475. Re-enacting Highways Act 1959, s. 59(1), which was based on Highway Act 1835, ss. 94, 95.
476. Highways Act 1980, s. 56(1).
477. *Ibid.*, s. 56(2), (4).
478. *Ibid.*, s. 56(6).
479. *Ibid.*, s. 56(7).
480. See above, pp. 84–5.

481. *Worcester C.C.* v. *Newman* [1975] 1 W.L.R. 901, 911 *per* Cairns L.J.; 913 *per* Lawton L.J.
482. *Ibid.*
483. *Riggall* v. *Hereford C.C.* [1972] 1 W.L.R. 171, 175 *per* Lord Widgery C.J.
484. *Williams* v. *Wilcox* (1838) 8 Ad. & El. 314, 329; 112 E.R. 857, 862 *per* Denman C.J.; *Attorney-General* v. *Simpson* [1901] 2 Ch. 671, 687 *per* Farwell J. Compare *Repair of Bridges, Highways, etc.* (1609) 13 Co. Rep. 33; 77 E.R. 1442, 1446; 1 Hawkins *Pleas of the Crown*, ch. 75, s. 13.
485. *Lynn Corporation* v. *Turner* (1774) 1 Cowp. 86, 87; E.R. 980, 981; Lofft. 555; 98 E.R. 796 *per* Lord Mansfield. See also *Repair of Bridges, Highways, etc.* (1609) 13 Co. Rep. 33; 77 E.R. 1442, 1446; 1 Hawkins *Pleas of the Crown*, ch. 75, s. 13. Compare *Attorney-General* v. *Simpson* [1904] A.C. 476, 491 *per* Lord Macnaghten.
486. 23 Hen 8, c. 5; *R.* v. *Westham Inhabitants* (1714) 10 Mod. 159; 88 E.R. 674; *Lord Rothschild* v. *Grand Junction Canal Co.* (1904) 91 L.T. 386, 393.
487. *Report from the Joint Select Committee of the House of Lords and the House of Commons on Railway Companies Amalgamation*, 1872, p. xxii. See, for example, the Leeds and Thirsk Railway Act 1845, discussed in *Blundy, Clark and Co. Ltd* v. *London and North Eastern Railway Co.* [1931] 2 K.B. 334.
488. Transport Act 1947, s. 14.
489. See H.L. Deb., 5th series, vol. 242, cols 168–71.
490. Transport Act 1962, s. 61(1).
491. *Ibid.*, ss. 1(1), 31(5).
492. Transport Act 1962, s. 64; Transport Finances Act 1966, s. 2.
493. Transport Act 1968, s. 105(5).
494. *Ibid.*, ss. 104, 105.
495. *Ibid.*, s. 104(1)(a), sched. 12, part 1.
496. *Ibid.*, s. 105(1)(a).
497. *Ibid.*, s. 104(1)(b), sched. 12, part 2.
498. *Ibid.*, s. 105(1)(b).
499. (1804) 10 Ves. 192; 32 E.R. 818, followed in *Cooke* v. *Chilcott* (1876) 3 Ch. D. 694; not followed in *Ryan* v. *Mutual Tontine Westminster Chambers Association* [1893] 1 Ch. 116. See also *Blakemore* v. *Glamorganshire Canal Navigation* (1832) 1 My. & K. 154, 183–4; 39 E.R. 639, 651; *Allport* v. *Securities Corporation* (1895) 64 L.J. Ch. 491.
500. See *Jackson* v. *Normanby Brick Co.* [1899] 1 Ch. 438. Note, however, that in *Willow Wren Canal Carrying Co. Ltd* v. *British Transport Commission* [1956] 1 W.L.R. 213, 214 the plaintiffs still sought a prohibitory injunction to restrain the Commission "from failing to maintain a proper depth of water in the [Kennet and Avon] canal or permitting the canal to be and remain impassable".
501. (1841) 2 Q.B. 64; 114 E.R. 27.
502. (1841) 2 Q.B. 64, 70; 114 E.R. 27, 30.
503. Transport Act 1968, s. 106(1).
504. *Ibid.*, s. 106(2)–(7).
505. *R.* v. *Montague* (1825) 4 B. & C. 598; 107 E.R. 1183; *R.* v. *Hornsea* (1854) 23 L.J.M.C. 59; *R.* v. *Greenhow* (1876) 1 Q.B.D. 703.
506. See *The Case of the Isle of Ely* (1609) 10. Co. Rep. 141a, 142a–142b; 77

E.R. 1139, 1141; *R.* v. *Warde and Lyme* (1632) Cro. Car. 266; 79 E.R. 832; *Ex parte Vennor* (1754) 3 Atk. 766; 26 E.R. 1239; *Ex parte Armitage* (1756) Amb. 294; 27 E.R. 199; *R.* v. *Russell* (1827) 6 B. & C. 566; 108 E.R. 560; Wellbeloved, p. 374; R.A. Glen, "Recent Writs of Ad Quod Damnum", (1928) 66 L.J. 79.

507. This maxim appears to have been coined by Byles J. in *Dawes* v. *Hawkins* (1860) 8 C.B. (N.S.) 848, 857; 141 E.R. 1399, 1401. For later uses of this maxim, see *Gerring* v. *Barfield* (1864) 16 C.B. (N.S.) 597, 603; 143 E.R. 1261, 1263 *per* Byles J.; *R.* v. *Platts* (1880) 49 L.J.Q.B. 848, 850 *per* Cockburn C.J.; *Eyre* v. *New Forest Highway Board* (1892) 56 J.P. 517; *Attorney-General* v. *Simpson* [1904] A.C. 476, 510 *per* Lord Lindley; *Redbridge London B.C.* v. *Jacques* [1970] 1 W.L.R. 1604, 1606 *per* Lord Parker C.J.; *Hubbard* v. *Pitt* [1976] Q.B. 142, 155; *Suffolk C.C.* v. *Mason* [1979] A.C. 705, esp. at p. 727 *per* Lord Fraser of Tullybelton.

508. *Harvey* v. *Truro R.D.C.* [1903] 2 Ch. 638, 644 *per* Joyce J.

509. *Vooght* v. *Winch* (1819) 2 B. & Ald. 622; 106 E.R. 507; *Hubbard* v. *Pitt* [1976] Q.B. 142, 155 *per* Forbes J.

510. See *Dawes* v. *Hawkins* (1860) 8 C.B. (N.S.) 848, 857; 141 E.R. 1399, 1401; *Harvey* v. *Truro R.D.C.* [1903] 2 Ch. 638, 644.

511. See, however, *R.* v. *Montague* (1825) 4 B. & C. 598, 605; 107 E.R. 1183, 1185 *per* Littledale J.; *Freeman* v. *Tottenham and Hampstead Junction Railway Co.* (1865) 11 L.T. 702.

512. See *Williams* v. *Eyton* (1858) 2 H. & N. 771; 157 E.R. 318; affmd. (1859) 4 H. & N. 357; 157 E.R. 878; *Leigh U.C.* v. *King* [1901] 1 Q.B. 747; *Esher and Dittons U.C.* v. *Marks* (1902) 71 L.J.K.B. 309; *Representative Church Body* v. *Barry* [1918] 1 I.R. 402.

513. See *Cababé* v. *Walton-upon-Thames U.D.C.* [1914] A.C. 103, 114; *Stockwell* v. *Southgate Corporation* [1936] 2 All E.R. 1343.

514. See *Yarmouth Corporation* v. *Simmons* (1878) 10 Ch. D. 518, 527 *per* Fry J.; *Attorney-General* v. *Shonleigh Nominees* [1981] 1 W.L.R. 1723, 1729– 30 *per* Goulding J.; [1972] 1 W.L.R. 577, 583 *per* Megaw L.J.

515. Under 14 & 15 Hen. VIII, c. 6, s. 3 (1552) and 26 Hen. VIII, c. 7 (1534) respectively, justices in Kent and Sussex were empowered to divert highways in these counties.

516. 13 Geo. 3, c. 78, ss. 19–22, amended by 55 Geo. 3, c. 68 (1815), re-enacted with certain modifications by the Highway Act 1835, ss. 84–91.

517. See also General Inclosure Act 1845, s. 62, discussed in *Crush* v. *Turner* (1877) 3 Ex. D. 303, 312–13; *Reynolds* v. *Barnes* [1909] 2 Ch. 361, 370.

518. Various Acts also make provision for temporary prohibitions on use of highways. See, for example Mineral Working Act 1951, s. 32; Opencast Coal Act 1958, s. 15; Road Traffic Regulation Act 1984, s. 14.

519. See Clayden & Trevelyan, pp. 77–8.

520. Highways Act 1980, s. 116(6), sched. 12, part 1.

521. *Ibid.*, s. 116(7).

522. *Ibid.*, sched. 6, para. 1(1).

523. *Ibid.*, ss. 118(1), (2), 119(1), (6).

524. *Ibid.*, ss. 118(1), (2), 119(1), (6), sched. 6, para. 2 (2).

525. Defence Act 1842, s. 16.

526. Defence Act 1860, s. 40.

527. See Highways Act 1980, ss 118(1), (2), (6), 119(1), (6).

528. See Civil Aviation Act 1982, s. 48(1); Town and Country Planning Act 1971, s. 214.
529. Local Government, Planning and Land Act 1980, sched. 28, para. 11.
530. New Towns Act 1981, s. 23.
531. See also Defence Act 1842, s. 16; Defence Act 1860, s. 40.
532. Highways Act 1980, s. 119(1).
533. *Ibid.*, s. 121(2).
534. *Ibid.*, ss. 29, 121(3).
535. *Ibid.*, s. 116(2). Under s. 117, the authorities may, however, bring applications on behalf of other persons.
536. Highways Act 1980, s. 116(1)(b).
537. See *R*. v. *Shiles* (1841) 1 Q.B. 919; 113 E.R. 1383.
538. [1983] J.P.L. 607.
539. *Stockwell* v. *Southgate Corporation* [1936] 2 All E.R. 1343, 1347 *per* Porter J.
540. 13 Geo. 3, c. 78, s. 19.
541. See *R*. v. *Kent Justices* [1905] 1 K.B. 378, 386 *per* Mathew J.
542. *Wright* v. *Frant Overseers* (1863) 4 B. & S. 118; 122 E.R. 404; *R*. v. *Phillips* (1866) L.R. 1 Q.B. 648, rejecting the view of Lord Denman C.J. in *R*. v. *Shiles* (1841) 1 Q.B. 919, 930–1; 113 E.R. 1383, 1388.
543. Highways Act 1980, s. 116(8)(a).
544. Compare Highways Act 1980, s. 121(2).
545. As documented by Sidney & Beatrice Webb, *English Local Government from the Revolution to the Municipal Corporations Act: The Parish and the County,* London, Longmans, Green, 1906, pp. 599–602; Webb, pp. 202–3, 230–1, early forms of this power was extensively abused in the early nineteenth century. See also, Wellbeloved, p. vii.
546. Wellbeloved, pp. viii-ix.
547. See W. Brunsdon Yapp, *Long-Distance Routes,* Countryside Commission, 1975, pp. 29, 52.
548. Highways Act 1980, s. 116(1)(a).
549. *Ibid.*, s. 118(1).
550. *Ibid.*, s. 118(2).
551. [1980] J.P.L. 174, 175.
552. See *Walsh* v. *Oates* [1953] 1 Q.B. 578, 581.
553. *Compton* v. *Somerset C.C.* (1982), unreported, discussed in Clayden & Trevelyan, p. 86.
554. See *R*. v. *Secretary of State for the Environment, Ex parte Stewart* [1980] J.P.L. 174, 175 *per* Phillips J.
555. Highways Act 1980, s. 118(2).
556. [1980] J.P.L. 174.
557. *Ibid.*, p. 175.
558. Highways Act 1980, s. 118(6).
559. [1980] J.P.L. 174, 176–7, rejecting the view earlier taken by Phillips J. in *Wood* v. *Secretary of State for the Environment* [1977] J.P.L. 307.
560. *Ibid.*, p. 176.
561. *Ibid.*
562. See above, pp. 93–4.
563. See Desmond Heap, *An Outline of Planning Law,* 8th ed., London, Sweet & Maxwell, 1982, pp. 163–4.
564. Highways Act 1980, s. 119(1).
565. National Parks and Access to the Countryside Act 1949, s. 42(1)

re-enacted with minor modifications by Highways Act 1959, s. 111(1).
566. [1976] 1 W.L.R. 371.
567. Highways Act 1980, s. 121(2).
568. *Ibid.*, s. 119(2)(a).
569. *Ibid.*, s. 119(2)(b).
570. See *Ibid.*, s. 119(6).
571. *Ibid.*
572. See above, pp. 92–6.
573. Town and Country Planning Act 1971, s. 209(1).
574. *Ibid.*, ss. 210(1), 217.
575. See, however, D.O.E. Circular 1/83, para. 14, which encourages authorities to publicize such applications.
576. This problem may arise in accentuated form where, following the grant of planning permission, the developer commences work without first obtaining an order diverting or stopping up the way. See *Ashby* v. *Secretary of State for the Environment* [1980] 1 W.L.R. 673.
577. Town and Country Planning Act 1971, s. 214; Acquisition of Land Act 1981, s. 32.
578. Military Lands Act 1892, s. 13; Defence Act 1842, s. 16. See also Defence Act 1860, s. 40.
579. Civil Aviation Act 1982, s. 48(1).
580. Land Powers (Defence) Act 1958, s. 8(1)(b).
581. Town and Country Planning Act 1971, s. 211. See also the alternative powers under the Highways Act 1980, ss. 14, 18.
582. Water Act 1945, s. 23; Water Resources Act 1963, s. 67.
583. Local Government, Planning and Land Act 1980, sched. 28, para. 11.
584. New Towns Act 1981, s. 23.
585. *In re Bradford Navigation Co.* (1870) L.R. 5 Ch. App. 600, 602 *per* James L.J. See also *In re Wey and Arun Junction Canal Co.* (1867) L.R. 4 Eq. 197; *In re Woking U.D.C. (Basingstoke Canal) Act 1911* [1914] 1 Ch. 300.
586. Railway and Canal Traffic Act 1888, s. 45(1).
587. See *Report of the Committee of Inquiry into Inland Waterways,* Cmnd. 486, 1958, Appendix J.
588. Transport Act 1968, s. 112(7).
589. *Ibid.*, s. 112(1)(a).
590. *Ibid.*, s. 112(1)(b), (c).
591. Railway and Canal Traffic Act 1888, s. 45(1).
592. Transport Act 1968, s. 112(5), sched. 13, para. 5(2)(b).
593. See also *ibid.*, s. 115(2).
594. H.L. Deb., 5th series, vol. 296, col. 1052, 8 October 1968, Lord Hailsham.
595. See above pp. 68–9.

Chapter 2

THE RIGHT TO RAMBLE

On both land and water, members of the public have certain rights to ramble which allow them to wander at large and navigate at will rather than simply to pass and repass. In relation to land, these rights are primarily a product of legislation and cover only a small area. The courts have only recently accepted that at common law the public can acquire *jura spatiandi* or rights to wander at large over particular pieces of land. By way of contrast, it has long been firmly established at common law that there is a general public right to navigate over all tidal waters. Although its basis remains unclear, there appears to be a similar right to navigate at will over many non-tidal lakes and rivers.

I. COMMON LAW

(A) LAND

As a matter of principle, it should be possible for rights to ramble to be created at common law. By analogy with the law concerning the creation of public rights of way,[1] members of the public should be able to acquire a *jus spatiandi* by either dedication or prescription (if the public can prescribe). At minimum the law should recognize express dedication of *jura spatiandi*.[2] In addition, it should be possible for a *jus spatiandi* to be created by implied dedication, though such dedication could be more difficult to imply than a right of way because of the greater right involved.

While these principles may seem quite straightforward and have won some support in North America, they have gained very limited acceptance in England. Although made up only of dicta, the weight of English authority has traditionally been against members of the public being able to acquire *jura spati-*

andi. It is only in the recent case, *R.* v. *Doncaster Metropolitan Borough Council; ex parte Braim* (1986),[3] that the creation at common law of a public right to ramble has for the first time been upheld, and the circumstances in which this right will be recognized in future remain unclear.

In North America, the authority in favour of recognizing the creation of public *jura spatiandi* by both express and implied dedication has gradually extended from the cities to the countryside. From the mid-nineteenth century, courts in both the United States and Canada held that squares and parks, as well as roads, could be dedicated to the public.[4] In the Ontario case, *Carpenter* v. *Smith* (1951),[5] it was held that a lakefront area, used by fishermen, picknickers and so on, had been dedicated by the landowner to public use. In a series of cases beginning in the mid-1960s, courts in a number of American coastal states have affirmed that "the rules governing implied dedication apply with equal force . . . to land used by the public for purposes other than as a roadway."[6] In holding that the public can aquire a "recreational easement" over beaches by implied dedication,[7] they have applied a test no different from that used in relation to rights of way. The substance of the "easement" has varied from case to case but it typically has included the right to wander at large over the whole dry sand area, with associated rights of picknicking and camping.[8]

In England, until recently, only three cases directly supported the proposition that the public can acquire *jura spatiandi*. In *Maddock* v. *Wallasey Local Board* (1886)[9] – a case concerning the foreshore and the immediate upland area – Grove J. stated "this is a private place over which the public have aquired some right of user, just as is done in certain places on the coast where the tide comes up above the foreshore. By constant user the public acquire a right to go here and there, and ride or drive, it may be, or walk, for recreation". In *Sandgate U.D.C.* v. *Kent C.C.* (1898),[10] which concerned a sea wall used not only as a highway but also as a promenade, Lord Watson in the House of Lords rejected the contention that "no part of a high road could ever be used for purposes of recreation"; he went on to say that "The use of the esplanade for any *jus spatiandi* or purposes of amusement is in no way inconsistent with its being a part of the road."[11] In *Tyne Improvement Commissioners* v. *Imrie* (1899), which concerned public rights on a pier, Phillimore J. inclined to the view "that dedication to the public is not restricted to the commonest form of dedication, which is that of a road over the soil as a highway".[12] The judge was "prepared to assume that an owner may dedicate his land for use by the public for bathing and for fishing" but he emphasized that "if there can be in law such a dedication . . . for other purposes than that of a highway, it is rather difficult to prove, and would require very conclusive evidence".[13] In particular, he stated that if a *jus spatiandi* can exist in law, which he described as a matter of "very great difficulty", it "requires such a case to prove it as that it practically can never be proved."[14]

These cases have been supported indirectly by a series of decisions, beginning with *In re Hadden* (1931),[15] concerning the law of trusts. In these cases the courts have held that dedication of land for public recreation is a purpose "beneficial to the community" and hence may constitute the object of a valid charitable trust. In reaching this conclusion and upholding the trusts in question, the judges have focused on the range of permissible charitable objects for trusts rather than the land law rules concerning the ambit of dedication. However, the effect of the decisions is to affirm that public *jura spatiandi* may be created at common law.

Ranged against these authorities is a long series of decisions – falling broadly into three categories – in which English courts have either implicitly or expressly rejected the proposition that members of the public can acquire a *jus spatiandi*.

Firstly, in cases concerning alleged customary rights to recreation, it has been held that "there can be no customary right for all the Queen's subjects to be present and to go and remain upon the land".[16] That this should be so is, of course, inherent in the idea of a local customary right as something which can be exercised only by the inhabitants of the relevant district. Consequently, these decisions need not have any bearing on the creation of public rights. However, it seems clear that the courts would have commented if they had felt that the public could have successfully claimed these rights if the actions had been framed in terms other than custom.

Secondly, in cases concerning alleged public rights of way, it has been held that evidence that members of the public wandered at large in the relevant area is not evidence which goes to show dedication of rights of way.[17] That this should be so can again be regarded as simply resulting from the fact that rights of way are defined routes. Consequently these decisions also do not of themselves necessarily indicate anything about the acquisition by the public of *jura spatiandi*.[18] However, it is implicit in most of these cases that the public could not have claimed this right. In two cases the courts expressly stated that a public "right to stray" was unknown to law and could not be acquired by the public.[19]

Finally, in a miscellany of cases, concerned in part with private rather than public rights, the courts have dismissed the possibility that members of the public might be able to acquire a *jus spatiandi* over dry land at common law. In *Blundell* v. *Catterall* (1821), Abbott C.J. remarked that "no one ever thought that any right existed" in favour of "those persons who reside in the vicinity of wastes and commons, [and] walk or ride on horseback, in all directions, over them, for their health and recreation".[20] In *International Tea Stores Co.* v. *Hobbs* (1903)[21] and then in *Attorney-General* v. *Antrobus* (1905),[22] Farwell J. similarly stated that a *jus spatiandi* was not known to English law. In *Johnston* v. *O'Neill* (1911) Lord Dunedin remarked that "Proprietors often admit indiscriminate trespass on their property . . . [because] they know . . . a general right of trespass cannot be acquired".[23] In *Re Ellenborough Park* (1955), Lord Evershed M.R. stated that "no right can be granted (otherwise than by Statute) to the public at large to wander at will over an undefined open space, nor can the public acquire such a right by prescription."[24]

Notwithstanding this mass of dicta, the various decisions do not constitute convincing authority as to whether members of the public may acquire a *jus spatiandi*. Apart from in *Attorney-General* v. *Antrobus* and *Re Ellenborough Park*, the courts provided no rationale for why the public should be unable to acquire a *jus spatiandi*. In *Antrobus*[25] Farwell J. based his view on the proposition that the public as such cannot prescribe, but even if correct,[26] this does not exclude the possibility of dedication to the public of a *jus spatiandi*. In *Re Ellenborough Park* Lord Evershed M.R. interpreted Farwell J. as having held that, "a jus spatiandi cannot be acquired by public user as an easement", a conclusion Lord Evershed agreed with "if only for the reason that there can be no dominant tenement to which the easement could be said to be appurtenant."[27] Whether there should be a requirement that easements be appurtenant to a dominant tenement is in fact open to question.[28] However, if a dominant tenement is necessary, then, just as public rights of way are not classified as easements under traditional theory precisely because there is no dominant tenement,[29] so a public *jus spatiandi* (like a public right of way) would not be classified in this way. Consequently, the rules governing the creation of easements are irrelevant in this context.

Scottish cases – especially the decision of the House of Lords in *Dyce* v. *Hay* (1852)[30] – provide an alternative basis for holding that the public cannot acquire a *jus spatiandi*. In *Dyce* v. *Hay* Lord St Leonards decided the issues in accordance with Scots law but noted that English law was "more decidedly" against the proponent of the public right "even than that of Scotland".[31] His main reason for rejecting the public right was that it was "a claim so large as to be entirely inconsistent with the right of property; for no man can be considered to have a right of property, worth holding, in a soil over which the whole world has the privilege to walk and disport itself at pleasure".[32]

This argument is not, in itself, convincing since both Scots and English law allow similar "sterilization" of private property in relation to public rights of way and village greens over which there are customary rights of recreation.[33] However, the argument is more persuasive if recast partly as a matter of degree. Whereas public ways and village greens characteristically take up a relatively limited area – which in the case of village greens cannot be expanded by modern use – the area over which the public might claim a *jus spatiandi* on the basis of implied dedication or long use is potentially vast, and the public right once obtained could prevent changes in land use. This problem appears to have been recognized in the Court of Session in *Dyce* v. *Hay* by Lord Justice-Clerk Hope who noted that "Frequent resort for . . . simply walking over and through the ground, and resting on it, could have been averred . . . as to . . . many other similar grounds along the shore [of the River Don] in other quarters, before they were levelled, manured, and tilled".[34] The difficulty with this type of argument is that it reflects a bias in favour of "productive" rather than recreational land use, and it is unclear why the common law should adopt this approach, rather than giving landowners the freedom to grant the public a *jus spatiandi* over their land.

These arguments were to some extent considered in the recent case, *R* v. *Doncaster Metropolitan B.C.; ex parte Braim* (1986),[35] which concerned Doncaster Common, best known as the site of the racecourse where the St Leger is run. The case arose because of the intention of the Council, the owner of the site, to grant a lease giving exclusive possession of part of the land to the Town Moot Golf Club. The question was whether the Council had power to grant the lease without first advertising its intentions. Under the relevant legislation, the Open Spaces Act 1972, this issue depended partly on whether there was a public right of recreation over the common.

The evidence submitted to McCullough J. indicated that there had been public use of the common since at least 1860. Such use had been continuous, and at no time during this period was "there even a hint that such use was regarded, either by the Corporation or the users or by anyone else, as use by mere tolerance or permission of the Corporation".[36] McCullough J. consequently concluded that if a public right of recreation could exist over the common, "the only reasonable factual inference to draw is that from some date prior to 1860 and at all times thereafter the public has of right used Doncaster Common for what can conveniently be called recreation".[37]

In considering the relevant law, McCullough J. began from the premise, derived from *Tyne Improvement Commissioners* and *In re Hadden* and accepted by counsel for both parties, that "a person is capable in law of dedicating his land to the use of the public for recreation, for example, by the express creation of a trust or by act of dedication".[38] In further support of this proposition, the judge suggested that if a right to recreation could be a valid easement (or private right) as established in *In re Ellenborough Park*, it should also be valid as a public right. Finally, he acknowledged that, since "a right to enjoy recreation on a particular piece of land includes the right to wander over it at will",[39] his conclusion was inconsistent with Farwell J.'s rejection of public *jura spatiandi* in *International Tea Stores* and *Antrobus*. However, McCullough J. rejected Farwell J.'s remarks as dicta.

In considering whether a public right of recreation could be established by implication, McCullough J. was principally influenced by *Goodman* v. *Mayor of Saltash* (1882),[40] a dispute over an oyster fishery in a tidal river. Title to the fishery was clearly in the Saltash Corporation, but local inhabitants claimed that they had a right to take the oysters. To establish this right, the inhabitants had to overcome the rule that there cannot be a local right of taking. Because the inhabitants had enjoyed the fishing "from time immemorial, under claim of right", they succeeded. The majority of the House of Lords held that they should find a local right of fishing if at all possible, and achieved this by implying that the Corporation held the fishing rights on trust for the inhabitants.

Against this background, McCullough J. implied that a public right of recreation existed over Doncaster Common. The judge held that since the Doncaster Corporation was a local corporation, the case was analagous to *Goodman*, which in his view applied equally to trusts for local inhabitants and trusts for the public. If the charter under which the Corporation apparently held the land did not in fact exist, there was no obstacle to implying that a public right had been created (since, by definition, there would be no documents inconsistent with the right). However, if the charter existed and did not mention the public right, McCullough J. held that he could presume that at some later date "the Corporation created in favour of the public a trust by means of an instrument now lost granting the rights in question".[41]

The result of the decision in the *Doncaster* case is therefore that public rights of recreation, and hence also *jura spatiandi* over dry land, can be created both expressly and by implication at common law. Yet so far as implied rights are concerned, it may be that the decision does not extend much beyond its own facts of long unchallenged use and land held by a local authority which "had an interest in affording the amenity [of its land] to its residents and a further interest in encouraging others from outside the borough to attend the races."[42] This narrow reading of the decision is consistent with *Goodman* v. *Mayor of Saltash* where Lord Selbourne stated that, regardless of length of use, a trust could not be implied on behalf of local inhabitants if the land was not held by a corporation but was privately owned and the title deeds did not refer to the trust.[43] However, the distinction between land held by private individuals and local authorities appears illogical if cast in this absolute form.[44] Consequently, the better view appears to be that implied dedication should be possible regardless of the identity of the landowner, though such dedication will be implied more readily if the land is in public ownership since a local authority is more likely than a private person to have received land on trust for local inhabitants (or the public) or to have dedicated rights to them.

(B) NON-TIDAL WATERS

There are no reported cases which directly concern the right of members of the public to navigate at will over non-tidal waters. However, the existence of this type of right was affirmed in relation to the Thames by legislation which was intended "to preserve existing rights, not to create new ones, or destroy old ones".[45] Under what is now section 79 of the

Thames Conservancy Act 1932, it is lawful between Tedding-
ton, where the Thames ceases to be tidal, and Cricklade

> for all persons to go pass and repass in vessels over or upon any
> and every part of the Thames . . . including all backwaters creeks
> side-channels bays and inlets connected therewith as form part of
> the said river.[46]

The existence of a public right to navigate at will over the
whole or a substantial part of the surface of non-tidal lakes has
also been accepted by both counsel and judges in a series of
cases in relation to Ullswater,[47] Windermere[48] and part of the
Norfolk Broads[49] as well as two Irish lakes, Lough Erne[50] and
Lough Neagh.[51] Such rights were probably also implicitly recognized in collision rules made under the Merchant Shipping
Act 1894[52] and in the Countryside Act 1968.[53]

Notwithstanding this authority, the existence of these public
rights to navigate at will appeared quite open to challenge until
recently. The various cases concerning the public right did not
examine its origin and it was arguable that if the public could
not acquire *jura spatiandi* by dedication over dry land, they
could not do so in relation to non-tidal waters, since the public
rights in both contexts depend on the acts or acquiescence of
the relevant landowners. On this basis, the dicta in cases such
as *Antrobus* could have been used to argue that the public
cannot acquire a right to navigate at will over non-tidal lakes.

With the decision in the *Doncaster* case, this problem has
lessened since it is now clear that rights to wander at large can
be created over dry land at common law. Even if such rights
can be created by implied dedication only over publicly (rather
than privately) owned land, this rule arguably should not apply
to rights of navigation over non-tidal waters since different
policy considerations apply. Whereas the courts may refuse to
imply *jura spatiandi* over privately held land because the existence of this right is generally inconsistent with development of
the land, a right to navigate at will is relatively compatible with
other forms of exploitation of rivers and lakes. Hence the
"productive" argument – which appears to be the main justification for non-recognition of *jura spatiandi* over land – is largely
inapplicable to non-tidal waters.

(C)   TIDAL WATERS

Apart from where a riparian landowner has excavated his own
land so as, for example, to create a boathouse,[54] there is a

public right to navigate over all tidal waters which are in fact navigable. This right of navigation is unlike the public rights of access over dry land or non-tidal water in that it exists independently of any dedication by the landowner or long enjoyment by members of the public. Where the soil under such waters is held by the Crown, as is *prima facie* the case, this ownership is "for the benefit of the subject, and cannot be used in any manner so as to derogate from, or interfere with, the right of navigation, which belongs by law to the subjects of the realm."[55] Even if the Crown has made a grant of part of the bed of an estuary or tidal river, the grantee takes subject to, and cannot lawfully interfere with, the public right.[56]

The nature of the public right of navigation on tidal waters has frequently been mis-stated. By more or less equating this right with the public's rights on highways, judges have suggested that the public right may be limited to passing and repassing[57] for limited purposes – trade and fishing.[58] As stated, however, by Lord Widgery C.J. in *Evans* v. *Godber* (1974):

> over land a right of way . . . can only exist if it goes from one point to another following a defined course. By contrast, the right of navigation in tidal waters is a right to move at will throughout the area where the water is tidal . . . [There is] no obligation to follow a particular route or have a motive or reason to come in; . . . the common law right [of members of the public] to navigate is a right to go in tidal waters as and when they please.[59]

II. UNDER STATUTE

Since the second half of the nineteenth century, proponents of public rights in the countryside have sought legislation granting members of the public the right to wander at large over two, somewhat overlapping, types of land. More narrowly, they have sought a public right of access to all common land; more broadly, they have sought a public right of access to all "open country" or uncultivated land. Neither of these campaigns has, as yet, been successful. However, members of the public have been granted rights to ramble over certain common land as well as some "open country".

(A)   COMMON LAND

In spite of its name, "common land" is not land which in some way is publicly owned. Rather it is land owned by some individual or other legal entity in which both the owner of the soil and a limited number of others – known as "commoners" –

have certain rights, in common, to take the natural produce of the soil. At common law, even commoners have a right to go on to common land only for purposes connected with their right of common;[60] members of the public, regardless of whether they are inhabitants of the parish or manor in which a common lies, have no general rights of access to common land.[61]

Until the mid-nineteenth century, Parliament's primary interest in common land was in its "inclosure" which in the present context denotes the extinguishment of all rights of common over a given area of land rather than, necessarily, the building of fences.[62] At common law there were a number of ways in which rights of common could be extinguished of which the most important were probably agreement (or collective release) and "approvement" which allowed a lord of the manor to extinguish rights of common over manorial waste if a sufficiency of common would remain for the commoners.[63] This process of approvement was given statutory form by the Commons Act 1236[64] and along with agreement was used extensively in medieval and Tudor England in order to extinguish rights of common.[65] However, approvement did not extend to the consolidation of the strips of open fields and meadows; agreement to such consolidation was not always forthcoming. Hence lords of the manor turned to Parliament for authorization of inclosure. The first local inclosure Act was passed in 1545 in relation to Hounslow Heath; a small number of such Acts were passed in the seventeenth century and the first half of the eighteenth century, but the great majority were enacted between 1760 and 1845 when Parliament finally obviated the need for obtaining private inclosure Acts by enacting a General Inclosure Act which provided that inclosure could be authorized by independent commissioners.[66]

Around the time that Parliament facilitated the inclosure of common land by enacting the General Inclosure Act, the importance of commons as public open spaces began to gain widespread recognition. Parliament consequently restricted the situations in which inclosure could lawfully take place. The Metropolitan Commons Act 1866 provided that the Commons Commissioners should not entertain applications for the inclosure of any common situated in whole or in part in the Metropolitan Police District.[67] The Commons Act 1876 provided that the Commissioners could authorize the inclosure of other commons only if such inclosure was both for the benefit of the neighbourhood and for the benefit of private interests.[68]

In a series of cases, initiated with the assistance of the Commons Preservation Society which had been founded in 1865,[69] certain areas of common land were preserved as *de facto* public recreation grounds by invoking the rights of individual commoners (rather than any public rights in the land).[70]

To a limited extent Parliament has also moved to legalize public access to common land. Under a series of Acts passed between 1878 and 1925, members of the public have been given rights to ramble over what is estimated as being about one-fifth of the remaining 1.5 million acres of common land.[71] Quite recently, after more than eight years of discussion,[72] Parliament enacted the Dartmoor Commons Act 1985 which gives members of the public "a right of access . . . on foot and on horseback for the purpose of open-air recreation" to the 100,000 acres of common land on Dartmoor.[73] Successive Governments have, however, ignored the recommendations of the 1958 Royal Commission on Common Land that "all common land should be open to the public as of right"[74] and that new organizations be established to manage common land. Parliament has acted on the 1958 report only in enacting the Commons Registration Act 1965 which, as its title suggests, simply established a scheme for the registration of common land. This Act was intended as, and will still probably form, the basis of "second-stage" legislation extending public access. But this legislation has repeatedly been delayed because the registration process has been very slow (as a result of Government appointing too few Commissioners to decide disputed registrations) and because commons legislation has in any event been a very low priority for Government.

There is, however, renewed prospect of second-stage legislation as a result of the 1986 report of the Common Land Forum, which was made up of representatives of 20 interested bodies, including the National Farmers' Union and the Country Landowners' Association. In its report, the Forum followed the Royal Commission of 1958 in endorsing a right of access to all common land "by persons on foot for the purpose of quiet enjoyment".[75] Where informal horse-riding already takes place on common land, it should be allowed to continue, while elsewhere it should be at the discretion of the associations established to manage the commons.[76] Rather than acting immediately on these proposals, the Government in January 1987 chose to issue a consultation paper. However in doing so, William Waldegrave, the Minister of State for the Environment announced: "The Government accepts the case for future legislation based broadly on the Common Land Forum report and intends to introduce legislation at a suitable opportunity when parliamentary time permits."[77]

(1) "Urban" commons

By far the most important right of access to common land was conferred by section 101 of fhe Law of Property Act 1922 which, in slightly amended form, was re-enacted as section 193 of the Law of Property Act 1925. The creation of this right of access appears superficially to have been unconnected with the primary object of the 1922 Act, which was to simplify the conveyancing of land. In fact, the two measures were linked since the need for a provision giving the public a right of access to common land was a direct result of the Act's "enfranchisement" or conversion of copyhold land into freehold. That enfranchisement was in turn intended to facilitate the conveyancing of land since copyhold land could not be conveyed by a single deed but only by a surrender and admittance in the relevant manor court.

Within this complicated context, copyhold land was connected to public rights of access to common land because copyholds had, prior to 1922, been the tenements to which rights of common were most frequently attached. As with earlier Copyhold Acts, the existing rights of common were preserved under the law of property legislation for the benefit of the enfranchised land.[78] Enfranchisement meant, however, that the manor rolls, which provided one of the main records of rights of common, would not be kept up to date. Hence, as noted by a Joint Select Committee, when examining the Law of Property Bill in 1920, it would become more difficult to ascertain the rights of commoners while inclosure would become easier.[79] Provision of a public right of access would not in itself preserve common land but the Committee agreed to a clause giving "members of the public . . . rights of user (not being *profits à prendre*) and access in respect of the surface of all commons and commonable land, *not inclosed at the commencement of this Act*".[80] These last words would have made the public right of access independent of any loss of rights of common. As stated by the Committee, the clause was intended "to secure that commons, particularly those near large towns, shall not be inclosed to the prejudice of the public".[81]

On a variety of grounds there was considerable controversy over the clause agreed to by the Joint Select Committee granting a public right of access over common land. The Land

Union initially rejected this proposal out of hand, and suggested that public rights of access to common land should instead be granted only by ministerial order made on application of the relevant owner of the soil in relation to those commons where members of the public had traditionally been permitted entry.[82] Other critics of the provision feared that because of imprecision in its drafting, the public's right of access might be "abused by gypsies or undesirables".[83] Ultimately Parliament agreed to a compromise clause – section 101 of the 1922 Act – which defined and restricted the nature of the public's right of access, limited this right to "urban" commons, and stipulated that certain forms of conduct by members of the public on "urban" commons should constitute summary offences.

As provided by what is now section 193(1) of the Law of Property Act 1925, members of the public have a right of access "for air and exercise" to the specified common land. This right of access clearly allows members of the public to roam unimpeded over the land on foot.[84] However, it does not include any right to draw or drive vehicles or to camp or light fires on the land, and a member of the public who without lawful authority engages in these activities commits a summary offence.[85] The main uncertainty over the public right concerns whether it extends to horseriding. Arguably horseriding falls within the right since "air and exercise" appears to cover all informal recreation. This view is supported by the fact that horseriding is not expressly excluded from the right, unlike for example camping. However, in *Mienes* v. *Stones* (1985)[86] Farquharson J. suggested that the right was limited to pedestrians since "If the right . . . had incorporated the use of a horse . . ., then it would have said so expressly."

Regardless of the extent of the right of "air and exercise", it is "subject to any Act, scheme, or provisional order for the regulation of the land, and to any byelaw, regulation or order made thereunder or under any other statutory authority".[87] Moreover, on application of the lord of the manor, the Secretary of State may make an order imposing "such limitations on and conditions as to the extent of the land to be affected" as the Secretary thinks necessary or desirable to protect the land.[88] The result is that the public right may be significantly restricted so long as the restriction is not discriminatory. Thus in *Conservators of Mitcham Common* v. *Cox* (1911)[89] – a case under the Metropolitan Commons Act 1866 but applicable to the 1925 Act – a byelaw was held invalid which provided that no person should use a golf course on Mitcham Common

unless he or she were a member of the golf club or an inhab-
itant of Mitcham holding a permit from the conservators. By
way of contrast, in *Mienes* v. *Stones* the court held that, even
assuming horseriding came within the public right, a local
authority could make a byelaw prohibiting horseriding on a
common unless a permit was obtained. It was open to any
member of the public to obtain a permit. Consequently, as
noted by Farquharson J. the permit system was "not a method
of extending privileges to a selected or restricted class of individuals; it is a system which has been operated simply to
control the common and to prevent excessive use thereof when
it was dangerous or detrimental to the common for riding to
take place."[90]

Under section 193(1), the rights of access of members of the
public are confined to

> any land which is a metropolitan common within the meaning of
> the Metropolitan Commons Act, 1866 to 1898, or manorial waste,
> or a common which is wholly or partly situated within a . . .
> borough or urban district. . .

What land actually falls within this formulation is, however,
far from clear. The Act did not define "common land" and
hence it is, for example, uncertain whether the provision
covers so-called "commonable land" over which rights of common are exercised only at particular times of year.[91] Furthermore, the Act also did not require the land over which the
right was exercisable to be mapped or demarcated.[92] This
failure probably has not been remedied by the Commons Registration Act 1965, because the definition of "common land" in
the 1965 Act is unlikely to correspond with that which would
be accepted by the courts in relation to the 1925 Act.[93] Hence
even if appropriately situated land is registered under the 1965
Act, there may be no public right of access over it.

These problems have been exacerbated by the misleading
impression created by the term "urban" common and the
reorganization of local government under the Local Government Act 1972. As noted by the Royal Commission on Common Land in 1958:

> Not all [urban commons] are compact spaces lying like Mid-
> summer Common in Cambridge in the heart of a built-up area.
> Ignoring the important but perhaps somewhat exceptional twenty-
> five square miles of common which are technically urban because
> they are situated within the Lakes Urban District, there are other
> predominantly rural commons which nevertheless come into the

same urban category merely because they overlap into a borough or urban district.[94]

With some prescience, the Commission also adverted to the confusion which would ensue if "any thorough-going reorganisation of local government" took place.[95] Under the Local Government Act 1972, all borough and urban districts were in fact abolished from 1 April 1974 when England and Wales were divided into new areas known as metropolitan and non-metropolitan counties. Rather, however, than redefining the commons to which the public right of access applied, the 1972 Act provided that section 193 should continue to benefit the identical geographical area as formerly.[96] That decision was, in itself, understandable because the reorganization of local government was not an appropriate occasion on which to reconsider the law relating to public access over common land.[97] However, the subsequent failure to re-examine the extent of the public's rights means that the public right of access is now defined in terms of administrative areas which are no longer generally recognized.

The final difficulty with section 193(1) concerns land which has ceased to be subject to rights of common at some date after 1 January 1926 when the Law of Property Act 1925 came into force. Where rights of common are extinguished "under any statutory provision", section 193(1)(d)(i) provides that members of the public automatically lose their right of access to the land in question. Consequently, where "urban" commons or the rights over them are unregistered under and hence extinguished by the Commons Registration Act,[98] the public right appears to be destroyed.[99] But where rights of common are otherwise extinguished – as by the lord of the manor purchasing the commoners' interests – the public right of access ceases only "if the council of the county or metropolitan district [or prior to April 1974 also the county borough] in which the land is situated by resolution assent to its exclusion from the operation of this section, and the resolution is approved by the Minister".[100] In the absence of such a resolution and ministerial approval – which frequently do not appear to have been sought – the public right of access continues even if, for example, the land is enclosed and then cultivated.

(2) Rural Commons

(a) Deeds granting access to rural commons
As part of the compromise by which section 193(1) of the Law

of Property Act 1925 was confined to "urban" commons, provision was made in section 193(2) that owners of the freehold of commons outside urban districts could by deed bring their land within the operation of section 193(1). The promoters of section 193(2) hoped that landowners would be prompted to execute such deeds by the prospect of being better able to control public misbehaviour on the land.[101] Instead of the landowner having to implement civil proceedings, abuses on land subject to a deed can be dealt with immediately by the police since on such land it is an offence to draw or drive vehicles or to camp or light fires whilst other activities may be controlled by a Ministerial order of limitations. At least partly because of the availability of these controls on the public, a small number of landowners between 1926 and 1939 granted deeds under section 193(2). However, since then, this provision has scarcely been utilized,[102] and only 120,000 acres of common land are now covered by deeds. Of this total 68,000 acres comprise common land owned by the Crown Estate Commissioners (primarily in Wales).[103]

So far as members of the public are concerned, the only difference between commons in urban districts and rural commons covered by deeds is that where the deeds are revocable – which is generally the case[104] – the landowner may put an end to public access. Examples of such revocation have been rare and were confined to private landowners until January 1983 when the Newbury District Council revoked a deed it had made in relation to Greenham Common.[105] The ostensible basis of the Council's action was to enable it to bring Greenham Common into line with other commons under the Council's control, all of which are managed under byelaws made under the Commons Act 1899. In fact, the decision appears to have been an unnecessary part of the Council's effort to remove the women's peace camp from the common. By revoking the deed, the Council made anyone who went on the common a trespasser and the Council subsequently obtained an injunction against certain women trespassing there. While the deed was in force, however, the women were already trespassing (as well as committing a summary offence) because they were camping, which is outside the public right of access for "air and exercise".[106] The Council could therefore have sought an injunction against the peace campers without depriving the public of its right of access over the common.

(b) Local Acts creating access to rural commons

Since the Epping Forest Act 1878 gave the public a right to use Epping Forest as an open space for recreation and enjoyment,[107] a succession of local Acts has given members of the public rights of access over common land. These Acts have been quite diverse both as to their general objects and as to their formulation of the public right. The existing legislation falls, however, into three main categories:

(i) COMMONS INCLOSED OR REGULATED UNDER THE COMMONS ACT 1876

The Commons Act 1876 provides for both the inclosure and the regulation of common land under a complex procedure whereby Inclosure Commissioners make a provisional order which is then confirmed by Parliament in the form of a private Act. In preparing a provisional order, the Commissioners are required, if appropriate, to provide for access to any particular points of view and for a privilege of playing games on part or all of the common.[108] This power to provide for access and games is to be exercised "for the benefit of the neighbourhood".[109] Consequently, when making orders in the late nineteenth and early twentieth centuries, the Commissioners in the majority of cases limited the right of access to the inhabitants of the neighbourhood.[110] In numerous provisional orders, however, the Commissioners provided for public rights of access. These rights were not restricted to particular viewing points but extended over large parts if not all of the common land.[111] They occasionally were limited to access on foot but more usually allowed access for "air, exercise and recreation".[112] The granting of these rights to all members of the public was arguably outside the Commissioners' duty to weigh "the benefit of the neighbourhood". Nevertheless, because the provisional orders were confirmed by Parliament, the public rights contained in these orders have statutory force independent of the terms of the 1876 Act.[113]

Because the 1876 Act remains in force, provisional orders can theoretically still be made which might confer public rights of access over common land. However, the last inclosure and regulation orders made under the Act were respectively confirmed in 1914 and 1919.[114] Since then, the main procedure for the authorisation of any type of construction on common land has been section 194 of the Law of Property Act 1925 which provides that Ministerial consent must be obtained if the building, fence or work will impede access to the land.[115] The regulation of commons has been achieved under the relatively simple procedure laid down in the Commons Act 1899 which requires no parliamentary action and, since 1980, has not even required the approval of the Secretary of State.[116] Schemes made under the 1899 Act may contain any of the provisions of the 1876 Act "for the benefit of the neighbourhood".[117] Under the 1899 Act, however, the prescribed form of scheme limits the right of access and privilege of playing games to the inhabitants of the district and neighbourhood.[118]

(ii) COMMONS IN WATER CATCHMENT AREAS

Although large-scale construction of reservoirs in England and Wales dates from the early nineteenth century, it was only in the second half of the century that many cities sought statutory powers to acquire compulsorily the extensive areas of uplands which form water catchment areas.[119] The cities sought these powers in order to be able to avoid water pollution by excluding members of the public from the gathering grounds and by controlling land use there. Such exclusion of the public was, however, fought by the Commons Preservation Society which, together with local interest groups, on a number of instances obtained provisions ensuring public access to the gathering grounds.[120]

The first water authority Act to make provision for public access was the Manchester Corporation Waterworks Act 1879 which simply prohibits the Corporation from restricting or interfering in any manner with "the access heretofore actually enjoyed on the part of the public and tourists to mountains and fells surrounding Lake Thirlmere. . . ".[121] The Birmingham Corporation Water Act 1892, which applies to the Elan and Claerwen valleys in Powys, goes further and gives

> The public . . . a privilege at all times of enjoying air exercise and recreation on such parts of any common or unenclosed land acquired by the Corporation . . . in the catchment area whether any common or commonable rights in or over such lands shall have been extinguished under the provisions of this part of the Act or not . . .[122]

This provision, which has become known as the "Birmingham clause", was included in a number of later water Acts including the Paignton Urban District Water Act 1900 (in relation to Holme Moor on Dartmoor)[123] and the Manchester Corporation Act 1919 (in relation to Haweswater in the Lake District).[124] As determined by Whitford J. in *Welsh Water Auth-*

ority v. *Clayden* (1984),[125] these sections prevent water authorities from fencing and ploughing common and unenclosed land in the catchment areas, since such actions would interfere with public access.

(iii) COMMONS OWNED BY THE NATIONAL TRUST

Although members of the public do not have an express right of access to common land owned by the National Trust, the 1907 Act which governs the Trust places it under a duty to keep common land which it owns "at all times . . . unenclosed and unbuilt on as open spaces for the recreation and enjoyment of the public".[126] If the Trust were to refuse unreasonably to allow members of the public access to its commons, it would be in breach of its duty and a member of the public might be able to obtain an order for judicial review ordering the Trust to keep its commons open for public enjoyment.[127]

(3) Registered Commons

In its 1958 Report, the Royal Commission on Common Land made two major sets of recommendations. The first concerned registration of all common land and rights of common so as to determine the extent, nature and ownership of such land and rights.[128] The second concerned public access to and management and improvement of common land in order to put the commons to better use.[129] The Commissioners clearly considered that members of the public should immediately be given a right of access to all common land.[130] However, they also noted that registration was "in a sense" a "preliminary" step to the promotion of schemes for the management and improvement of common land, [131] and this last idea was adopted by the then Conservative government which proposed that legislation in relation to common land should be in two stages beginning with registration.[132] The result of this policy, albeit under the Wilson Labour government, was the enactment of the Commons Registration Act 1965.

Under the 1965 Act, any person was entitled, within a period now elapsed, to apply to register any land as common land and to register any rights of common over such land.[133] The relevant council which served as a registration authority was then obliged to register the land or right of common provisionally.[134] If there was no objection to the provisional registration, it became final at the end of another specified period.[135] However, if there was an objection to a provisional registration the matter fell, and continues to fall, to be determined by

Commons Commissioners with the onus of proof (as determined in a series of cases) lying on the applicant for registration.[136] In the event of this onus not being discharged, the Commissioners refuse to confirm the registration in which case it becomes void, while if the onus is discharged, they confirm the registration in which case it becomes final.[137] Such registration is conclusive evidence of the matters registered.[138] Only registered rights of common may be exercised, while land which could have been registered is no longer deemed to be common land unless it was registered.[139]

This procedure was deficient in a number of fundamental respects. Because of the perceived difficulty in ascertaining the owners of common land, the Act did not require that notice be given to an owner that an application had been made to register his land as a common. As a result some unwary landowners found that their land had been irrevocably and wrongly registered as common land, without the matter ever having been brought to their attention.[140] Unlike the register kept under the Land Registration Act 1925, which shows all current incumbrances on the title of registered land except for what are known as "overriding interests",[141] the commons registers provide a conclusive record of all common land and rights of common only at the date of registration.[142] Interested parties may notify any changes in the status of or rights in the land but they are not obliged to do so; hence the value of the registers as a record of common land is gradually diminishing.[143] Contrary to the proposals of the Royal Commissioners,[144] the 1965 Act also fails to provide that land should not cease to be common land by reason of either the extinction of the rights of common or their coming into the possession of the owner of the soil. Consequently, far from protecting common land as the Commissioners intended, registration has accelerated the loss of common land by making it easier for farmers and others to ascertain the commoners and then buy out their interests.[145]

These weaknesses in the registration system have been compounded by the ambiguity of a number of the crucial provisions of the Act. In the mass of consequent litigation, the courts have in part adopted interpretations of the Act which are different from those previously adopted by the Commons Commissioners. The result is that land and rights of common have been registered or rejected for registration on different principles at different times.[146] These inconsistencies cannot generally be rectified under the Act in its present form. Where land or rights of common have been wrongly registered, the courts have at most a limited power to amend and rectify the register. Where land or rights of common have wrongly been rejected for registration, there is no procedure under which they can be registered.

The most significant disputes under the Act have arisen where the only property interest involved has been that of landowners because no rights of common have been registered. In these cases, the conflict has been, in effect, between landowners and the public at large. The substantial matter at issue has been registration which, as noted by Oliver L.J., "clearly affects the value of the land and subjects it to whatever consequences may be provided for common land in the future by the legislature."[147] The precise question before the courts has been what land, which is not subject to registered rights of common, comes within the Act, which defines "common land" as including both "land subject to rights of common" and "waste land of a manor not subject to rights of common".[148]

In *Central Electricity Generating Board* v. *Clwyd* (1975),[149] the issue was whether rights of common are rendered un-exercisable or are extinguished by non-registration. The Act is silent in this respect, and the Commons Commissioner had held that non-registered rights of common cannot be exercised but are not extinguished. He consequently had held that provisionally registered land is "common land" within the meaning of the Act, so long as there were rights of common over the land before the deadline for the provisional registration of such rights. However, by reference to sections dealing with the inter-relationship between the 1965 Act and sections 193 and 194 of the Law of Property Act 1925, Goff J. held that un-registered rights of common were extinguished. He therefore decided that, where no rights of common were provisionally registered, land which was not waste of a manor ceased to be common land on the date of provisional registration and hence the registration of the land should not be confirmed.[150]

In *Box Parish Council* v. *Lacey* (1979)[151] the issue was the date at which land had to be waste of a manor in order to satisfy the definition of "common land" in the 1965 Act. In an earlier case, Slade J. had read the legislation expansively in holding that land satisfied the definition if it had been waste of a manor in the days when copyhold tenure existed, that is prior to 1926. He argued that to hold that land needed to be part of a manor when it was registered "would involve the conclusion that the lord of a manor could remove waste land of that manor not subject to commonable rights entirely out of the ambit of the Act by the simple device of conveying the lordship to another person, while retaining the land, or vice versa."[152] In the *Lacey* case, however, the Court of Appeal rejected Slade J.'s interpretation of the definition as artificial. On a literal reading of the Act, the court held that land must be parcel of a manor at the date of registration in order to be "common land". Because few manors remain intact, there is little waste land which satisfies this requirement and any waste land which is still owned by the lord of the manor can probably be brought outside the Act either by cultivating, enclosing or occupying it (in which case it ceases to be "waste")[153] or, as noted by Slade J., by transferring either the land or the lordship into different ownership.[154]

Finally, in *Corpus Christi College, Oxford* v. *Gloucestershire C.C.* (1982),[155] the issue was whether land can be deregistered when it has been registered as common land but it is not waste land of a manor and no rights of common have been registered over it. This issue is of considerable importance because it appears that about four-fifths of all registered commons have no registered rights over them.[156] Apparently influenced by the fact that the meadow in question had been subject to some rights of common, the Court of Appeal rejected the College's application on the basis that registration conclusively established that the meadow was common land even if the meadow in fact satisfied neither limb of the statutory definition. Nothing had occurred since registration to change the status of the land and hence it could not be deregistered. However, it may be possible to circumvent even this decision by transfer of the land into different ownership. The land then would be neither subject to rights of common nor waste land of a manor and, within the meaning of the Act, would therefore arguably cease to be common land and could be deregistered.[157]

Because of these problems, the Commons Registration Act has been subject to intense criticism,[158] which in 1983 finally prompted the Countryside Commission to establish the Common Land Forum. The task of the Forum was to make proposals for commons legislation commanding the support of all major interest groups. Apart from affirming the need for a general right of access to common land and suggesting mechanisms for better management of the commons, the Forum reviewed the operation of the Registration Act. In its report released in mid-1986, it recognized that "the application of the

Act has resulted in some genuine common land escaping the net of registration whilst other land, not common land at all, has been caught in it."[159] However, the Forum concluded:

> it would be altogether unsatisfactory to propose general reopening of the registers. The passage of nearly twenty years since the registration process began, and the inferred waste of substantial resources of time, thought and money expended, would rule out such a prospect even were a general reopening of its registers desirable in principle; and we have firmly concluded that it is not.[160]

The Forum therefore suggested that land should be open to deregistration only where "an applicant shows that the land was at the date of provisional registration neither waste land of a manor nor subject to rights of common and that the land is either occupied with a house or building or is, and was, used for a purpose compatible with its existence as a common".[161] If a registered common fails to satisfy the statutory definition of common land – for example, because no rights of common exist over it or because it ceases to be waste of a manor – it shall not be liable to deregistration as currently appears to be the case. Rather, it shall become statutory common land. Finally, commons registration authorities will be under a duty to maintain registers which show current interests in common land.

If government acts on its promises and soon implements the Forum's recommendations, the effect will be that "the last uncommitted reserve of land in England and Wales . . . [will] be preserved in the public interest",[162] as the Royal Commission on Common Land proposed three decades ago. However, until such legislation is enacted, the current Act will simply facilitate the destruction of common land, and hence will diminish the area of land which ultimately may be subject to public rights of access.

(B) OPEN COUNTRY

For a century, private members have introduced Bills into Parliament which, if passed, would have given members of the public a general right of access to uncultivated parts of the countryside. More than 25 Bills of this type have been introduced into the House of Commons, but only three have received a second reading and no such legislation has been enacted.

Instead Parliament has twice passed unsuccessful compromise measures which, far from granting a right of access to all uncultivated land, have merely established machinery for obtaining public access to specified areas. The first such measure, the Access to Mountains Act 1939, was never implemented. The current National Parks and Access to the Countryside Act 1949 avoids many of the faults of its predecessor but has resulted in the public obtaining a right of access to only a very small part of the countryside.

Apart from one Bill in relation to Wales,[163] early attempts to gain a statutory right of access to uncultivated land were all made in relation to Scotland where many owners of moorland, who had previously run sheep and cattle on their land, turned in the second half of the nineteenth century to stocking deer for hunting. With this change in land use, the landowners sought to exclude the public from their traditional enjoyment of the moors. In an attempt to prevent this exclusion, James Bryce in 1884 introduced the first of thirteen Access to Mountains (Scotland) Bills, all of which provided that "no owner or occupier of uncultivated mountains or moorlands shall be entitled to exclude any person from walking on such lands for the purposes of recreation or scientific or artistic study, or molest him so walking".[164]

Because of the difficulties faced by members of the public in obtaining access to many regions in England and Wales, Bryce's Bill was presented in 1908 in relation to all of Great Britain. Thirty years later a Bill of this type, but not applicable to Scotland, was radically recast at the Committee stage in the House of Commons and enacted as the Access to Mountains Act 1939. As noted by John Dower, what had started as "a simple two-page measure . . . finally emerged . . . [as] an elaborate and entirely different fourteen-page measure, actually opposed by many rambling organizations and disappointing to all".[165]

The main departure of the 1939 Act from Bryce's original Bill was that the Act did not create a general right of access to all mountains and moorland; instead it applied only to land covered by access orders made by the Minister of Agriculture under a highly complex procedure. Although landowners, local authorities and amenity organizations were entitled to apply for such orders,[166] amenity organizations believed that only ramblers would do so and regulations made under the Act imposed a heavy financial burden on applicants by requiring them to bear the cost of the application procedure in all cases[167] and to purchase, erect and maintain elaborately worded notice boards if successful in obtaining an order.[168] No provision was made to compensate landowners whose land was made the subject of an order. Most controversially, the Act created 15 conditions – such as shutting gates and keeping dogs under control – which were to be observed by members of the public on land covered by an access order.[169] A person who breached these conditions did not simply commit trespass but could be convicted of a summary offence even if he caused no damage.[170] Because of these deficiencies in the legislation as well as the outbreak of war, no applications for access orders were made under the 1939 Act.

In their reports issued in 1945 and 1947 respectively, John Dower and the Hobhouse Committee recommended that there be a statutory right of public access to all uncultivated land.[171] On lines similar to the survey of rights of way,[172] the Hobhouse Committee proposed that planning authorities should within a year draw up draft maps of uncultivated land and that after a period for objections all land shown in the maps should become subject to a right of public access "for air and pedestrian exercise".[173] However, the Labour government – almost without parliamentary opposition[174] – refused to take this step. According to Lewis Silkin, then Minister of Town and Country Planning, where the public already enjoyed *de facto* access it would be better "to let sleeping dogs lie" than to make access a matter of right.[175]

Like the Access to Mountains Act which it repealed, Part V of the 1949 Act merely establishes procedures whereby public access can be created in relation to particular parts of the countryside. However, the 1949 Act has overcome some of the problems of the earlier legislation through the relative simplicity of its procedures for securing access and by improving the position of both ramblers and the relevant landowners in relation to access land.

Under the 1949 Act (as amended), the procedures for creating public rights of access may be applied to all "open country" apart from "excepted land". "Open country" is defined as areas consisting "wholly or predominantly of mountain, moor, heath, down, cliff or foreshore" as well as woodlands and lakes and certain rivers and canals in the countryside;[176] all waterways in National Parks also come within the ambit of Part V.[177] The most important form of "excepted land" is "agricultural land, other than such land which is agricultural land by reason only that it affords rough grazing for livestock".[178] As a result

of this exception, the procedures for creating public access
apply, as under the 1939 Act, only to uncultivated land.

Local planning authorities can create a public right of access
to appropriate parts of the countryside by making either an
access agreement with or an access order against the relevant
landowners.[179] Where such agreements or orders are in force,
members of the public may lawfully enter and remain on the
land for the purpose of "open-air recreation".[180] Special restrictions on public activities on access land may be imposed by
the relevant agreement or order,[181] but if this is not done the
right of "open-air recreation" allows the public to ride horses
and even to go camping on the land. In all cases the 1949 Act,
like its predecessor, imposes 15 conditions on members of the
public on access land.[182] However, under the 1949 Act, a
person who breaches these conditions merely becomes a trespasser. He commits an offence only if he is in breach of whatever byelaws may have been made by the local planning authority in relation to the land.[183]

In return for their land being subject to a public right of
access, landowners typically receive the assistance of wardens[184] as well as monetary payments from local planning authorities. In general, the function of the wardens is to control
and advise the public and to work with landowners so as to
make good any physical damage to fences and gates and to
minimize disturbance of livestock. The nature and timing of
the payments vary according to whether an order or agreement
is in force. Where land is covered by an order, a local planning
authority is generally required to wait five years before paying
the landowner an amount equal to any depreciation in the
value of the land caused by the public access.[185] Such depreciation is frequently difficult to establish. Hence a landowner is
generally better off under the clauses of the model access
agreement issued by the Countryside Commission in 1970.[186]
Under an agreement of this type, the relevant authority pays
the landowner an annual consideration determined before the
agreement commences by the District Valuer who has regard
to such factors as the value of the land for the purposes secured
by the agreement and any diminution in the value of the
holding caused by the agreement.[187]

The main weakness of both access agreements and orders is
that they are of limited duration. Under the 1949 Act, owners
of land subject to agreements or orders were free to put an end
to public access by, for example, ploughing the relevant land
and hence converting it from "open country" to "excepted

land".[188] The Countryside Act 1968 empowers local planning authorities to make access agreements prohibiting or restricting the conversion of "open country" into "excepted land".[189] However, such conditions appear to be rarely included in agreements.[190] Moreover, agreements and orders can still last only so long as the ownership of the relevant land does not change, since both agreements and orders impose positive obligations on landowners and at common law such obligations cannot "run with the land".[191]

Local planning authorities can avoid these difficulties if they exercise their power under section 76 of the 1949 Act to acquire land compulsorily within their area. The Secretary of State for the Environment has a similar power in relation to land within national parks.[192] In both cases, the Act does not give members of the public an express right of access to the land which is acquired. However, if an authority acquires land, it is required by section 76(4)

> so to manage the land as to give to the public access for open-air recreation to so much thereof as appears to the authority to be practicable, having regard to the nature of the different parts of the land, to anything done thereon which may result in danger to the public or to persons employed thereon unless public access to the land . . . is restricted, and to all other relevant circumstances.

If the Minister acquires land, he is under no such duty. He may retain the land in which case the Act leaves him free to determine how the land should be managed. Alternatively, he may transfer the land to a suitable person on such trusts or conditions as will secure public access to so much of the land as is practicable having regard to the matters specified in section 76(4).[193]

In enacting the 1949 legislation, the intention of the Labour Government was that access would be obtained "first by agreement, then by order and, if all else fails, by compulsory purchase".[194] Consistent with this statement, the 1949 Act imposed no restraints on the making of access agreements other than the need to obtain ministerial approval,[195] a requirement which was removed in 1974.[196] The 1949 Act also made clear that access orders are a reserve power, available only where an agreement cannot adequately secure public access.[197] However, the 1949 Act did not place any such preconditions on the compulsory acquisition of land for access. Instead, it simply specified that land could be acquired if it "is requisite that the public should have access thereto for open-air recreation" and

"in the circumstances it is expedient that such access . . .
should be secured by the acquisition of the land".[198] The authorities' and ministerial powers of compulsory acquisition consequently appear not as powers of last resort but as alternatives to the making of access agreements.

Although planning authorities initially favoured access
agreements, over the last two decades acquisition has become
increasingly popular and now accounts for just over half of the
access arrangements which have been made.[199] However,
more than 80% of access land is covered by access agreements
since acquisition has been favoured in relation to small low-
land sites under considerable recreational pressure whereas
agreements have been made primarily in relation to extensive
tracts of rough grazing country in the uplands. Only two access
orders have been made and the power to make such orders has
been significant at most as a means of inducing landowners to
make access agreements. The ministerial power of compulsory
acquisition appears never to have been used.

For a variety of reasons – including the lack of interest of
planning authorities, cost, the opposition of landowners and
the extent of de facto access[200] – only about 100,000 acres or
just over 0.3% of the total area of England and Wales is
covered by access arrangements.[201] Around half of the access
land is in the Peak District where the Peak Park Joint Planning
Board has made an exceptional effort to overcome the access
problems which in the 1930s resulted in the "mass trespasses"
in protest at the exclusion of members of the public from such
areas as Kinder Scout and Bleaklow. Several planning authorities have failed to make any access arrangements whatsoever. Almost no agreements have been made in relation to
woodlands and waterways.[202]

NOTES TO CHAPTER 2

1. See above, especially, pp.19, 30-2.
2. For authority concerning the recognition of certain types of rights over
   land only if they are expressly created, see Hamilton v. Aikman (1832)
   6 W. & S. 64, 76 per Lord Wynford; Dempster v. Cleghorn (1813) 2
   Dow. 40, 62; 13 E.R. 780, 787; Dyce v. Hay (1852) 1 Macq. 305, 312;
   Bourke v. Davis (1889) 44 Ch. D. 110, 121.
3. The Times, 11 October 1986; CO/1455/85 transcript.
4. See, for example, Cincinnati v. White 6 Pet. 431 (1832); Brooklyn Park

Commissioners v. *Armstrong* 6 Am. Rep. 70 (1871); *Guelph* v. *Canada Co.* (1853) 4 Gr. 632.
 5. [1951] 2 D.L.R. 609, 622.
 6. *Gion* v. *City of Santa Cruz* 465 P. 2d 50, 58 (1970).
 7. *Seaway Co.* v. *Attorney-General* 375 S.W. 2d 923 (1964); *Gion* v. *City of Santa Cruz* 465 P. 2d 50 (1970); *County of Los Angeles* v. *Berk* 605 P. 2d 381 (1980).
 8. *Seaway Co.* v. *Attorney-General* 375 S.W. 2d 923, 925 (1964); *Gion* v. *City of Santa Cruz* 465 P. 2d 50, 54 (1970).
 9. (1886) 55 L.J.Q.B. 267, 270.
10. (1898) 79 L.T. 425.
11. *Ibid.*, p.428.
12. (1899) 81 L.T. 174, 179. Compare *Ex parte Lewis* (1888) 21 Q.B.D. 191, 197 *per* Wills J.
13. (1889) 81 L.T. 174, 179.
14. *Ibid.*, p.182.
15. [1932] 1 Ch. 133. See also, *In re Morgan* [1955] 1 W.L.R. 738; *Inland Revenue Commissioner* v. *Baddeley* [1955] A.C. 572.
16. *Earl of Coventry* v. *Willes* (1863) 9 L.T. 384, 385 *per* Cockburn C.J. See also *Schwinge* v. *Dowell* (1862) 2 F. & F. 845, 849; 175 E.R. 1314, 1316 *per* Wightman J.; *Hammerton* v. *Honey* (1876) 24 W.R. 603, 604 *per* Jessel M.R.
17. *Schwinge* v. *Dowell* (1862) 2 F. & F. 845; 175 E.R. 1314; *Chapman* v. *Cripps* (1862) 2 F. & F. 864; 175 E.R. 1323; *Eyre* v. *New Forest Highway Board* (1892) 56 J.P. 517; *Robinson* v. *Cowpen Local Board* (1892) 62 L.J.Q.B. 619; (1893) 63 L.J.Q.B. 235; *Great Western Railway Co.* v. *Solihull R.D.C.* (1902) 66 J.P. 772, 773; *Attorney-General* v. *Sewell* (1918) 120 L.T. 363. See also *Attorney-General* v. *Hemingway* (1916) 81 J.P. 112, 114.
18. In *Robinson* v. *Cowpen Local Board* (1892) 62 L.J.Q.B. 619, 620, Bruce J. expressly stated that the point for decision was "not whether a general right of stray may exist in law".
19. *Eyre* v. *New Forest Highway Board* (1892) 56 J.P. 517, 518 *per* Wills J.; *Attorney-General* v. *Sewell* (1918) 120 L.T. 363, 368 *per* Duke L.J.; 370 *per* Eve J.
20. 5 B. & Ald. 268, 315; 106 E.R. 1190, 1217.
21. [1903] 2 Ch. 165, 172.
22. [1905] 2 Ch. 188, 198, approved in *Alfred F. Beckett Ltd* v. *Lyons* [1967] Ch. 449, 479 *per* Winn L.J. That Farwell J.'s comments concerning the *jus spatiandi* were dicta is most evident from the report of the case in (1905) 21 T.L.R. 471, 472.
23. [1911] A.C. 552, 592.
24. [1956] Ch. 131, 184. Perhaps significantly Lord Ellenborough did not address the question of acquisition by the public of *jura spatiandi* over *defined* open spaces, such as Doncaster Common, the subject of the litigation in *R.* v. *Doncaster Metropolitan Borough Council; ex parte Braim* (1986). See below pp. 127–9
25. [1905] 2 Ch. 188, 198.
26. See above pp. 38–9.
27. [1956] Ch. 131, 183.
28. See Michael F. Sturley, "Easements in Gross", (1980) 96 L.Q.R. 557.
29. See *Rangeley* v. *Midland Railway Co.* (1868) L.R. Ch. 306; *Hawkins* v. *Rutter* [1892] 1 Q.B. 668.

30. (1852) 1 Macq. 305.
31. *Ibid.*, p.315.
32. *Ibid.*, p.309 See also *Dempster* v. *Cleghorn* (1813) 2 Dow. 40, 49, 60, 61; 3 E.R. 780, 783, 787 *per* Lord Eldon. For a similar principle in relation to the English law of easements, see *Copeland* v. *Greenhalf* [1952] Ch. 488; *Re Ellenborough Park* [1956] Ch. 131, 176; *Thomas W. Ward Ltd* v. *Alexander Bruce (Grays) Ltd* [1959] 2 Lloyd's Rep. 472.
33. See *Hall* v. *Nottingham* (1875) L.R. 1 Ex. D. 1, 3 *per* Kelly, C.B.; *Truro Corporation* v. *Rowe* [1901] 2 K.B. 870, 878 *per* Wills J.
34. (1849) 11 Dun. 1266, 1269.
35. *The Times*, 11 October 1986; CO/1455/85 transcript.
36. *Ibid.*
37. *Ibid.*
38. *Ibid.* McCullough J. had some reservations about whether "dedication" was the correct word as he felt its proper use may be only in relation to highways. As suggested, however, by the judgment of Phillimore J. in *Tyne Improvement Commissioner* v. *Imrie* (1889) 81 L.T. 174, 179, these reservations are unfounded.
39. *The Times,* 11 October 1986; CO/1455/85 transcript.
40. (1882) 7 App. Cas. 633.
41. *The Times*, 11 October 1986; CO/1455/85 transcript.
42. *Ibid.*
43. (1882) 7 App. Cas. 633, 647; applied in *Attorney-General* v. *Antrobus* [1905] 2 Ch. 188, 198-9.
44. See, albeit from a different perspective, *Goodman* v. *Mayor of Saltash* (1882) 7 App. Cas. 633, 662 *per* Lord Blackburn.
45. *Smith* v. *Andrews* [1891] 2 Ch. 678, 697 *per* North J. in relation to the Thames Preservation Act 1885 which was the first Act to confirm the public's right of navigation over the non-tidal Thames. In *William Stevens & Sons* v. *Thames Conservators* [1958] 1 Lloyd's Rep. 401, 407, 408, Streatfeild J. stated incorrectly that the public's rights were first confirmed by the Thames Conservancy Act 1857.
46. Thames Conservancy Act 1932, s. 79. The fact that this right extends over all parts of the Thames and is a right to "go" as well as "pass and repass" suggests that it is a right to navigate at will rather than a right of passage.
47. *Marshall* v. *Ulleswater Steam Navigation Co.* (1863) 3 B. & S. 732; 122 E.R. 274; *Marshall* v. *Ulleswater Steam Navigation Co.* (1871) L.R. 7 Q.B. 166, 172. See also *Iveagh* v. *Martin* [1961] 1 Q.B. 232, 274. Compare *Bourke* v. *Davis* (1889) 44 Ch. D. 110, 120-1.
48. *Attorney-General* v. *Furness Railway Co.* (1897) discussed in Michael Burke-Gaffney, "Report of the Public Local Inquiry into Byelaws as to the Lakes known as Ullswater, Conistonwater and Derwentwater made by the Lake District Special Planning Board", March 1977, p.18 (copy of report held by Home Office, London).
49. *Micklethwait* v. *Vincent* (1892) 67 L.T. 225.
50. *Bloomfield* v. *Johnston* (1868) I.R. 8 C.L. 68. Compare *Bourke* v. *Davis* (1889) 44 Ch. D. 110, 121.
51. *Bristow* v. *Cormican* (1876) I.R. 10 C.L. 398, 432 *per* Whiteside C.J. See also *O'Neill* v. *Johnston* [1908] 1 I.R. 358, 382 *per* Ross J.; [1909] 1 I.R. 237, 238 *per* Holmes L.J.; *Toome Eel Fishery (Northern Ireland) Ltd* v. *Cardwell* [1963] N.I. 92, 113 *per* McVeigh J.
52. Lake Windermere (Collision Rules) Order 1961 (S.I. 1961/343) and

Lake Ullswater (Collision Rules) Order 1966 (S.I. 1966/1413) made under the Merchant Shipping Act 1894, s.421(2).

53. Section 13(5) of the Countryside Act 1968 provides that the power of local planning authorities under section 13(1) of the Act to make byelaws prohibiting or restricting traffic on lakes in National Parks cannot be exercised "so as to extinguish any public right of way over any waters". This provision was intended to protect the public right of navigation on Ullswater, Derwentwater, Conistonwater and Windermere. See H.C. Deb., 5th series, vol. 762, cols 1215-22, 9 April 1968; H.L. Deb., 5th series, vol 291, cols 1587-99, 9 May 1968. However, as a result of poor drafting it may not do so, because it simply protects "rights of way" rather than the right to navigate at will over these lakes. See, in this respect, *Evans* v. *Godber* [1974] 1 W.L.R. 1317.

54. See *Lynn Corporation* v. *Turner* (1774) 1 Cowp. 86; 98 E.R. 980, 981 *per* Lord Mansfield; *Miles* v. *Rose* (1814) 5 Taunt. 705; 128 E.R. 868; *R.* v. *Montague* (1825) 4 B. & C. 598; 107 E.R. 1183; *Sim E. Bak* v. *Ang Yong Huat* [1923] A.C. 429.

55. *Gann* v. *Free Fishers of Whitstable* (1865) 11 H.L.C. 192, 207-8; 11 E.R. 1305, 1312 *per* Lord Westbury L.C. See also *Mayor of Colchester* v. *Brooke* (1845) 7 Q.B. 339, 374; 115 E.R. 518, 531 *per* Denman C.J.

56. *Attorney-General* v. *Parmeter* (1811) 10 Price 378, 400-1; 147 E.R. 345, 352 *per* MacDonald C.B.; *Mayor of Colchester* v. *Brooke* (1845) 7 Q.B. 339, 374; 115 E.R. 518, 531 *per* Denman C. J.; *Gann* v. *Free Fishers of Whitstable* (1865) 11 H.L.C. 192, 208; 11 E.R. 1305, 1312 *per* Lord Westbury L.C.

57. For example, *Williams* v. *Wilcox* (1838) 8 Ad. & El. 314, 329, 333; 112 E.R. 857, 862, 864 *per* Denman C.J.; *Mayor of Colchester* v. *Brooke* (1845) 7 Q.B. 339, 373; 115 E.R. 518, 531 *per* Denman C.J.; *Denaby and Cadeby Main Collieries Ltd* v. *Anson* [1911] 1 K.B. 171, 198-9 *per* Fletcher Moulton L.J.; *Iveagh* v. *Martin* [1961] 1 Q.B. 232, 272-3 *per* Paull J.

58. *Blundell* v. *Catterall* (1821) 5 B. & Ald. 268, 294; 106 E.R. 1190, 1199 *per* Holroyd J.; *Lord Fitzhardinge* v. *Purcell* [1908] 2 Ch. 139, 168 *per* Parker J.

59. [1974] 1 W.L.R. 1317, 1326. See also *Peltier* v. *Darwent* (1870) 9 S.C.R. 133, 150 (N.S.W.); *Tate and Lyle Industries Ltd* v. *Greater London Council* [1983] 2 A.C. 509, 537 *per* Lord Templeman; 545 *per* Lord Diplock.

60. *Spilman* v. *Hermitage* 5 Vin. Abr. 35.

61. *Conservators of Mitcham Common* v. *Cox* [1911] 2 K.B. 854, 870 *per* Phillimore and Hamilton JJ.

62. See Harris & Ryan, pp. 71-80.

63. *Arlett* v. *Ellis* (1827) 7 B. & C. 346, 369; 108 E.R. 752, 761 *per* Bayley J.

64. See Charles Elton, *A Treatise on Commons and Waste Land,* London, Wildy, 1868, pp. 177-86; Thomas Edward Scrutton, *Commons and Common Fields*, Cambridge University Press, 1887, pp.61-7.

65. See *Royal Commission on Common Land 1955-1958: Report*, Cmnd. 462, 1958, App. II, paras 27, 44; App. III, para. 25.

66. *Ibid.*, App. II, para. 45.

67. Metropolitan Commons Act 1866, ss. 4, 5.

68. Commons Act 1876, preamble, s.7. See *Royal Commission on Common Land 1955-1958: Report*, Cmnd. 462, 1958, p. 177.

69. See Octavia Hill, *Our Common Land*, London, Macmillan, 1877, p.11;

Lord Eversley, *Commons, Forests and Footpaths*, London, Cassell, 1910.

70. See *Smith* v. *Earl Brownlow* (1870) L.R. 9 Eq. 241; *Warwick* v. *Queen's College, Oxford* (1870) L.R. 10 Eq. 105; (1871) L.R. 6 Ch. App. 716; *Betts* v. *Thompson* (1871) L.R. 6 Ch. App. 732. See also *Willingale* v. *Maitland* (1866) L.R. 3 Eq. 103; *Commissioners of Sewers of the City of London* v. *Glasse* (1872) L.R. 7 Ch. App. 456; (1874) L.R. 19 Eq. 134.

71. *Common Land: Preparations for Comprehensive Legislation: Report of an Inter-Departmental Working Party 1975/77,* Department of the Environment, 1978, p.1.

72. See Mark Blacksell & Andrew Gilg, *The Countryside: Planning and Change*, London, Allen & Unwin, 1981, pp. 211-13.

73. Dartmoor Commons Act 1985, s.10(1). Public rights of access were also extended by section 21 of the Ashdown Forest Act 1974 which gives members of the public a right of "access on foot to and over the forest for quiet recreation". This provision extends the much more limited rights conferred on the public by the Commons Regulation (Ashdown Forest) Provisional Order Confirmation Act 1885. By way of contrast, Section 15 of the Epsom and Walton Downs Regulation Act 1984, which gives the public certain rights of access "for air and exercise on horseback" over the Downs, appears to reduce the rights of the public previously conferred by the Epsom and Walton Downs Act 1936, s. 4.

74. *Royal Commission on Common Land*, para. 314. This recommendation was endorsed in 1973 by the House of Lords Select Committee on Sport and Leisure, in 1977 by the inter-departmental working party on common land and in 1984 by the Countryside Commission. See *Second Report from the Select Committee of the House of Lords on Sport and Leisure,* 1973, para. 256; *Common Land*, p. 3; Countryside Commission, *A Better Future for the Uplands*, C.C.P. 162, Cheltenham, 1984, para. 176.

75. Countryside Commission, *Common Land: The Report of the Common Land Forum*, C.C.P. 215, para. 2.8.

76. *Ibid*, para. 4.17

77. H.C. Deb., 29 January 1987.

78. Law of Property Act 1922, s. 128(2), sched. 12, para. 4.

79. *Report from the Joint Select Committee of the House of Lords and the House of Commons on the Law of Property Bill*, 1920, p. 4.

80. *Ibid.* (Emphasis added).

81. *Ibid.*

82. H.L. Deb., 5th series, vol. 45, cols 323-24, 24 May 1921, Lord Dynesor.

83. H.L. Deb., 5th series, vol. 44, col. 654, 17 March 1921, Lord Birkenhead.

84. See *Attorney-General* v. *Southampton Corporation* (1969) 21 P. & C.R. 281.

85. Law of Property Act 1925, s. 193(1)(c), (4).

86. 1985, unreported; CO/1217/84 transcript, discussed in J.R. Montgomery, "Rural Rides: Horseriding and Common Land", (1985) Conv. 415-7; *Open Space*, vol. 22, no. 4, autumn 1985, p.11; Alec Samuels, "Horses on the Common", (1986) 150 Local Government Review 591-2. See also H.L. Deb., 5th series, vol. 292, col. 159, 13 May 1968; col. 609, 21 May 1968, Lord Kennet.

87. Law of Property Act 1925, s.193(1)(a).

88. *Ibid*, s.193(1)(b).
89. [1911] 2 K.B. 854. See, also, *De Morgan* v. *Metropolitan Board of Works* (1880) 5 Q.B.D. 155; *Harris* v. *Harrison* (1914) 78 J.P. 398.
90. 1985, unreported; CO/1217/84 transcript.
91. *R* v. *Minister of Health, Ex parte Villiers* [1936] 2 K.B. 29, 45 *per* Hewart C.J.; *Royal Commission*, para. 86. Compare Harris & Ryan, pp. 5, 241-2. The Government's intention in 1921 was to exclude "commonable land" from the operation of section 193. See H.L. Deb., 5th series, vol. 44, col. 653, 17 March 1921, Lord Birkenhead.
92. *Royal Commission*, para. 87.
93. The definition of "common land" in section 22(1) of the 1965 Act departs in several respects from the common law definition of "common land". See Harris & Ryan, pp. 7-8.
94. *Royal Commission on Common Land*, para. 89.
95. *Ibid.*, para 87.
96. Local Government Act 1972, s. 189(4).
97. *Common Land*, p. 2.
98. See *Central Electricity Generating Board* v. *Clwyd C.C.* [1976] 1 W.L.R. 151, 155-6 *per* Goff J.
99. See *R* v. *Doncaster Metropolitan Borough Council; ex parte Braim* (1986), *The Times*, 11 October 1986; CO/1455/86 transcript.
100. Law of Property Act 1925, s. 193(1)(d)(ii); Local Government Act 1972, s. 189(4); Local Government Act 1985, sched. 8.
101. See Lawrence W. Chubb, "The Law of Property Act, 1925", *Journal of the Commons, Open Spaces and Footpaths Preservation Society*, 1926, p. 9.
102. Between 1926 and 1939, 109 deeds were executed as against 18 between 1940 and 1955 and 16 between 1956 and 1978. The area covered by these deeds increased only by 1,500 acres between 1956 and 1978. See *Royal Commission on Common Land, Minutes of Evidence*, London, H.M.S.O., 1956-7, pp. 37-8; *Royal Commission on Common Land*, para. 93; *Common Land*, p. 1.
103. Royal Commission on Common Land, *Minutes of Evidence*, London, H.M.S.O., 1956-7, pp. 966, 978.
104. *Open Space*, vol. 21, no. 7, summer 1983, p. 4.
105. *The Times*, 14 March 1983, p. 10; Duncan Mackay, "Common Causes: Greenham Common 1938-84", *Open Space*, vol.21, no. 9, spring 1984, pp. 9-17.
106. Law of Property Act 1925, s. 193(1)(d), (4). See, also, *Hipperson* v. *Newbury Electoral Officer* [1985] Q.B. 1060, esp. 1071.
107. Epping Forest Act 1878, s. 9. See generally, Robert Hunter, *The Epping Forest Act 1878*, London, Davis, 1878.
108. Commons Act 1876, s. 7(1), (3).
109. *Ibid.*, s. 7.
110. See, for example, Commons Regulation (Stoke) Provisional Order Confirmation Act 1878; Commons Regulation Order (Laindon) Confirmation Act 1887; Commons Regulation (Therfield) Provisional Order Confirmation Act 1888.
111. Compare *Harlow* v. *Minister of Transport and the Rugby Portland Cement Co. Ltd* [1951] 2 K.B. 98.
112. See, for example, Inclosure and Regulation (Matterdale) Provisional Orders Confirmation Act 1879; Commons Regulation (Crosby Garrett and Stivichall Commons) Provisional Order Confirmation Act 1882;

Inclosure (Arkelside) Provisional Order Confirmation Act 1882; Inclosure (Bettws Disserth) Provisional Order Confirmation Act 1882; Inclosure (Hildersham) Provisional Order Confirmation Act 1883.

113. See *Collis* v. *Amphlett* [1918] 1 Ch. 232, 241.
114. *Royal Commission on Common Land*, p. 177.
115. See further, *Attorney-General* v. *Southampton Corporation* (1969) 29 C. & P.R. 281.
116. Local Government, Planning and Land Act 1980, s. 1(3), sched. 3, para. 2(1).
117. Commons Act 1899, s. 1(2).
118. See paragraph 4 of the scheme set out in the Commons (Schemes) Regulations 1982.
119. See M.F. Tanner, *The Recreational Use of Water Supply Reservoirs in England and Wales*, Water Space Advisory Council Research Report no. 3, 1977, p. 4.
120. Lord Eversley, *Commons, Forests and Footpaths*, London, Cassell, 1910, pp. 267-9.
121. Manchester Corporation Waterworks Act 1879, s. 62.
122. Birmingham Corporation Water Act 1892, s. 53.
123. Paignton Urban District Water Act 1900, s. 27.
124. Manchester Corporation Act 1919, s. 43.
125. See *Open Space*, spring 1984, pp. 22-4; *Daily Telegraph*, 14 January 1984, p. 8.
126. National Trust Act 1907, s.29(A).
127. See above, p. 70–1.
128. *Royal Commission on Common Land*, chapter 7.
129. *Ibid.*, chapter 8.
130. *Ibid.*, paras 312-16.
131. *Ibid.*, para. 311.
132. H.C. Deb., 5th series, vol. 627, col. 134 (written answers), 26 July 1960, Mr. Hare; vol. 648, cols 15-16 (written answers), 6 November 1961, Mr. Soames.
133. Commons Registration Act 1965, s. 4(2).
134. *Ibid.*, s. 4(1), (5).
135. *Ibid.*, s. 7(1).
136. See *In re Sutton Common* [1982] 1 W.L.R. 647, 656; *In re Ilkley and Burley Moor* (1983) 47 P. & C.R. 324, 328; *Corpus Christi College, Oxford* v. *Gloucestershire C.C.* [1983] Q.B. 360, 369; *In re West Anstey Common* [1985] 2 W.L.R. 677, 687. Compare, Denning M.R. in the *Corpus Christi* case at 367.
137. Commons Registration Act 1965, s. 6.
138. *Ibid.*, s. 10.
139. *Ibid.*, s. 1(2).
140. See Common Land Forum, pp. 12, 37.
141. Land Registration Act 1925, ss. 69, 70.
142. Commons Registration Act 1965, s. 10.
143. *Common Land*, p. 25.
144. *Royal Commission on Common Land*, para. 230.
145. Anne & Malcolm MacEwen, *National Parks: Conservation or Cosmetics?*, London, Allen & Unwin, 1982, p. 206.
146. This problem has arisen, most notably, as a result of *Central Electricity Generating Board* v. *Clwyd C.C.* [1976] 1 W.L.R. 151 discussed below, p. 143.

147. *Corpus Christi College, Oxford* v. *Gloucestershire C.C.* [1983] Q.B. 360, 370.
148. Commons Registration Act 1965, s. 22(1).
149. [1976] 1 W.L.R. 151.
150. [1976] 1 W.L.R. 151, 155-6. This view is consistent with the intention of the Labour government in 1965. See H.C. Standing Committee A, 1964-5, vol. 1, col. 239, Mr. Skeffington; H.L. Deb., 5th series, vol. 263, col. 91, 9 February 1965; col. 716, 23 February 1965, Lord Mitchison. However, the Department of the Environment, like the Commons Commissioner, subsequently took the view that the rights simply ceased to be exercisable. See [1976] 1 W.L.R. 151, 156-7. Goff J.'s decision has been doubted by Lord Denning M.R. in *Corpus Christi College, Oxford* v. *Gloucestershire C.C.* [1983] Q.B. 360, 368.
151. [1979] 2 W.L.R. 177.
152. *In re Chewton Common* [1977] 1 W.L.R. 1242, 1249. See also *In re Yately Common* [1977] 1 W.L.R. 840, 853 per Foster J.; *Corpus Christi College, Oxford* v. *Gloucestershire C.C.* [1983] Q.B. 360, 368 per Lord Denning M.R.
153. *Baxendale* v. *Instow Parish Council* [1982] Ch. 14, 18 per Megarry V.-C. Land does not cease to be "waste" merely because the lord of the manor takes its produce and cuts the grass for hay and silage. See *In re Britford Common* [1977] 1 W.L.R. 39, 47-8.
154. *In re Chewton Common* [1977] 1 W.L.R. 1242, 1249. Compare, Common Land Forum, pp. 72-3.
155. [1983] Q.B. 360.
156. See Alec Samuels, "Common Land and Rights of Common: How the Commons Registration Act 1965 has worked out", (1985) Conv. 24, 29.
157. Compare, Common Land Forum, pp. 72-73.
158. See, for example, *Corpus Christi College* v. *Gloucestershire C.C.* [1983] Q.B. 360, 369-70 per Denning M.R.; 378 per Oliver L.J.
159. Common Land Forum, p. 11.
160. *Ibid.*, p. 12.
161. *Ibid.*, p. 38.
162. Royal Commission on Common Land, para. 403.
163. Welsh Mountain, River and Pathway Bill, 1888.
164. Access to Mountains (Scotland) Bill, 1884, cl. 2.
165. Dower, para. 51. For a detailed discussion of the background to the 1939 Act, see Gordon E. Cherry, *National Parks and Recreation in the Countryside*, London, H.M.S.O., 1975, pp. 16-24.
166. Access to Mountains Act 1939, s. 3(1).
167. *Ibid.*, s. 3(12); Schedule of Fees in respect of transactions under this section, 1940.
168. Access to Mountains Regulations 1940, reg. 6.
169. Access to Mountains Act 1939, s. 6.
170. *Ibid.*, s. 7.
171. Dower, para. 52; Hobhouse, part 2.
172. See above, pp. 71–2.
173. Hobhouse, para. 159.
174. Only two members of Parliament, H.D. Hughes and A.L. Symonds, spoke in favour of a general right of access to uncultivated land. See H.C. Deb., 5th series, vol. 463, cols 1563, 1642, 1 April 1949.
175. H.C. Standing Committees, 1948-9, vol. 2, col. 834, 19 May 1949.
176. National Parks and Access to the Countryside Act 1949, s. 59(2);

Countryside Act 1968, s. 16; Transport Act 1968, s. 111.
177. National Parks and Access to the Countryside Act 1949, s. 74.
178. *Ibid.*, s. 60(5)(a).
179. *Ibid.*, ss. 64, 65.
180. *Ibid.*, s. 60(1).
181. *Ibid.*, s. 60(3).
182. *Ibid.*, s. 60(1), (4), sched. 2.
183. *Ibid.*, s. 90(1).
184. *Ibid.*, s. 92.
185. *Ibid.*, ss. 70-3; Countryside Act 1968, s. 21(3).
186. Countryside Commission, *Access to Open Country: Model Clauses for an Access Agreement*, 1970. For further discussion of these financial provisions, see M.J. Feist, *A Study of Management Agreements*, Cheltenham, Countryside Commission, 1978, paras 8.8, 8.9.
187. See Countryside Commission, *Access to Open Country*, 1970, p. 1.
188. National Parks and Access to the Countryside Act 1949, s. 66(1).
189. Countryside Act 1968, s. 18. Section 17 of the 1968 Act also provided that the conversion of land subject to an access order into agricultural land would put an end to the public right of access only if the Minister so directed. This provision was repealed by the Local Government, Planning and Land Act 1980, s. 1(3), sched. 3, para. 8.
190. R.S. Gibbs & M.C. Whitby, *Local Authority Expenditure on Access Land*, Monograph 6, Agricultural Adjustment Unit, University of Newcastle-upon-Tyne, 1975, pp. 31-2.
191. Megarry & Wade, p. 741. For proposed reforms of the law, see Law Commission, *Transfer of Land: the Law of Positive and Restrictive Covenants*, H.C. 201, 1984.
192. National Parks and Access to the Countryside Act 1949, s. 77(1). Under section 77(4) of the 1949 Act, the Minister of Agriculture could, with the agreement of the Secretary of State for the Environment, also exercise this power of compulsory purchase. The power of the Minister of Agriculture to do so was, however, removed by the Local Government, Planning and Land Act 1980, s. 118, sched. 23, part II.
193. National Parks and Access to the Countryside Act 1949, s. 77(3).
194. H.C. Deb., 5th series, vol. 463, col. 1664, 1 April 1949.
195. National Parks and Access to the Countryside Act 1949, s. 64(1).
196. Local Government Act 1974, s. 42(2), sched. 8.
197. National Parks and Access to the Countryside Act 1949, s. 65(2).
198. *Ibid.*, ss. 76(1)(a), (b), 77(1)(a), (b).
199. Gibbs & Whitby, *op. cit.;* Feist, *op. cit.*, paras 7.12-13.
200. Marion Shoard, "Opening up the Countryside to the People", [1974] J.P.L. 266, 270; Christopher Hall, "Country Matters", *Vole*, vol. 3, no. 6, 13 March 1980, p. 29; MacEwen & MacEwen, *op. cit.*, p. 20.
201. Hall, *op. cit.*, p. 29.
202. *Ibid.*

Chapter 3

ACCESS UNDER LICENCE

In the absence of a right of way or right to ramble, a member of the public may enter land lawfully if the relevant landowner gives him permission to do so. As stated by Vaughan C.J. in *Thomas* v. *Sorrell* (1673)[1], the effect of such licence is to make "an action lawful, which without it had been unlawful". Unlike a right of access, however, a licence to enter may be revoked at will by the landowner, in which case the entrant must leave within a reasonable time or become a trespasser.[2]

In order for members of the public to have a licence to enter land, the landowner may either expressly or impliedly permit such access. While the law governing express licences is relatively straightforward, the issue of whether a licence should be implied is more complex. This issue has arisen in reported cases only in relation to occupier's liability. Because the common law traditionally made occupiers liable to trespassers in only a very narrow range of circumstances,[3] the courts were sometimes quite liberal in finding that entrants, especially children, who came on to land without the landowner's express permission, were not trespassers but rather were implied licensees.[4] If the law had not been so severe in relation to trespassers, the courts might not have found that these entrants were licensees. Consequently, it has been suggested that since trespassers can now recover in a somewhat greater (albeit still narrow) range of situations,[5] "it is likely that implied permission will be rather less readily found [in relation to occupiers' liability]".[6] Nevertheless, the broad principles laid down in the occupiers' liability cases in relation to when a licence should be implied still appear to be good law.

The cases on occupiers' liability indicate that whether a landowner has impliedly consented to an entry on his land is determined according to an objective test. Regardless of the landowner's frame of mind, he will be treated as having given the necessary permission if members of the public habitually go on to the land and "a reasonable owner would feel that unless he acted to stop the trespass, the belief would naturally be induced in those who used the land that they had his tacit permission to do so".[7]

In interpreting the conduct of a landowner, it is clear that "knowledge of itself is not enough to constitute a licence: there is a distinction between toleration and permission".[8] Consequently, the fact that a landowner knows of the entries on his land and does not take such measures as effectively prevent them does not necessarily mean that he should be treated as having licensed this conduct.[9] The landowner need not erect a wall around his land or bring legal actions against the entrants.[10] However, if a landowner fails to take any steps to prevent persistent intrusions, his conduct will amount to licence.[11] Moreover, even if he takes some "half-hearted" measure, such as "a mere putting up of a notice 'No Trespassers Allowed' or 'Strictly Private', followed, when people often come, by no further steps", he may still be found to have impliedly permitted the entries.[12]

In areas where the public has traditionally enjoyed undisturbed access, it therefore seems that members of the public are implied licensees rather than trespassers. This view was adopted by Pollock who stated that

> where the public enjoyment of . . . lands for sporting or other recreation is notorious, . . . a licence . . . would be implied. Often-- times warnings or requests are addressed to the public to abstain from going on some specified part of open land or private ways, or from doing injurious acts. In such cases there seems to be a general licence to use the land or ways in conformity with the owner's will thus expressed.[13]

On the basis of "custom and usage", American courts have similarly been willing to infer that landowners have consented to members of the public wandering at will over open areas. In delivering the opinion of the Supreme Court in *McKee* v. *Gratz* (1922), Holmes J. stated that "with regard to the large expanses of uninclosed and uncultivated land in many parts . . . of this country . . . it is customary to wander, shoot, and fish at will until the owner sees fit to prohibit it. A licence may be implied from the habits of the country".[14]

NOTES TO CHAPTER 3

1. (1673) Vaugh. 330, 351; 124 E.R. 1098, 1109.
2. See *Cornish* v. *Stubbs* (1870) L.R. 5 C.P. 334; *Minister of Health* v. *Bellotti* [1944] K.B. 298.
3. See *Robert Addie & Sons (Collieries) Ltd* v. *Dumbreck* [1929] A.C. 358.
4. See, for example, *Cooke* v. *Midland Great Western Railway Co.* [1909] A.C. 229; *Lowery* v. *Walker* [1911] A.C. 10.
5. See *Herrington* v. *British Railways Board* [1972] A.C. 877 and now the Occupiers' Liability Act 1984, discussed below, p. 164.
6. *Winfield and Jolowicz on Tort*, 12th ed., London, Sweet and Maxwell, 1984, p. 211.
7. *Phipps* v. *Rochester Corporation* [1955] 1 Q.B. 450, 456 *per* Devlin J.
8. *Ibid.*, p. 455 *per* Devlin J. See also *Edwards* v. *Railway Executive* [1952] A.C. 737, 744 *per* Lord Porter.
9. *Robert Addie & Sons (Collieries) Ltd* v. *Dumbreck* [1929] A.C. 358, 372 *per* Viscount Dunedin.
10. *Edwards* v. *Railway Executive* [1952] A.C. 737, 746 *per* Lord Goddard. See also *Lowery* v. *Walker* [1910] 1 K.B. 173, 200 *per* Kennedy L.J.; *Robert Addie & Sons (Collieries) Ltd* v. *Dumbreck* [1929] A.C. 358, 372 *per* Viscount Dunedin.
11. *Edwards* v. *Railway Executive* [1952] A.C. 737, 744 *per* Lord Porter, adopted in *Phipps* v. *Rochester Corporation* [1955] 1 Q.B. 450, 455 *per* Devlin J.
12. *Robert Addie & Sons (Collieries) Ltd* v. *Dumbreck* [1929] A.C. 358, 372 *per* Lord Dunedin.
13. Frederick Pollock, *The Law of Torts*, London, Stevens, 1887, p. 280. This view is not contradicted by the statement of Devlin J. in *Phipps* v. *Rochester Corporation* [1955] 1 Q.B. 450, 455: "The owner of moorland or downland, for example, in any favoured part of the country may know quite well that people are walking on his land for pleasure, but he cannot be held merely by that fact to licence them to do so." Within the context of the judgment, it is clear that Devlin J. was considering land subject to only occasional trespasses.
14. 260 U.S. 127, 136. See also *Marsh* v. *Colby* 33 Am. Rep. 439 (1878).

Chapter 4

TRESPASS

Because the tort of trespass seeks, at least in principle, to preserve the right of landowners to exclusive possession of their land, it has a very broad ambit. As noted by Lord Morris in *British Railways Board* v. *Herrington* (1972),[1]

> the wicked and the innocent: the burglar, the arrogant invader of another's land, the walker blithely unaware that he is stepping where he has no right to walk, or the wandering child – all may be dubbed as trespassers.

However, the courts have to a significant extent differentiated between "innocent" and "wicked" trespassers in determining the powers of landowners to exclude such entrants as well as in deciding whether (and to what extent) landowners should be able to use the judicial process to achieve this object. Thus, landowners can use force to exclude "bare" trespassers in a much narrower range of situations than in relation to burglars or trespassers entering forcibly.[2] While a substantial range of legal remedies is available against trespassers who cause damage, a bare trespasser may in practice be "dispunishable",[3] since he may not be open to an effective civil action and generally will not have committed a criminal offence.

I. THE POWER OF LANDOWNERS TO EXCLUDE THE PUBLIC

At common law it has generally been accepted that the right to prevent intrusion is "essential to the rights of property" and hence "every proprietor is allowed to use the force that is absolutely necessary to vindicate it[4]." Legislation has curtailed this right to a limited extent but landowners retain very substantial powers to exclude members of the public from their land. They can prevent access by erecting barriers; they may deter entrants by keeping guard dogs; and may themselves expel trespassers in the event of any unlawful entries.

In order to exclude the public, landowners may erect barriers of any height around their land. These walls or fences may be topped with additional safeguards such as broken glass and iron spikes – at least so long as these devices are visible in ordinary daylight[5] – and the fact that the barriers are consequently dangerous to intruders will not make them a nuisance.[6] Moreover, if a trespasser climbing a barrier is injured by some form of obvious deterrent such as spikes, the landowner will not be liable in damages on the basis that the trespasser voluntarily subjected himself to the risk of injury.[7] The only significant restriction on landowners in this context exists not out of any concern for public access to land but in order to prevent interferences with lawful uses of adjoining land. If a wall is likely to injure animals turned out in neighbouring fields or people on an adjacent highway – as may be the case with barbed wire fences[8] or iron fences with spikes jutting out[9] – it is a nuisance which the landowner may be liable to abate as well as be liable for in damages.

The freedom to keep guard dogs which landowners enjoyed at common law[10] has been curtailed by legislation. Under the Guard Dogs Act 1975, it is an offence for any occupier or owner of commercial property not to display a notice warning of the presence of a guard dog.[11] It is also an offence for such an owner or occupier not to have the dog secured or under the control of a handler[12] (in which case, as noted by one commentator, the dog is either useless or redundant).[13] However, the definition of "premises" in the Act excludes agricultural land and dwelling-houses,[14] so farmers and householders are entitled to have guard dogs roaming free.

A trespasser who is injured by a guard dog may seek to recover damages under either the Animals Act 1971 or the Occupiers' Liability Act 1984 but in both cases is unlikely to succeed; such actions may possibly fail even where the owner of the dog has committed an offence under the 1975 Act.[15] Because a guard dog is not classified as belonging to a "dangerous species"[16] – even if it is an alsatian or doberman[17] – its owner may be liable under the Animals Act only if three statutory preconditions for liability for "non-dangerous" animals are satisfied.[18] Even then, the landowner can escape liability if it was reasonable to keep the dog[19] or if the trespasser voluntarily accepted the risk of damage,[20] which would probably be held to be the case where the landowner had erected signs warning of the dog's presence. Under the Occupiers' Liability Act, an occupier owes a duty to a trespasser only if

> (a)　he is aware of the danger or has reasonable grounds to believe that it exists (which, of course, will be the case here);
> (b)　he knows or has reasonable grounds to believe that the trespasser is in the vicinity of the danger concerned or that he may come into the vicinity of the danger; and
> (c)　the risk is one against which, in all the circumstances of the case, he may reasonably be expected to offer the trespasser some protection.[21]

The occupier may discharge this duty "by taking such steps as are reasonable in all the circumstances of the case to give warning of the danger concerned or to discourage persons from incurring the risk".[22] Moreover, as under the Animals Act, an occupier is not liable under the Occupiers' Liability Act "in respect of risks willingly accepted as his" by the trespasser.[23]

Landowners finally have certain powers to remove trespassers who come on to their land. If a trespasser has entered land peaceably, the landowner must request him to leave and allow a reasonable time for compliance before using force to remove him.[24] Even then, the landowner can use only such force as is reasonably necessary[25] and in any event may not be able to use more than "moderate" force which falls short of the intentional or reckless infliction of death or grievous bodily harm.[26] If the trespasser made a forceful entry, the landowner need not request the trespasser to leave;[27] he can simply expel the trespasser, although again using no more force than is necessary. If the trespasser assaults the owner in order to retain his unlawful possession, the owner may meet force with force.[28]

II.　CIVIL LAW

Any member of the public who intentionally enters on to land without lawful justification commits trespass. An entry is intentional if the defendant desired to go on to the land (as opposed, for example, to being carried there against his will).[29] Even the slightest crossing of the boundary is sufficient. There is no requirement that the trespasser have caused any damage, and it is no defence that the trespasser honestly and reasonably believed the entry was lawful, because for example he mistakenly thought he had the consent of the owner or a legal privilege to enter.

In relation to animals the law should arguably be the same.

In other words, "when hounds enter or cross forbidden land the only question is whether such intrusion is voluntary or involuntary . . . Accordingly . . . where the organizers of a hunt take a pack of hounds out . . . and foresee that as a consequence there is a real risk that any of the pack of hounds may enter or cross land on which no permission is given by the landowner, the organisers become liable in trespass."[30] However, in a weakly argued judgment in *League against Cruel Sports Ltd* v. *Scott* (1985),[31] one of a series of remarkable post-war decisions in favour of hunts,[32] Park J. rejected this approach. He held that the owner of animals is liable in trespass only if he either intended the animals' entries or was negligent.[33] According to the judge, intention does not exist simply because a master of hounds knows that there is a real risk that the hounds might enter prohibited land.[34] Nor apparently will intention necessarily be inferred in the extreme situation where "it is virtually impossible, whatever precautions are taken, to prevent hounds from entering . . . [the] land, . . . yet the master knowing that to be the case, nevertheless persists in hunting in its vicinity, with the result that hounds frequently trespass on the land". The court simply may infer that the master's "indifference to the risk of trespass amounted to an intention that hounds should trespass on the land."[35]

In the event of someone, whether man or beast, committing trespass in the countryside, the critical issue is the nature of the defendant's liability. While a trespasser who causes physical damage to land is liable for the loss suffered by the landowner, even a trespasser who inflicts no harm is liable for nominal damages[36] – generally between 50 pence and £2[37] – which in effect symbolize the infringement of the landowner's rights. Contrary to popular belief, the trespasser cannot avoid such an action by "tendering amends", since this defence is restricted by the Limitation Act 1623 to "involuntary" trespasses[38] which do not even include trespasses occurring by mistake.[39] However, to discourage landowners from suing bare trespassers, the courts may refuse to award costs or award them against the landowner, just as they can probably refuse to grant injunctions in this situation. The judicial exercise of these discretions is of critical importance to members of the public seeking access to the countryside in the absence of public rights of way or a right to wander at large.

(A) ACTIONS FOR NOMINAL DAMAGES

The rule that trespass is actionable *per se* is generally justified in one of two ways. It is either said that every wrongful entry necessarily involves damage[40] – at minimum the treading down and bruising of the herbage[41] – but this is a manifest fiction.[42] Alternatively, the rule is justified on the basis that, if landowners could not bring such actions, repeated acts of going over land might be used as evidence of a right to do so.[43] This rationale is more cogent – especially now that members of the public can clearly acquire both rights of passage and rights to ramble at common law. Yet even so it is arguable that, as in Scotland, landowners should not be able to recover damages for trespass unless they have suffered actual loss,[44] with the result that they could seek only declarations and injunctions where they have suffered no damage.

This approach is unlikely to be adopted at common law, because there is such strong authority that trespass is actionable *per se* in all cases.[45] However, first Parliament and, more recently, the courts have attempted to discourage unnecessary trespass actions through the refusal or adverse award of costs. Beginning in 1601,[46] Parliament passed a series of Acts which ultimately provided that in actions for trespass, where the damage was less than 40 shillings, the plaintiff could not recover costs unless "the action was really brought to try a right besides the mere right to recover damages for the trespass or grievance for which the action shall have been brought, or that the trespass or grievance in respect of which the action was brought was wilful and malicious".[47] Since the second half of the nineteenth century,[48] the courts have had a discretion in the granting of costs.[49] As a general rule, they have been awarded to successful plaintiffs,[50] but a plaintiff who recovers nominal damages is not necessarily regarded as a "successful" plaintiff in this context.[51] In an action against a rambler who had committed bare trespass, the landowner would probably be ordered to pay costs "for seeking empty vindication".[52] He consequently would in effect have lost the action, notwithstanding that technically his right would have been upheld.

(B) INJUNCTIONS

The primary issue for the courts in determining whether to grant an injunction is the extent to which the law should help landowners to exclude the public from their land instead of leaving the landowner to do so himself by means of his "self-help" remedies. This issue is most clearly illustrated by the Scottish case, *Winans* v. *Macrae* (1885),[53] in which an American millionaire, who was the tenant of 200,000 acres of shootings, sought to have a cottar interdicted from grazing any animals on his estate. The millionaire sought the interdict because the cottar had a pet lamb which strayed off the public road on to the millionaire's land which was unenclosed. The court refused to grant the interdict even though the cottar had declined to give an undertaking that he would not in future place livestock on the millionaire's land. Lord Young stated:

> If a man wants to protect his lands from being invaded in this way – against children toddling on to the grass at the roadside, or a lamb going on to it, or a cat, or a kitten – . . . he must do so by other means – by fencing the lands, for example – but not by applying to Her Majesty's Judges for interdict.[54]

In England the one situation in which it seems clear that the courts will refuse to grant an injunction against bare trespassers is where the trespass has ceased before trial and there is no intention of renewing it. The leading case in this respect is *Fielden* v. *Cox* (1906)[55] in which the defendants were four boys who had trespassed on a highway and adjacent land while catching moths. The defendants had neither threatened nor intended to infringe any rights of property and desisted from doing so when requested. Buckley J. consequently held that "the writ ought never to have been issued against these four schoolboys . . . after they had given their word of honour, and the action was oppressive to the last degree."[56] He awarded nominal damages of one shilling against the defendants, but refused to grant an injunction and awarded costs against the landowner.

In relation to trespasses which cause no damage but where the trespassers threaten to continue their wrongdoing, the courts have also affirmed their discretion to grant injunctions. First in *Llandudno U.D.C.* v. *Woods* (1899),[57] a local authority failed to obtain an injunction to restrain a clergyman from giving sermons on the foreshore. Cozens-Hardy J. thought the litigation to be

> wholly unnecessary, and one which ought never to have been brought. It is no part of the duty of the council, as lessees from the Crown for an unexpired term of two years, to prevent a harmless use of the shore . . . I cannot refuse to make a declaration . . . But

I decline to go further. I decline to grant an injunction. That is a
formidable legal weapon which ought to be reserved for less trivial
occasions.[58]

Then in *Behrens* v. *Richards* (1905)[59] the court granted a declaration that certain public paths were not public rights of way
but refused to grant an injunction because the plaintiff was not
injured by public use of the ways in question. Buckley J.
considered that

> The existing security of the tenure of land in this country is largely
> maintained by the fact that the owners of the land behave reason-
> ably in the matter of its enjoyment. It would . . . be a disastrous
> thing, not for the public only, but for the landowners also, if this
> Court, at the caprice of the landowner, not because circumstances
> have altered, but merely because he was minded that it should be
> so, entertained every trivial application to restrain persons by
> injunction from using paths which, though not public highways,
> have in fact been used by the permission of the owners for many
> generations, and whose user is no injury to the owner of the land.
> The landowner, if he be wise, will rather erect upon the road or
> path a notice expressive of permission or even of invitation to
> persons who make use of the way so long as they conduct them-
> selves in an orderly and reasonable manner.[60]

These decisions may appear at variance with a line of cases
concerning boundary disputes between adjoining landowners
in which the courts have emphasized that

> the very fact that no harm is done is a reason for rather than
> against the granting of an injunction: for if there is no damage
> done the damage recovered in any action will be nominal and if the
> injunction is refused the result will be no more nor less than a
> licence to continue the tort of trespass in return for a nominal
> payment.[61]

In the most recent boundary dispute *Patel* v. *W.H. Smith
(Eziot) Ltd* (1987),[62] Balcombe L.J. suggested that this approach be adopted in all cases of trespass causing nominal damage, which would destroy the public's *de facto* rights in the
countryside. However, this dicta is not even supported by
decisions in disputes between adjoining landowners.[63] Moreover in *Patel* even Balcombe L.J. acknowledged that "there
may be exceptional circumstances, such as those considered by
the court in *Behrens* v. *Richards*, when the court will not think
it appropriate to grant an injunction."[64] In the same case Neill
L.J. was "prepared to assume that there may be exceptional
cases, of which *Behrens* v. *Richards* is one, where not-

withstanding that a continuing trespass is proved or admitted, the court can properly decline to grant an injunction."[65]

In relation to trespasses which may cause damage and which the trespassers threaten to repeat, the courts will almost always issue injunctions.[66] Thus injunctions have frequently been granted in order to restrain opponents of blood sports from interfering with grouse shooting.[67] However, hunts have again been treated more generously by the courts because judges have focussed on the fact that the master of hounds typically does not threaten to repeat trespasses on the plaintiff's land instead of emphasizing that invasions of the land may be recurrent because of the master's inability to control the hounds while hunting on adjoining ground.[68] Thus in the *League against Cruel Sports* case,[69] where the Devon and Somerset Staghounds did not threaten to invade the *League's* land, Park J. held that injunctions were unnecessary and therefore should not be granted in relation to three parcels of land, each of which had been subject to one negligent trespass. He granted an injunction only in relation to one parcel of land which had been subject to three trespasses, one of which appeared to be intentional. Only in this instance was the League entitled "to ensure that the sport was not carried out on its land."[70]

III. CRIMINAL LAW

As demonstrated in 1982 by the Queen's unwanted nocturnal visitor, Michael Fagan, trespass on land is not in general an offence. At common law trespass is not a crime unless it is accompanied by or tends to create a breach of the peace. Whereas in most common law jurisdictions there are petty trespass Acts which make it an offence to trespass either on any type of land after notice or warning[71] or on cultivated land regardless of notice,[72] England has no legislation of this type. Instead, trespass is an offence only under a miscellany of statutes, each of which operates in narrowly defined situations. Most of these Acts apply to bare trespasses on certain limited classes of land, such as railways,[73] licensed aerodromes,[74] military lands[75] and areas of special protection for wild birds.[76] Other statutes apply to trespassers carrying weapons.[77] A third type of legislation makes it an offence to trespass with certain proscribed ends in view, such as pursuit of game[78] or deer.[79]

Members of the public may in general therefore commit trespass in the countryside without being intimidated by notices warning that "Trespassers will be prosecuted". With some judicial support, the adventurous may even take the "wooden falsehoods"[80] found in these notices as an incitement to trespass. In 1894 an unidentified judge was reported as having "recently intimated from the bench that when he saw a notice of this nature, he always took it as an invitation to walk over the protected land".[81] At the Chester Assizes in 1933, Mac-Kinnon J. remarked amid laughter, "people know the notices cannot be enforced. I trespass about once a week".[82]

Over the past 150 years, however, the general immunity of trespassers from prosecution has frequently been threatened. First, landowners sought to bring trespass within the malicious injuries to property legislation by arguing that malicious damage occurred whenever a trespasser walked across land. Notwithstanding some notable successes, the better view was that a bare trespasser did not commit an offence, and this is clearly the case under the current Criminal Damage Act. More recently, there has been a strong campaign for general criminal trespass legislation. This campaign has not, as yet, been successful, though it has led to certain extensions in the criminal law.

The most striking application of the malicious injuries legislation to a bare trespasser is *Gayford* v. *Chouler* (1898).[83] In that case the defendant had seen notices that there was "no road" and was warned by the landowner that he had no right of passage. Nevertheless, he went on, asserting that he would go across the field in question as often as he liked. The defendant's lack of deference to the landowner was probably his undoing. The Queen's Bench Division upheld the decision of local justices that the trespass was wilful and malicious and had caused actual damage to the value of sixpence. Because "the grass was deep, . . . it was inevitable that if a person walked across it some damage would be done."[84]

The weight of authority clearly indicates, however, that a trespasser did not commit an offence under the malicious injuries legislation simply by walking across land. The more important reason for this view was that walking over grass did not cause "damage" within the meaning of the legislation. As stated by Best C.J. in *Butler* v. *Turley* (1827),[85] an unsuccessful prosecution of a man who walked over a grassed field:

> An Act of Parliament which puts the liberty of the subject in danger, ought to receive a strict construction; and . . . not every walking over another man's land for recreation, if no damage is done, . . . constitutes a case within the meaning of this Act. You

must make out actual, positive damage: imaginary damage will not do. There is imaginary damage in every walking over grass land; and for this you may bring your [civil] action if you are sufficiently ill-natured; but you cannot proceed under this Act of Parliament.

A further reason for holding that a trespasser did not commit malicious damage – ignored by the court in *Gayford* v. *Chouler*[86] – was that the relevant provision probably applied only to damage to the realty itself rather than the products of the realty.[87]

Under the Criminal Damage Act 1971, which repealed the old provisions relating to malicious injuries,[88] bare trespassers appear to be safe from successful prosecution. The Act makes it an offence for any person without lawful excuse to destroy or damage any property belonging to another.[89] As with the earlier legislation, the defendant must have caused "damage" which, following the judgment of Best C.J., should be interpreted as meaning appreciable damage. There is also provision that a person shall not be guilty where he has a "lawful excuse" which includes where "at the time of the act or acts alleged to constitute the offence he believed that the person or persons whom he believed to be entitled to consent to the destruction of or damage to the property in question had so consented, or would have so consented to it if he or they had known of the destruction or damage and its circumstances".[90] Finally, "property" is defined in the Act as excluding "flowers, fruit or foliage of a plant growing wild on any land",[91] which suggests that a rambler who walks across uncultivated land will not interfere with "property" in the relevant sense.

The recent campaign for general trespass legislation has been fuelled by a number of widely publicized trespasses. Most notably, the squatting crisis of the late 1960s and early 1970s led the Law Commission to produce a working paper proposing a new offence of continuing trespass after being warned off the land by a person entitled to occupy it.[92] In the wake of the Fagan episode, private members' Bills were introduced into both the House of Commons and the House of Lords which would have created an offence of trespass on residential premises.[93] In response to the hippy convoy of 1985 and 1986, the Country Landowners' Association and National Farmers' Union, together with many Tory M.P.s, argued for an offence of wilful trespass.[94]

These campaigns have resulted in some extensions of criminal trespass. The Criminal Law Act 1977 made offences of a wide range of activities by squatters. The Public Order Act

1986 created the highly convoluted offence of failing to leave land after being directed to do so by a policeman, who reasonably believes that two or more persons have entered land as trespassers with the common purpose of residing there, and who further believes that they have either damaged the property, threatened, abused or insulted its legitimate inhabitants or brought 12 or more vehicles on to the land.[95] But Parliament has refused to enact general criminal trespass legislation because "simple trespass does not always, or even often, entail actions so hostile to the interest of an occupier or the general public that criminal sanctions are appropriate. Moreover, such trespass does not necessarily demonstrate a clearly discernible infringement of rights, still less conscious wrong-doing".[96] Finally, as stated by Lord Glenarthur for the government in debate on the Public Order Bill 1986, "No one wants to criminalise the activities of ramblers and birdwatchers, and no-one wants to harass genuine gypsies."[97]

NOTES TO CHAPTER 4

1. [1972] A.C. 877, 904.
2. See David Lanham, "Defence of Property in the Criminal Law", [1966] Criminal L.R. 366–74.
3. Sir William Harcourt in debating the Commons Bill 1876, quoted by George H. Whybrow, *The History of Berkhamsted Common*, London, Commons, Open Spaces and Footpaths Preservation Society, n.d., p. 119.
4. *Ilott* v. *Wilkes* (1820) 3 B. & Ald. 304, 317; 106 E.R. 674, 679 *per* Best J.
5. See *Deane* v. *Clayton* (1820) 7 Taunt. 489, 521, 534; 129 E.R. 196, 209, 214; *Ilott* v. *Wilkes* (1820) 3 B. & Ald. 304, 318; 106 E.R. 674, 680; *The Calgarth* [1927] P. 93, 109.
6. *Elgin County Road Trustees* v. *Innes* 1886–7 14 S.C. 48, 52 *per* Lord Inglis.
7. Occupiers' Liability Act 1984, s. 1(6). See also *Ilott* v. *Wilkes* (1820) 3 B. & Ald. 304; 106 E.R. 674; *Quigley* v. *Clough* 53 N.E. 884 (1889).
8. *Elgin County Road Trustees* v. *Innes* 1886–7 14 S.C. 48; *Stewart* v. *Wright* (1893) 9 T.L.R. 480. See also Highways Act 1980, s. 164 which provides a special procedure for the abatement of nuisances to highways caused by barbed wire fences.
9. *Fenna* v. *Clare & Co.* [1895] 1 Q.B. 199; *Gibson* v. *Plumstead Burial Board* (1897) 13 T.L.R. 273, 274 *per* Lopes L.J.; *Morton* v. *Wheeler* (Bar Library Transcript No. 33 of 1956), noted in *Dymond* v. *Pearce* [1972] 1 Q.B. 496, 501.
10. *Sarah* v. *Blackburn* (1830) 4 C. & P. 297, 300; 172 E.R. 712, 714.
11. Guard Dogs Act 1975, s. 1(3).
12. *Ibid.*, s. 1(1), (2), discussed in *Hobson* v. *Gledhill* [1978] 1 W.L.R. 215.
13. J.R. Spencer, "Protection of Property and Protection of Trespassers – which principle prevails?" [1977] C.L.J. 39, 43.
14. Guard Dogs Act 1975, s. 7.

15. See Bernard S. Jackson, "Cave Canem", (1977) 40 M.L.R. 590, 594.
16. Animals Act 1971, s. 6(2).
17. See *Cummings* v. *Granger* [1977] Q.B. 397, 406–7 *per* Ormrod L.J.
18. Animals Act 1971, s. 2(2), discussed above at pp. 112–13. See also *Cummings* v. *Granger* [1977] Q.B. 397, 404 *per* Denning M.R. Compare at 407 *per* Ormrod L.J., 409 *per* Bridge L.J.
19. Animals Act 1971, s. 5(3)(b). See *Cummings* v. *Granger* [1977] Q.B. 397, 405, 408, 410.
20. Animals Act 1971, s. 5(2). See *Cummings* v. *Granger* [1977] Q.B. 397, 405–6, 408, 410.
21. See Occupiers' Liability Act 1984, s. 1(3), discussed by R.A. Buckley, "The Occupiers' Liability Act 1984 – has *Herrington* survived?", [1984] Conv. 413–22; Michael A. Jones "The Occupiers' Liability Act 1984: The Wheels of Law Reform turn slowly", (1984) 47 M.L.R. 713–26.
22. Occupiers' Liability Act 1984, s. 1(5).
23. *Ibid.*, s. 1(6).
24. *Green* v. *Goddard* (1702) 2 Salk. 641; 91 E.R. 540; *Tullay* v. *Reed* (1823) 1 C. & P. 6; 171 E.R. 1078; *Polkinhorn* v. *Wright* (1845) 8 Q.B. 197; 115 E.R. 849.
25. *R.* v. *Hinchcliffe* (1823) 1 Lew. 161, 162; 168 E.R. 998; *R.* v. *Wild* (1837) 2 Lew. 214; 168 E.R. 1132. See also *Ilott* v. *Wilkes* (1820) 3 B. & Ald. 304, 317; 106 E.R. 674, 679 *per* Best J.
26. See Williams, *Textbook of Criminal Law*, pp. 515–16.
27. See the cases cited in note 24 above.
28. *Weaver* v. *Bush* (1798) 8 T.R. 78; 101 E.R. 1276.
29. *Smith* v. *Stone* (1647) Style 65; 82 E.R. 533.
30. Argument of Blom Cooper Q.C. in *League against Cruel Sports Ltd* v. *Scott* [1985] 3 W.L.R. 400, 406–7. See, also, *Sanders* v. *Teape* (1884) 51 L.T. 263, 264 *per* Williams J.
31. [1985] 3 W.L.R. 400. One of Park J.'s two principal authorities was *Calvert* v. *Gosling* (1889) 5 T.L.R. 185 where the court did not address the question of whether entry by hounds was a trespass. Rather it held that an interim injunction should not be granted where the hunt did not threaten to enter the land. Park J.'s other main authority was *Read* v. *Edwards* (1864) 17 C.B.N.S. 245; 144 E.R. 99 which was an action based on *scienter* rather than for trespass to land. Moreover, insofar as *Read* v. *Edwards* may have been relevant, it does not support Park J.'s conclusions. Rather, as noted by Williams, *Liability*, p. 311, the case suggests a much greater liability – that, for example, "a person who knows that his dog is prone to scratch up his neighbour's flower beds should be held liable for any recurrence of the wrong".
32. See *Winder* v. *Ward, The Times*, 27 February 1957; *Chamberlain* v. *Sandeman* [1962] C.L.Y. para. 3083.
33. [1985] 3 W.L.R. 400, 408–9.
34. *Ibid.*, p.408.
35. *Ibid.*, p.409.
36. See, for example, *Ashby* v. *White* (1703) 6 Mod. 45, 54; 87 E.R. 810, 816 *per* Holt C.J.; *Entick* v. *Carrington* (1765) 19 St. Tr. 1029, 1066 *per* Lord Camden C.J.; *Morris* v. *Beardmore* [1981] A.C. 446, 464 *per* Lord Scarman.
37. *Rawson* v. *Peters* (1972) 116 S.J. 884 (50p.); *Boaks* v. *Associated Newspapers Ltd* (1967) 111 S.J. 703 (£1); *Sykes* v. *Midland Bank Executor & Trustee Co.* [1971] 1 Q.B. 113 (£2). Compare *League against*

Cruel Sports Ltd v. *Scott* [1985] 3 W.L.R. 400 where it was "not alleged that any damage was caused by any trespass", yet the damages awarded for the various infringements ranged from £5 to £50.

38. 21 Jac. 1, c. 16, s. 5.
39. See *Basely* v. *Clarkson* (1681) 3 Lev. 37; 83 E.R. 565.
40. See *Ashby* v. *White* (1703) 6 Mod. 45, 54; 87 E.R. 810, 816 *per* Holt C.J.
41. 3 Bl. Comm. 210.
42. See *McGregor on Damages*, 14th ed., London, Sweet & Maxwell, 1980, pp. 221–2.
43. See, for example, *Patrick* v. *Greenway* (1796) 1 Wm. Saund. 346; 85 E.R. 498, 499; *Marzetti* v. *Williams* (1830) 1 B. & Ad. 415, 426; 109 E.R. 842, 846; *Embrey* v. *Owen* (1851) 6 Ex. 353, 368; 155 E.R. 579, 585.
44. See *Hill* v. *Merricks* (1813) Hume 397; *Baird* v. *Thomson* (1825) 3 S. 448; *Graham* v. *Duke of Hamilton* (1868) 6 M. 965; *Lord Advocate* v. *Glengarnock Iron and Steel Co. Ltd* 1909 1 S.L.T. 15.
45. See, for example, *Ashby* v. *White* (1703) 6 Mod. 45, 54; 87 E.R. 810, 816; *Embrey* v. *Owen* (1851) 6 Ex. 353, 368; 155 E.R. 579, 585.
46. 43 Eliz. 1, c. 6, s. 2 (1601).
47. 3 & 4 Vict. c. 24, s. 2 (1840). For a detailed account of this legislation (and the way in which it was subverted by the courts which were eager to award costs to plaintiffs), see Humphrey W. Woolrych, *A Treatise on the Law of Certificates*, London, Clarke, 1826, pp. 137–77.
48. 3 & 4 Vict., c. 24 was repealed only in 1879, but it was superseded by the County Courts Act 1867, s. 5 which provided that a plaintiff recovering less than 10 guineas damages in an action founded in tort was to receive no costs in a Superior Court unless by a special certificate or order. The Supreme Court of Judicature Act 1873, s. 67 extended this provision to all actions commenced or pending in the High Court in which the relief sought could be given in a county court. By the Supreme Court of Judicature Act 1890, s. 5 the Court was given a discretion as to costs, subject to the earlier Judicature Acts.
49. As to the High Court, see now Supreme Court Act 1981, s. 51(1) together with R.S.C., Ord. 62, esp. r. 2(4); as to the county court, see County Court Rules, Ord. 47, r. 1.
50. See *Cooper* v. *Whittingham* (1880) 15 Ch. D. 501.
51. *Anglo-Cyprian Trade Agencies Ltd* v. *Paphos Wine Industries Ltd* [1951] 1 All E.R. 873, 874 *per* Devlin J.
52. *Harrison* v. *Carswell* (1975) 62 D.L.R. (3d) 68, 73 *per* Laskin C.J. As, for example, in *Fielden* v. *Cox* (1906) 22 T.L.R. 411, discussed below at p.167. See also *Harrison* v. *Duke of Rutland* [1893] 1 Q.B. 142, 156 *per* Kay L.J.
53. 1885 12 S.C. 1051.
54. *Ibid.*, p. 1064.
55. (1906) 22 T.L.R. 411.
56. *Ibid.*, p.412.
57. [1899] 2 Ch. 705.
58. *Ibid.*, pp. 709–10.
59. [1905] 2 Ch. 614.
60. *Ibid.*, p.622, endorsed in *Williams-Ellis* v. *Cobb* [1935] 1 K.B. 310, 322 *per* Lord Wright.
61. *Woollerton and Wilson* v. *Costain Ltd* [1970] 1 W.L.R. 411, 413 *per* Stamp J. See also *Charrington* v. *Simmons & Co. Ltd* [1971] 2 All E.R.

588, 591; *John Trenberth Ltd* v. *National Westminster Bank Ltd* (1979) 39 P. & C.R. 104.
62. [1987] 1 W.L.R. 853, 858–9.
63. See *Tollemache and Cobbold Breweries Ltd* v. *Reynolds* (1983) 268 E.G. 52.
64. [1987] 1 W.L.R. 853, 859.
65. *Ibid.*, p.863.
66. See, for example, *Stanford* v. *Hurlstone* (1873) 9 Ch. App. 116.
67. See *The Guardian*, 13 August 1982, p.3. Note also the Canadian cases, *Irving Pulp & Paper Ltd* v. *McBrine* (1973) 9 N.B.R. (2d) 194; *Gilbert* v. *Butler* (1986) 71 N.B.R. (2d) 101.
68. See *Calvert* v. *Gosling* (1889) 5 T.L.R. 185, 186 *per* Lord Coleridge; *League against Cruel Sports Ltd* v. *Scott* [1985] 3 W.L.R. 400.
69. [1985] 3 W.L.R. 400.
70. *Ibid.*, p.412.
71. See, for example, Trespass Act 1980, s. 3(1) (N.Z.); Petty Trespass Act, R.S.M. 1970, c. P50, s. 2 (Manitoba); 87 C.J.S., para. 151.
72. See, for example, Inclosed Lands Protection Act 1901, s. 4(1) (N.S.W.); 87 C.J.S., para. 150.
73. British Transport Commission Act 1949, s. 55.
74. Civil Aviation Act 1982, s. 39.
75. Military Lands Act 1892, ss. 14, 17(2).
76. Wildlife and Countryside Act 1981, s. 3(1)(b).
77. Firearms Act 1968, s. 20; Criminal Law Act 1977, s. 8.
78. Night Poaching Act 1828, s. 1; Game Act 1831, s. 30.
79. Deer Act 1980, s. 1(1).
80. F.W. Maitland, *Justice and Police*, London, Macmillan, 1885, p.13. These notices have never been strictly accurate, although they were of legal significance under the legislation relating to costs discussed above which sought to discourage litigation over trivial trespasses. From 1697 until 1867 a landowner could recover costs, regardless of the extent of damage, if the trespass was "wilful and malicious" (see 8 & 9 Will. 3, c. 11, s. 4, re-enacted in this respect by 3 & 4 Vict., c. 24, s. 2). In a series of cases culminating in *Reynold* v. *Edwards* (1794) 6 T.R. 11; 101 E.R. 408 the courts held that trespass after notice was wilful and malicious. It appears to have been generally accepted that "Notice by a board would be sufficient if it could be proved that the defendant had read it." (Edward Christian, *A Treatise on the Game Laws*, London, Clarke, 1817, p. 94. See also *Sherwin* v. *Swindall* (1843) 12 M. & W. 783, 790; 152 E.R. 1416, 1418 *per* Parke B.) For the use to which these notices were put, see P.B. Munsche, *Gentlemen and Poachers: The English Game Laws 1671-1831*, Cambridge, Cambridge University Press, 1981, p.41.
81. See "Trespassers will be Prosecuted", (1894) 58 J.P. 829.
82. See (1933) 77 S.J. 806; 52 Law Notes 355.
83. [1898] 1 Q.B. 316. For a similar case in relation to a party of ramblers from Sheffield and Barnsley, see (1952) 96 S.J. 670; (1952) 116 J.P. 716; *Manchester Guardian*, 13 October 1952, p.2.
84. [1898] 1 Q.B. 316, 317–18.
85. (1827) 2 C. & P. 585, 589; 172 E.R. 266, 268, approved in *Gardner* v. *Mansbridge* (1887) 19 Q.B.D. 217, 221. See also *Eley* v. *Lytle* (1885) 50 J.P. 308; 2 T.L.R. 44.

86. [1898] 1 Q.B. 316, 317.
87. See *Gardner* v. *Mansbridge* (1887) 19 Q.B.D. 217, discussed below at pp. 203-4.
88. Criminal Damage Act 1971, s. 11(8), sched. 1.
89. *Ibid.*, s. 1(1).
90. *Ibid.*, s. 5(2)(a).
91. *Ibid.*, s. 10(1)(b).
92. Law Commission, *Criminal Law: Offences of Entering and Remaining on Property*, working paper no. 54, 1974, esp. paras 49, 73.
93. See Peter Vincent-Jones, "Private Property and Public Order: The Hippy Convoy and Criminal Trespass", (1986) 13 Journal of Law and Society 343, 358–9.
94. See *Ibid.*, pp. 359–63; "Trespass and the Public Order Act 1986", (1987) 151 Local Government Review 225, 226.
95. Public Order Act 1986, s. 39, discussed in D.G.T. Williams, "Processions, Assemblies and the Freedom of the Individual", [1987] Crim. L.R. 167, 176–7; "Trespass and the Public Order Act 1986", (1987) 151 Local Government Review 225–7.
96. See Home Office, *Trespass on Residential Premises: a Consultation Paper*, 1983, para. 8.
97. H.L. Deb., 13 June 1986.

PART THREE

TAKING FROM THE COUNTRYSIDE

In its broadest legal sense, "land" (whether or not covered with water) denotes not only the soil but also all those things above and below the surface, at least to some finite level in both directions.[1] However, "landowners" are far from being the owners of all these things. Instead, some of the constituent elements of land – most significantly, oil, coal, royal mines of gold and silver, and treasure trove – belong to the Crown under statute or the prerogative. Other things – including fish and shellfish in tidal waters, floating seaweed and sea-coal, and abandoned things – are *res nullius*, which means that they are ownerless but subject to being owned by any member of the public who reduces them into possession. The air (rather than air space) is probably best classified as *res communes*, which means that it is open to public use but as a general rule is not the subject of or susceptible to private ownership.

The most significant rights of taking from the environment enjoyed by members of the public relate to things which are *res nullius* and *res communes*. However, members of the public also have rights in relation to certain things which are owned by landowners or the Crown. Thus, in certain situations they may take minerals on payment of a royalty (that is, a form of compulsory purchase); if they find treasure trove or salvage wreck and then deliver these things to the appropriate authority, they may be entitled to a reward. Furthermore, there are certain things which members of the public have no right to take – namely running water, the flowers, fruit and foliage of certain wild plants, and also certain wild animals – but the taking of which is a tort not a crime. If the taking of these things causes the landowner anything more than trivial damage, he clearly is entitled to recover his loss, obtain costs and so on. However, if the taking involves only trivial damage, it may be treated by the courts as having caused the landowner no loss at all.[2] In that case, the landowner will still be able to recover nominal damages, but, as with bare trespass to land, this may be an empty vindication of the landowner's right as costs may not be awarded or may even be awarded against him.[3]

If the things which are the subject of these different public rights (or *de facto* rights) are considered together, it will be seen that they are all either constituent parts of the environment in its natural condition or abandoned, hidden or lost things. While far from the complete explanation of why members have certain rights in relation to these things, it is significant that there is arguably no-one with an obvious, strong moral claim to them, because they are either the product of no-one's labour or (with the partial exception of wreck) their owner is out of consideration but has no intention to transfer them to any specific person. Consequently, the claim of a member of the public who actually reduces these things into possession may be no smaller and may in fact be greater than that of landowners or the Crown who are the two other main potential claimants.

Rather than taking a rights-based approach as in Part Two, this part examines the law governing the taking by members of the public of nine types of property which make up the environment in its natural condition – soil, minerals, water, air, wild plants, seaweed, wild animals, fish and shellfish – as well as abandoned, hidden and lost things and "wreck" which is a form of lost property governed by special rules. In relation to all but one of these types of property, members of the public have certain rights of taking or taking by members of the public is only tortious rather than criminal. The one exception is soil – the central element within the things owned by landowners – which members of the public have no right to take and the taking of which is not only a tort but a crime.

NOTES TO PART THREE

1. For the upward limits to the rights of landowners, see *Baron Bernstein of Leigh* v. *Skyviews and General Ltd* [1978] Q.B. 479. There is considerable authority that there is no lower limit to the rights of landowners. However, the better view may be that the rights of surface owners extend only so far downwards as they can take "effective possession". See *Boehringer* v. *Montalto* 254 N.Y.S. 276 (1931), discussed in (1932) 30 Michigan L.R. 1126-7; (1937) 37 Columbia L.R. 503, 505. See also George A. Thomp-

son, *Commentaries on the Modern Law of Real Property*, Indianapolis, Bobbs-Merrill, 1964, vol. 1A, pp. 1-2.

2. See *St Helen's Smelting Co.* v. *Tipping* (1865) 11 H.L.C. 642, 654; 11 E.R. 1483, 1488 *per* Lord Wensleydale; *McGregor on Damages*, 14th ed., London, Sweet & Maxwell, 1980, p. 223.

3. See above, p. 166. Unlike trespass to land, there are no reported cases specifically dealing with this issue.

Chapter 1

SOIL

The only context in which there has been any suggestion that members of the public might have a right to take such things as soil and sand has been in relation to the foreshore. Under an Act of 1609, it is

> lawful to and for all persons whatsoever resident and dwelling within . . . Devon and Cornwall, to fetch and take sea-sand at all places under the full sea-mark, where the same is or shall be cast by the sea, for the bettering of their land, and for the increase of corn and tillage, at their wills and pleasures.[1]

Partly on the basis that this statute was declaratory of previous law, Robert Gream Hall argued that there was a public right to take sand from the foreshore.[2] However, in two Irish cases, the courts have characterized the Act of 1609 as enacting rather than declaratory.[3] Consistent with the view that members of the public have only limited rights over the foreshore, it is now clearly established that there is no public right to take sand and gravel from the shore, whether it is owned by the Crown or by a private individual.[4]

In the absence of any right to do so, the taking of soil by members of the public is a trespass. Until 1968 members of the public who took soil were only vulnerable to such an action in tort because soil, as something savouring of realty, was not a subject of larceny at common law, and Parliament had not intervened to bring the taking of soil within the ambit of the criminal law. However, following the proposals made by the Criminal Law Revision Committee in 1966,[5] the taking of soil was to a significant extent brought within the scope of the Theft Act 1968. Section 4(2)(b) of the Act provides that things forming part of land can be stolen by any person who "when he is not in possession of the land . . . appropriates anything forming part of the land by severing it or causing it to be

severed, or [by appropriating it] after it has been severed".
Hence, any member of the public other than a squatter may
now commit theft if he dishonestly appropriates soil or sand.

NOTES TO CHAPTER 1

1. 7 Jac. 1, c. 18.
2. Hall, pp. 206-14. See also H. Gallienne Lemmon, *Public Rights in the Seashore,* London, Pitman, 1934, ch. 7.
3. *Howe* v. *Stawell* (1833) Alc. & Nap. 348, 356; *Macnamara* v. *Higgins* (1854) 4 I.C.L.R. 326, 332.
4. *Hamilton* v. *Attorney-General* (1880) 5 L.R. (Ireland) 555, 573-5 *per* Chatterton V.-C.; *Attorney-General* v. *Emerson* [1891] A.C. 649, 662 *per* Lord Herschell.
5. See Criminal Law Revision Committee, *Eighth Report: Theft and Related Offences,* Cmnd. 2977, 1968, paras 41-4.

Chapter 2

MINERALS

As analyzed by the Hoovers, there have historically been four principal claimants for the title to minerals – "that is, the Overlord, as represented by the King, Prince, Bishop . . .; the Community or the State, as distinguished from the Ruler; the Landowner; and the Mine Operator to which class belongs the Discoverer".[1] In England the common law – to some extent modified by statute – has divided the ownership of minerals between the Crown and landowners. Apart from its prerogative right to "Royal Mines" of gold and silver,[2] the Crown owns petroleum and coal which were nationalized in 1934[3] and 1938[4] respectively. All other minerals are owned at common law by the proprietor of the soil.[5] Such limited rights as members of the public have to take minerals depend on what survives of the custom of "free mining" and on a statutory process under the Mines (Working Facilities and Support) Act 1966.

Both free mining and the rights obtainable under the 1966 Act involve a form of compulsory purchase whereby members of the public may take minerals without the consent of the relevant landowner in return for monetary compensation. The main difference between the two forms of mining is that free mining is restricted to specified minerals in limited areas but is done as of right, whereas the statutory right is applicable to almost all minerals throughout England but depends on judicial approval. Both rights are now rarely exercised and are of primary importance as a means to induce landowners to grant mining leases.

I. FREE MINING

Although its origins are to some extent obscure, free mining was widely established in the thirteenth century across both continental Europe and England where it was practised in the most important mining areas – Cornwall, Devon, the Forest of Dean, Derbyshire, the Mendip Hills and Alston Moor.[6] In the Forest of Dean free mining was restricted to the sons of miners born in the Hundred of St Briavels.[7] Elsewhere free mining was open to all. Every member of the public had the right to stake out a claim of limited size and start mining on payment of a portion of the proceeds of the mine to the Crown or to the local possessor of seignorial rights.

The substantial rights enjoyed by the free miners were, at least initially, in the overlord's interest since they facilitated the working of the mines; the portion of produce claimed by the overlord was in reality part of a bargain made with the miner in lieu of demanding a rent for the mines.[8] From the fourteenth century, however, the rights of the free miners were gradually challenged. Wealthy individual miners used force to turn other miners into their employees. More importantly, the smelters, ore dealers and buyers of minerals used their economic power to bring the miners into a position of increasing dependence.[9] On Alston Moor, free mining had ceased by the seventeenth century.[10] In the Mendip Hills, where free mining was restricted to unenclosed waste land, the parliamentary inclosure of nearly all open land towards the end of the eighteenth century extinguished what remained of the custom.[11] In Cornwall, where tin bounding was similarly restricted to common land, both legal and illegal inclosures contributed to the demise of free mining in the early decades of the nineteenth century.[12] At the same time, new mining methods resulted in abandonment of the custom in Derbyshire.[13]

The Forest of Dean – where the Free Mining Association still boasts about 100 members – is the one area where free mining continues (although the right was recently under threat as a result of the proposed closure of the one maternity hospital in the Hundred which could lead to no births in the area and hence no one satisfying the definition of a free miner).[14] In other areas where free mining was established, the discontinuance of the custom does not mean that members of the public can no longer take advantage of it.

As in relation to the Forest of Dean in 1838,[15] the customary rights of free mining in the High Peak and Wirksworth districts of Derbyshire were given statutory force by enactments of 1851 and 1852.[16] The key provision in both Acts states:

> It is lawful for all the subjects of this realm to search for, sink, and
> dig mines or veins of lead ore, upon, in, or under all manner of

lands, of whose inheritance soever they may be (churches, churchyards, places for public worship, burial grounds, dwelling houses, orchards, gardens, pleasure grounds and highways excepted.)[17]

In return, free miners must pay the Crown the duty called "lot" which, depending on the exact location of the mine, is either one-thirteenth or one-ninth of all the ore raised. Miners must also pay the Crown the duty called "cope" which is either four or six pence for every load of ore measured at the mine.[18]

In Cornwall and Devon (and for that matter the Mendip Hills and Alston Moor) where free mining does not have direct statutory endorsement,[19] rights of free mining, if otherwise lawful, are not extinguished by non-use since customary rights cannot be lost by abandonment or disuse.[20] However, the legality of the custom is uncertain. The problem is that free mining does not satisfy two of the general rules governing customary rights – that a custom must not involve taking a profit from land[21] and that it must be limited to the inhabitants of a particular district.[22] When the first of these issues was raised in *Attorney-General* v. *Mathias* (1858)[23] in relation to free mining in the Forest of Dean, Byles J. suggested that the custom would have been unlawful in the absence of the Dean Forest (Mines) Act 1838. However, on both practical and theoretical grounds the better view is probably that free mining should not be judged in the same terms as other customs. In *Rogers* v. *Brenton* (1847)[24] Denman C.J. considered it a matter of "necessity"[25] to uphold the custom of tin-bounding in Cornwall because

> the mine is parcel of the soil . . . which to discover and bring to the surface may ordinarily require capital, skill, enterprise and combination; which, while in the bowels of the earth, is wholly useless to the owner as well as to the public; and the bringing of which into the market is eminently for the benefit of the public. If, therefore, the owner of the soil cannot or will not do this for himself, he shall not be allowed to lock it up from the public . . .[26]

As recognized by Elton, free mining may also be distinguished from other customs to take profits on the basis that it "does not involve any right of common being vested in a fluctuating body of inhabitants" but rather results in a species of private property in the free miner.[27] Furthermore, the main reason for holding that customs to take profits are unreasonable and therefore invalid – that such customs may lead to the extinguishment of renewable resources[28] – is manifestly inapplicable to non-renewable resources such as minerals.

Even if the custom of free mining is upheld, the situations in which a member of the public might seek to exercise this right are, in fact, few. The lead mines of Derbyshire are largely worked out as are those in the Mendip Hills and on Alston Moor. In Cornwall and Devon, the most important deposits of tin are mixed with lodes of copper and only the former mineral can be claimed by a free miner under the custom. Any copper or other metal, even if extracted by a member of the public who had struck "bounds", would belong to the landowner. Tin bounding is consequently "a practical proposal only for streamworks near stream and river beds which still bear mine waste washed away from the deep mines years ago . . . The capital costs of prospecting and shaft sinking are too great to hazard work on so flimsy a title".[29]

II.   THE MINES (WORKING FACILITIES AND SUPPORT) ACTS

(A).   THE HISTORY OF THE LEGISLATION

The need for legislation giving members of the public a right to acquire mining rights by compulsory purchase was recognized in 1919 by Leslie Scott's Committee on the Acquisition and Valuation of Land. In its third report,[30] the Committee identified 14 causes, primarily related to actions by landowners, which resulted in minerals being lost or their development impeded. The Committee consequently recommended the establishment of a process whereby individuals or companies could obtain orders from a "sanctioning authority" for "the compulsory acquisition or working of minerals . . . wherever the best development of the nation's minerals resources is impeded by the rights of private property".[31]

Parliament partially implemented the Scott Committee report when it passed the Mines (Working Facilities and Support) Act 1923, the first legislation to empower a tribunal to compel a landowner to allow the minerals in his land to be worked without his consent and on terms to which he did not necessarily agree.[32] However, instead of conferring rights on members of the public as such, the Act restricted the right of compulsory purchase to two quite limited classes of people. Persons already having an interest in minerals could apply where the concurrence of two or more persons was needed before the mineral could be worked.[33] Likewise, persons owning adjacent minerals could apply where the minerals were owned in such small parcels that they could not be properly or conveniently worked by themselves.[34]

A right to acquire mining rights compulsorily was first conferred on all members of the public in relation to coal by the Mining Industry Act 1926.[35] That legislation was enacted in response to a suggestion of Sir Lewis Coward who, in an appendix to the Samuel's Royal Commission's report on the coal industry, dwelt on the success of the 1923 Act in facilitating the working of coal, and proposed that "power should be given to any person or company to be at liberty to lodge an application . . . for a right to work minerals".[36]

Although there have been few applications since the late 1920s for the right to acquire minerals compulsorily,[37] Parliament has gradually extended the legislation on the basis that the "mere existence" of the statutory process may induce landowners to allow mining.[38] First, in 1934 Parliament extended the right of compulsory purchase to nine non-ferrous metals.[39] Then in 1974 it again expanded this right so that it now applies to all minerals other than coal and peat cut for purposes other than sale.[40]

(B) APPLICATIONS FOR THE RIGHT TO WORK MINERALS

In order to obtain a right to work minerals, a member of the public must first apply to the Secretary of State who, unless "of opinion that a *prima facie* case is not made out", must refer the matter to the High Court.[41] The High Court must grant the mining rights if satisfied of the two requirements of section 3 of the Mines (Working Facilities and Support) Act 1966, which is a consolidation of all the earlier working facilities legislation. Section 3(1) provides that the court must be "satisfied that the grant is expedient in the national interest". Section 3(2) provides that it must be "shown that it is not reasonably practicable to obtain the right by private arrangement for one of the following reasons":

(a)   the mineral owners are numerous or have conflicting interests;
(b)   the mineral owners cannot be ascertained or found;
(c)   the mineral owners lack the necessary powers of disposition;
(d)   the mineral owners unreasonably refuse to grant mining rights or demand terms which are unreasonable.

The initial problem with section 3 is the determination of

the onus of proof. Probably some burden rests on the applicant, at least in relation to section 3(2).[42] However, as suggested by Lord Mackay in *Archibald Russell Ltd* v. *Nether Pollock Ltd* (1937),[43] "technical ideas of onus" seem
inappropriate in this context: "The whole code looking to the
national interest as overriding the individual reluctance, one
would expect to find in the objector . . . not only a full and
candid statement of the bare fact of his refusal . . . but a clear
statement of the motives which led him so to do."[44]

The main difficulty with section 3 is determining at what
point and to what extent the court should consider the interests
of the mineral owner. These interests can be assessed most
easily in determining whether the mineral owner's refusal to
grant the rights or the terms which he demanded were
"unreasonable" in accordance with section 3(2)(d). But the
better view is that it is necessary for the applicant to bring
himself within only one of the paragraphs of section 3(2).[45]
Consequently, the requirement of paragraph (d) may not
come under consideration. In this event, the mineral owner's
interests may only be considered in determining the "national
interest" under section 3(1). However, at that point the mineral owner's interests are likely to count for little.

When the court grants a right to work minerals, it may do so
on such terms, subject to such conditions and for such period
as it thinks fit.[46] This general discretion is subject to the court
having "regard to all the circumstances of the case, and in
particular to the extent to which the retention of any minerals
is required for the protection of any mines or other works from
flooding, or for any other mining purpose".[47] The court must
also, so far as relevant, have regard to the royalties, covenants
and conditions customary in mining leases in the district.[48] The
key to the compensation to be awarded is that it be assessed
"on the basis of what would be fair and reasonable between a
willing grantor and a willing grantee, having regard to the
conditions subject to which the right . . . is to be granted".[49]

NOTES TO CHAPTER 2

1. Georgius Agricola, *De Re Metallica*, (translated by Herbert Clark & Lou
   Henry Hoover), London, Mining Magazine, 1912, p.82.
2. See *R.* v. *Earl of Northumberland* (1567) 1 Plowd. 310; 75 E.R. 472. The
   Crown's prerogative was cut back first by the statute 1 Wm. & M., c. 30
   (1688) and then by 5 Wm. & M., c. 6 (1693). See *Attorney-General* v.
   Morgan [1891] 1 Ch. 432.

3. Petroleum (Production) Act 1934.
4. Coal Act 1938.
5. *R.* v. *Earl of Northumberland* (1567) 1 Plowd. 310, 336; 75 E.R. 472, 511.
6. See John U. Nef, "Mining and Metallurgy in Medieval Civilization" in M. Postan & E.E. Rich (eds), *The Cambridge Economic History of Europe*, Cambridge, Cambridge University Press, 1952, vol. 2, pp.446-7, 486-9.
7. Chris Fisher, *Custom, Work and Market Capitalism: the Forest of Dean Colliers 1788-1888*, London, Croom Helm, 1981, p.7.
8. Arthur Raistrick & Bernard Jennings, *A History of Lead Mining in the Pennines*, London, Longmans, Green, 1965, p.95.
9. M. Dodd, *Studies in the Development of Market Capitalism*, London, Routledge & Kegan Paul, 1949, p.245.
10. Raistrick & Jennings, *op. cit.*, p. 182.
11. J.W. Gough, *The Mines of Mendip*, Newton Abbot, David & Charles, 1967, p. 109.
12. D.B. Barton, *A History of Tin Mining and Smelting in Cornwall*, Truro, Barton, 1967, p. 68.
13. Raistrick & Jennings, *op. cit.*, p. 174.
14. John Ezard, "Ancient Freedom put in Jeopardy", *The Guardian*, 21 October 1983, p. 26.
15. Dean Forest (Mines) Act 1838. The statutory rights of free miners were preserved by the Coal Nationalization Act 1946, s. 63(2). See also Coal (Registration of Ownership) Act 1937, s. 6(3); Coal Act 1938, s. 43.
16. High Peak Mining Customs and Mineral Courts Act 1851; Derbyshire Mining Customs and Mineral Courts Act 1852.
17. High Peak Mining Customs and Mineral Courts Act 1851, sched. 1, para. 1; Derbyshire Mining Customs and Mineral Courts Act 1852, sched. 1, para. 1.
18. High Peak Mining Customs and Mineral Courts Act 1851, sched. 1, para. 9; Derbyshire Mining Customs and Mineral Courts Act 1852, sched. 1, para. 9.
19. The rights of the free miners of Cornwall and Devon were, however, recognized by various charters. See George Randall Lewis, *The Stannaries: a Study of the English Tin Miner*, Boston, Houghton, Mifflin, 1908, especially appendices B and D.
20. *New Windsor Corporation* v. *Mellor* [1975] Ch. 380, 391 *per* Lord Denning M.R.
21. For this rule, which is derived from *Gateward's Case* (1607) 6 Co. Rep. 59b; 77 E.R. 344, see, for example, *Commissioners of Sewers of the City of London* v. *Glasse* (1872) L.R. 7 Ch. App. 456, 465 *per* James L.J.; *Chilton* v. *London Corporation* (1878) 7 Ch. D. 735, 740 *per* Jessel M.R.
22. See *Fitch* v. *Rawling* (1795) 2 H. Bl. 393, 398; 126 E.R. 614, 616-17 *per* Buller J.; *Gifford* v. *Lord Yarborough* (1828) 5 Bing. 163, 164; 130 E.R. 1023 *per* Best C.J.; *Coventry* v. *Willes* (1863) 12 W.R. 127.
23. 4 K. & J. 579; 70 E.R. 241.
24. 10 Q.B. 26; 116 E.R. 10.
25. 10 Q.B. 26, 61; 116 E.R. 10, 24.
26. 10 Q.B. 26, 50; 116 E.R. 10, 20.
27. Charles I. Elton, *A Treatise on Commons and Waste Lands*, London, Wildy, 1868, p. 115.
28. See *Race* v. *Ward* (1855) 4 El. & Bl. 702, 709; 119 E.R. 259, 262 *per*

Lord Campbell C.J.; *Lord Rivers* v. *Adams* (1878) 3 Ex. D. 361, 364 *per* Kelly C.B.; *Lord Chesterfield* v. *Harris* [1908] 2 Ch. 397, 410 *per* Cozens-Hardy M.R.

29. Robert R. Pennington, *Stannary Law: a History of the Mining Law of Cornwall and Devon*, Newton Abbot, David & Charles, 1973, p. 100.
30. Ministry of Reconstruction, *Third Report of the Acquisition and Valuation of Land Committee on the Acquisition for Public Purposes of Rights and Powers in Connection with Mines and Minerals*, Cmd. 156, 1919.
31. *Ibid.*, pp. 7, 25 (paras 5, 47).
32. *Consett Iron Co.* v. *Clavering Trustees* [1935] 2 K.B. 42, 65-6 *per* Slesser L.J.
33. Mines (Working Facilities and Support) Act 1923, s. 1(1)(a).
34. *Ibid.*, s. 1(1)(b).
35. Mining Industry Act 1926, s. 13.
36. *Report of the Royal Commission on the Coal Industry (1925), Appendices and Index*, London, H.M.S.O., 1926, p. 147.
37. *First Report of the House of Lords and the House of Commons in the present session appointed to consider all Consolidation Bills . . . being a Report upon the Mines (Working Facilities and Support) Bill* (1965-66) H.L. 25-I, H.C. 34-I, p. 1; H.L. Deb., 5th series, vol. 353, col. 382, 15 July 1974.
38. See, for example, H.L. Deb., 4th series, vol. 81, col. 657, 18 April 1934, Earl of Munster.
39. Mines (Working Facilities) Act 1934, s. 1.
40. Mines (Working Facilities and Support) Act 1974, s. 1.
41. Mines (Working Facilities and Support) Act 1966, s. 4(3).
42. *Archibald Russell Ltd* v. *Nether Pollock Ltd* 1938 S.C. 1, 12 *per* Lord Aitchison.
43. *Ibid.*, p. 18 *per* Lord Mackay.
44. *Ibid.*
45. *Ibid.*, p. 18 *per* Lord Mackay; p. 24 *per* Lord Pitman. *Cf.* p. 26 *per* Lord Aitchison.
46. Mines (Working Facilities and Support) Act 1966, s. 5(1).
47. *Ibid.*, s. 5(4).
48. *Ibid.*
49. *Ibid.*, s. 8(2).

Chapter 3

WATER

English law draws a fundamental distinction between running water in rivers or the ocean and water which has been "severed" so that it is contained, for example, in buckets, pipes or even a pond.[1] Probably only riparian landowners are entitled to abstract running water, but it is not regarded as "property". Consequently, if members of the public take only a relatively small quantity of running water they will be liable only to an action in trespass. By way of contrast, water which has been abstracted is regarded as "property" so long as it is reduced into possession. A member of the public who takes such water is open to prosecution for theft as well as an action for damages.

The English rule that running water is not property has its basis in Justinian's *Institutes* in which water was classified as *res communes* along with air, the sea and the seashore.[2] Things falling within this category were regarded not only as open to public use but also as inherently incapable of private ownership (which means that the concept of *res communes* was based on a misconception since "insusceptibility of ownership is a matter of legal prohibition rather than an inherent characteristic of common things'[3]). All members of the public appear to have had a right to abstract running water so long as they did not interfere with the "public use" of the river, which seems to have meant its navigability.[4]

The classification of water as *res communes* was adopted by Bracton[5] and as late as the nineteenth century there is authority which suggests that members of the public may, at least in certain places, have a right to abstract running water. In *R. v. Bristol Dock Co.* (1810)[6] a brewery which had abstracted water from the River Avon brought an action for damages against the dock company for polluting the river. On the clear assumption that there was a public right to abstract water from the river, the court rejected the brewery's action because "the injury, if any, . . . [was] to all the king's subjects".[7] In *R.* v. *Metropolitan Board of Works* (1869)[8] it was admitted that at a certain point on the Thames "there was a common and public right from time immemorial for all persons freely to dip for and take water from the river for their own use without payment, and that there was a right of way or access to the river for that purpose."[9] Hayes J. described this right as being "like the right of the public to a road. All the Queen's subjects have a right to go and take the water, but it so happens that the claimants, because they live near, use it more frequently than others, but others have the same right to use it."[10]

Partly because a right to take water is generally classified as an easement,[11] it is possible that, as admitted in the *Board of Works* case, members of the public may have certain local rights at common law to abstract water: the authority that members of the public cannot acquire local rights of taking by long use is directly concerned only with profits à prendre.[12] However, as a result of disputes between competing landowners (rather than between members of the public and landowners), it has been clearly established since the mid-nineteenth century that members of the public have no general right to abstract running water. Rather, this right is limited to "riparians" who own land through or along which water flows.[13]

As stated by Cave J. in *Ormerod* v. *Todmorden Mill Co.* (1883),[14] the common law's departure from the Roman classification of water as *res communes* was probably a result of "the greater demand for water for manufacturing purposes" which made it "necessary in our law to limit the right to running water". The courts' conferral of exclusive water rights on riparian owners may be explained on the basis that "in an age when administrative organization was rudimentary, the institution of private property was perhaps the most convenient method of making use of, and allocating resources, including water flowing in streams and other bodies of water".[15] Nevertheless, there are strong arguments for a limited public right of abstraction as found in certain Australian and American jurisdictions[16] and also in South Africa where any person, while "lawfully at any place where he has access to a public stream, may take and use water from such stream for the immediate purpose of watering stock or drinking or cooking, or use in a vehicle at that place".[17] Just as Parke B. in *Embrey* v. *Owen* (1851)[18] considered that common sense would be shocked if a riparian owner could not dip a watering pot into a stream in order to water his garden, so it is absurd that a child playing on the seashore is not entitled to take a pail of water or that a rambler walking by a stream is not free to take a drink.

Within this context, the main alleviating feature of English law is that a member of the public who takes running water is generally vulnerable to at most two relatively ineffectual actions in tort. Such taking of water is a trespass against all lower riparian owners. Because the taking of water is not part of the right of passage, a member of the public who takes water also commits trespass by being wrongfully on land or water even if he is on a highway or a river subject to a public right of navigation.[19] These torts are both actionable without proof of actual injury,[20] but in the absence of proof of such injury, a member of the public will be liable to pay only nominal damages.

A member of the public who takes running water does not commit theft because, as in Roman law,[21] such water does not fall within the category of things which can be stolen: the Theft Act 1968 applies only to "property"[22] which does not include running water.[23] Consequently, the taking of running water is an offence only if it contravenes the Water Resources Act 1963. As a general rule, that Act provides that a person who abstracts water from any "inland water" commits an offence unless he has obtained a licence from the relevant water authority.[24] Under section 27(2) of the Act, the only persons who may apply for such a licence are occupiers of land contiguous with the inland water or those who have a right of access to such land. Members of the public are therefore, without more, unable to obtain a licence to make abstractions from inland water unless the existence of either a public right of way leading to the water or a public right of navigation over the water satisfies this provision. However, members of the public will not commit an offence under the 1963 Act if the abstraction is "by machinery or apparatus installed on a vessel, where the water is abstracted for use on that, or any other, vessel".[25] They also will not commit an offence if the abstraction is "of a quantity of water not exceeding one thousand gallons, if it does not form part of a continuous operation, or of a series of operations, whereby in the aggregate more than one thousand gallons of water are abstracted".[26]

NOTES TO CHAPTER 3

1. See especially, *Race* v. *Ward* (1855) 4 El. & Bl. 702, 708, 712; 119 E.R. 259, 261, 263 *per* Lord Campbell C.J.
2. 2 Justinian, *Institutes*, tit. 1, s. 1.
3. A.N. Yiannopoulos, *Louisiana Civil Treatise: Property*, 2nd ed., St Paul, Minn., West, 1980, p. 85.
4. D.39.3.10.2, 43.12.2, 43.20.3.1., in Eugene F. Ware, *Roman Water Law*, St Paul, Minn., West, 1905, ss. 30, 38, 39. See also "Water Rights in Roman Law", (1903) 20 South African L.J. 266, 267; Ludwik A. Teclaff, "What you have always wanted to know about riparian rights, but were afraid to ask", (1972) 12 Natural Resources Journal 30, 31.
5. Bracton, vol. 2, p. 39.
6. 12 East 429; 104 E.R. 167.
7. 12 East 429, 431; 104 E.R. 167, 169 *per* Lord Ellenborough C.J., discussed in *East and West India Docks and Birmingham Junction Railway Co.* v. *Gattke* (1851) 3 M. & G. 155, 168; 42 E.R. 220, 225; *McCarthy* v. *Metropolitan Board of Works* (1872) L.R. 8 C.P. 191, 200.
8. (1869) L.R. 4 Q.B. 358.
9. *Ibid.*, p. 359.
10. *Ibid.*, p. 365.
11. See *Manning* v. *Wasdale* (1836) 5 Ad. & El. 758; 111 E.R. 1353; *Race* v.*Ward* (1855) 4 El. & Bl. 702; 119 E.R. 259; *Alfred F. Beckett Ltd* v. *Lyons* [1967] Ch. 449, 481-2.
12. See especially *Neill* v. *Duke of Devonshire* (1882) 8 App. Cas. 135, 154 *per* Lord Selbourne L.C.
13. See *Lyon* v. *Fishmongers' Co.* (1876) 1 App. Cas. 662, 683 *per* Lord Selbourne.
14. (1883) 11 Q.B.D. 155, 160.
15. Gerald V. La Forest, *Water Law in Canada: the Atlantic Provinces*, Ottowa, Information Canada, 1973, p. 175.
16. Water Act 1928 (Qld) s. 6; Water Act 1958 (Tas.) s. 83(5); Water Act 1958 (Vict.) s. 6(1). Massachussets, Maine, New Hampshire and Florida, in relation to the "great ponds" within these states. See *West Roxbury* v. *Stoddard* 7 Allen 158 (1863); Lincoln Smith, "The Great Pond Ordinance – Collectivism in Northern New England", (1950) 30 Boston U.L.R. 178, 185.
17. Water Act 1956, s. 7(a) (South Africa).
18. 6 Exch. 353, 372; 155 E.R. 579, 587.
19. See above, pp. 55–8.
20. For this issue in relation to the taking of water, see *Embrey* v. *Owen* (1851) 6 Ex. 353, 368-9; 155 E.R. 579, 585-6.
21. Buckland, p. 185, esp. note 9.
22. Theft Act 1968, s. 1(1).
23. See, for example, *Wright* v. *Howard* (1823) 1 Sim. & St. 190, 203; 57 E.R. 76, 82; *Mason* v. *Hill* (1833) 5 B. & Ad. 1, 24; 110 E.R. 692, 701; *Embrey* v. *Owen* (1851) 6 Ex. 353, 369; 155 E.R. 579, 585; *Race* v. *Ward* (1855) 4 El. & Bl. 702, 708-9; 119 E.R. 259, 261; *John White and Sons* v. *J. & M. White* [1906] A.C. 72, 83; *Alfred F. Beckett Ltd* v. *Lyons* [1967] Ch. 449, 481. "Severed" water is a subject of theft. See *Ferens* v. *O'Brien* (1883) 11 Q.B.D. 21.

24. Water Resources Act 1963, s. 23(1).
25. *Ibid.*, s. 24(7).
26. *Ibid.*, s. 24(1). On the meaning of this provision, see *Cargill* v. *Gotts* [1980] 1 W.L.R. 521, 527 *per* H.E. Francis, Q.C.; reversed on this issue [1981] 1 W.L.R. 441, 446 *per* Templeman L.J.

Chapter 4

AIR

In Roman law air was classified as *res communes* which meant that it was regarded as subject to public use but was thought to be incapable of ownership.[1] Unlike running water and for that matter the seashore, which were also classified by the Romans in this way, it is probably still appropriate to regard air as *res communes* since it remains open to public use and, in its ordinary state, is not the subject of property rights. However, air may be the subject of qualified ownership when transformed and, to this extent, it may be thought of as *res nullius*.

When air is "at large" in the atmosphere, it is not the subject of property rights. Regardless of the rights which a landowner has to control the use of the space above his land,[2] his interest in the actual air is no greater than that of any other member of the public.[3] On account of its superabundance, there are no restrictions on the quantity or circumstances in which anyone may take air. As stated by the Earl of Halsbury in *Colls* v. *Home and Colonial Stores Ltd* (1904), air "is the common property of all, or, to speak more accurately, it is the common right of all to enjoy it, but it is the exclusive property of none."[4]

In his *Commentaries* Blackstone recognized that air was something which must "unavoidably remain in common"[5] but twice stated that it could be the subject of qualified property while subject to use or occupation.[6] Blackstone made these statements in the context of discussing easements and then nuisance rather than capture of air by placing it in a container and – although hardly of great practical importance – the better view appears to be that mere capture of air does not result in property rights since the air cannot be enjoyed in that form.[7] However, if air is not only reduced into possession but is also in some way transformed – as where air is compressed or liquified – it is the subject of qualified ownership which lasts so long as it remains in that state.[8]

NOTES TO CHAPTER 4

1. 2 Justinian, *Institutes*, tit. 1, s. 1.
2. See *Baron Bernstein of Leigh* v. *Skyviews and General Ltd* [1978] Q.B. 479.
3. See John Cobb Cooper, "Roman Law and the Maxim *Cujus Est Solum* in International Law", (1952) 1 McGill L.J. 24, 36-8.
4. [1904] A.C. 179, 182-3. See also *Millar* v. *Taylor* (1769) 4 Burr. 2303, 2356, 2357; 98 E.R. 201, 230 *per* Yates J.; *Chasemore* v. *Richards* (1859) 7 H.L.C. 349, 379; 11 E.R. 140, 152 *per* Lord Cranworth; *Lacroix* v. *The Queen* (1954) 4 D.L.R. 470, 476 *per* Fournier J.; *Re the Queen in Right of Manitoba and Air Canada* (1978) 86 D.L.R. (3d) 631.
5. 2 Bl. Comm. 14.
6. *Ibid.*, pp. 14, 395.
7. Compare *Palmer* v. *Railroad Commissioner of California* 138 P. 997, 999 (1914).
8. See *Clark* v. *State* 170 P. 275, 276 (1918).

Chapter 5

WILD PLANTS

At common law all plants – whether wild or cultivated – form part of the relevant landowner's property since they are attached to his land. Members of the public consequently have no right to take uncultivated plants or their fruit, and if they do, they cannot gain title to them. Nevertheless, if members of the public take only mushrooms and the fruit, foliage or flowers of "wild plants", they are not liable to prosecution for theft or criminal damage. If they take only the fruit, foliage or flowers of "unscheduled" species of plant, they also do not commit an offence under conservation legislation unless the plant is in an especially protected area such as a national or local nature reserve. Instead they are open only to an action for trespass or conversion, which is likely to be ineffectual so long as the things taken are of little value. In practice members of the public may therefore be able to take these products of the soil with impunity.

This substantial freedom to take the fruit, foliage and flowers of wild plants exists because these things generally have little monetary value and because their taking is regarded as part of ordinary enjoyment of the countryside. Thus the Conservative Lord Chancellor, Lord Hailsham, argued in debate over the Criminal Damage Bill 1971 that landowners "ought to put up with a certain amount" of taking of wild plants. He suggested that it would be "ridiculous" if the making of daisy chains could be a crime.[1] It would have revolted his social conscience and shocked him to the core had the picking of wild flowers, blackberries and mushrooms come within the Act.[2]

I. WHAT ARE "WILD PLANTS"?

(A)   THE MEANING OF "WILD"

In order to establish that a plant is "growing wild" within the meaning of the Theft Act 1968[3] and the Criminal Damage Act 1971[4] and is a "wild" plant "growing wild" within the Wildlife and Countryside Act 1981,[5] three factors are potentially significant:

(a)   Species: For a plant to come within the scope of the Wildlife and Countryside Act, it must be "of a kind which ordinarily grows in Great Britain in a wild state".[6] There is no such requirement under the Theft and Criminal Damage Acts.

(b)   Manner of propagation: Under all three Acts, the plant must be "growing wild".[7] If a shrub has been planted, it will not satisfy this test.[8]

(c)   Extent of interference by man: Even if a plant is self-sown, it will not be "growing wild" if it has been cultivated by man. But the degree of husbandry required to change the legal status of such a plant is unclear. Possibly something more than pruning or the spreading of fertilizer is necessary, since otherwise it would "be criminal to pick blackberries because the owner took care of bramble bushes in clipping the hedge".[9]

(B) THE MEANING OF "PLANT"

In both the Theft and Criminal Damage Acts "plant" is defined as including "any shrub or tree".[10] The Wildlife and Countryside Act contains no such definition and the Act consequently fails to make clear whether it means "plant" in its technical sense of a member of the vegetable kingdom or in its popular, more restricted sense in which it denotes the smaller, especially herbaceous, plants to the exclusion of trees and shrubs. By reference to the general principle that criminal offences should be read restrictively, it may be argued that "plants" in the Wildlife and Countryside Act should be interpreted in its narrow, popular sense. The absence of an expansive definition section from the Act may also be taken as evidence that "plants" should be interpreted in this way. Yet the presence of the definition section in the Theft and Criminal Damage Acts can be explained on the basis that in both the old larceny and malicious injuries to property legislation separate provisions had governed plants and roots on the one hand and trees, saplings, shrubs and underwood on the other.[11] An expansive definition of "plants" was therefore necessary in the Theft and Criminal Damage Acts if trees and shrubs were to be included within this term, whereas, in the absence of such previous legislation, an expansive definition may not have been essential in the Wildlife and Countryside Act. As a matter of public policy there appears to be no reason why a person who uproots an oak should be in a better position than one who uproots a daisy. On this basis, the legislation should be interpreted as covering all wild members of the vegetable kingdom regardless of size.

II. THE TAKING OF WILD PLANTS

(A) TRESPASS AND CONVERSION

The taking of uncultivated plants from any land is a trespass to that land because it involves removing part of the realty. It is also conversion because the removed plant can be considered as a chattel to which the landowner had a right of possession.[12] In actions for both conversion and trespass, the taker will be liable for the value of the plants he has removed. In most instances, it is not worth the trouble and possible expense for a landowner to bring such an action.

(B) THEFT

At common law, a member of the public who took wild plants did not commit larceny because plants fell within the general principle that things viewed technically as immovables, that is land and things attached to land, could not be stolen. While the principle that the taking of land was not a crime had been part of Roman law, the inclusion within this rule of things attached to land was an English innovation.[13] In deciding cases involving the transfer and descent of land, English judges had held that trees, growing grain and *fructus industriales* in general were part of the realty. When these same judges came to decide criminal cases involving the felonious taking of such property, they applied the same definition of realty. They consequently held that the unlawful taking of products of the soil was not larceny unless these products had previously been severed from the land.[14] It was a crime only to take growing things which had already been gathered or harvested.

The rule excluding plants from larceny, which apears to have been settled by the late fourteenth century,[15] was inconsistent with the importance of agriculture to medieval English society. Nevertheless, the stealing of growing things was only made an offence more than 200 years later. By an Act of 1601, any person who took corn, grain, fruit or vegetables, or uprooted, cut or damaged any tree was obliged to pay damages or was liable to be whipped.[16] The statute – reflecting the strength of the traditional view that a man cannot steal part of the freehold – did not make the offence a felony;[17] the provision for whipping in default of paying damages was the one material change to the civil law of trespass.

The punishment provided by the Act of 1601 not surprisingly proved to be too small to achieve its object of preventing the stealing of growing things. Later Acts consequently created more substantial penalties for the stealing of certain specified plants. The legislation was piecemeal and thus an Act of 1750 which imposed a penalty on persons stealing or destroying turnips growing in private grounds[18] was extended first to potatoes, cabbages, parsnips, peas and carrots[19] and then to certain other field crops and fruit trees in orchards.[20] Under the Larceny Act 1861, which substantially remained in force until 1968, it was an offence to steal, destroy or damage any tree, sapling, shrub or underwood worth at least a shilling, any cultivated plant regardless of value, and any uncultivated plant growing in such places as orchards, pleasure grounds and nurseries.[21] Members of the public who, however, took uncultivated plants, roots, fruits or vegetables from outside these various types of garden or took trees, saplings, shrubs or underwood worth less than a shilling did not commit an offence.

In its 1966 report on theft, the Criminal Law Revision Committee considered whether the stealing of uncultivated plants should be a crime. The Committee had "no doubt that . . . growing things . . . if cultivated, should be the subject of theft". It was less certain about wild plants, suggesting that "On the one hand a person should not ordinarily be guilty of theft by picking wild flowers and the like. On the other hand it may be right that this should be theft in some cases. Examples are cutting holly at Christmas to sell and perhaps picking sloes which the owner of the land wants to keep in order to make sloe gin."[22] After some hesitation, the Committee recommended that "a person should not be guilty of theft by picking mushrooms or other fungi, or flowers, fruit or foliage, growing

wild unless he does so for reward or for sale or another commercial purpose".[23]

This view was adopted by Parliament in section 4(3) of the
Theft Act 1968, which provides that

> A person who picks mushrooms [or any other fungi] growing wild
> on any land, or who picks flowers, fruit or foliage from a plant
> growing wild on any land, does not . . . steal what he picks, unless
> he does it for reward or for sale or other commercial purpose.

The burden is on the prosecution to establish commercial purpose, which is difficult except where a known market trader is
caught in the act of amassing a large quantity of flowers, fruit
or foliage.[24] However, a person who uproots a wild plant is
guilty of theft because the plant falls within the Act's definition
of "property",[25] and the provision protecting the taker of the
flowers, fruit or foliage of the plant does not extend to protecting the taker of the plant itself.[26]

(C) CRIMINAL DAMAGE

Apart from arson, the offence of criminal damage to property
(formerly known as "malicious damage") is a creature of
statute. By a piecemeal process, analogous to the legislative
expansion of larceny, statutes enacted primarily in the eighteenth century made it an offence to injure maliciously a considerable range of property.[27] These Acts were consolidated
first in 1827 and then again in 1861. Like the Larceny Act 1861,
both of these consolidation Acts included provisions specifically directed against malicious injury to trees, saplings, shrubs
and underwood worth more than a shilling,[28] cultivated
plants,[29] and uncultivated plants growing in such places as
gardens and orchards.[30] Neither of these Acts dealt specifically
with either trees worth less than a shilling or uncultivated
plants growing outside such places as gardens. However, both
Acts contained general provisions applicable to persons who
wilfully or maliciously damaged "any real or personal property
whatsoever . . . for which no punishment is hereinbefore provided".[31]

The scope of these general provisions was first considered in
Charter v. *Greame* (1849),[32] in which it was held that the
general provision of the 1827 Act – section 24 – did not apply
where injury to trees had resulted in a shilling or more of
damage. Denman C.J. stated:

The statute containing specific enactments and penalties for malicious injuries to the trees, where the damage is to the extent of 1s. or upwards, we are strongly inclined to thing that the 24th section of the statute was not intended to apply to trees at all; and that if the injury be less in amount than 1s., it is too inconsiderable to be made the subject of prosecution. But in any view of the case, . . . the 24th section can only be applicable in case the damage is less than 1s.[33]

Possibly on account of this decision Parliament added a proviso to section 52, the general provision in the Malicious Injuries to Property Act 1861. Under this proviso, which was section 53, the general provision was extended to "any person who shall wilfully or maliciously commit any injury to any tree, sapling, shrub or underwood for which no punishment" had otherwise been provided. Thus, it clearly became an offence to injure trees maliciously, even if the damage was less than a shilling, and in *Hamilton* v. *Bone* (1888),[34] the defendant was convicted under section 52 of the 1861 Act for having knocked blossom worth 11 pence off a horse-chestnut tree. Field J. referred to *Laws* v. *Eltringham* (1882)[35] – in which it had been held that boys playing football while trespassing had not committed malicious injury to the grass – and stated that he

hoped that that case would not be understood to extend to the length that anybody might commit a trifling act of damage with impunity merely because it was trifling. It would be absurd to bring an action for a trifle like this in the County Court [for trespass], and the result of whittling down the effect of section 52 [the general provision] would therefore be to leave a large number of acts of trifling damage remediless.[36]

This approach was contrary to that adopted in the previous year in *Gardner* v. *Mansbridge* (1887).[37] In the *Gardner* case the court held that the taking of wild mushrooms did not come within section 52.[38] The judges reached this decision partly by reference to the proviso in relation to trees, saplings, shrubs and underwood which they felt tended "to shew that the legislature did not consider the damage to things growing upon the realty was damage to the realty itself."[39] The judges also argued that the sections in the malicious injuries legislation protecting specific types of growing things would have been unnecessary if "real property" in section 52 included products of the realty. They considered it "impossible" that the legislature could have "intended that for simply gathering mushrooms growing wild in a field and uncultivated, a person might be liable to two months' hard labour, whereas for maliciously destroying cultivated roots or plants used for the food of man, he was only to be liable to one month".[40] Damage to wild plants and roots growing outside such places as gardens was therefore not an offence under the Act.

Following the abolition of larceny by the Theft Act 1968, the Law Commission examined the operation of the Malicious Injuries to Property Act and recommended the enactment of new criminal damage legislation. The Law Commission followed the Criminal Law Revision Committee in proposing that a person who took mushrooms or the fruit, foliage or flowers of uncultivated plants should not commit the new offence of criminal damage.[41] This proposal was adopted by Parliament in the Criminal Damage Act 1971 which provides that for the purposes of the Act "property" does not include any fungus or the flowers, fruit or foliage of any plant growing wild on land.[42]

The main difference, in the present context, between the Theft and Criminal Damage Acts is that under the latter Act there is no test of commercial purpose. Hence the taking of wild fungi and the flowers, fruit or foliage of wild plants is not criminal damage even if done for reward. The main difference between the Criminal Damage Act and the earlier malicious injuries to property legislation is that under the 1971 Act it is now an offence to damage an uncultivated plant itself (rather than simply its flowers, fruit or foliage) regardless of where the plant is growing. A member of the public who without lawful excuse intentionally or recklessly digs up a wild plant consequently commits criminal damage.

(D)   CONSERVATION LEGISLATION

The first measures aimed at conserving wild plants sought to prevent the despoliation of plants in places to which members of the public had a right of access such as roadside wastes. Although George Shaw-Lefevre was unsuccessful in introducing two Bills into the House of Commons in the late 1880s which would have protected wild plants in these "public places",[43] over the next 50 years most county and borough councils made byelaws to this effect under their general power to make byelaws under the Municipal Corporations Act 1882 and the Local Government Act 1888.[44] Then, in the National Parks and Access to the Countryside Act 1949 and the Conservation of Wild Creatures and Wild Plants Act 1975 (which was superseded by the Wildlife and Countryside Act 1981), Parliament finally enacted a series of provisions protecting all wild plants wherever located, as well as conferring special protection on endangered species and habitats of particular scientific significance.

(1) General protection

Under the Wildlife and Countryside Act all wild plants are protected from being intentionally uprooted,[45] that is being dug up or otherwise removed from the land on which they were growing.[46] The clear intention of Parliament was that, as under the Theft and Criminal Damage Acts, it should not be an offence for members of the public simply to pick the flowers or fruit of common species as part of what might be termed "ordinary countryside recreation".[47] The problem with the Wildlife and Countryside Act is that the picking of mushrooms, which is part of such recreation, almost always involves the uprooting of the plant.[48] Consequently, it is now an offence – punishable by a fine not exceeding £500[49] – for any member of the public to pick wild mushrooms without the consent of the relevant landowner.

(2) Species protection

The Wildlife and Countryside Act gives special protection to certain scheduled plants which, to be categorized in this way, must be either in danger of extinction or likely to become so endangered unless conservation measures are taken.[50] Instead of making the uprooting of these plants the subject of a heavier penalty than is the case with ordinary plants, the Act protects scheduled plants not only from being uprooted but also from being destroyed or picked.[51] As defined in the Act, "pick" means to "gather or pluck any part of the plant without uprooting it".[52]

(3) Habitat protection

Under the National Parks and Access to the Countryside Act 1949 and the Wildlife and Countryside Act 1981, the Nature Conservancy Council (NCC) and local authorities are authorized to make byelaws in relation to land which they respectively have declared to be national nature reserves[53] and local nature reserves.[54] The NCC and the local authorities have a general power to make byelaws for the protection of these reserves[55] but they are also specifically empowered to make byelaws prohibiting or restricting "the taking of, or intereference with, vegetation of any description in a nature reserve".[56]

NOTES TO CHAPTER 5

1. H.L. Deb., 5th series, vol. 316, cols 266-7, 15 March 1971.
2. *Ibid.*, col. 1268, 30 March 1971.
3. Theft Act 1968, s. 4(3).
4. Criminal Damage Act 1971, s. 10(1)(b).
5. Wildlife and Countryside Act 1981, s. 27(1).
6. *Ibid.*
7. Theft Act 1968, s. 4(3); Criminal Damage Act 1971, s. 10(1)(b); Wildlife and Countryside Act 1981, s. 27(1).
8. Glanville Williams, *Textbook of Criminal Law*, 2nd ed., Stevens, London, 1983, p. 906.
9. (1884) 19 L.J. 551.
10. Theft Act 1968, s. 4(3); Criminal Damage Act 1971, s. 10(1).
11. Larceny Act 1861, ss. 32, 33 (trees); ss. 36, 37 (plants); Malicious Injuries to Property Act 1861, ss. 21, 22 (trees); ss. 23, 24 (plants).
12. *Mills* v. *Brooker* [1919] 1 K.B. 555, 558.
13. Jerome Hall, *Theft, Law and Society*, 2nd ed., Bobbs-Merrill, Indianapolis, 1952, pp. 87-8.
14. See *Halsbury's Laws of England*, 2nd ed., vol. 9, p. 508; *R.* v. *Foley* (1889) 17 Cox C.C. 142.
15. See *Emmerson, Executor of Fisher* v. *Annison* (1384) 1 Mod. 89; 86 E.R. 755; James Fitzjames Stephen, *A History of the Criminal Law of England*, Macmillan, London, 1888, vol. 3, p. 136; Hall, *op. cit.*, pp. 83-4.
16. 43 E. 1, c. 7, s. 1.
17. Hall, *op. cit.*, p. 90.
18. 23 G. 2, c. 26, ss. 13, 14.
19. 13 G. 3, c. 32 (1773).
20. 42 G. 3, c. 67 (1802).
21. Larceny Act 1861, ss. 32, 33, 36, 37.
22. Criminal Law Revision Committee, *Eighth Report: Theft and Related Offences*, Cmnd. 2977. 1966. pp. 22-3.
23. *Ibid.*, p. 23.
24. Edward Griew, *The Theft Acts 1968 and 1978*, 3rd ed., Sweet & Maxwell, London, 1978, p. 11.
25. Theft Act 1968, s. 4(1).
26. *Ibid.*, s. 4(3).
27. See Stephen, *op. cit.*, pp. 188-91.
28. Malicious Injuries to Property Act 1827, s. 20; Malicious Injuries to Property Act 1861, s. 22.
29. Malicious Injuries to Property Act 1827, s. 22; Malicious Injuries to Property Act 1861, s. 24.
30. Malicious Injuries to Property Act 1827, s. 21; Malicious Injuries to Property Act 1861, s. 23.
31. Malicious Injuries to Property Act 1827, s. 24; Malicious Injuries to Property Act 1861, s. 52.
32. (1849) 13 J.P. 232.
33. *Ibid.*, p. 235.
34. (1888) 4 T.L.R. 450.
35. (1882) 8 Q.B.D. 283.
36. (1888) 4 T.L.R. 450.
37. (1887) 19 Q.B.D. 217.

38. The Court had indicated that it might adopt this approach in *R. v. Justices of Hexham* (1887) 3 T.L.R. 465.

39. (1887) 19 Q.B.D. 217, 220.

40. *Ibid.*, p. 222.

41. Law Commission, *Criminal Law: Report on Offences of Damage to Property*, (H.C. 91, 1970-71), para. 35.

42. Criminal Damage Act 1971, s. 10(1)(b).

43. Footpaths and Roadside Wastes Bill 1888, clause 9. This Bill was reintroduced in 1889 but was not printed.

44. Municipal Corporations Act 1882, s. 23; Local Government Act 1888, s. 16. See John Sheail, *Nature in Trust: the History of Nature Conservation in Britain*, Blackie, Glasgow, 1976, pp. 39-40.

45. See Wildlife and Countryside Act 1981, s. 13(1)(b).

46. *Ibid.*, s. 27(1).

47. See, for example, the views of Lord Hailsham, quoted above, p. 198.

48. *Cf.* Conservation of Wild Creatures and Wild Plants Act 1975, s. 15(2) which excluded mushrooms, among with all fungi and algae, from the scope of the Act.

49. Wildlife and Countryside Act 1981, s. 21(3). Under section 21(6)(a), the court is also required to order forfeiture of the mushrooms.

50. Wildlife and Countryside Act 1981, s. 22(3)(a).

51. *Ibid.*, s. 13(1)(a).

52. *Ibid.*, s. 27(1).

53. National Parks and Access to the Countryside Act 1949, s. 20; Wildlife and Countryside Act 1981, s. 35.

54. National Parks and Access to the Countryside Act 1949, ss. 20, 21.

55. *Ibid.*, ss. 20(1), 21(4); Wildlife and Countryside Act 1981, s. 35(3).

56. National Parks and Access to the Countryside Act 1949, ss. 20(2)(b), 21(4); Wildlife and Countryside Act 1981, s. 35(4).

Chapter 6

SEAWEED AND SEA COAL

In 1966 a dispute over the right of members of the public to take sea coal from the foreshore in County Durham – where about 100,000 tons of coal are washed ashore each year – resulted in the Court of Appeal's decision in *Alfred F. Beckett Ltd* v. *Lyons*.[1] Probably because the mineral and vegetable products of the sea found on the foreshore elsewhere in England are of relatively little value, there has been almost no other reported English litigation over the rights of members of the public to take these things. English decisions consequently provide only limited guidance as to the law in this area. However, especially in Ireland, as well as in Canada and the United States, there was frequent litigation during the nineteenth century over seaweed which was an important form of fertilizer and which remains significant in this respect in Ireland[2] where it is sometimes also eaten – particularly in the more remote areas.

Together with *Beckett* v. *Lyons*, the cases from these other jurisdictions suggest that property rights in mineral and vegetable products of the sea depend on whether these things are floating in the water or are stranded on land. If they are floating, they are probably open to taking by members of the public. If they are stranded, there is no public right to enter on the dry foreshore to take them. However, a member of the public who takes these things from the dry foreshore does not necessarily commit either wrongful interference to goods or theft.

I. FLOATING v. FIXED PRODUCTS OF THE SEA

As suggested by the Massachusetts case *Anthony* v. *Gifford* (1861)[3] and the judgment of Winn L.J. in *Beckett* v. *Lyons*,[4] property rights in products of the sea depend on whether these things have become part of land. Both cases indicate that products of the sea are only to be regarded as part of land if they are "fixed" to the soil, which will be the case if they are stranded, even if some water remains round them.[5] However, they are not to be regarded as part of land simply because "they occasionally, by the motion of the waves or the rise of tide, touch or rest on the beach".[6]

II.   FLOATING PRODUCTS OF THE SEA

In *Blundell* v. *Catterall* (1821)[7] the majority of the Court of King's Bench held that the public's rights over the foreshore were limited to navigation and fishing and things incidental thereto. On the basis of this authority, it can be argued that members of the public have no right to take floating products of the sea, in which case these products would presumably be owned by the owner of the subjacent soil, that is *prima facie* the Crown. However, as noted by Fitzgerald J. in the Irish case, *Brew* v. *Haren* (1877), "there is no instance to be found in the books . . . of any assertion by the Crown to the property in . . . seaweed [or, for that matter, other floating products of the sea] . . . before it had touched the sea shore".[8] By way of contrast, following the arguments of counsel in the first reported Irish case concerning seaweed, *Howe* v. *Stawell* (1833),[9] the courts in a series of cases in Ireland,[10] Canada[11] and the United States[12] have recognized a public right to take floating seaweed which they have considered to be analogous to the public right of fishing. As stated by Seymour C.J. in the Connecticut case, *Mather* v. *Chapman* (1873)[13]:

> We see no reason for making a distinction between the vegetable and animal products of the ocean. Neither, in the state of nature, is the property of any one; the title to both depends on the first occupancy. It is agreed that while afloat both are alike common. . .

Consequently, the views of the majority in *Blundell* v. *Catterall* should probably be distinguished on the basis that the court there was concerned with the public's right to bathe in tidal waters rather than their rights of taking. Just as members of the public *prima facie* have a right to fish in tidal waters,[14] so they should be regarded as *prima facie* having a right to take vegetable and mineral products of the sea floating in the same area.

III. FIXED PRODUCTS OF THE SEA

The law concerning products of the sea which are washed on to
the foreshore is clearly settled only in relation to those things
such as gravel, stones and sand which, when washed ashore,
either "become part of the soil" or are "in the nature of the
soil".[15] As established in *Blewett* v. *Tregonning* (1835),[16] such
things become part of the land and hence the property of the
landowner. Because they become personal property once severed from the land, a member of the public who takes them
may commit wrongful interference to goods.[17] Unless he is a
squatter, a member of the public who takes them may also
commit theft since a person who is not in possession of land
may commit theft by appropriating "anything forming part of
the land by severing it".[18]

In relation to other products of the sea, such as seaweed and
sea coal,[19] it has been settled since *Howe* v. *Stawell* (1833)[20]
that members of the public have no right to enter on the
foreshore to take these things when they are deposited by the
tide. However, this rule simply concerns rights of access to the
foreshore. The law concerning property rights in seaweed and
sea coal cast ashore is unclear, and so consequently is the law
governing members of the public who take these things.

In the first American case concerning rights in seaweed,
Emans v. *Turnbull* (1807),[21] Kent C.J. developed what has
been the main argument in favour of the owner of the foreshore owning things such as seaweed washed on to his land.[22]
The judge relied on what he recognized was a "liberal" construction of the doctrine of accretion to land, stating that:

> Seaweed . . . thrown up by the sea may be considered as one of
> those marine increases arising by slow degrees; and according to
> the rule of common law it belongs to the owner of the soil.[23]

The difficulty with this view is that there is strong English
authority that the principle of accretion is limited to changes in
the boundaries of land and water rather than additions to the
top of land.[24] Moreover, Kent C.J.'s main rationale for vesting
the seaweed in the landowner does not hold. He stated that
giving the landowner this property right "forms a reasonable
compensation to him for the gradual encroachment of the sea,
to which other parts of his estate may be exposed".[25] However, quite apart from vegetable and mineral products of the
sea, such compensation is already made as part of the traditional doctrine of accretion which balances the loss of land by
erosion by providing that the landowner's title extends to any

gradual additions to his land from what was previously water.[26]

An alternative basis on which it has been argued that the owner of the foreshore owns seaweed cast on to his land rests on the clearly established rule that a party who claims ownership of the soil of the foreshore may rely on evidence that he and his predecessors regularly, and to the exclusion of others, collected seaweed.[27] As stated by Morris C.J. in the Irish case *Brew* v. *Haren* (1877)[28]:

> It would appear to be a contradiction in terms, while exclusive user of the foreshore by the taking of the seaweed is acceptable as proof of the ownership of the soil, that, when the ownership of the soil is established, the owner of the foreshore has not the property in the seaweed.

However, this argument also does not necessarily hold. Just as a landowner has an exclusive right to take – but no absolute property in – wild animals on his land,[29] so it may be that the owner of the foreshore simply has the exclusive right to take certain products of the sea rather than property in them.[30]

The judicial authority which supports the view that the owner of the foreshore does not own products of the sea cast on to his land rests principally on the Irish case, *R.* v. *Clinton* (1869).[31] There the court, by a majority of six to one, held that seaweed, which had been cast on to the foreshore, was not the subject of larceny. Unfortunately, the majority judgment of Whiteside C.J. is not particularly lucid. He made a number of remarks consistent with the notion of landowners having some form of qualified property in seaweed insufficient to form the basis of larceny. For example, he twice stated "although one may have a property in certain things, it does not follow that felony can be committed in respect of them".[32] He also appears to have drawn an analogy between seaweed and wild animals,[33] suggesting thereby that a landowner might have the exclusive right to take seaweed but no absolute property in it. At no point did the judge expressly state that the owner of the foreshore had no rights in seaweed cast on to his land, yet this was how *Clinton* was interpreted by one member of the Court of Exchequer[34] and two of the six members of the Exchequer Chamber[35] in *Brew* v. *Haren*.

The most recent discussion of rights in products of the sea cast on to the foreshore took place in *Beckett* v. *Lyons*.[36] While Harman L.J. expressly chose not to resolve the property issue,[37] Winn L.J. made inconsistent remarks about the question of property. He intitially suggested that a landowner might have property in sea coal cast ashore – when stating that "the coal which is found in, on and off the beaches . . . is probably not the property of any person until any particular piece of it has been reduced into possession *or has at least become fixed on the shore.*"[38] However, he then distinguished *Blewett* v. *Tregonning* from the case before him,[39] which would make sense only if property rights in sea coal were different from property rights in sand, stones and gravel washed ashore. Finally, he stated that he had earlier suggested that sea coal "belongs to no one until it has been physically reduced into possession of some person[40]," which appears to mean that taking of the coal is necessary to obtain rights in it and that merely owning the relevant strip of foreshore is insufficient.

Other approaches to this problem are possible. It could be argued that it is illogical to draw a distinction between rights in gravel on the one hand and sea coal on the other (although the distinction between land and chattels is firmly established, as is the distinction in the law of finding between things under or attached to land and things simply on land). Alternatively, the rules developed in the finding cases could, themselves, be applied in relation to such things as seaweed. The general issue in the finding cases is the obtaining of first possession of the chattel which may be regarded as analogous to occupancy of products of the sea. Just as a landowner may have possession of a lost chattel without physically reducing it into possession, so it may be that a landowner with the relevant intention to control things on his land may be able thereby to gain ownership of products of the sea cast on to his land.

Because the courts are very reluctant to allow a person wrongly on land to profit from this wrong,[41] the one likely result in this area is that a member of the public trespassing on the foreshore will not be entitled to take products of the sea such as seaweed. Either the courts will hold that these products belong to the landowner in which case their taking will be both a tort and a crime. Or the courts will hold that these products are not property before they are taken and hence their taking is not theft; but that just as the trespassing taker of a wild animal turns the landowner's qualified into absolute property, so the trespassing taker of products of the sea at the instant of taking vests property in the landowner and hence in carrying the things away may be guilty of conversion.

The law in relation to a member of the public lawfully on the foreshore, as in excercise of a public right of way, is equally unpredictable. If the products of the sea are the property of the relevant landowner, then, as above, it will be both a tort and a crime for a member of the public to take such products of the sea as seaweed. However, if these products are *res nullius*, a member of the public on a public right of way could take seaweed or sea coal lawfully,[42] just as one may take lost or abandoned chattels which are found while exercising a public right of passage.

NOTES TO CHAPTER 6

1. [1967] Ch. 449.
2. See *Mahoney* v. *Neenan* [1966] I.R. 559.
3. 2 Allen 549, 550 (1861).
4. [1967] Ch. 449, 479.
5. *R.* v. *Two Casks of Tallow* (1837) 3 Hag. Adm. 294, 298; 166 E. R. 414, 416 *per* Sir John Nicholls, applied in this context by Winn L.J. in *Alfred F. Beckett Ltd* v. *Lyons* [1967] Ch. 449, 479; *Anthony* v. *Gifford* 2 Allen 549, 550 (1861). See also *R.* v. *Forty-nine Casks of Brandy* (1836) 3 Hag. Adm. 257, 292-3; 166 E.R. 401, 414 *per* Sir John Nicholls.
6. *Anthony* v. *Gifford* 2 Allen 549, 550 (1861).
7. 5 B. & Ald. 268; 106 E.R. 1190.
8. I.R. 11 C.L. 198, 205.
9. Alc. & Nap. 348, 349.
10. *R.* v. *Clinton* (1869) I.R. 4 C.L. 6, 16 *per* Whiteside C.J.; *Brew* v. *Haren* (1877) I.R. 11 C.L. 198, 202 *per* Lawson J. (with whom Keogh J. at 213 agreed); 208 *per* Fitzgerald J. Compare at 214 *per* Morris C.J.
11. *R.* v. *Lord* (1864) 1 P.E.I. 245, 251 *per* Peters J.; *Young* v. *McIsaac* (1897) 8 E.L.R. 245, 249 *per* Sullivan C.J.; 254 *per* Hodgson J.
12. *Anthony* v. *Gifford* 2 Allen 549 (1861); *Mather* v. *Chapman* 16 Am. Rep. 46, 48, 49, 50 (1873) *per* Seymour C.J.
13. 16 Am. Rep. 46, 50. See also *Brew* v. *Haren* (1877) I.R. 11 C.L. 198, 202 *per* Lawson J.; *Young* v. *McIsaac* (1897) 8 E.L.R. 245, 254 *per* Hodgson J.
14. See below, p. 246.
15. *Blewett* v. *Tregonning* (1835) 3 Ad. & El. 554, 574; 111 E.R. 524, 532 *per* Littledale J. and Patteson J.
16. 3 Ad. & El. 554, 111 E.R. 524.
17. See John G. Fleming, *Law of Torts*, 6th ed., Sydney, Law Book Co., 1983, p. 49, note 27; *Prosser and Keeton on the Law of Torts*, 5th ed., St Paul, Minn., West, 1984, pp. 90-1.
18. Theft Act 1968, s. 4(2)(b).
19. The distinction between sea coal on the one hand and sand, gravel and stones on the other is drawn in *Alfred F. Beckett Ltd* v. *Lyons* [1967] Ch. 449, 479-80 *per* Winn L.J.
20. (1833) Alc. & Nap. 348. See also *Healy* v. *Thorne* (1870) I.R. 4 C.L. 495, 499 *per* Morris J.; *Mulholland* v. *Killen* (1874) 9 I.R.Eq. 471, 482.
21. 3 Am. Dec. 427.
22. Apart from in later American cases, Kent C.J.'s views have been

adopted in both Ireland and Canada. See *Brew* v. *Haren* (1877) I.R. 11
C.L. 198, 201 *per* Lawson J. (with whom Keogh J. agreed at 213); 214
per Morris C.J.; 216-17 *per* May C.J.; *R.* v. *Lord* (1864) 1 P.E.I. 245,
250-1 *per* Peters J.; *Young* v. *McIsaac* (1897) 8 E.L.R. 245, 248-9 *per*
Sullivan C.J. (with whom Fitzgerald J. at 255 agreed); 254 per *Hodgson*
J.
23. *3 Am. Dec. 427, 430.*
24. *See Southern Centre of Theosophy Inc.* v. *State of South Australia* [1982]
    A.C. 706, 716 *per* Lord Wilberforce.
25. 3 Am. Dec. 427, 431.
26. See 2 Bl. Comm. 26; *Southern Centre of Theosophy Inc.* v. *State of South*
    Australia [1982] A.C. 706, 716 *per* Lord Wilberforce, discussed by Paul
    Jackson, "Alluvio and the Common Law", (1983) 99 L.Q.R. 412-31.
27. Hale, p. 27; *Calmady* v. *Rowe* (1848) 6 C.B. 861; 136 E.R. 1487; *Healy*
    v. *Thorne* (1870) I.R. 4 C.L. 495; *Lord Advocate* v. *Blantyre* (1879) 4
    App. Cas. 770; *Daly* v. *Murray* (1885) 17 L.R. (Ireland) 185.
28. I.R. 11 C.L. 198, 214. See also at 216 *per* May C.J.
29. See below, pp. 224–5.
30. See *R.* v. *Clinton* (1869) I.R. 4 C.L. 6, 15-16 *per* Whiteside C.J.; *Brew* v.
    Haren (1874) I.R. 9 C.L. 29, 42 *per* Fitzgerald B.; 45 *per* Dowse B.
    Compare, however, *Brew* v. *Haren* (1874) I.R. 9 C.L. 29, 43-4 *per* Deasy
    J. On appeal to the Exchequer Chamber (I.R. 11 C.L. 198), none of the
    judges in *Brew* v. *Haren* adopted this analogy.
31. (1869) I.R. 4 C.L. 6.
32. *Ibid.*, pp. 14, 15.
33. *Ibid.*, pp. 15-16 quoting Gabbett.
34. (1874) I.R. 9 C.L. 29, 43 *per* Deasy B.
35. (1877) I.R. 11 C.L. 198, 205 *per* Fitzgerald J.; 210-11 *per* O'Brien J. For
    reasons noted previously the other four judges held that the seaweed was
    property.
36. [1967] Ch. 449.
37. *Ibid.*, p. 473.
38. *Ibid.*, p. 479 (emphasis added).
39. *Ibid.*, p. 480. *Blewett* v. *Tregonning* is discussed above, p. 210.
40. *Ibid.*, p. 481.
41. See below, pp. 220, 279.
42. See *Brew* v. *Haren* (1877) I.R. 11 C.L. 198, 211 *per* O'Brien J.

Chapter 7

WILD ANIMALS

Under Roman Law, wild animals – tagged in Latin, animals *ferae naturae* – were the subject of ownership only while they were effectively held; otherwise they became the property of any member of the public who took them, even if, at the relevant time, he was on land without permission.[1] In English law, this principle of occupancy as the basis of title in wild animals regardless of trespass appears to have been established until the end of the fourteenth century[2] but does not appear to have remained significant for long thereafter.[3] Already in the reign of William I, the importance of wild animals as sources of food and objects of sport had resulted in their lawful taking being restricted in favour of the Crown and the landed gentry; until the early nineteenth century the right to take game remained limited in this way, while since then it has been enjoyed by all landowners.

As part of its prerogative powers, the Crown from Norman times enjoyed two different sorts of rights over wild animals. The more limited of these was its ownership of royal fish and all swans except those on private waters.[4] The more important was its power to declare areas in which specified persons had exclusive hunting rights. In exercise of this power, William I carved out vast districts called "forests" in which only the king and persons acting with his permission had the right to hunt deer and wild boar.[5] Out of generosity as well as political necessity, successive kings granted franchises of similar hunting rights to favoured individuals: "chases" were private forests; "parks" were enclosed areas containing deer; "warrens" involved exclusive rights over animals other than beasts of the forest – most importantly hares, but also rabbits, foxes and probably all those birds which were taken by snares, hounds or hawks.[6]

Until recently, it has generally been argued that the importance of the Crown's prerogative over wild animals declined from the late fourteenth century[7] and that the organization of the royal forests had largely decayed by the time John Manwood wrote his *Treatise and Discourse of the Lawes of the Forrest* (1598).[8] However, documentary evidence available for the New Forest and a more careful reading of Manwood suggest that the forest laws remained effective until the mid-seventeenth century.[9] Until at least the 1690s the Crown continued to grant franchises of park and free warren.[10] But then even this power fell into desuetude. Having had no effect for more than two and a half centuries, the Crown's prerogative to set aside land or water for the breeding, support or taking of wild creatures was abolished in 1971, as were also all franchises of forest, chase, park and free warren. Only the Crown's right to swans and royal fish was preserved.[11]

Apart from the franchises which they received of chase, free warren and park, the landed gentry's rights in wild animals depended on a series of statutes beginning in 1389.[12] These Acts made it an offence to hunt "game" – that is, most importantly, hares, partridges, pheasants and moor fowl[13] – unless certain property qualifications were satisfied. The culmination of this legislation, the Game Act 1671, remained in force for 160 years and, as described by Thomas Lund, even the sale of game was restricted during this period in such a way "as to disclose a vigorous intent to preserve game from contact with a base gullet".[14] While purchase for consumption in itself remained legal, a statutory presumption was established that any unqualified person who possessed game held it for the purpose of resale which was an offence. This presumption "sealed inviolate the gastronomic preserve of the upper classes".[15]

With the repeal of the property qualifications by the Game Act 1831, the lapse and then abolition of most of the Crown's prerogative rights, as well as the development at common law of what is known as "qualified" ownership of wild animals,[16] landowners now generally enjoy an exclusive right to take wild animals on their land. The principle of occupancy survives – but in such attenuated form that it is of only very limited benefit to members of the public. A member of the public who takes a wild animal without the permission of the relevant landowner will generally commit a variety of torts if not crimes.

I. WHAT ARE WILD ANIMALS?

(A)   THE MEANING OF "ANIMAL"

For the purpose of determining property rights, the common law distinguishes what may loosely be termed "animals" from "fish". This distinction depends primarily on genus – thus all birds, insects and reptiles and probably also amphibians are classified as "animals". However, in relation to mammals the distinction also has a geographic basis which means that at least the cetaceans – whales, sturgeon, porpoise and so on – are characterized as fish along with the usual members of this class.

(B)   THE MEANING OF "WILD"

At common law animals are classified as either "tame" or "wild". Whether alive or dead, tame animals – in Latin, animals *mansuetae* or *domitae naturae* – are the subject of absolute property which does not depend on possession and continues even if the animals stray or are lost. Wild animals are also the subject of absolute ownership when dead, but while alive they can be the subject of only qualified ownership. So long as it continues, qualified ownership confers the same rights as absolute ownership, but it is defeasible in certain circumstances.

For the purpose of determining property rights, the distinction between wild and tame animals depends on the extent to which the animals are domesticated rather than their ferocity.[17] Those animals which by habit or training live in association with or in the service of man are generally defined as "tame";[18] the remainder are "wild". This definition appears to be without intrinsic problems but it is unclear whether it is to be applied in relation to particular animals or to sub-species or species of animals. While any form of class test has the advantage of simplicity and generality, it will fail to take into account the fact that there are many species (and even sub-species) of animal, of which only some members live in association with or in the service of man.

Although Roman Law (expressly)[19] and such classical writers as Blackstone (implicitly)[20] adopted a species test for determining property rights, there is little judicial authority as to which test is now law.[21] The only judge to consider the application of a species as against a sub-species rule has been

Boyd J. who, when dissenting in the Irish case, *Brady* v.
Warren (1900),[22] held that "all deer are alike, *ferae naturae*,
and that the mere difference of breed can make no distinction
. . . [T]hat one species of the same genus can be more easily
tamed 'by the art and industry of man' can surely make no
difference in their original nature."[23] In the two most recent
English property cases concerning animals, *Kearry* v. *Pattinson* (1938)[24] and *Hamps* v. *Darby* (1948),[25] the courts implicitly applied a species test in holding the animals in question to
be wild. They consequently failed to consider that the animals
should have been classified as tame under the accepted definition – that the bees in *Kearry* v. *Pattinson* were of considerable
economic importance and so were "in the service of man";
that the pigeons in *Hamps* v. *Darby* were the progeny of birds
bred in captivity for several generations and hence could be
classed as living in association with man.

A more considered line of authority, stemming from the
decision in *Davies* v. *Powell* (1738)[26] has developed in cases
concerning deer. In *Davies* v. *Powell* the litigation concerned
deer which the defendant landlord had taken as distress for
rent owed by the plaintiff tenant. Only goods and chattels may
be seized for rent in arrears and hence animals *ferae naturae*
cannot be the subject of distress. Previous decisions had held
that deer were wild animals but Willes J. decided that various
changes in the circumstances in which deer were kept meant
that the old property classification of deer should no longer
always apply:

> When the nature of things changes, the rules of law must change
> too. When it was holden that deer were not distrainable, it was
> because they were kept principally for pleasure, and not for profit,
> and were not sold and turned into money as they are now. But now
> they are become as much a sort of husbandry as horses cows sheep
> or any other cattle. Whenever they are so and it is universally
> known, it would be ridiculous to say that when they are kept
> merely for profit they are not distrainable as other cattle, though it
> has been holden that they are not so when they were kept only for
> pleasure.[27]

On the facts before him, Willes J. held that the deer, which
were kept for profit, were chattels and so could be distrained.
In two later English cases, *Morgan* v. *Earl of Abergavenny*
(1849)[28] and *Ford* v. *Tynte* (1861),[29] as well as the Irish decision *Brady* v. *Warren* (1900),[30] the courts similarly examined
the characteristics of the deer in question and held that as they
were kept in parks they should be classified as tame.

II. QUALIFIED OWNERSHIP OF WILD ANIMALS

(A) THE FORMS OF QUALIFIED OWNERSHIP

There are purportedly three situations in which wild animals may be subjects of qualified ownership.[31] All three are generally referred to under Latin tags but only one has a Roman law heritage while another is broadly consistent with Roman law. The third, a novelty of English jurisprudence, is by far the most important, having rendered the other two rules largely redundant.

According to Bracton,[32] following Roman law,[33] animals were the subject of ownership only so long as they were under effective control (or had an *animus revertendi*[34]). Restating this rule, English courts in the fifteenth and sixteenth centuries held that someone who had tamed or reclaimed a wild animal had qualified property in it so long as it was confined (property *per industriam*).[35] Broadly consistent with this rule, the courts also held that landowners had qualified property in the young of wild animals on their land until they could fly or run away (property *ratione impotentiae et loci*).[36]

In the leading *Case of Swans* (1592),[37] Coke J. held that qualified property in wild animals could be obtained only by industry or by reason of the infancy of the animals. However, there was already considerable authority in the fifteenth century that a landowner had qualified property in wild animals simply by virtue of their being on his land (that is, *ratione soli*).[38] The latter rule was applied in *Boulston's Case* (1598)[39] and *Newton and Richard's Case* (1611)[40] and was then endorsed by Holt C.J. in *Sutton* v. *Moody* (1697).[41] Over 150 years later, the House of Lords in *Blades* v. *Higgs* (1865)[42] affirmed that landowners have qualified property in wild animals on their land.

The common law's creation of property *ratione soli* has been recognized as a departure from Roman law,[43] but neither judges nor commentators have fully considered the relation of qualified property in wild animals *ratione soli* with property *per industriam* and *ratione impotentiae*. The one judge to advert to this question has been Lord Westbury who in *Blades* v. *Higgs* distinguished the last two types of qualified property on the basis that they "apply to animals which are not in the proper sense *ferae naturae*".[44] This comment conveys the degree of control over wild animals exercised by a person who has qualified property *per industriam* or *ratione impotentiae*, but it wrongly suggests that the rules derived from Roman law have ambits distinct from property *ratione soli*. In fact qualified property *ratione soli* altogether subsumes property *ratione impotentiae* as it generally does property *per industriam*.

The practical effect of the rule of property *ratione soli* is that wild animals are generally, if not always, subjects of qualified property and hence, so far as the civil law is concerned, are not open to taking by members of the public. Only the decision of the House of Lords in *Blades* v. *Higgs* offers some judicial explanation of the conferment of this property on landowners to the exclusion of members of the public. In that case, Lords Westbury and Chelmsford considered that a trespasser should not be able to profit from his wrongdoing and gain title to wild animals killed or reduced into possession while trespassing; in the absence of any other appropriate claimant, property in the wild animal should go to the person on whose ground the animal is taken or killed.[45]

Wildfowl over tidal waters are possibly the only animals which may not be subjects of qualified property. In *Carrington* v. *Taylor* (1809)[46] counsel for the defendant argued that the defendant had a right to shoot wildfowl while in a boat on tidal waters, and this claim was not contested. In *Allen* v. *Flood* (1898)[47] Lords Watson and Herschell both affirmed the correctness of this argument. However, in *Lord Fitzhardinge* v. *Purcell* (1908)[48] Parker J. held that there was no public right of wildfowling on tidal waters. Parker J. reached this decision partly on the incorrect basis that there was no authority in favour of the public right.[49] He also reached this decision on the basis that, consistent with the judgment of Holroyd J. in *Blundell* v. *Catterall* (1821),[50] the public's only rights on tidal waters are rights of fishing and navigation.[51] However, as suggested by the cases concerning floating seaweed and seacoal, the majority in *Blundell* v. *Catterall* probably understated the public's rights of taking from the foreshore.[52] Consequently, members of the public may have a right to take wildfowl while on tidal waters – at least where (unlike in *Lord Fitzhardinge* v. *Purcell*) ownership of the soil remains in the Crown.[53]

(B)   THE LIMITS OF QUALIFIED OWNERSHIP

The distinctive aspect of "qualified", as opposed to "absolute", ownership is that a person's rights in wild animals generally exist only so long as the animals are either on his land or under his physical control. While the subject of this type of possession, wild animals are much as chattels and their owner can bring an action for wrongful interference to goods if another person takes them. But before he has obtained possession of the animals or if they escape, the putative owner has no rights in the animals.

The determination of the point at which qualified ownershp in wild animals begins is primarily of importance to competing hunters or fishermen. Apart from cases concerning whales decided on the basis of customary law,[54] only two reported English decisions have considered this question. In line with the Roman principle that capture of a wild animal is necessary in order to obtain property in it – "for many factors may arise by reason of which you do not take it"[55] – Archer J. in *Geary* v. *Bearcroft* (1666)[56] stated that "actual possession" was necessary in order to obtain property in wild animals. In *Young* v. *Hichens* (1844)[57] the Court of Queen's Bench adopted the same view, holding that the plaintiff, who had partially encompassed pilchards with a net, had neither possession of nor property in the fish.

By analogy, it seems clear that even if a hunter wounds an animal, he gains no property in it until he has reduced it into possession. If a second hunter intervenes during the chase and captures the wounded animal, the second hunter gains property in the animal even if the first hunter would have been successful had it not been for the interference.[58] Anomalously, however, this second hunter, who on civil principles had property in the animal, may be guilty of stealing the property of the first since under the Theft Act 1968 it is not necessary that a stolen animal have been in another person's possession; it is sufficient if that person was in the course of reducing the animal into possession at the time it was taken.[59]

The point at which qualified property ends is most contentious when someone has invested time or money in animals which nevertheless are classified as wild. Arguably, the rights of owners of such animals should not cease merely because the animals escape or their owners let them loose, and this view has to a certain extent been recognized by the courts in a series of exceptions which modify the general rule that the ownership of wild animals ends when possession is lost.

(1) Animus revertendi

Following Roman law, the owner of a wild animal which is out of his physical control retains his qualified property when the animal has an *animus revertendi*, literally the intention to return. An owner can consequently let loose such animals as bees and homing pigeons and retain his rights in them, so that, for example, he can bring an action for wrongful interference to goods against anyone who shoots the pigeons.[60] The obvious difficulty with this rule is in determining whether an animal has an *animus revertendi*. As noted by G.W. Paton, the law has sufficient difficulties in determining the intention of people – it does not attempt to consider whether an animal intended to return.[61] Instead the test is whether the animal is in the habit of returning.[62]

(2)   Hot pursuit

The owner of a wild animal outside his physical control also retains his qualified property where he is in "hot pursuit" of the animal. In its narrowest form, this rule allows a person to retain qualified ownership of an animal which he is lawfully pursuing and which he retains in sight.[63] Yet the better view is that sight of the animal should only be relevant to the question of identification of the animal, and that if there are other means of identifying the animal, continuous sight of it should be unnecessary.[64] Equally it is arguable that since a landowner who hunts an animal from his own land on to the land of another can probably gain property in the animal in spite of his trespass,[65] so persons who have invested time and money in wild animals should be able to pursue them on to land in other ownership and retain their qualified property in the animals.

(3)   Exotic species

A person may possibly retain qualified ownership of a wild animal outside his physical control if the animal belongs to a species which is not indigenous to England. Authority for continuance of qualified property in this situation is provided by Blackstone's statement that qualified property in a wild animal only ceases when the animal returns to its "ancient wildness" or to its "proper element". A non-indigenous animal cannot of course return to its "proper element".[66] As noted by Thomas Beven, an escaped tiger in England "is not indigenous; he is an importation. He is merchandise. He is property with the marks of his identity as such indelibly stamped on him, by his rareness, if not by his individuality".[67]

(4)   Captive animals

The final situation in which a person might retain qualified property in wild animals out of his possession relate to indigenous animals which are farmed, kept in zoos, laboratories or as pets. Notwithstanding the decision to the contrary in the Canadian case *Campbell* v. *Hedley* (1917),[68] these animals could reasonably be held to remain subjects of qualified property if they remain identifiable after they escape.[69] Recognition of qualified property in this situation would be desirable not only because it would take account of the plaintiff's expenditure on such animals but also because it would prevent a disjunction between the civil and criminal law similar to that which can exist when a wild animal is captured. If qualified property in a pet or farmed "wild" animal ceases when it escapes, then a second person who takes or kills it will respectively gain qualified or absolute property in the animal. But this second party may be guilty of stealing the animal since for the purposes of the Theft Act it will remain the property of its former keeper. Under that Act property which can be stolen includes "wild creatures" which have been "tamed" and "those ordinarily kept in captivity".[70]

III. THE TAKING OF WILD ANIMALS

An unfortunately complex jumble of laws governs members of the public who take wild animals. Apart from two basic principles of tort liability developed at common law, at least eight statutes have created offences which may be committed by persons who take wild animals. This proliferation of legislation has occurred partly because few general legal principles apply to the taking of wild animals – even the ordinary rules of trespass to land may not apply in all situations; wild animals were not subjects of larceny at common law and generally may not be stolen under the Theft Act. The law has also become more complex because it has sought to achieve an increasing number of objects – not only the protection of wild animals as subjects of property rights but also the conservation of wild animals, the prevention of cruelty to animals and the protection of the public through firearms control.

(A) CIVIL LAW

Because of changes in the common law over the last 400 years, the only substantial right which members of the public may have to take wild animals is in relation to wildfowl on tidal waters.[71] Otherwise, a member of the public, who takes a wild

animal without permission of the relevant landowner, will now
in most if not all cases commit two separate torts. By going on
to land without permission, he will commit trespass to land. By
taking the wild animal, he will wrongfully interfere with goods.

(1)   Trespass to land

That hunting without permission on the land of another should
be a trespass appears as an obvious application of the general
rule that it is trespass for a person to enter on to land without
lawful justification. However, on the basis that hunting for
animals classified as vermin was "for the good of the commonwealth", cases decided up to the eighteenth century established that persons hunting foxes could justify their trespasses and hence escape liability regardless of whether their
purpose was in fact laudable advancement of "the common
profit" or mere sport.[72] As a result of three decisions in the
nineteenth century,[73] this exemption from liability for hunters
of vermin has been significantly narrowed if it now exists at all.
The only situation in which hunting on another's land without
permission may now be justifiable is where the hunter starts
vermin lawfully (as on his own land) and then continues the
pursuit on to the other land solely in order to destroy the
animal.[74] If, as is likely, even such hunting is held to be
trespass, it would simply be consistent with the considerable
reluctance of the common law to excuse entries on land made
without permission.

(2)   Property rights in wild animals

Because landowners generally have qualified property in wild
animals on their land,[75] a trespasser cannot gain title to a wild
animal which he starts and kills on the ground of one landowner. In this situation, the trespasser is cast by law as the
landowner's agent who turns the landowner's qualified property into absolute property. The landowner can recover either
the animal or, more likely, its value from the trespasser by
bringing an action against him for wrongful interference to
goods.[76] Under the common law of recaption of goods, he can
alternatively retake the animal from the trespasser and, if he
does so peaceably, he need not make a prior demand for the
animal's return. If, however, he has to use force – which in any
event is limited to what is reasonably necessary – he must in
general first request the animal's return in order to justify what
would otherwise be an assault.[77] Probably because these rules
concerning recaption were only settled in the second half of

the nineteenth century,[78] the Game Act 1831 expressly provides that where a trespasser is apprehended, while in pursuit of game and with game in his possession which appears to have been recently killed, the landowner may demand to be given the animals and if the trespasser does not do so immediately, the landowner may take the game from him.[79]

A different rule probably applies at common law when a trespasser starts a wild animal on the land of one person and kills it on the land of another. According to Holt C.J. in *Sutton* v. *Moody*, the trespasser obtains absolute property in the animal in this situation.[80] However, in *Blades* v. *Higgs* Lord Chelmsford suggested that the second landowner should obtain property in the animal by analogy with the situation where the animal voluntarily quits one piece of land for another.[81] This principle would remove the apparent anomaly of a trespasser obtaining property in a wild animal only when he hunts the animal over land in different ownership. Nevertheless, the rule, as declared by Holt C.J., follows from the principles that the first landowner's property is lost when the animal leaves his land unless he himself pursued it; the second landowner obtains no property in an animal hunted on to his land so long as it is being hunted.[82] If landowners are entitled to benefit from hot pursuit, it is not inappropriate that trespassers should also.

The one possible statutory modification of this rule applies to game. Various text writers have suggested that the power of landowners under the Game Act to seize game recently killed[83] applies where a trespasser has hunted game from the land of one landowner on to that of another and that this power of seizure confers title to the game on the landowner.[84] No cases have, however, determined this point and arguably the trespasser retains property in the game in this situation. The power of seizure can plausibly be read down so that it operates only where the game belongs to the landowner at common law and hence applies only to game hunted and killed on his land. Alternatively, even if the power of seizure applies where game has been hunted across land boundaries, nothing in the section confers title to the game on the landowner. If a landowner seized game under this section, a trespasser who had hunted the game on to the land could still bring a civil action to recover it as his property.

(B)   CRIMINAL LAW

(1)   Restrictions on taking

The criminal statutes restricting the taking of wild animals restrict either the period during which or the manner in which wild animals may lawfully be taken.

(a)   *Proscribed times*

(i) CLOSE SEASONS

The imposition of close seasons, coinciding with the breeding seasons of specific species, is the most important form of limitation on the periods during which animals may be taken. Such seasons are imposed to allow quarry species to replenish for subsequent hunting, and game, deer and wildfowl are protected in this way.[85] Foxes – on account of their status as vermin – are the only "sport target" species which are not protected by a close season.

(ii) PROSCRIBED DAYS

The other main restriction on when wild animals may be taken relates to certain specified species on particular days. Under the Game Act 1831, it is an offence to "kill or take any game, or use any dog, gun, net, or other engine or instrument for the purpose of killing or taking any game, on a Sunday or Christmas Day".[86] Under the Wildlife and Countryside Act 1981, the Secretary of State may prescribe areas in which it is an offence to take wildfowl on Sundays.[87] The object of these provisions is unclear and there probably is little rationale for their existence in their present form. The prohibition on taking game on Sunday was possibly introduced as an expression of Evangelical sentiment,[88] but in a society made up of diverse religions this is not a persuasive reason for its existence. The power to prohibit Sunday sport in specified areas appears to have been intended as a means of protecting endangered species of wildfowl,[89] but isolated safe days have only limited conservation benefits for wildfowl.

(b)   *Proscribed means for taking*

The legislation which restricts the way in which members of the public may take wild animals is designed to achieve three different objects – the prevention of crime and preservation of public safety, the conservation of wild animals and the prevention of cruelty to animals.

(i) PREVENTION OF CRIME AND PRESERVATION OF PUBLIC SAFETY

Although the Bill of Rights 1688[90] and Blackstone[91] recognized a right in members of the public to keep arms for their defence, Parliament has subsequently imposed substantial controls on the circumstances in which persons may keep, as well as the places where they may lawfully carry and use, firearms.[92] Current legislation is largely found in the Firearms Act 1968 which, in attempting to prevent crime and to preserve public safety, also restricts the manner in which members of the public may take wild animals.

The Firearms Act seeks to control the keeping of firearms by requiring that a person in possession of a firearm (other than an air weapon) obtain a certificate from the police.[93] While shotgun certificates can be obtained by members of the public with little difficulty,[94] an applicant must show "good reason" in order to obtain a certificate for other firearms. Members of the public, who wish to use a rifle for shooting wild animals but do not have an authority to shoot over the land in question, do not satisfy this test.[95]

The most general restraint on members of the public carrying firearms when hunting wild animals applies to persons trespassing. Under the Firearms Act, a person commits an offence if, while he has a firearm with him, he enters or is on any land as a trespasser and without reasonable excuse.[96] This provision extends to "land covered with water"[97] but its main purpose is to protect farmers.

A narrower restraint on persons carrying firearms when hunting is imposed by both the Prevention of Crime Act 1953 and the Firearms Act in relation to "public places", which the legislation defines as including highways and other premises or places to which at the material time the public have or are permitted to have access.[98] As a result of these provisions, even if members of the public have a right to take wildfowl on tidal waters, they cannot use firearms in exercise of this right. Thus in *Ross* v. *Collins* (1982),[99] the respondent was convicted under the Firearms Act for having been in possession of and having discharged a shot gun at ducks and seagulls while on the River Thames.

The main justification for the overlapping provisions under the Prevention of Crime and the Firearms Acts is that the firearms legislation allows for the imposition of a much greater penalty.[100] The Acts also cover different ranges of weapons. The Prevention of Crime Act makes it an offence – in the absence of lawful authority or reasonable excuse – to carry "offensive weapons" which are defined as articles which are made or adapted for use for causing injury to the person, or are intended for such use by persons carrying them.[101] It may be that firearms commonly used for game are not offensive *per se* and so would only fall within the Prevention of Crime Act if a person carrying them intended to cause injury to the person.[102] But the Firearms Act specifically applies to any person who, again without justification, has with him a loaded shot gun or loaded air weapon or any other firearm (whether loaded or not) together with ammunition suitable for use in that firearm.[103]

Finally, a range of legal restraints apply to the use of firearms in or near places to which members of the public have a right of access. At common law, a person who uses a firearm in a public place such as a street, and hence "frightens or terrorizes" other members of the public, commits a public nuisance.[104] Legislation makes it an offence to discharge a firearm on a highway "to the damage or danger" of any person[105] or to discharge a firearm within 50 feet of the centre of a highway and either damage the highway or injure, interrupt or endanger a user of the highway.[106]

(ii) CONSERVATION OF WILD ANIMALS

In order to conserve wild animals, Parliament has restricted the implements which can lawfully be used by hunters. Such legislation has traditionally been directed at methods of hunting considered to be wasteful, excessively successful or unsporting.[107] However, provisions have increasingly been aimed also at indiscriminate forms of destruction which affect not only the intended quarry but also other species. Thus, the Wildlife and Countryside Act 1981 prohibits a wide range of methods of taking animals ranging from such obviously destructive weapons as automatic and semi-automatic firearms to what might seem more subtle devices such as artificial lighting, mirrors and decoys.[108]

(iii) PREVENTION OF CRUELTY TO ANIMALS

Although the first Cruelty to Animals Act was passed in 1835, the Wild Birds Protection Act 1904 was the first legislation to prohibit particular methods of taking wild animals on account of the cruelty of these methods. The 1904 Act made it an offence to "set any spring, trap, gin, or other similar instrument calculated to cause bodily injury to any wild bird coming in contact therewith".[109] In 1908 and 1925 this legislation against cruelty to wild birds was extended to encompass first the use of hooks,[110] and then live decoys and bird lime.[111] With minor extensions, these offences are now found in section 5 of the Wildlife and Countryside Act 1981. Under the 1981 Act there are also for the first time similar general prohibitions in relation to the taking of wild animals other than birds.[112] Under the Badgers Act 1973 it is an offence to dig for badgers or use badger tongs.[113]

The activities which have, most controversially, remained outside the scope of the legislation are hare coursing, stag hunting and fox hunting. Although the Protection of Animals Act 1911 applies to wild animals in captivity, there is a substantial exemption in relation to cruelty to animals which occurs as part of hunting or coursing.[114] While fox hunting has not even been the subject of Parliamentary debate, since the 1930s a series of Bills have been introduced directed at prohibiting hare coursing and stag hunting. The issue has become party-political with Labour supporting prohibition and the Conservatives opposing abolition. In 1975-6 a Bill to abolish coursing was passed by the Labour-controlled Commons but was defeated in the Lords. Since 1979, because of the Conservative's opposition to such legislation, no further Bills against field sports have been introduced.[115]

(2) Prohibitions on taking

The statutes which prohibit the taking of wild animals (or which empower the making of regulations to this effect) take one of two forms. Either they impose general prohibitions on the taking of particular species of wild animals, in which case the prohibitions apply to all land. Or they prohibit the taking of all or some animals within specified areas. Such prohibitions are generally, although not always, part of a package of protections intended to preserve the habitat of the areas in question.

(a) Protected species

The various statutes which impose general prohibitions on the taking of wild animals are intended either to protect the rights of those persons who have qualified ownership of wild animals or to conserve wild animals. In analytic terms, the difference between property protection and conservation legislation depends on the class of persons bound by the various provisions. Legislation which prohibits taking in order to protect private property binds all members of the public apart from the owners of the animals and persons acting with their permission. Legislation intended to conserve wild animals – if designed to achieve this object regardless of other considerations – would bind all members of the public including landowners.

In practice almost no English conservation legislation is cast in the absolute mould of binding all members of the public. Under most conservation legislation, landowners enjoy a substantial exemption from the prohibitions on taking wild animals.[116] In one extreme case – the Badgers Act 1973 until its amendment in 1981 – legislation, which was introduced into Parliament with conservationist objectives, was "wrecked" by amendments in the House of Commons[117] with the result that landowners were completely exempted from the Act's prohibition on taking, killing or injuring badgers.[118] The Act consequently operated like property protection legislation, and was amended only after certain landowners were shown to have abused their freedom to take badgers.[119]

(i) OFFENCES AGAINST PRIVATE PROPERTY

(a)   Theft
At common law it was not larceny to take or kill wild animals because the animals, until taken or killed, were not regarded as being subjects of sufficient property; when taken or killed the animals were in the possession of the taker who consequently could not steal them.[120] The Theft Act 1968, which abolished the common law of larceny,[121] contains the bold statement that "Wild creatures, tamed or untamed, shall be regarded as property".[122] However, the Act goes on to provide that, subject to two exceptions, wild animals cannot be stolen. The first of these exceptions covers wild animals which have been tamed or are ordinarily kept in captivity such as pets and laboratory and zoo animals. The second exception covers wild animals which have been reduced into possession and which remain in the possession of another person or which are in the course of being so reduced as by a hunter whether poaching or acting with the permission of the landowner.[123]

(b)   Poaching Acts
Rather than being specifically directed at the taking of another person's property, poaching legislation is concerned with the taking of certain specified animals while being a trespasser on land. The Night Poaching Act 1828 provides against the poach-

ing of game birds, hares and rabbits at night; the Game Act 1831 provides against the taking of these animals during the daytime; the Deer Act is, predictably, concerned with the taking of deer. Under the Night Poaching and Game Acts a lone poacher of "game" is liable to a smaller penalty than a group of poachers, while a poacher who takes these animals by day may commit a lesser offence than one who takes them by night.[124] These distinctions, based on the number of poachers working together and the time of day when they take the animals, do not specifically apply to deer although they may be weighed by the courts in determining sentence. The Deer Act 1980 provides, however, that where a person is convicted of taking or attempting to take more than one deer he may be fined as if he had been convicted of a separate offence in respect of each animal.[125]

The main uncertainty in the application of this poaching legislation is whether it extends to persons hunting on the highway. The Night Poaching Act 1828 applied initially to persons on any land, whether open or enclosed".[126] However, in 1844 the Act was amended so as to apply additionally to "any public road, highway, or path, or the side thereof",[127] where poachers "through a defect in the law, carried on their practices unmolested".[128] This express provision against poaching on highways in the 1844 Act casts doubt on the ambit of the Game Act 1831 and the Deer Act 1980, both of which – like the Night Poaching Act 1828 – apply to "any land".[129] If the 1844 Act is to be given any significance, then, by analogy, the Game Act 1831 and the Deer Act 1980 do not apply to highways unless the words "whether open or enclosed" in the 1828 Act are thought to exclude highways. This issue has not been addressed in either of the two reported decisions under the 1831 Act in which defendants have been convicted for having trespassed in pursuit of game while on highways.[130] Consequently, it may be that a person on a highway does not commit an offence by taking game during the daytime or deer at any time.

(ii) CONSERVATION LEGISLATION

Legislation which prohibits the taking of wild animals on conservation grounds may take one of two forms. It can rest on the positive identification of the species to be protected in which case the protected species are likely to be in danger of extinction. Alternatively it can rest on the principle known as "reverse listing" which involves a general prohibition on the

taking of a genus of animal which is then subject to qualifications in relation to certain listed species. Legislation of this
type tends to protect not only endangered species but also
many common species which are in no danger of extinction, or
at least all species other than those which are either quarry or
pests.

Reverse listing provides the only sound basis for bird protection laws "since it minimizes recurring indentification problems and avoids difficulties with accidental species and species
new to national lists".[131] In England, wild birds have been
protected by reverse listing since 1954. Other species of wild
animal are protected, if at all, by positive listing.

The Wildlife and Countryside Act 1981 protects "any bird of
a kind which is ordinarily resident in or is a visitor to Great
Britain in a wild state".[132] It does not protect poultry or, as a
general rule, game birds.[133] It also does not apply to "any bird
which is shown to have been bred in captivity" but a bird is not
treated as bred in captivity "unless its parents were lawfully in
captivity when the egg was laid".[134]

Subject to these matters of definition, the Act makes it an
offence intentionally to kill, injure or take any wild bird; to
take, damage or destroy the nest of any wild bird while that
nest is in use or being built; and to take or destroy an egg of
any wild bird.[135] These general prohibitions are reinforced in
relation to certain scheduled endangered and vulnerable birds
by the existence of a special penalty.[136] The prohibitions are
relaxed in relation to certain scheduled "food" birds such as
mallards and golden plover which may be taken lawfully outside their close season.[137]

With the exception of the Badgers Act which makes it an
offence for a member of the public wilfully to kill, injure or
take badgers,[138] the Wildlife and Countryside Act is the only
statute to protect wild animals by positive listing. The Act
makes it an offence intentionally to kill, injure or take any
scheduled wild animal which is "living wild", and in proceedings for such an offence the animal in question will be
presumed to have been a wild animal unless the contrary is
shown.[139] When the Act was passed, 36 species – made up
primarily of butterflies, lizards, moths, snails and spiders as
well as otters and all bats – were protected in this way. Further
species may be added to the schedule if they either are in
danger of extinction in Great Britain or are likely to become so
endangered unless conservation measures are taken.[140]

(b) Protected habitats

Prohibitions on the taking of wild animals within specified areas were first developed in exercise of the prerogative – in relation to forests, warrens, chases and parks. These areas can in certain respects be considered as prototypes for and predecessors to contemporary protected habitats.[141] Like the medieval forests, habitats which are now protected tend to the preservation of wild animals. But in the case of the forests, the prohibition on taking deer was intended to protect the Crown's property in these animals. In the case of almost all modern legislation prohibiting the taking of wild animals in particular habitats, the prohibitions bind the landowner along with the general public. The prohibition is imposed in the public interest in order to conserve the animals.

Areas of special protection for wild birds, which may be created by ministerial order under the Wildlife and Countryside Act, are exceptional among contemporary protected habitats in that their creation depends on the acquiescence of the relevant landowners whose use of the land then remains unrestricted and who are also partly exempt from the special prohibitions on interfering with wild birds in these areas.[142] But members of the public who intentionally kill, injure or take a wild bird within an area of special protection may – depending on the terms of the ministerial order – be liable to a special penalty over and above that applicable to all land.[143] Persons who take quarry birds in the open season – which is generally not an offence under the Act – may similarly be subject to a special penalty if they take these birds in a protected area, and persons who commit other forms of generally permissible conduct, such as disturbing a wild bird while it is building a nest, are similarly liable.[144]

In nature reserves, the taking of wild animals is generally prohibited as part of a greater design intended to preserve the existing environment. In relation to national and local reserves respectively, the Nature Conservancy Council and the relevant local authority are empowered to make byelaws which prohibit the killing, taking, molesting or disturbance of living creatures of any description in a reserve.[145] They may also prohibit or restrict the shooting of birds within such areas surrounding or adjoining the reserves as appear requisite to them for the protection of the reserves.[146]

NOTES TO CHAPTER 7

1. Thomas, *Institutes*, pp. 66, 77; Thomas, *Textbook*, p. 167.
2. G.J. Turner, *Select Pleas of the Forest*, S.S. 13, 1899, p. cxxiii; Charles Petit-Dutaillis, *Studies and Notes supplementary to Stubbs' Constitutional History*, Manchester, Manchester University Press, 1914, vol. 2, pp. 155–6.
3. See below, p. 219.
4. *The Case of Swans* (1592) 7 Co. Rep 15b; 77 E.R. 435. See also Norman F. Ticehurst, *The Mute Swan in England*, London, Cleaver-Hume, 1957. For royal fish, see below, p. 240.
5. Turner, *op. cit.*, pp. x-xiv. Roe deer ceased to be classified as beasts of the forest in 1389 as a result of a decision of the Court of King's Bench.
6. *Ibid.*, p. cxvi. This was the position at least from the Tudor period.
7. See, for example, Chester & Ethyn Kirby, "The Stuart Game Prerogative", *English Historical Review*, vol. 46, 1931, pp. 239–54.
8. See Charles R. Young, *The Royal Forests of Medieval England*, Leicester, Leicester University Press, 1979, p. 149.
9. See D.J. Stagg (ed.), *A Calendar of New Forest Documents: The Fifteenth to Seventeenth Centuries*, vol. 5, Hampshire Record Series, Hampshire County Council, 1983.
10. Kirby & Kirby, *op. cit*, pp. 293–4.
11. Wild Creatures and Forest Laws Act 1971, s. 1(1)(a).
12. 13 Rich. 2, c. 13, s. 1.
13. Different statutes included different animals within the definition of "game". The definition of "game" in the text is that which prevailed under the Game Act 1671 between 1692 and 1831. See P.B. Munsche, *Gentlemen and Poachers: the English Game Laws 1671–1831*, Cambridge, Cambridge University Press, 1981, pp. 3–5.
14. Thomas A. Lund, "British Wildlife Law before the American Revolution: Lessons from the Past", (1975) 74 Michigan L.R. 49, 57.
15. *Ibid.*, p. 58.
16. See below, pp. 219–20.
17. Compare the law of liability for harm caused by animals, where wild and tame animals were distinguished at common law according to their ferocity, and now under the Animals Act 1971 are categorized according to whether or not they belong to a "dangerous species". See Williams, *Liability;* North, *The Modern Law of Liability for Animals*.
18. *Buckle* v. *Holmes* (1926) 134 L.T. 284, 285 *per* Shearman J.; *McQuaker* v. *Goddard* [1940] 1 K.B. 687, 696 *per* Scott L.J. See also Halsbury, vol. 2, para. 202.
19. See Thomas, *Textbook*, p. 167.
20. 2 Bl. Comm. 390.
21. This issue was raised but not resolved in *Falkland Islands Co.* v. *R.* (1863) 2 Moore N.S. 266, 274; 15 E.R. 902, 905. See also Williams, *Liability*, p. 149; *Reeve* v. *Wardle* [1960] Q.R. 143; *R.* v. *Drinkwater* (1981) 27 S.A.S.R. 396, 401. Halsbury, vol. 2, para. 202 cites *McQuaker* v. *Goddard* [1940] 1 K.B. 687 as authority for a species test but that case strictly concerned only liability for animals and in any event has been strongly criticized. See Glanville Williams, "The Camel Case", (1940) 56 L.Q.R. 354.

22. [1900] 2 I.R. 632.
23. *Ibid.*, p. 639. For this issue in relation to liability for animals, see *Behrens* v. *Bertram Mills Circus Ltd* [1957] 2 Q.B. 1; Animals Act 1971, s. 11; North, pp. 36–8.
24. [1939] 1 K.B. 471.
25. [1948] 2 K.B. 311.
26. Willes 46; 125 E.R. 1048.
27. Willes 46, 51; 125 E.R. 1048, 1051.
28. 8 C.B. 768; 137 E.R. 710.
29. 2 J. & H. 150; 70 E.R. 1008.
30. [1900] 2 I.R. 632, 648–50, 651–8 *per* Johnson J. and Palles C.B.
31. A fourth type of qualified property, property *ratione privilegi*, which applied at common law to land covered by franchises granted by the Crown (see *Blades* v. *Higgs* (1865) 11 H.L.C. 621, 631; 11 E.R. 1474, 1479 *per* Lord Westbury), was abolished by the Wild Creatures and Forest Laws Act 1971, s. 1(1)(b).
32. Bracton, vol. 2, p.42.
33. Buckland, p. 205; Thomas, *Textbook*, p. 167.
34. See below, pp. 221–2.
35. See the authorities cited by J.H. Baker (ed.), *The Reports of Sir John Spelman*, vol. 2, S.S. 94, p. 211, which can be found in translation in Joseph Chitty, *A Treatise on the Game Laws and on Fisheries*, London, 1812, vol. 2.
36. See Baker, p. 211.
37. 7 Co. Rep. 15b, 17b; 77 E.R. 435, 438.
38. See Holdsworth, vol. 7, p. 492, esp. at note 11, citing T. 22 H. 6, pl. 11; Baker, p. 215.
39. 5. Co. Rep. 104b; 77 E.R. 216.
40. Godbolt 174; 78 E.R. 106.
41. 5 Mod. 375; 87 E.R. 715; 12 Mod. 144; 88 E.R. 1223; 12 Mod. 145; 88 E.R. 1224; Comerbach 458; 90 E.R. 590; Holt 608; 90 E.R. 1236; 2 Salk. 556; 91 E.R. 470; 3 Salk. 290; 91 E.R. 831; 1 Ld. Raym. 250; 91 E.R. 1063; 1 Comy. 34; 92 E.R. 945.
42. 11 H.L.C. 621; 11 E.R. 1474.
43. See, for example, *Blades* v. *Higgs* (1862) 12 C.B. (N.S.) 501; 142 E.R. 1238.
44. 11 H.L.C. 621, 631; 11 E.R. 1474, 1478.
45. 11 H.L.C. 621, 632, 641; 11 E.R. 1474, 1479, 1482.
46. 2 Camp. 258; 170 E.R. 1148; 11 East 571; 103 E.R. 1126.
47. [1898] A.C. 1, 103, 136.
48. [1908] 2 Ch. 139.
49. *Ibid.*, pp. 165, 167. Neither *Carrington* v. *Taylor* nor *Allen* v. *Flood* was cited in argument.
50. 5 B. & Ald. 268; 106 E.R. 1190.
51. [1908] 2 Ch. 139, 165–6.
52. See above, p. 209.
53. See [1908] 2 Ch. 139, 167. Compare the position in Scotland where members of the public probably have a right to shoot wildfowl on the foreshore even where it has been alienated. See *Hope* v. *Bennewith* (1904) 12 S.L.T. 243, 246, 248; *Burnet* v. *Barclay* 1955 S.L.T. 282.
54. *Littledale* v. *Scaith* (1788) 1 Taunt. 243n.; 127 E.R. 826; *Fennings* v. *Lord Grenville* (1808) 1 Taunt. 241; 127 E.R. 825; *Hogarth* v. *Jackson* (1827) 2 C. & P. 595; 172 E.R. 271; *Skinner* v. *Chapman* (1827) M. &

M. 59n; 173 E.R. 1081. See also *Aberdeen Arctic Co.* v. *Sutter* (1862) 4 Macq. H.L. 335.

55. 2 Justinian, *Institutes*, tit. 1, s. 13.
56. Carter 57, 58; 124 E.R. 822, 823.
57. 6 Q.B. 606; 115 E.R. 228.
58. *Pierson* v. *Post* 2 Am. Dec. 264 (1805); *Dapson* v. *Daly* 153 N.E. 454 (1926). Compare *Liesner* v. *Wanie* 145 N.W. 374 (1914).
59. Theft Act 1968, s. 4(4).
60. *Hamps* v. *Darby* [1948] 2 K.B. 311. See also *Tutton* v. *A.D. Walter Ltd* [1985] 3 W.L.R. 797, 806.
61. G.W. Paton, "Bees and the Law", (1939) 2 Res Judicata 22.
62. *Hamps* v. *Darby* [1948] 2 K.B. 311, 323 *per* Evershed L.J.
63. *Kearry* v. *Pattinson* [1939] 1 K.B. 471, 478, 479 *per* Slesser L.J.
64. See *The Case of Swans* (1592) 7 Co. Rep. 15b, 17b; 77 E.R. 435, 438; *Vincent* v. *Lesney* (1625) Cro. Car. 18; 79 E.R. 621; *Quantrill* v. *Spragge* (1907) 71 J.P. 425, 426 *per* Mulligan J. explaining *Harris* v. *Elder* (1893) 57 J.P. 553; *Brown* v. *Eckes* 160 N.Y.S. 489, 493 (1916).
65. See *Gedge* v. *Minne* (1613) 2 Bulst. 60, 61; 80 E.R. 958, 960 *per* Dodderidge J.; *Sutton* v. *Moody* (1697) Holt 608; 90 E.R. 1236. See also Game Act 1831, s. 35; Malicious Injuries to Property Act 1861, s. 52; *Kearry* v. *Pattinson* [1939] 1 K.B. 471, 481 *per* Goddard L.J. Compare Slesser L.J. in the same case at p. 479, and the medieval position, discussed by Morris S. Arnold (ed.), *Select Cases of Trespass from the King's Courts 1307–1399*, S.S. 100, 1985, vol. 1, pp. lxxii-lxxiii.
66. 2 Bl. Comm. 393. American authority on this issue is conflicting. According to *Mullett* v. *Bradley* 53 N.Y.S. 781 (1898) and *Hughes* v. *Reese* 109 So. 731 (1926), qualified property does not continue in exotic animals which escape. The contrary view was taken in *E.A. Stephens and Co.* v. *Albers* 256 P. 15 (1927) and *Kelser* v. *Jones* 296 P. 773 (1931). For a discussion of this issue, see (1927-8) 12 Minnesota L.R. 172–3.
67. Thomas Beven, "The Responsibilities at Common Law for the Keeping of Animals", (1909) 22 Harvard L.R. 465, 481.
68. (1917) 39 O.L.R. 528.
69. Beven, *op. cit.*, 481. Compare Williams, *Liability*, p. 338.
70. Theft Act 1968, s. 4(4).
71. See above, p. 220.
72. 12 Hen. 8, p. 9 (1521) *per* Brooke J.; *Gedge* v. *Minne* (1613) 2 Bulst. 60, 61; 80 E.R. 958, 960 *per* Dodderidge J. *Gundry* v. *Feltham* (1786) 1 T.R. 334; 99 E.R. 1125.
73. *Earl of Essex* v. *Capel* (1809) in Chitty, *A Treatise on the Game Laws and on Fisheries*, vol. 2, pp. 1381–3; *Paul* v. *Summerhayes* (1878) 4 Q.B.D. 9; *Calvert* v. *Gosling* (1887) 5 T.L.R. 185.
74. *Paul* v. *Summerhayes* (1878) 4 Q.B.D. 9, 11–12 *per* Coleridge C.J.
75. See above, pp. 219–20.
76. See *Toome Eel Fishery (Northern Ireland) Ltd* v. *Cardwell* [1966] N.I. 1, 29 *per* Lord MacDermott L.C.J.
77. *R.* v. *Mitton* (1827) 3 C. & P. 31; 172 E.R. 309; *Blades* v. *Higgs* (1861) 10 C.B. (N.S.) 713, 721; 142 E.R. 634, 637 *per* Erle C.J. Compare *Whatford* v. *Carty* [1960] C.L.Y. 3258. See generally Law Reform Committee, *Eighteenth Report: Conversion and Detinue*, Cmnd. 4774, 1971, paras 116–26.
78. The common law on recaption remained largely unclear until *Blades* v.

Higgs (1861) 10 C.B. (N.S.) 713; 142 E.R. 634. In *The Game Laws of the United Kingdom*, London, Shaw, 1861, p. 64, which was published slightly later than and in ignorance of this decision, James Paterson still considered that "At common law the owner or occupier of lands, . . ., a *fortiori*, the mere owner of shootings, has no right to take away any property from a trespasser."

79. Game Act 1831, s. 36. Note also the police powers to seize animals and the courts' power to order forfeiture of animals under the Game Laws (Amendment) Act 1960, s. 4; Deer Act 1980, s. 7, sched. 2.
80. 3 Salk. 290; 91 E.R. 831. Affirmed in *Churchward* v. *Studdy* (1811) 14 East 249; 104 E.R. 596 *per* Lord Ellenborough; *Deane* v. *Clayton* (1817) 7 Taunt. 489, 510–11; 129 E.R. 196, 205 *per* Park J. See also *Earl of Lonsdale* v. *Rigg* (1856) 11 Exch. 654, 672; 156 E.R. 992, 1000 *per* Martin B.
81. (1865) 11 H.L.C. 621, 639–40; 11 E.R. 1474, 1482.
82. Holdsworth, vol. 7, p. 496.
83. Game Act 1831, s. 36.
84. Joshua Williams, *Principles of the Law of Personal Property*, 18th ed., London, Sweet & Maxwell, 1926, p. 169; Vaines, p. 429.
85. Game Act 1831, s. 3; Deer Act 1963, s. 1, sched. 1; Wildlife and Countryside Act 1981, s. 2(1), (4), sched. 2, part I.
86. Game Act 1831, s. 3.
87. Wildlife and Countryside Act 1981, s. 2(3).
88. Munsche, p. 221, note 39. See also Thomas Lund, "British Wildlife Law before the American Revolution: Lessons from the Past", (1975) 74 Michigan L.R. 49, 65.
89. *Minutes of Evidence before the Departmental Committee on the Protection of Wild Birds*, Cmd. 189, 1919, para. 218; *Report of the Departmental Committee on Wild Birds*, Cmd. 295, 1925, p. 27. Orders protecting birds on Sundays were first made under the Wild Birds Protection Act 1896, s. 1 and then under the Protection of Birds Act 1954, s. 2(1), (2), (5).
90. 1 W. & M. 2, c. 2.
91. 1 Bl. Comm. 143–4.
92. See Colin Greenwood, *Firearms Control: a Study of Armed Crime and Firearms Control in England and Wales*, London, Routledge & Kegan Paul, 1972, especially at pp. 11–14.
93. Firearms Act 1968, ss. 1, 2.
94. Greenwood, *op. cit.*, pp. 213–14.
95. *Ibid.*, p. 206.
96. Firearms Act 1968, s. 20(2).
97. *Ibid.*, s. 20(3).
98. Prevention of Crime Act 1953, s. 1(1), (4); Firearms Act 1968, ss. 19, 57(4).
99. [1982] Crim. L.R. 368.
100. H.C. Deb., 5th series, vol. 707, col. 1151, 2 March 1965, Sir Frank Soskice.
101. Prevention of Crime Act 1953, s. 1(4).
102. Alec Samuels, "Gun Law – II", (1963) 107 S.J. 145.
103. Firearms Act 1968, s. 19.
104. *R.* v. *Meade* (1903) 19 T.L.R. 540.
105. Metropolitan Police Act 1839, s. 54; Town Police Clauses Act 1847, s. 28.

106. Highways Act 1980, ss. 131(1)(d), 161(2).
107. See Thomas A. Lund, "British Wildlife Law before the American Revolution: Lessons from the Past", (1975) 74 Michigan L.R. 49, 66.
108. Wildlife and Countryside Act 1981, s. 11(2).
109. Wild Birds Protection Act 1904, s. 1.
110. Wild Birds Protection Act 1908, s. 1.
111. Protection of Birds Act 1925, s. 1.
112. Wildlife and Countryside Act 1981, s. 11.
113. Badgers Act 1973, s. 2(1)(b).
114. Protection of Animals Act 1911, s. 15(a). See *Steele* v. *Rodgers* (1912) 106 L.T. 79; *Rowley* v. *Murphy* [1964] 2 Q.B. 43.
115. See Richard H. Thomas, "Hunting as a Political Issue", *Parliamentary Affairs*, vol. 39, no. 1, January 1986, pp. 19–30.
116. See Deer Act 1963, s. 10A (introduced by the Wildlife and Countryside Act 1981 s. 12, sched. 7); Badgers Act 1973, ss. 8(1A), (1B), 9(1)(e) (introduced by the Wildlife and Countryside Act 1981, s. 12, sched. 7); Wildlife and Countryside Act 1981, ss. 2(2), 4(2)(c), 4(3), 10(3)(c), 10(4), 16(1)(k). For a prosecution of a farmer under the repealed Protection of Birds Act 1954, see *Robinson* v. *Whittle* [1980] 1 W.L.R. 1476.
117. H.L. Deb., 5th series, vol. 341, col. 66, Lord Somers, col. 72, Earl of Arran, 2 April 1973. For a more positive view of the original Act, see Peter Hardy, *A Lifetime of Badgers*, London, David & Charles, 1975.
118. Badgers Act 1973, s. 7(1).
119. Nature Conservancy Council, *Fifth Report*, London, H.M.S.O., 1979, p. 34; H.L. Deb., 5th series, vol. 416, col. 1125, Lord Melchett, col. 1129, Earl of Ferrers, 3 February 1981. The amendments were made by the Wildlife and Countryside Act 1981, s. 12, sched.7.
120. *R.* v. *Townley* (1871) 12 Cox C.C. 59.
121. Theft Act 1968, s. 32(1)(a).
122. *Ibid.*, s. 4(4).
123. *Ibid.*
124. Night Poaching Act 1828, ss. 1, 3; Game Act 1831, s. 30.
125. Deer Act 1980, s. 1(6).
126. Night Poaching Act 1828, s. 1.
127. Night Poaching Act 1844, s. 1.
128. P.D., vol. 75, col. 146, 3 June 1844. See also Night Poaching Act 1844, preamble.
129. Game Act 1831, s. 30; Deer Act 1980, s. 1(1).
130. *R.* v. *Pratt* (1855) in which the matter was raised in argument at 4 El. & Bl. 860, 863–4; 119 E.R. 319, 321; *Mayhew* v. *Wardley* (1863) 14 C.B. (N.S.) 550; 143 E.R. 561.
131. John Temple Lang, "The European Community Directive on Bird Conservation", *Biological Conservation*, vol. 22, 1982, 11, 19.
132. Wildlife and Countryside Act 1981, s. 27(1).
133. *Ibid.*
134. *Ibid.*, ss. 1(6), 27(2).
135. *Ibid.*, s. 1(1).
136. *Ibid.*, s. 1(4), sched. 1.
137. *Ibid.*, s. 2(1), sched. 2, part 1.
138. Badgers Act 1973, s. 1(1). Because of the widespread continuance of digging for badgers and the difficulties of obtaining convictions against the offending parties, the Wildlife and Countryside (Amendment) Act

1985 effected a partial reversal of the onus of proof in the offence of taking badgers. Section 1(1A) of the Badgers Act now provides that if "there is evidence from which it could reasonably be concluded that at the material time the accused was attempting to kill, injure or take a badger, he shall be presumed to have been attempting to kill, injure or take a badger unless the contrary is shown." See, further, Alec Samuels, "The Wildlife and Countryside (Amendment) Act 1985", [1986] J.P.L. 174–6.

139. Wildlife and Countryside Act 1981, ss. 9(1), (6), 27(1), sched. 5.
140. *Ibid.*, s. 22(3)(a).
141. See Thomas A. Lund, "British Wildlife Law Before the American Revolution: Lessons from the Past", (1975) 74 Michigan L.R. 49, 67.
142. Wildlife and Countryside Act 1981, s. 3(2), (3), (4), (5).
143. *Ibid.*, s. 3(1)(a)(i).
144. *Ibid.*, s. 3(1)(a)(iv).
145. National Parks and Access to the Countryside Act 1949, ss. 20(2)(b), 21(4); Wildlife and Countryside Act 1981, s. 35(4).
146. National Parks and Access to the Countryside Act 1949, ss. 20(2)(c), 21(4); Wildlife and Countryside Act 1981, s. 35(4).

Chapter 8

FISH

The right to fish is the most substantial of the rights of members of the public to take things from the environment. However, there is considerable uncertainty about the extent of the waters subject to the public right, the legal basis of this right is unclear, and there are also significant limitations on the manner in which the right may be exercised.

I. THE EXTENT OF THE PUBLIC RIGHT OF FISHING

Apart from "royal fish" – whales and sturgeon – which belong to the Crown,[1] fishing rights in England are divided between all members of the public (in "public" fisheries) and landowners and the recipients of Crown grants (in "private" fisheries). This type of division of fishing rights has, with one exception,[2] been consistently recognized in English law since at least medieval times. However, the extent of the public right is in many respects unclear.

The main basis on which fishing rights are divided is according to whether or not the waters are tidal or non-tidal. However, in tidal waters, where members of the public have *prima facie* a right to fish, the common law recognizes that there may be private fisheries so long as they were created prior to Magna Carta. In non-tidal waters, members of the public do not have a general right to fish, though there possibly are local public rights of fishing in certain non-tidal lakes. In relation to all exclusive fisheries – whether in tidal or non-tidal waters – it is unclear why the owner of the fishery should not be able to dedicate his rights to the public but at least in relation to non-tidal fisheries the law is clearly against recognition of such transfers of fishing rights.

(A) THE DIVISION BETWEEN PUBLIC AND PRIVATE FISHERIES ON THE BASIS OF TIDALITY

In determining the upper limit of the public right of fishing in rivers, the courts were faced with two main alternatives. They could have held that the public right of fishing is co-extensive with the area in which the Crown *prima facie* owns the soil in rivers, and so is restricted to the tidal reaches of rivers. Alternatively, they could have held that the public right of fishing is co-extensive with the public right of navigation which in relation to many rivers goes far beyond the upper limits of the tide. The public right of fishing might then extend even to those parts of rivers which are not tidal but have been made navigable by statute.

Until the mid-nineteenth century, judges and writers used diverse terminology to describe the point where fishing in a river ceased being *prima facie* public and instead became private and was generally the property of the adjacent landowners. According to Bracton, there was a public right to fish in all "permanent" rivers.[3] In *Warren* v. *Matthews* (1703)[4] and *Carter* v. *Murcot* (1768),[5] Holt C.J. and Lord Mansfield respectively stated that the public right of fishing existed in "navigable" waters. In texts on the law of waters and fishing written in the first half of the nineteenth century, writers similarly linked the public right of fishing to either "public" or "public navigable" waters.[6] However, in the *Case of the Royal Fishery of the Banne* (1610)[7] the Privy Council divided royal and private (rather than public and private) fishing rights on the basis of whether or not the waters were tidal. In *Lord Fitzwalter's Case* (1674),[8] his unpublished essay on Admiralty jurisdiction[9] and *De Jure Maris*[10] (which remained unpublished until 1787), Hale C.J. adopted tidality as his basis for dividing public from private fishing rights. In *Carter* v. *Murcot* (1768)[11] Yates J. equated navigable and tidal waters. Some later English dicta also supported the division of fishing rights by reference to tidality,[12] while American cases decided in the early nineteenth century adopted the same view of the common law (while sometimes rejecting the test of tidality as inappropriate for American conditions).[13]

The question of the extent of the public's right of fishing was therefore still open in the United Kingdom in the mid-nineteenth century. However, when this issue first arose for decision – which happened in Ireland rather than England – the courts exhibited little hesitation in adopting the test of tidality. In *Ashworth* v. *Browne* (1860),[14] Smith M.R. followed Hale in holding that when "it is said in some books that the public right of fishing exists in navigable rivers, . . . by that is meant so far as the sea flows and re-flows". Eight years later in another Irish case, *Murphy* v. *Ryan*,[15] O'Hagan J. – without reference to *Ashworth* v. *Browne* – adopted the same view. Following a statement in James Kent's *Commentaries*[16] based on the Bann case and Hale's *De Jure Maris,* O'Hagan J. held that at common law "navigable"

> has a popular, and also a legal and technical meaning, and that, whilst the former would be satisfied by the existence of a public right of transit on the surface of the stream, the latter involves the assumption of the "fluxum et refluxum maris", wherever the royal prerogative and the general right exist.[17]

He consequently held that the various authorities which referred to a public right of fishing in "navigable" rivers meant that the public's right extended only so far as the rivers were tidal.

In *R.* v. *Burrow* (1869),[18] the first English decision to consider *Murphy* v. *Ryan,* Cockburn C.J. rejected the contention that it was "a clearly settled point that the public could not have a right to fish in a navigable river above the flow of the tide". He noted that *Murphy* v. *Ryan* "may be taken by appeal to a higher court" (which did not in fact occur) and suggested that because "it is a point of so much importance . . . it should be taken if necessary to the highest court in the realm".[19] However, in *Mayor of Carlisle* v. *Graham* (1869)[20] Kelly C.B. quoted with approval a passage from O'Hagan J.'s judgment in which he had described the right of fishing in freshwater rivers as exclusive. In *Hargreaves* v. *Diddams* (1875)[21] and then *Mussett* v. *Birch* (1876)[22] the courts held that there was no public right of fishing in rivers which private companies had made navigable. In 1882 the Queen's Bench Division twice affirmed that the public had no right of fishing in rivers which were navigable but not tidal.[23]

In response to this series of decisions, E.P. Dove wrote an opinion in 1887 for the Corporation of Nottingham which was then engaged in disputes with landowners over fishing rights in the Trent. In this opinion, which was published as a pamphlet, *Public Rights in Navigable Rivers,*[24] Dove argued that the public had a right of fishing in the navigable reaches of rivers, except for where a grant of exclusive fishing rights had been made prior to Magna Carta. Dove's argument now appears unconvincing insofar as he wrongly assumed that Magna Carta had deprived the Crown of its power to grant exclusive fisheries.[25] His opinion was also weak in that it was largely devoted to establishing the public's right of navigation and he failed to demonstrate that the public's rights of navigation and fishing were co-extensive. The most interesting aspect of his opinion were extracts from the Hundred Rolls (c.1285) which showed that it was then unlawful for a private person to take possession of fisheries in navigable waters which previously had been "common". These extracts were, however, unclear as to whether fisheries which had been "common" had been public or had been enjoyed only by commoners.

Dove's opinion was widely discussed in contemporary newspapers and legal journals, which all regarded the matter as one of public importance and some of which found Dove's opinion to be persuasive.[26] It is consequently surprising that Dove's opinion does not appear to have been relied on in *Smith* v. *Andrews* (1891),[27] which concerned fishing rights in the navigable but non-tidal reaches of the Thames. In that case it was argued, for what appears to have been the last time, that members of the public *prima facie* have a right to fish in navigable rivers. In accordance with the views expressed by O'Hagan J. in *Murphy* v. *Ryan,* North J. stated in *Smith* v. *Andrews* that

> Some few passages may be found in the books in which Judges are reported to have said that subjects have a right to fish in navigable rivers, just as in the sea; but on investigation it will always be found that they are referring to navigable rivers where the tide ebbs and flows, and nothing else.[28]

(B) PRIVATE FISHERIES IN TIDAL WATERS

Since at least medieval times, the extent of the public right of fishing in tidal waters has been diminished by the Crown exercising its prerogative to create private fisheries. Since the early nineteenth century it has been settled (albeit incorrectly) that Magna Carta deprived the Crown of this prerogative, and hence that all private fisheries should have been created as early as the reign of Henry II. The development of this rule has not made it significantly more difficult to establish the lawful existence of private fisheries. Rather proof of the existence of a private fishery is relatively easy, at least in relation to settled fisheries. Although no recent surveys have been made, it appears that private fisheries occupy a considerable proportion of England's tidal waters.[29]

In their major study of fishing rights in England, *The History and Law of Fisheries* (1903), Stuart A. and Hubert Stuart Moore make contradictory statements as to whether exclusive fisheries in tidal waters already existed when the Domesday Book was compiled in 1086.[30] Nevertheless, they clearly conclude that very many such fisheries existed prior to the death of Henry II in 1189.[31] Their researches apparently also showed "that all, or almost all, tidal rivers and estuaries were in ancient times . . . covered by several fisheries in the hands of the subject . . . [T]he whole of the foreshore of the kingdom, wherever it was fit for fishing by weirs, was covered by several fisheries".[32] Although uncertain as to the basis on which these fisheries were created, the Moores suggest that the Crown did not specifically make grants of fisheries but rather granted the soil in tidal waters which carried the profits of the soil, that is the exclusive right to fish.[33]

There appear to be few recorded instances of several fisheries being created in English tidal waters after the twelfth century. On the evidence produced by the Moores, this change was simply the result of the prior creation of fisheries in most tidal waters (rather than the development of limitations on the Crown's power to create such fisheries) and following the conquest of Ulster in 1603, the Crown made extensive grants of exclusive fishing rights in the major rivers of northern Ireland. Most significant was the agreement of January 1610 under which members of the City of London undertook the "plantation" (that is, colonization) of the county of Coleraine (which was renamed Londonderry) and in return received extensive privileges including the fisheries of the Bann and the Foyle. Although this agreement gave rise to the case of *The Royal Fishery of the Banne* (1610),[34] the Crown's power to grant exclusive fisheries in tidal waters was not questioned in the litigation. The case turned on whether an earlier Crown grant of lands adjoining the Bann had already passed title to the fishery.

The weight of English seventeenth and eighteenth century authority supports the proposition that exclusive fisheries could be created in tidal waters either by royal grant[35] or by prescription.[36] Yet there was some dissent from this view. Already in *Warren* v. *Matthews* (1703),[37] Holt C.J. stated that the Crown was entitled to make grants in relation only to royal fish and could not deprive the public of their fishing rights. Then, in the unreported case, *Kelsey* v. *Baker* (1803),[38] Heath J. held that the Crown had no power to create exclusive fisheries:

> If the King possessed it exclusively, he could grant it exclusively. If
> he had it as a trustee, he could not grant it. The King is prima facie
> seized in trust for his subjects.

In his essay published in 1811, Henry Schultes similarly
attacked the Crown's power to grant fisheries in tidal waters on
the basis that the existence of such a power was inconsistent
with the Crown's prerogative over fish being in the nature of a
public trust.[39]

Finally, during the course of the nineteenth century, an
alternative theory prevailed which allowed the courts to uphold
existing exclusive fisheries while holding that new exclusive
fisheries could be created only by Parliament. This theory
implicitly rejected the possibility of prescription, and wrongly
contended that Magna Carta had deprived the Crown of its
power to grant private fishing rights in tidal waters, so that any
private fishery in these waters must have been created before
the death of Henry II in 1189.[40]

The immediate basis of the theory that Magna Carta acted as
a barrier to the creation of exclusive fisheries in tidal waters
was Blackstone who in his *Commentaries*[41] relied on an
unsatisfactory passage in Coke's *Institutes*[42] which in turn was
derived from the much impugned *Mirror of Justices* (c. 1285).[43]
The relevant provision of Magna Carta is chapter 16:

> Let no river be defended [i.e. be made exclusive] henceforth
> except those which were in defence at the time of our grandfather
> King Henry in the same places and by the same bounds as they
> were wont to be in his time.[44]

Although the *Mirror of Justices* and one early fourteenth
century case[45] suggest the contrary, the weight of contemporary evidence shows that chapter 16 of Magna Carta was not
meant to deal with grants by the Crown of fishing rights in
either tidal or non-tidal waters. Rather its object was to
restrain the writ *de defensione ripariae* whereby, when the King
was about to come into a county, all persons might be
forbidden from approaching the banks of the rivers so that the
King might enjoy undisturbed sport. Contemporary documents
indicate that the King only went hawking and fowling but later
authorities describe this prerogative as extending to the
prevention of fowling and fishing.[46]

Although chapter 16 of Magna Carta was therefore clearly
not concerned with the granting of fishing rights, Blackstone's
interpretation of this provision was accepted without argument
by Bayley J. in *Duke of Somerset* v. *Fogwell* (1826)[47] and then

by the House of Lords in *Malcolmson* v. *O'Dea* (1862).[48] The inconsisencies between the Magna Carta rule and Hale's *De Jure Maris* were raised for the first time in the House of Lords decision *Neill* v. *Duke of Devonshire* (1882) by Lord Blackburn who also recognized that chapter 16 probably did no more than restrain the King's sport.[49] In *Attorney-General for British Columbia* v. *Attorney-General for Canada* (1913),[50] Viscount Haldane also acknowledged that the House of Lords in *Malcolmson* v. *O'Dea* may have misinterpreted Magna Carta. Nevertheless, like Lord Blackburn in the *Neill* case, he affirmed the decision in *Malcolmson* v. *O'Dea*.

Because the Crown had long since ceased to exercise its prerogative to grant exclusive fishing rights, the adoption of the Blackstonian view of Magna Carta was not significant as a curtailment of the Crown's powers. Even though chapter 16 of Magna Carta was repealed by the Statute Law (Repeals) Act 1969,[51] the prerogative did not then revive since the Interpretation Act provides that such repealing of an enactment does not "revive anything not in force or existing at the time at which the repeal takes effect".[52] That the Crown lacks power to create exclusive fisheries was made certain by the Wild Creatures and Forest Laws Act 1971 which abolished "any prerogative right of Her Majesty to set aside land or water for the breeding, support or taking of wild creatures".[53]

The adoption of the Magna Carta rule has also not significantly affected proof of the existence of private fisheries in tidal waters. Because members of the public *prima facie* have a right to fish in tidal waters,[54] the party who claims the fishery bears the onus of establishing his claim, but he is not required to show an express grant or charter from the Crown pre-dating Magna Carta. Just as in the case of prescription, the party claiming exclusive rights under the Magna Carta rule can discharge the onus of proof if he produces sufficient evidence of long, exclusive enjoyment of the fishery – 140 years in the most recent reported case.[55] The courts will then presume that the Crown granted a private fishery as early as the reign of Henry II, and the onus shifts to the proponents of the public right to show otherwise.[56] This onus has never been discharged in a reported English case.

(C) PUBLIC FISHERIES IN NON-TIDAL LAKES

Although it is generally assumed that there is no public right of fishing in any non-tidal waters (whether rivers or lakes),[57] the question of public fishing rights in non-tidal lakes is still not settled. When the Irish case *Bristow* v. *Cormican* (1878) was on appeal to the House of Lords, Lord Cairns L.C. stated that the existence of such a right might "be a fit question to raise in some other case". [58] In deciding another Irish case, *Johnston* v. *O'Neill* (1911), three members of the House of Lords held that "no right can exist in the public to fish in the waters of an inland non-tidal lake";[59] an equal number of members of the court expressly chose not to resolve this issue.[60]

In view of this authority, there are two main obstacles to establishing a public right of fishing in non-tidal lakes (apart from the dearth of case law actually in favour of the public right rather than simply leaving this issue open). The first is the difficulty in formulating a rationale for recognizing public fishing rights in non-tidal lakes but not in non-tidal rivers. The second is the absence of settled rules by which it could be determined where exactly the public right in non-tidal lakes exists, since it is clear that not all such lakes are subject to this right.[61]

(1) Non-tidal lakes v. Non-tidal rivers

The main rationale for recognizing a public right of fishing in non-tidal lakes (but not in non-tidal rivers) rests on the size and nature of the potential fishing grounds.[62] While it may be proper to consider proprietary rights in rivers as incidental to proprietary rights in the adjacent land, decided cases indicate that at least in relation to lakes surrounded by land owned by a number of different persons, property rights should not necessarily be regarded in the same way. Whereas riparian proprietors *prima facie* own the soil and hence the fishing to the median point of non-tidal rivers,[63] Lord Blackburn twice stated that it would be "very inconvenient" if the same rule applied to such non-tidal lakes so that, for example, "each proprietor of a few acres fronting on Lough Neagh should have a piece of the soil of the lough many miles in length tacked on to his frontage".[64] The resulting absence of authority in relation to private fishing rights in many large non-tidal lakes may itself support the case for a public right of fishing, especially since other bases for allocating private fishing rights in these lakes may be unsatisfactory.[65]

There may, however, be no need for a convincing rationale for recognizing public rights of fishing in non-tidal lakes but not in non-tidal rivers. As noted by Whiteside C.J. in the Exchequer Chamber in *Bristow* v. *Cormican,* to hold that there can be no public right of fishing in non-tidal lakes simply because they do not contain salt water would itself be "An arbitary rule, repugnant to reason, convenience, and the common sense of mankind."[66] Furthermore, it is not as if in the absence of a public right in lakes there would be a perfect geographical division between public and private fisheries. The situation in tidal waters is already rather patchwork because of the number of private fisheries. It could be even regarded as a matter of symmetry if there was also a public right of fishing in at least some non-tidal waters.

(2) The extent of the possible public right

If a public right of fishing can exist in non-tidal lakes, the extent of this right is unclear. Probably the courts would resolve this issue by extending various rules and presumptions developed in relation to fishing in both tidal and non-tidal waters. However, these rules are frequently conflicting and the manner in which they would be applied is therefore largely a matter of speculation.

Where the soil of a non-tidal lake is in private ownership, it would probably be difficult but not impossible to establish a public right of fishing. Just as the ownership of soil in a non-tidal river creates a presumption of ownership of the fishing over it,[67] so ownership of the soil in a non-tidal lake probably creates a presumption of the ownership of the relevant fishery. Nevertheless, a public right of fishing could still exist since, just as a grant of the foreshore does not necessarily convey the right to a private fishery over it,[68] so the Crown might have granted the soil of lakes while retaining the fishing for the public.

Where the soil of a non-tidal lake is in the Crown, it would probably be relatively easy to establish a public right of fishing. As with tidal waters, the Crown could have granted exclusive fishing rights in non-tidal lakes without granting the soil.[69] However, if a public right of fishing in non-tidal lakes is recognized, it could well be that where the soil of such lakes is owned by the Crown, there is *prima facie* a public right of fishing. The Crown's ownership of the soil would then be subject to a public trust in the same way as in tidal waters. The main difference•between public rights in the two areas would be one of evidence rather than substance. Whereas the Crown is *prima facie* entitled to the soil in tidal waters,[70] the House of Lords has twice held that the Crown does not *prima facie* have title to the soil of non-tidal lakes.[71]

(D) DEDICATION OR ABANDONMENT OF PRIVATE FISHERIES TO THE PUBLIC

Because the public as such is regarded as being too large and indefinite a body to receive a grant,[72] it is firmly established that a public right of fishing cannot be created by prescription.[73] However, there is authority for the proposition that the owner of a private fishery in tidal waters may transfer his rights to the public by "dedication" or "abandonment" which appear to be used as synonyms in this context.[74] In principle there appears to be no reason why the owner of a fishery in non-tidal waters should not be able to do so also, unless there is an absolute rule that there cannot be a public right to fish in non-tidal waters (or, at least, non-tidal rivers) and such a rule would itself require explanation. Nevertheless, there is considerable authority that public fishing rights cannot be acquired in non-tidal waters at common law, and some of this authority is in such wide terms that it may even undermine the authority in relation to dedication to the public of fishing rights in tidal waters.

In relation to tidal waters the issue of creation of public fishing rights by dedication or abandonment is of limited importance since, if there has been such long use by the public as to show dedication or abandonment, the putative owner of the fishery will in any event probably be unable to discharge the onus of establishing the existence of private fishing rights.[75] The issue of such creation of public fishing rights arose, however, in *Rogers* v. *Allen* (1808)[76] in which there was documentary evidence of an exclusive right to both "floating" fish and shellfish in the tidal reaches of the Burnham River but there was also evidence that members of the public had fished without interruption for "floating" fish. Heath J. stated:

> Part of a fishery may be abandoned, and another part of more value may be preserved. The public may be entitled to catch floating fish in the river Burnham; but it by no means follows that they are justified in dredging for oysters, which may still remain private property.[77]

In *Mayor of Carlisle* v. *Graham* (1869)[78] it was accepted in argument that there could be abandonment to the public of an exclusive fishery in tidal waters, and, although this issue was not decided, Kelly C.B. noted that "if it be possible . . . by non-user, to dedicate a fishery in a tidal river to the public, the facts of this case afford some evidence of such a dedication between the years 1780 and the present time".[79] In the

Exchequer Chamber in the Irish case *Bristow* v. *Cormican* (1876), which concerned fishing rights in the non-tidal lake, Lough Neagh, Lawson J. distinguished *Rogers* v. *Allen* on the basis that it applied only to tidal waters,[80] while Whiteside C.J. stated that public rights of fishing could be created in all waters by dedication or abandonment.[81]

In relation to non-tidal waters – where the question of creation of public fishing rights is of considerable practical importance – the courts have held that the owners of private fisheries cannot transfer their rights to the public by either dedication[82] or abandonment.[83] However, the courts have generally not explained why this should be so, except by referring to the rule that there cannot be a public fishery in non-tidal waters (or at least non-tidal rivers),[84] which the courts in turn have made no effort to justify. The only specific explanation which the courts have given for not recognizing abandonment of fishing rights to the public is wrong. In the House of Lords in *Neill* v. *Duke of Devonshire* (1882),[85] Lord Selbourne stated that " 'abandonment' . . . is a term which has no legal meaning as to an incorporeal hereditament, such as a several fishery, which can only pass by deed". However, it is in fact clearly established that profits *à prendre*, which are incorporeal hereditaments, can pass by abandonment (that is, without a deed.)[86]

In principle, the better view appears to be that members of the public should be able to acquire fishing rights in non-tidal waters on the same basis as they can acquire rights of passage. However, even if they cannot do so, the long use by the public which would act as evidence of dedication is not altogether without legal significance. Thus, if members of the public have fished in a stretch of non-tidal water over a long period without interruption and as of right, they may argue that there must be a defect in the title of any party who asserts ownership of the fishery because otherwise the party would not have tolerated fishing by the public.[87] Consequently, it may be that no one will be able to establish ownership of the fishery (even though the courts will assume that an owner of the fishery exists somewhere).[88] Hence no one will be able to bring actions in tort to prevent members of the public from fishing in the waters.[89]

This state of affairs is most likely to arise in relation to non-tidal lakes since, as noted above, there may be no legal rule which *prima facie* awards title to this land.[90] However, it may also arise in relation to non-tidal rivers. According to

North J. in *Smith* v. *Andrews* (1891), "there are large portions of the *Thames* in which the public are at liberty to fish without interference: not from any right of their own, but because the real proprietors of the soil and fishery are not in a position to trace and establish . . . their title".[91]

II. THE BASIS OF THE PUBLIC RIGHT IN TIDAL WATERS

Since at least medieval times, conflicting views have been expressed as to whether the public right of fishing in tidal waters is enjoyed directly by members of the public or is vested in the Crown on behalf of the public. Notwithstanding early dicta to the contrary, the balance of relatively modern authority clearly supports the proposition that at common law the right was vested in the Crown on behalf of the public. However, as a result of the Wild Creatures and Forest Laws Act 1971 it appears that this right is now enjoyed directly by the public.

In the earliest English authority on fishing rights – Bracton and a decision of Choke J. in 1466 – the public right of fishing is simply described as "common to all"[92] and a matter of "common right"[93]; there is no suggestion that the public right is in any way derived from or dependent upon the Crown. This view of fishing rights was rejected in the elaborately argued Irish case, *The Royal Fishery of the Banne* (1610),[94] which involved a dispute over rights to the Bann which was then regarded as the best eel fishery in Europe and which also yielded a rich salmon harvest. The Crown had confiscated six of the nine Ulster counties following the English conquest of Ulster in 1603. It had also laid claim to most of the region's tidal fisheries, and the principles arrived at by the Privy Council in *The Royal Fishery of the Banne* served the Crown's interest in having title to as much valuable property in northern Ireland as possible as the basis for plantation of the region by English and Scottish settlers. The court held that

> Every navigable river, so high as the sea flows and ebbs in it, is a royal river, and the fishery of it is a royal fishery, and belongs to the king by his prerogative; but in every other river not navigable, and in the fishery of such river, the ter-tenants [that is, the occupants of the land] on each side have an interest of common right.[95]

The judges recognized that the fishing in tidal waters was "not

commonly taken and appropriated by the King".[96] They
therefore presumably recognized that as a matter of practice
members of the public fished extensively in tidal waters.
However, by finding that fisheries were owned either by the
Crown or by riparians, the court implicitly rejected the
existence of any form of public right of fishing.

In *Lord Fitzwalter's Case* (1674),[97] an unpublished essay on
Admiralty jurisdiction,[98] as well as *De Jure Maris*[99] (published
1787), Lord Hale stated that members of the public were
entitled to fish in tidal waters, except for where a subject has "a
private interest or property exclusive of others".[100] In both
Lord Fitzwalter's Case and his essay on Admiralty jurisdiction,
Hale made no mention of the Crown's rights in relation to fish,
and instead simply stated that the public right was "common to
all".[101] However, in *De Jure Maris* he argued that the court in
the Bann case had misunderstood the notion of "royal river" as
applied to navigable rivers. A royal river was not one in which
the soil (and hence also the fishing) was necessarily owned by
the Crown. Rather such rivers were termed "royal" because
they were open to public use under the king's care, supervision
and protection. The prerogative over fish was simply a vehicle
through which the public right was expressed. Although the
right of fishing in tidal waters was

> originally lodged in the Crown . . . [and] the King is the owner of
> this great waste, and as a consequence of his property hath the
> primary right of fishing in the sea and the creeks and the arms
> thereof; yet the common people of England have regularly a
> liberty of fishing in the sea or creeks or arms thereof, as a public
> common of piscary, and may not without injury to their right be
> restrained of it . . .[102]

Hale therefore reconciled the prerogative and public right of
fishing in tidal waters by largely sterilizing the Crown's right.

In the eighteenth century judicial authority on the basis of
the public right of fishing continued to be conflicting.[103]
However, following the publication of *De Jure Maris* in 1787,
Hale's interpretation of the Crown prerogative over fish as
some form of public trust became firmly established. The
arguments in favour of this view were painstakingly rehearsed
by Henry Schultes who, in his influential *Essay on Aquatic
Rights* (1811),[104] sought to demonstrate that "the right of
fishing never was vested in the Crown exclusively, and . . . is
not to be considered as a legal franchise. As a public right,
belonging to the people, it *prima facie* vests in the Crown; but
such legal investment does not diminish the right or counteract

its exertion". This passage from Schultes was taken up by Joseph Chitty in his *Treatise on the Game Laws and on Fisheries* (1812) who added that the public's right of fishing was "merely reposed in the Crown for the sake of regulation and government".[105]

Schultes is the last English writer to have seriously examined the legal basis of the public right of fishing in tidal waters. Subsequent commentators in the nineteenth century briefly noted that public fishing in tidal waters might be either of common right or derived from the Crown.[106] However, they tended to the latter view[107] and the correctness of this approach was affirmed twice by the House of Lords in 1882 and then by the Privy Council in 1914. In all three cases, the courts cited Hale's *De Jure Maris* with approval and accepted that the right of fishing in tidal waters originally lodged in the Crown.[108]

There the matter rested until the enactment of the Wild Creatures and Forest Laws Act 1971 which abolished "any prerogative right of Her Majesty to wild creatures (except royal fish and swans)".[109] The Bill for this Act was drafted by the Law Commission pursuant to its duty to promote the repeal of obsolete and unnecessary enactments and to simplify and modernize the law. The primary purpose of the Act was the repeal of many enactments relating to the forest laws and to do so it was felt necessary to delimit the royal prerogative over wild creatures.[110]

It was clearly not the intention of either the Law Commission or Parliament to affect the public right of fishing in tidal waters. The better view therefore is probably that as a result of the 1971 Act the public right survives but now stands by itself regardless of its origins and earlier rationalizations. Nevertheless, it can be argued that if the prerogative acted as the foundation of the public right, the removal of this foundation must have destroyed the public right as traditionally recognized at common law. However, even if this argument is correct, members of the public can still fish lawfully in "public" fisheries as the 1971 Act did not create any exclusive rights in these waters. Hence, on this view also members of the public should probably be regarded as directly enjoying a right to fish in tidal waters.

III. THE EXERCISE OF THE PUBLIC RIGHT

In waters where a public right of fishing exists, members of the public generally are not entitled to fish where, how and when they please. While it is settled that the public may use boats to fish in tidal waters, the extent of their rights, if any, to fish from the adjacent land is unclear. As a result of both statutory provisions and local byelaws designed to conserve fish stocks, there are substantial restrictions on the type and size of fish which members of the public may lawfully take in tidal waters as well as the implements they may use and the periods during which fishing may occur.

(A) USE OF THE FORESHORE AND RIVER BANKS

There is conflicting authority as to whether members of the public have a general right to cross the foreshore in order to exercise their right of fishing in tidal waters. Probably influenced by the decision in *Blundell* v. *Catterall* (1821)[111] – that members of the public have no general rights to cross the foreshore in order to bathe in the ocean – Kekewich J. in *Earl of Ilchester* v. *Rashleigh* (1889)[112] held that there is no general right for fishermen to cross over the foreshore. However, in *Brinckman* v. *Matley* (1904) Buckley J. stated "For the purpose of exercising the right of fishing it may be that there is . . . a right to cross the foreshore in order to launch a boat . . . [T]he right of fishing tends to the sustenance and beneficial enjoyment of individuals, and for these purposes it would seem that there are special rights to cross the foreshore."[113]

It is also unclear whether members of the public are entitled to stand on the foreshore (when wet or dry) and fish from there. Again, following the restrictive view of the public's rights over the foreshore adopted in *Blundell* v. *Catterall*,[114] it may be that the public has no such right. However, the decision of the Court of Common Pleas in *Bagott* v. *Orr* (1801)[115] proceeds on the footing that the public has a right to take shellfish from the foreshore when the tide is out.[116] If this view is accepted, it would be illogical if members of the public could not also fish in the ocean from there.[117]

Finally, there is no direct authority as to whether members of the public are entitled to use public rights of way for fishing. As noted previously,[118] the courts on different occasions have adopted a narrow and a broad view of the extent to which the public may use rights of way for activities other than passage. On the narrow view, members of the public have no right to fish from public paths because fishing is not "incidental" to passage. However, on the broad view, which seems preferable, members of the public may use highways to carry out an otherwise lawful activity such as fishing in tidal waters so long as they do not thereby interfere with other members of the public exercising their right of passage. On this view, members of the public should, at least in certain situations, be entitled to fish from public rights of way which run along or across the foreshore or along the banks of tidal waters.

(B) TAKE LIMITATIONS

The common law imposes only minimal restrictions on the manner in and extent to which members of the public can take fish in tidal waters. Members of the public may not exercise their right of fishing in such a way as to be a nuisance to navigation.[119] They may not use implements such as kiddles which are attached to the soil of the seashore, since to do so would be a trespass against the Crown or individual who owns the soil.[120] It has also been suggested that the common law requires the public to exercise their right of fishing "reasonably",[121] but this requirement appears meaningless as the common law imposes no restrictions on the quantity or size of fish which can be taken[122] or the implements which may be used other than the prohibition on fixed engines. It is likely in fact that the suggestion that the right of fishing be exercised reasonably is no more than a restatement of this prohibition since fixed engines can be excessively destructive of fish.

The main restrictions on the exercise of the public right of fishing have been imposed by Parliament in order to conserve fish stocks. These restrictions take a variety of forms. A small number apply to fish of any species in all waters. Thus the Salmon and Freshwater Fisheries Act 1975 prohibits the use of explosives, poisons and electrical devices to destroy fish in any waters.[123] Other statutes protect certain species of aquatic mammals. Thus the Conservation of Seals Act 1970 imposes close seasons for grey and common seals and also prohibits certain methods of killing these animals throughout the year;[124] the Wildlife and Countryside Act 1981 prohibits certain methods of killing bottlenosed and common dolphins and common porpoises.[125] The 1981 Act also provides for the establishment of marine nature reserves in which "the killing, taking, destruction, molestation or disturbance of animals . . . of any description" may be prohibited or restricted under byelaws made by the Nature Conservancy Council.[126] However, the bulk of the restrictions on taking fish have been imposed in the form of byelaws made either by Local Fisheries

Committees in relation to coastal waters or by Water Authorities in relation to rivers and estuaries.[127] The Sea Fisheries
Regulation Act 1966 authorizes these committees and authorities to make byelaws regulating a wide range of matters
including the periods during which all or any specified kinds of
fish may be taken and the methods of fishing and implements
which may be used.[128]

IV. INTERFERENCE WITH PRIVATE FISHERIES

Where a fishery is privately owned, the civil and criminal law
which protects the rights of the owner of the fishery is in large
measure the same as that which governs the taking of wild
animals discussed in the previous chapter. Regardless of
whether he catches any fish, a member of the public who fishes
in a private fishery is likely to be liable in tort both for
personally trespassing and for disturbing the fishery. If
succcessful in landing any fish, he will either be liable in
damages for the value of the catch or absolute property in the
fish will go to the owner of the fishery. Such fishing may also
breach provisions aimed at conserving fish in the Salmon and
Freshwater Fisheries Act 1975; in all cases it will be an offence
under Schedule One of the Theft Act 1968 which, in modified
form, preserves section 24 of the Larceny Act 1861.

(A) CIVIL LAW

(1) Trespass by being wrongfully on land or water

A member of the public who fishes in a private fishery commits
trespass by being on the water or adjacent land without
permission. Even if a public right of navigation exists over the
water, a member of the public who fishes from a boat commits
trespass against the owner of the soil of the river[129] since his act
of fishing is tortious if not criminal (unlike in tidal waters where
he *prima facie* has a right to fish). Equally, if there is a public
right of way alongside the fishery, a member of the public who
fishes from that path will not be exercising his right of
passage[130] and hence will be trespassing as against the owner of
the soil of the highway.

(2) Interference with the fishery

If a member of the public fishes without success in waters in
which the owner of the fishery owns the subjacent soil, the

wrongful acts of fishing are also trespasses against the soil. Like all trespasses, such fishing appears to be actionable without proof of actual damage and regardless of the extent to which the fishery was disturbed.[131] However, where the owner of the fishery does not own the subjacent soil – and the fishery is therefore an incorporeal hereditament – he cannot bring an action in trespass unless the member of the public is successful in his fishing.[132] Instead he can bring an action in the nature of trespass which also can be brought without proof of financial loss[133] but which does require that there has been a substantial interference with the fishery.[134]

(3) Property rights in fish in private fisheries

Just as a landowner has qualified property in wild animals on his land, so the owner of a private fishery has qualified property in the fish that are found within the limits of the fishery.[135] If fish within a private fishery are taken and killed by a member of the public, then, as with wild animals killed by a poacher, the fish appear to become the absolute property of the owner of the fishery who may recover them either by invoking his self-help remedies or by bringing an action for wrongful interference to goods.[136] Even if the fish are kept alive – as in the case of eels being taken to market – the fishery owner has the same remedies.[137]

(B) CRIMINAL LAW

(1) Restrictions on taking

Compared to the muddle of statutes which impose restrictions on the taking of wild animals, the position in relation to fish is straightforward. The only restrictions on taking fish from private fisheries in tidal waters are those noted above in the section dealing with the exercise of the public right of fishing in tidal waters.[138] The only restriction on taking fish in non-tidal waters are imposed in order to conserve fish stocks by the Salmon and Freshwater Fisheries Act 1975. This Act prohibits the use of various instruments for catching salmon, trout and freshwater fish.[139] While specifying minimum close seasons and weekly close times for salmon and trout (other than rainbow trout), the statute also imposes a duty on water authorities to make byelaws in relation to these matters.[140] In the case of rainbow trout and freshwater fish, a water authority has a discretion to make byelaws either fixing or altering the statutory annual close season or dispensing with it.[141]

(2) Prohibitions on Taking

Because theft applies only to those wild animals which have been or were in the course of being reduced into a person's possession,[142] a person who takes fish from a non-tidal river does not commit theft. However, he will commit an offence under section 32(1) of the Theft Act 1968 which with some modifications preserves the offence under section 24 of the Larceny Act 1861 of unlawfully taking or destroying (or attempting to take or destroy) any fish in water which is private property or in which there is a private right of fishery. Unlike theft, this offence can be committed without an intention to deprive permanently, with the unfortunate result that the offence can be committed even by anglers who intend to return their catch to the water.[143]

NOTES TO CHAPTER 8

1. The Prerogativa Regis, c. 11 as amended by the Merchant Shipping Act 1894, s. 745, schedule 22 gives the King whales and sturgeons taken in the sea or elsewhere in the realm. According to *R. v. Earl of Northumberland* (1567) 1 Plowd. 310, 315; 75 E.R. 472, 480 the Prerogativa Regis is declaratory of the common law. "Royal fish" are similarly defined as whales and sturgeons in *The Case of Swans* (1592) 7 Co. Rep. 15b, 16a; 77 E.R. 435, 436; *The Case of the Royal Fishery of the Banne* (1610) Davies 149, 152 and *Lord Warden of the Cinque Ports v. R.* (1831) 2 Hagg. Adm. 438, 441; 166 E.R. 304, 305. However, Hale, p. 43 gives an expanded definition of "royal fish" – that is, not only whales and sturgeons but also porpoise and grampus.
2. *The Case of the Royal Fishery of the Banne*, Davies 149.
3. Bracton, vol. 2, p. 40. Contrary to the view expressed in Moore, *Fisheries*, p. xxxix, there is nothing in Bracton which indicates that by "permanent" he meant "tidal" rivers.
4. 6 Mod. 73; 87 E.R. 831; 1 Salk. 357; 91 E.R. 312.
5. 4 Burr. 2162, 2164; 98 E.R. 127, 128.
6. Henry Schultes, *An Essay on Aquatic Rights*, London, Clarke, 1811, p. 68; Woolrych, *Waters*, p. 56.
7. Davies, 149.
8. 1 Mod. 105; 86 E.R. 766, 767.
9. See Moore, *Fisheries*, p. 283.
10. Hale, p. 5.
11. 4 Burr. 2162, 2164–5; 98 E.R. 127, 128–9.
12. See, for example, *Mayor of Orford v. Richardson* (1791) 4 T.R. 437; 100 E.R. 1106.
13. See, for example, *Carson v. Blazer* 4 Am. Dec. 463 (1810); *Adams v. Pease* 2 Conn. (N.S.) 481, 483 (1818).
14. (1860) 10 Ir. Ch. R. 421, 438.
15. (1868) I.R. 2 C.L. 143.

16. 3 Commentaries 412. See also Joseph K. Angell, *A Treatise on the Right of Property in Tide Waters,* 2nd ed., Boston, Little & Brown, 1847, p. 75.
17. (1868) I.R. 2 C.L. 143, 153.
18. (1869) 34 J.P. 53.
19. *Ibid.*
20. (1869) L.R. 4 Ex. 361, 367.
21. (1875) L.R. 10 Q.B. 582.
22. (1876) 35 L.T. 486.
23. *Reece* v. *Miller* (1882) 8 Q.B.D. 626; *Pearce* v. *Scotcher* (1882) 9 Q.B.D. 162.
24. P. Edward Dove, *Public Rights in Navigable Rivers,* London, Cox, 1887. A Fishing in Rivers Bill promoted by the Corporation, which declared the law to be as stated in Dove's opinion, was also introduced into the House of Commons annually from 1887 until 1890 but failed to obtain a second reading.
25. See below, pp. 245–6.
26. *The Field,* 21 May 1887; (1887) 22 L.J. 683; (1887) 3 L.Q.R. 357; *Law Times,* 21 May 1887; *Sheffield Independent,* 25 May 1887; (1887) 31 S.J. 504.
27. [1891] 2 Ch. 678, 692.
28. *Ibid.,* p. 696.
29. Moore, *Foreshore,* p. 908; Moore, *Fisheries,* p. 406. Compare *Attorney-General for British Columbia* v. *Attorney-General for Canada* [1914] A.C. 153, 171 where Viscount Haldane described private rights of fishing in tidal waters as "rare exceptions to the public right".
30. Moore, *Fisheries,* pp. xliii, 3. Compare pp. 4–5.
31. *Ibid.,* pp. 7, 26.
32. *Ibid.,* p. 406.
33. *Ibid.,* pp. vi, 14, 26.
34. Davies, 149. See below, pp. 251–2.
35. Hale, p. 17; *Carter* v. *Murcot* (1768) 4 Burr. 2162, 2165; 98 E.R. 127, 129 *per* Yates J.
36. *Lord Fitzwalter's Case* (1674) 1 Mod. 105; 86 E.R. 766, 767 *per* Hale J.; Hale, p. 18; *Carter* v. *Murcot* (1768) 4 Burr. 2162, 2164–5; 98 E.R. 127, 128–9 *per* Lord Mansfield and Yates J. See also Schultes, *op. cit.,* p. 69.
37. 6 Mod. 73; 87 E.R. 831.
38. Discussed by Geoffrey Marston, *The Marginal Seabed: United Kingdom Legal Practice,* Oxford, Clarendon Press, 1981, p. 18.
39. Schultes, *op. cit.,* pp. 61, 68.
40. This misinterpretation of Magna Carta was first recognized by the Moores in *The History and Law of Fisheries* (1903). It has subsequently been discussed by Henry Phillip Farnham, *The Law of Water and Water Rights,* Rochester, Lawyers' Co-operative, 1904, vol. 2, pp. 1368–72; Bryan Murphy, "The Lawyer as Historian: Magna Carta and Public Rights of Fishery", (1968) 3 Irish Jurist 131–45.
41. 2 Bl. Comm. 39.
42. Coke, *Institutes,* Magna Carta, Cap. XVI.
43. See Frederic William Maitland, "Introduction" to William Joseph Whittacker (ed.), *The Mirror of Justices,* S.S. 7, 1893.
44. Translation taken from Bryan Murphy, "The Lawyer as Historian: Magna Carta and Public Rights of Fishery", (1968) 3 Irish Jurist 131, 132.

45. Moore, *Fisheries*, pp. 16–18.
46. *Ibid.*, p. 8.
47. (1826) 5 B. & C. 875, 884; 108 E.R. 325, 328.
48. 10 H.L.C. 593, 618; 11 E.R. 1155, 1165–6. See also *Gann* v. *Free Fishers of Whitstable* (1865) 11 H.L.C. 191; 11 E.R. 1305; *Duke of Northumberland* v. *Houghton* (1870) L.R. 5 Ex. 127; *Edgar* v. *Special Commissioners for English Fisheries* (1871) 23 L.T. 732; *Mayor of Saltash* v. *Goodman* (1880) 5 C.P.D. 431, 440 *per* Grove J.; (1881) 7 Q.B.D. 106, 112 *per* Baggallay L.J.; 119—20 *per* Brett L.J.
49. (1882) 8 App. Cas. 135, 177–8.
50. [1914] A.C. 153, 170.
51. Statute Law (Repeals) Act 1969, s. 1, sched. 1, part 1.
52. Then Interpretation Act 1889, s. 38(2)(a); now Interpretation Act 1978, s. 16(1)(a).
53. Wild Creatures and Forest Laws Act 1971, s. 1(1)(a).
54. *Malcolmson* v. *O'Dea* (1863) 10 H.L.C. 593, 618; 11 E.R. 1155, 1165.
55. *Loose* v. *Castleton* (1981) 41 P. & C.R. 19.
56. *Malcolmson* v. *O'Dea* (1863) 10 H.L.C. 593, 618; 11 E.R. 1155, 1166; *Edgar* v. *Special Commissioners for English Fisheries* (1871) 23 L.T. 732, 736 *per* Willes, J.; *Loose* v. *Casterton* (1981) 41 P. & C.R. 19, 37 *per* Ormrod L.J.
57. See, for example, Halsbury, vol. 18, para. 610.
58. (1878) 3 App. Cas. 641, 651. See also at 671 *per* Lord Gordon.
59. [1911] A.C. 552, 577 *per* Lord Macnaghten. See also at 568 *per* Earl of Halsbury; 592–3 *per* Lord Dunedin.
60. [1911] A.C. 552, 567 *per* Earl Loreburn L.C.; 572–3 *per* Lord Ashbourne; 605–6 *per* Lord Shaw. See also *Toome Eel Fishery (Northern Ireland) Ltd* v. *Cardwell* [1966] N.I. 1, 12 discussed by E. Tenebaum, "Fishing in Lough Neagh", (1966) 17 Northern Ireland Legal Quarterly 433–8.
61. See, for example, *Marshall* v. *Ulleswater Steam Navigation Co.* (1863) 3 B. & S. 732; 122 E.R. 274.
62. A further rationale, resting on the Irish plantation and hence probably restricted to Ireland, was advanced by Lord Shaw in *Johnston* v. *O'Neill* [1911] A.C. 552, 605–6.
63. See, for example, *Ecroyd* v. *Coulthard* [1898] 2 Ch. 358, 367 *per* Lindley M.R.; *Jones* v. *Llanrwst U.D.C.* [1911] 1 Ch. 393 *per* Chitty L.J.; *Attorney-General of British Columbia* v. *Attorney-General for Canada* [1914] A.C. 153, 167 *per* Viscount Haldane.
64. *Bristow* v. *Cormican* (1878) 3 App. Cas. 641, 666–7; *Mackenzie* v. *Bankes* (1878) 3 App. Cas. 1324, 1340–1.
65. The main alternative appears to be the Scottish rule that if no party can establish exclusive possession of a lake, then rights such as fishing are "to be enjoyed over the whole water space, by all the riparian proprietors in common, subject if need be to judicial regulation". See *Mackenzie* v. *Bankes* (1878) 3 App. Cas. 1324, 1338 *per* Lord Selbourne. This distribution of fishing rights is vulnerable to problems of excessive fishing as a result of riparians granting fishing licences to other persons, and the courts may also not be a very suitable forum in which to establish fishing quotas. See *Menzies* v. *Wentworth* (1901) 3 F. 941.
66. (1876) I.R. 10 C.L. 398, 434. See also at 411–12 *per* Dowse B.
67. *Hanbury* v. *Jenkins* [1901] 2 Ch. 401.

68. *Attorney-General* v. *Emerson* [1891] A.C. 649, 655 *per* Lord Herschell.
69. *Scratton* v. *Brown* (1825) 4 B. & C. 485, 503; 107 E.R. 1140, 1147 *per* Littledale J.; *Attorney-General* v. *Emerson* [1891] A.C. 649, 654 *per* Lord Herschell.
70. *Malcomson* v. *O'Dea* (1863) 10 H.L.C. 593, 617; 11 E.R. 1155, 1165 *per* Willes J.
71. *Bristow* v. *Cormican* (1878) 3 App. Cas. 641; *Johnston* v. *O'Neill* [1911] A.C. 552. Compare *Marshall* v. *Ulleswater Steam Navigation Co.* (1863) 3 B. & S. 732, 742; 122 E.R. 274, 278 *per* Wightman J. (with whom Mellor J. agreed).
72. See above, p. 104, n. 92.
73. See *Murphy* v. *Ryan* (1868) I.R. 2 C.L. 143, 154–5 *per* O'Hagan J.; *Hargreaves* v. *Diddams* (1875) L.R. 10 Q.B. 582, 586 *per* Quinn J.; *Neill* v. *Duke of Devonshire* (1882) 8 App. Cas. 135, 154–5 *per* Lord Selbourne L.C.; *Smith* v. *Andrews* [1891] 2 Ch. 678, 700 *per* North J.
74. See especially *Bristow* v. *Cormican* (1876) I.R. 10 C.L. 398, 416 *per* Lawson J., 433 *per* Whiteside C.J. The meaning of "abandonment" in this context is therefore different from its meaning in relation to chattels, where as discussed below at pp. 270–1, it connotes renouncing title without transferring it to anyone else.
75. See *Mayor of Carlisle* v. *Graham* (1869) L.R. 4 Ex. 361, 369 *per* Kelly C.B.
76. 1 Camp. 309; 170 E.R. 967.
77. 1 Camp. 309, 313; 170 E.R. 967, 969.
78. (1869) L.R. 4 Ex. 361.
79. *Ibid.*, p. 370 *per* Kelly C.B. Compare at p. 372 *per* Bramwell B.
80. (1876) I.R. 10 C.L. 398, 416.
81. *Ibid.*, p. 433.
82. *Bristow* v. *Cormican* (1876) I.R. 10 C.L. 398, 416 *per* Lawson J.
83. *Neill* v. *Duke of Devonshire* (1882) 8 App. Cas. 135, 154–5 *per* Lord Selbourne L.C.; *O'Neill* v. *Johnston* [1908] 1 I.R. 358, 380 *per* Ross J.; [1909] 1 I.R. 237, 242 *per* Holmes L.J., 257 *per* Walker L.C., 264 *per* Fitzgibbon L.J. See also *Smith* v. *Andrews* [1891] 2 Ch. 678, 703–4 *per* North J.
84. See, for example, *Bristow* v. *Cormican* (1876) I.R. 10 C.L. 398, 416.
85. (1882) 8 App. Cas. 135, 154–5. See also *O'Neill* v. *Johnston* [1909] 1 I.R. 237, 242, 257, 264.
86. See Paul Jackson, *The Law of Easements and Profits,* London, Butterworth, 1978, pp. 196–203; Megarry & Wade, pp. 897–8.
87. *Smith* v. *Andrews* [1891] 2 Ch. 678, 707 *per* North J.
88. See *Johnston* v. *O'Neill* [1911] A.C. 552, 594 *per* Lord Dunedin.
89. However, the criminal law protecting private fisheries could still be invoked because it does not depend on title being shown in any particular person. See below, p. 258.
90. See above, p. 247.
91. [1891] 2 Ch. 678, 698.
92. Bracton, vol. 2, p. 40.
93. Year Book, Mich. 8, Edw. IV, plea 30, quoted in Moore, *Foreshore,* p. 166.
94. Davies, 149.
95. *Ibid.*, p. 152.
96. *Ibid.*, p. 155.
97. 1 Mod. 105; 86 E.R. 766.

98. See Moore, *Foreshore*, p. 283.
99. Hale, p. 11.
100. Moore, *Foreshore*, p. 283.
101. 1 Mod. 105; 86 E.R. 766, 767.
102. Hale, p. 11.
103. Contrast *Warren* v. *Matthews* (1703) 6 Mod. 73; 87 E.R. 831; 1 Salk. 357; 91 E.R. 312 *per* Holt C.J. (the public right of fishing is enjoyed directly by members of the public) with *Carter* v. *Murcot* (1768) 4 Burr. 2162, 2164; 98 E.R. 127, 128 *per* Lord Mansfield (the Crown's prerogative forms the basis of the public right).
104. Schultes, *op. cit.*, p. 15.
105. J. Chitty, *A Treatise on the Game Laws and on Fisheries*, London, Clarke, 1812, vol. 1, p. 244. See also Joseph Chitty, *A Treatise on the Law of the Prerogatives of the Crown*, London, Butterworth, 1820, p. 142.
106. See Hall, p. 46; Woolrych, *Waters*, p. 55.
107. Woolrych, *Waters*, p. 55; James A. Paterson, *A Treatise on the Fishery Laws of the United Kingdom*, London, Macmillan, 1863, p. 14.
108. *Goodman* v. *Mayor of Saltash* (1882) 7 App. Cas. 633, 651 *per* Lord Blackburn quoted with approval in *Johnston* v. *O'Neill* [1911] A.C. 552, 605 *per* Lord Shaw; *Neill* v. *Duke of Devonshire* (1882) 8 App. Cas. 135, 157–8, 177 *per* Lords Blackburn and O'Hagan; *Attorney-General for British Columbia* v. *Attorney-General for Canada* [1914] A.C. 153, 168–9.
109. Wild Creatures and Forest Laws Act 1971, s. 1(1)(a).
110. Law Commission, *Statute Law Revision Second Report: Draft Wild Creatures and Forest Law Bill*, London, H.M.S.O., 1970, p. 1.
111. 5 B. & Ald. 268; 106 E.R. 1190.
112. (1889) 61 L.T. 477, 478.
113. [1904] 2 Ch. 313, 316.
114. See, especially, 5 B. & Ald. 268, 301–2; 106 E.R. 1190, 1202 *per* Holroyd J.
115. 2 Bos. & Pul. 472; 126 E.R. 1391.
116. See *Brinckman* v. *Matley* [1904] 2 Ch. 313, 327 *per* Romer L.J. and below, pp. 264–5.
117. Hall, pp. 174–5.
118. See above, pp. 56–8.
119. *Mayor of Colchester* v. *Brooke* (1845) 7 Q.B. 339, 375; 115 E.R. 518, 532 *per* Denman C.J.
120. *Attorney-General for British Columbia* v. *Attorney-General for Canada* [1914] A.C. 153, 171 *per* Viscount Haldane; *Attorney-General for Canada* v. *Attorney-General for Quebec* [1921] 1 A.C. 401, 428 *per* Viscount Haldane.
121. Halsbury, vol. 18, para. 613.
122. *Corporation of Saltash* v. *Goodman* (1881) 7 Q.B.D. 106, 116 *per* Baggallay L.J.; *Goodman* v. *Mayor of Saltash* (1882) 7 App. Cas. 633, 653 *per* Lord Blackburn.
123. Salmon and Freshwater Fisheries Act 1975, s. 5(1).
124. Conservation of Seals Act 1970, ss. 1, 2.
125. Wildlife and Countryside Act, s. 11, sched. 6.
126. *Ibid.*, s. 37(2)(ii). However, see John Gibson, "Marine Nature Reserves", [1984] J.P.L. 699–706, esp. at p. 704. No marine nature reserves have yet been established.

127. Sea Fisheries Regulation Act 1966, s. 18(1).
128. *Ibid.,* s. 5(1).
129. See *Grant* v. *Henry* (1894) 21 R. 358, 363 *per* Lord Kinnear.
130. See *Fergusson* v. *Shireff* (1844) 6 D. 1363, 1371 *per* Lord Moncrieff; 1375 *per* Lord Cockburn.
131. *Child* v. *Greenhill* (1639) Cro. Car. 553; 79 E.R. 1077.
132. See *Nicholls* v. *Ely Beet Sugar Factory Ltd* [1936] Ch. 343, 347 *per* Lord Wright M.R.
133. *Ibid.,* pp. 349–53 *per* Lord Wright M.R.; p. 356 *per* Romer L.J.
134. *Fitzgerald* v. *Firbank* [1897] 2 Ch. 96, 104 *per* Rigby L.J.; *Nicholls* v. *Ely Beet Sugar Factory Ltd* [1936] Ch. 343, 353 *per* Lord Wright M.R.
135. *Nicholls* v. *Ely Beet Sugar Factory Ltd* [1936] Ch. 343, 347 *per* Lord Wright M.R.
136. *Ibid.*
137. *Toome Eel Fishery (Northern Ireland) Ltd* v. *Cardwell* [1966] N.I. 1, 29.
138. See above, pp. 225–6.
139. Salmon and Freshwater Fisheries Act 1975, ss. 1, 3, 5.
140. *Ibid.,* s. 19, sched. 1, para. 1.
141. *Ibid.,* s. 19, sched. 1, paras 3, 4; sched. 3, para. 20.
142. Theft Act 1968, s. 4(4).
143. *Wells* v. *Hardy* [1964] 2 Q.B. 447. See Criminal Law Revision Committee, *Eighth Report: Theft and Related Offences,* 1966, Cmnd. 2977, para. 55.

Chapter 9

SHELLFISH

In a number of jurisdictions statutes have altered property rights in certain species of animal – such as bees and silver foxes – by either extending the circumstances in which a keeper of these species retains his qualified property in the animals[1] or by making these species the subject of absolute rather than qualified property (and hence treating the animals as tame rather than as wild).[2] In England the only legislation broadly of this type – consolidated in the Sea Fisheries (Shellfish) Act 1967 – applies to mussels, oysters and clams. This Act does not apply in all geographical areas; in certain areas it transforms qualified property in these molluscs into absolute property; elsewhere it operates more radically so as to change these species from being *res nullius* into absolute property.

The changes effected by statute in England result in property rights in shellfish much the same as those created by the courts in other jurisdictions. Thus, because oysters and mussels spend their adult life fixed to the soil of tidal waters, Scottish law treats them as part of the soil and hence as the absolute property of the relevant landowner.[3] In the United States shellfish such as oysters and clams in private fisheries are similarly treated as subjects of absolute property.[4] However, because such shellfish "do not require to be reclaimed and made tame by art, industry or education" and "have neither the inclination nor power to escape", they are considered to be like domesticated animals and hence are classified as personal property rather than as part of realty.[5]

In England property rights in shellfish at common law are the same as those in relation to "floating" fish.[6] As part of the public right of fishing, members of the public *prima facie* have a right to take oysters and mussels (along with other shellfish) in tidal waters.[7] Furthermore, as affirmed by a succession of cases beginning with *Bagott* v. *Orr* (1801),[8] the public can even take shellfish from the dry foreshore, and for this purpose have presumably a right of access over the foreshore. Where private shellfisheries exist (as a result of grants prior to Magna Carta), the owner of the fishery has qualified property in the shellfish but – as with floating fish – a person who wrongfully takes them generally does not commit theft.[9] He possibly will commit the offence of unlawfully taking or destroying fish under section 24 of the Larceny Act 1861, although in *Leavett* v. *Clark* (1915)[10] both Lord Reading C.J. and Avory J. suggested that shellfish were not "fish" within the meaning of the 1861 Act.[11]

The statutory alteration of property rights in shellfish occurred because of a drop in the supply of oysters in the mid-nineteenth century which, according to the Commissioners on Sea Fisheries (1866), resulted "not from overfishing but from the very general failure of the spat [that is, the young of the oyster]".[12] The Commissioners consequently recommended the creation of exclusive oyster beds in order to "promote the application of labour to the beds, with a view to ultimate rather than immediate returns".[13] This recommendation was adopted by Parliament in the Sea Fisheries Act 1868 which applied not only to oysters but also to mussels[14] and which in 1884 was extended so as to apply to cockles.[15] The legislation initially applied only to fisheries "on the shore and bed of the sea, or of an estuary or tidal river, above or below, or partly above and partly below, low water mark";[16] in 1981 it was extended so as also to apply to "any structure floating on, or standing or suspended in, water for the propagation of shellfish or . . . oysters".[17]

In property terms the Sea Fisheries (Shellfish) Act protects two different types of fishery. It applies firstly to private oyster beds owned by any person independently of the Act, which are sufficiently marked out or known as such.[18] It applies also to areas where at common law there typically was a public right of fishing[19] but which have been the subject of a ministerial order creating an exclusive fishery.[20] In each case the Act confers absolute property in the shellfish on the owner (or grantee) of the fishery;[21] hence a member of the public who takes the shellfish may commit theft. In each case, the Act also makes a range of activities unlawful[22] – the broadest of which is to disturb or injure the shellfish, bed or fishery in any manner except for a lawful purpose of navigation or anchorage.[23] Any person who "knowingly" (that is not accidentally)[24] does any of these things not only commits an offence but also is liable to make full compensation to the owner or grantee for all damage sustained by him as a result of the unlawful act.

NOTES TO CHAPTER 9

1. Bees Act, R.S.O. 1980, c. 42, ss. 2–4 (Ontario).
2. California Civil Code, s. 996 (1949) in relation to silver foxes, discussed in John C. Hogan, "The Distraint of Animals Ferae Naturae", (1955) 34 Oregon L.R. 217, 222–3.
3. *Duchess of Sutherland* v. *Watson* (1868) 6 M. 199, 213 *per* Lord Neaves; 216 *per* Lord Patton; *Parker* v. *Lord Advocate* [1904] A.C. 364, 372 *per* Lord Kincairney; 377–8 *per* Lord Kinross. Compare *Hall* v. *Whillis* (1852) 14 D. 324.
4. See *State* v. *Taylor* 72 Am. Dec. 347 (1858); *Peo,le* v. *Morrison* 86 N.E. 1120 (1909); 35 Am. Jur. 2d 649.
5. *State* v. *Taylor* 72 Am. Dec. 347, 348 (1858).
6. See *Goodman* v. *Mayor of Saltash* (1882) 7 App. Cas. 633, 646 *per* Lord Selbourne.
7. *Corporation of Truro* v. *Rowe* [1902] 2 K.B. 709, 716 *per* Cozens-Hardy L.J.; *Ullman* v. *Cowes Harbour Commissioners* [1909] 2 K.B. 1, 5 *per* Channell J.
8. 2 Bos. & Pul. 472; 126 E.R. 1391; accepted as correct in *Howe* v. *Stawell* (1833) Alc. & Nap. 348; *Corporation of Saltash* v. *Goodman* (1881) 7 Q.B.D. 106, 116 *per* Baggallay L.J.; *Alfred F. Beckett Ltd* v. *Lyons* [1967] Ch. 449, 481 *per* Winn L.J.; followed in the Canadian case *Donnelly* v. *Vroom* (1907) 40 N.S.R. 585; (1908) 42 N.S.R. 327.
9. Shellfish in most private fisheries would probably not satisfy the test of being "kept in captivity" or "reduced into possession" in the Theft Act 1968, s. 4(4). See *R.* v. *Howlett* [1968] Criminal L.R. 222. However, where shellfish are placed in special beds or ponds, such as artificial oyster layings, they may satisfy this test. See *The Swift* [1901] P. 168, 171 *per* Jeune P.; *Foster* v. *Warblington U.D.C.* [1906] 1 K.B. 648, 671 *per* Stirling L.J.; and especially, 681–2 *per* Fletcher Moulton L.J.
10. [1915] 3 K.B. 9, 12.
11. The third member of the court, Lush J., thought that shellfish should be regarded as fish. Notwithstanding this divergence of views, all three judges held that winkles were "fish" within the meaning of the Act, since they were bound by *Caygill* v. *Thwaite* (1885) 49 J.P. 614 in which "crayfish" had been held to be "fish".
12. *Report on the Commissioners appointed to inquire into the Sea Fisheries of the United Kingdom*, H.M.S.O., 1866, vol. 1, p. cv.
13. *Ibid.,* p. xcix.
14. Sea Fisheries Act 1868, part III.
15. Sea Fisheries Act 1884, s. 1.
16. Sea Fisheries Act 1868, s. 29, now Sea Fisheries (Shellfish) Act 1967, s. 1(1).
17. Fisheries Act 1981, s. 34.
18. Sea Fisheries (Shellfish) Act 1967, s. 7(1)(b).
19. *Ibid.,* s. 1(5) provides that no ministerial order "shall take away or abridge any right of several fishery or any right on, to or over any portion of the sea shore, being a right enjoyed by any person under any local or special Act of Parliament or any Royal charter, letters patent, prescription, or immemorial usage, except with the consent of that person".
20. *Ibid.,* ss. 1(1), 7(1)(a). In 1980 there were twenty such orders in existence. See Water Space Amenity Commission, *Conservation and Land Drainage Guidelines*, London, 1980, p. 60.

21. Sea Fisheries (Shellfish) Act 1967, s. 7(2).
22. *Ibid.*, s. 7(4).
23. *Ibid.*, s. 7(4)(e).
24. *Smith* v. *Cooke* (1914) 84 L.J.K.B. 959.

Chapter 10

ABANDONED, HIDDEN AND LOST THINGS

When a member of the public takes such things as a stray domesticated animal, a ring lying on the ground or a hoard of coins, his rights in the thing fall within one of three categories. In relatively rare circumstances he may become owner of the thing. Alternatively, he may have a better claim to the thing than anyone except for its original owner. Or he may be required to give the thing up to the Crown or the occupier of the land where he found it. In the first case, he can deal with the thing with the freedom of an owner, but otherwise he will incur certain obligations in relation to it.

I. RIGHTS IN ABANDONED, HIDDEN AND LOST THINGS

(A) FINDER v. OWNER

Where an owner of a chattel loses or hides his property, it remains his even though out of his possession. No lapse of time, however great, between the hiding or losing and the finding of the chattel by a member of the public can bar the owner's claim to recover his property. In the event of the original owner being dead, his successors may claim the chattel.

Contrary to popular belief, the owner of lost or hidden chattels is also never barred from recovering them from an honest finder regardless of the period which has elapsed since the finding of the chattels. The Statute of Limitations only runs against the owner of lost and hidden goods in two situations. If the finder of the goods converts them to his own use, the owner is not able to bring an action to recover his things six years from the conversion.[1] If the original taking of the thing was theft, but it was then bought by someone else in good faith, the original owner is again barred from recovering his property six years after that purchase.[2]

The one situation where the honest finder of a thing can probably succeed against its original owner is where the latter has abandoned the thing. The law concerning abandonment of chattels in English law is, however, highly confused and has been the subject of little serious consideration.[3] It is not only uncertain whether a person may in fact divest himself of ownership of chattels by abandonment; it is also unclear what combination of act and intention is necessary to establish abandonment and when abandonment takes effect.

(1) Does abandonment divest ownership?

In Roman law ownership of a chattel was divested by abandonment *(derelictio),* which occurred if possession of a thing was intentionally relinquished by its owner without desire of recovery.[4] In American jurisdictions, this rule also prevails[5] as a result of the influence of Blackstone.[6] However, in England as in some Commonwealth jurisdictions, the law is unclear[7] and there is some suggestion that abandonment does not divest ownership[8] which would mean that the "original" owner of an abandoned chattel could reclaim it even though it had been taken by someone else.

In early English law there are conflicting authorities concerning the consequences of abandonment. Following Roman law, the medieval English writers Bracton[9] and Fleta[10] considered that ownership of a chattel could be divested by abandonment. However, in a discussion of wreck in *Doctor and Student* (1523–31), St German expressly rejected the rule as stated by Bracton. According to St German, "though a man waive possession of his goods and said he forsaketh them yet by the law of the realm the property remaineth still in him and he may seize them after when he will".[11] This proposition was adopted by Viner in his *Abridgement* (1745)[12] but was rejected by Blackstone who, without discussing the views of St German and Viner, returned in his *Commentaries* (1765)[13] to the Roman and medieval English view that abandonment was a means of divesting ownership.

The only reported English decision which unambiguously supports the proposition that ownership of chattels cannot be divested by abandonment is *Steel* v. *Houghton* (1788)[14] in which Heath J. held that "By the law of England, no property can be lost by abandonment, for the owner may at any time resume the possession."[15] Otherwise, over the last 140 years, English courts have consistently either held or accepted that ownership of chattels can be divested by abandonment. In a series of maritime cases the courts have held that the owner of a sunken ship may relinquish all interest in it by abandonment and thereby escape certain obligations and liabilities in relation to the wreck.[16] In a number of criminal cases, the courts have accepted that if a chattel was abandoned, its taking was not larceny since the thing taken did not belong to someone other than the accused.[17] In *Elwes* v. *Brigg Gas Co.* (1886)[18] Chitty J. impliedly indicated that property rights could be divested by abandonment. In the relatively recent finding case, *Moffatt* v. *Kazana* (1967),[19] Wrangham J. expressly referred to abandonment as one of the recognized methods by which a person can rid himself of ownership of a chattel.

The only weakness of this modern authority is that the courts have not referred to, let alone rejected, the rule against abandonment first stated in *Doctor and Student*. Possibly for this reason, some modern writers have sought to read restrictively decisions in favour of effective abandonment, especially the maritime cases.[20] Nevertheless, the better view appears to be that abandonment should be effective. This proposition is not only supported by the weight of judicial authority; it also accords with the general expectations of the community, and cases of real injustice could otherwise result if, for example, the "retiring" owner reasserts his rights long after his "abandonment".[21]

(2) What constitutes abandonment?

In order that ownership be divested by abandonment, there must be a combination of the requisite act and intention: the owner of the thing must relinquish possession with the intention of renouncing his entire interest in it and without intending to confer an interest on anyone else.[22] Consequently, so long as the thing remains on the owner's land, it cannot be abandoned;[23] a person who does not intend to use a thing again does not abandon it if he also intends that no one else should use it;[24] equally, a person who stops searching for something he has lost does not thereby necessarily abandon it.[25]

Although the requirement of an act of abandonment could create difficulties because of confusion surrounding the issue of "possession", argument in reported decisions has consistently concerned the intention to abandon. In spite of some judicial uncertainty,[26] it appears clear that the intention which is relevant for abandonment is the actual (subjective) intention of the owner of the thing.[27] However, apart from in relation to wrecked ships, instances of express abandonment are rare, and frequently the owner of the thing is not even available to give evidence of his intention. In this type of situation, the owner's intention must be inferred from the surrounding circumstances and the courts enjoy considerable latitude in their findings.

While a wide variety of factors may be relevant in inferring the owner's intention, the two most important considerations generally are the value of the thing and the period which has elapsed since the putative act of abandonment. As stated by Rolfe B. in *R.* v. *Peters* (1843), "If I had an apple and dropped it, it might be presumed that I had abandoned it, but if I drop £500, the presumption is that I do not mean to abandon it."[28] According to Stephen J. in the Australian High Court decision in *Robinson* v. *Western Australian Museum* (1977), the mere passing of time without any attempt to assert possession may possibly be regarded as involving abandonment of title.[29]

On the basis of these considerations, the courts could (and should) sometimes infer an intention to abandon.[30] Yet, as illustrated by *Williams* v. *Phillips* (1957),[31] English courts have been reluctant to do so. In that case, garbagemen were charged with larceny for having appropriated refuse from garbage bins. The primary intention of the relevant householders was clearly to be rid of the refuse. While expecting the local authority to take it, they may not have cared who did, and so could have been held to have abandoned the garbage. However, Lord Goddard C.J. considered that this was a "wholly untenable proposition". In a remarkable passage, the judge deemed it only "very likely" that a householder who puts refuse out to be taken away "does not want it himself and that is why he puts it in the dustbin".[32] He inferred that the householders intended only the local authority to take the refuse, and consequently upheld the garbagemen's conviction. Because of the difference in the onus of proof in civil proceedings (whereby the person who asserts abandonment must establish it),[33] English judges in actions for wrongful interference to goods are even less likely than Lord Goddard C.J. in *Williams* v. *Phillips* to find that an owner has abandoned chattels.

(3) When is abandonment effective?

The point at which abandonment becomes effective is the subject of conflicting authority. According to Roman law[34] and a number of maritime cases,[35] an owner's abandonment of his property is effective when the thing is out of the owner's possession and he has the requisite intention to abandon it. However, *Haynes' Case* (1614)[36] supports the view that abandonment is effective only when a member of the public actually takes the thing and that until then property remains in the original owner. The court stated "a man cannot relinquish the property he hath to his goods, unless they be vested in another".[37]

The issue of when abandonment is effective is of considerable theoretical interest. If abandonment is effective when there is a combination of the requisite act and intention, the thing then becomes *res nullius* until someone takes it. On this view, abandonment is a distinctive method by which an owner may relinquish his interest in things. However, if abandonment is effective only when the thing is taken by a member of the public, an abandoned thing is never *res nullius*. If this approach is accepted, abandonment is no more than a form of gift where the owner intends that any person (rather than a specific individual or class of individuals) may take his property. Like a gift of a chattel in the absence of a deed, the abandonment of a thing will require delivery to be effective.

The question of when abandonment becomes effective may also be significant in relation to the original owner's obligations in relation to his property.[38] However, the incidence of such liabilities has no effect on a member of the public who finds an abandoned thing. Regardless of when abandonment is effective, he can only gain rights over the thing when he takes it into his care and control.

(B) FINDER v. CROWN OR OCCUPIER

In the absence of the owner, a finder's rights over lost or hidden things are the same as his rights over abandoned things. In both cases, the finder's right to the things depend on whether it was found under or attached to the soil as opposed to on the surface of land. The legal basis of this distinction is that things found under or attached to the surface of land are in possession of the occupier of the land regardless of whether he knows of their existence; things simply resting on the surface of land may not be in the possession of the occupier of the land. The practical basis of this distinction is that members of the public generally only find things under or attached to the soil as a result of deliberate search; the discovery of things on the surface of land is likely to be accidental.

(1) Things found under or attached to the soil

From the perspective of members of the public, the question of rights in things found under (or attached) to land arises primarily from the use of metal detectors to search for buried treasure – a hobby which has become increasingly popular since the late 1960s. Notwithstanding considerable controversy over the use of metal detectors by amateur treasure hunters, there are only very limited restrictions on their use. However, to dig for treasure without the permission of the relevant landowner may be both a tort and a criminal offence. An even more important restriction on members of the public who wish to search for treasure is that they have, of themselves, no rights in things under or attached to the surface of land.

(a) The use of metal detectors

Over the past decade, amateur treasure hunters using metal detectors have made many finds of considerable archaeological importance and great value including the so-called Mildenhall and Thetford treasures, the most significant recent discoveries of material relating to Roman Britain. The very success of the amateurs has given archaeologists cause for concern, since the unskilled extraction of treasure "inevitably causes extensive damage to archaeological deposits and deprives the find of its archaeological context, thereby preventing a full understanding of the object and the site".[39]

When members of the public began using metal detectors extensively in search of treasure, the only restriction on their use was imposed by the Wireless Telegraphy Act 1949 which required users of metal detectors to obtain a licence in order to ensure that the detectors did not interfere with radio frequencies.[40] On administrative grounds, quite removed from the debate over treasure hunting,[41] regulations which came into force at the beginning of January 1981 abolished the licence requirement.[42] Metal detectors must still, however, operate within certain frequency specifications.[43]

According to various newspaper reports, several local councils over the last ten years have considered banning the use of metal detectors on land which they control while other councils have already purportedly banned the use of metal detectors on such land.[44] The basis on which councils have sought to effect such bans is not clear but it seems that they have been legally unenforceable. The councils could only ban the use of metal detectors through byelaws which need to be confirmed by the Secretary of State in order to come into force.[45] On the ground that the use of metal detectors, as such, does not cause damage to land or interfere unduly with its enjoyment by other people, the Home Office has refused to confirm byelaws forbidding the use of metal detectors in pleasure grounds, open spaces and on beaches.[46]

The archaeologists' only success in the debate over legal control of treasure hunting came in 1979. In section 42 of the Ancient Monuments and Archaeological Areas Act, Parliament made it an offence to use a metal detector in protected places[47] – that is, designated areas of archaeological importance and the sites of scheduled monuments in the ownership or guardianship of the Secretary of State.[48] Using a metal detector in such places without the written permission of the Secretary of State is punishable by a fine not exceeding £200.[49] It is also an offence punishable by an unlimited fine to remove any object of archaeological or historical interest located by using a metal detector in a protected place.[50]

(b) Digging for treasure

To dig for treasure without the permission of the occupier of the land is a trespass for which the treasure hunter can be liable in damages. Where the land in question is an open space controlled by a local authority, digging for treasure will probably be an offence under byelaws which commonly provide that "a person shall not remove, cut or displace any soil, turf . . .". In relation to all land, digging for treasure without the relevant permission will generally also be an offence under the Criminal Damage Act 1971 since the digging will involve damage to property belonging to another intending to damage such property or being reckless as to whether any such property would be damaged.[51]

(c) The meaning of "treasure trove"

Any rights or claims existing in members of the public who find things under or attached to the surface of land derive from either the occupier of the land or the Crown. The critical question is whether or not the things found fall within the Crown's prerogative rights to treasure trove. While the meaning of "treasure trove" is a matter of law to be determined by the courts, application of the definition to particular objects and resolution of any disputes surrounding the identification of the finders of the objects are matters for coroners in exercise of their original function of protecting the financial interests of the realm.[52]

In the recent case, *Attorney-General of the Duchy of Lancaster* v. *G.E. Overton (Farms) Ltd* (1981), which resolved many longstanding questions concerning the definition of treasure trove, the Court of Appeal held that treasure trove is restricted to objects of gold or silver.[53] At one point in his judgment, Lord Denning M.R. suggested that an object should "be 50 per cent or more gold or silver before it could be described as a gold or silver object".[54] However, this would mean that even 9 carat gold (which contains 37½% gold) would not fall within treasure trove. Partly for this reason, the better view seems to be that an object should simply contain a "substantial" amount of gold – a view endorsed by Dunn L.J. as well as by Lord Denning earlier in his judgment.[55] Both judges chose not to define "substantial" as a percentage although Lord Denning emphasized that he used the term in the sense of considerable, solid, big.[56] Debased silver coins in which there was no more than eighteen per cent silver were therefore not treasure trove. A coroner has subsequently held that a sixteenth-century coin from the Spanish Netherlands which contained 31% fine silver was not treasure trove.[57] The fact that the coins were intended to pass as silver is irrelevant; their actual metal content is critical.[58]

To be treasure trove, the objects must also have been hidden in the earth, a house or some other private place.[59] According to the Scottish Divisional Court in *Lord Advocate* v. *Aberdeen University* (1963),[60]

> The epithet "hidden" when used in connection with treasure means no more than "concealed" and refers to the state or condition in which the goods or articles are found by the finder . . .

Following Joseph Chitty, however, English courts and coroners have unfortunately embarked on the speculative inquiry whether "the owner, instead of hiding the treasure, casually lost it, or purposely parted with it, in such a manner that it is evident he intended to abandon the property altogether".[61] Inevitably, there is no direct evidence to whether or not the objects were deliberately hidden and the coroners and courts consequently infer this intention "from the relevant surrounding circumstances, and the motives that usually influence persons acting under such circumstances, according to the ordinary dictates of human nature".[62] If the objects were of considerable value at the time of their assumed burial, and if they are found close together, the courts will infer that "they were intentionally concealed for the purpose of security".[63]

The Crown must establish a *prima facie* case that the objects were hidden,[64] but it seems that even very slight evidence may discharge this onus,[65] and then the burden falls on the landowner to establish that the objects were not intentionally concealed with a view to later recovering them.

The problem with this definition of treasure trove is that it does not fully achieve the modern function of the prerogative "as a means of preserving interesting antiquities for the benefit of the nation as a whole"[66] as opposed to a means of defraying the cost of government, as was formerly the case. Because of the restriction of the prerogative to objects containing a substantial amount of gold or silver, it obviously does not cover many items of great archaeological importance such as precious stones and jewellery, stone or bronze statuary or textiles. Equally, because of the restriction to "hidden" goods, it does not extend to lost or, for that matter, abandoned objects, such as the Sutton Hoo burial ship. Yet it covers objects of no antiquarian or historical interest such as a gold cigarette case stolen and concealed by a thief a few decades ago.[67]

As noted by Dillon J. at first instance in the *Overton* case, the resolution of this problem is a matter for Parliament:

> The Crown cannot unilaterally extend its prerogative rights . . .
> The fact that the object achieved by the law of treasure trove is now different cannot warrant the courts, without Parliamentary sanction, either in expanding the prerogative to articles not of gold or silver, or in adopting a wider or more relaxed definition of what are articles of [gold or] silver.[68]

Both Dillon J. and Denning M.R. suggested that legislation be enacted to give the Crown significantly expanded rights over objects of archaeological interest.[69] However, the Bills introduced to achieve this object have been unsuccessful, at least partly because Government has been reluctant to see private property rights curtailed.[70]

(d) Rights in treasure

Where the objects found are not treasure trove, the occupier of the land where they are discovered has best claim to them.[71] The occupier's right has been explained on a variety of bases. It has been suggested that either the objects become part of the realty and consequently are "incapable of being lost";[72] or that a trespasser cannot succeed as against a landowner because a trespasser can take these things only "by further acts of trespass involving spoil and waste of the inheritance";[73] or that by virtue of the things being in or attached to the soil, they are already in the occupier's possession prior to their actual discovery.[74] In any event, the superior right of the occupier means that he can recover the objects from a finder who removes them from his land without his permission. Members of the public should therefore both obtain the occupier's consent before digging on land and seek to enter a contract with him as to the sharing of any finds.

Where the things found are treasure trove, the landowner is entitled to them only if he can show that one of his predecessors in title to the land received a franchise from the Crown expressly granting the right to treasure trove found on the land.[75] From at least the late eleventh until the early nineteenth centuries, the Crown made such grants to individual landowners, to corporate bodies like the Cities of London and Bristol, and to feudal entities like the Duchies of Cornwall and Lancaster.[76]

Subject to this exception, the Crown is absolutely entitled to all treasure trove. The finder has no right to the things he has discovered, but the Crown's practice since 1931 has been such as to turn its prerogative over treasure trove into a power of compulsory purchase with full compensation now being paid to the finder who at once reports his discovery to the police, coroner or other proper authority such as a local museum.[77] If a museum wishes to retain the treasure trove, the finder receives an *ex gratia,* tax-free payment which is meant to represent the market value of the objects. If no museum wants the objects, they are returned to the finder.

The Crown deals with treasure trove in this fashion in order to discourage finders from concealing, secretly dispersing and even melting down objects of archaeological interest which they find. The British Museum consequently emphasizes in its most recent note on treasure trove that the reward is made to the actual finder and not to the owner or occupier of the land, or to the employer, if found by an employee in the course of his work.[78] Even trespassing finders of treasure trove have been rewarded by the Crown.[79] Moreover, in a 1982 case, a man who discovered two pots containing coins in woods near Bradford was rewarded notwithstanding that he was thought to have breached a local council byelaw in digging up the pots in a public open space.[80]

The only requirement which appears to concern the Crown in its administration of rewards is the speed with which the finder reports his discovery. If he reports the find at once, he will be entitled to the reward; if he fails to report the reward, he is likely to receive either only a small percentage of the treasure's market value or no reward at all.[81] Between these two extremes, the Crown's attitude is unclear. In a recent case involving the discovery of silver coins at Taunton, the finder had initially shared the coins with two workmates and taken his share home, but after talking to a policeman friend he collected the coins again and gave them to the authorities; for this action he was paid the full value of the coins.[82] In the case of the Thetford treasure, the finder only reported his discovery six months after he had made it. He delayed reporting his find partly out of illness and partly out of uncertainty as to his legal position. By the time the Crown came to make its *ex gratia* payment, the finder had died. The Crown paid one third of the value of the treasure to his widow. Under some criticism, the Chief Secretary to the Treasury then promised to be tougher on any future occasion on persons who concealed treasure trove.[83]

(2) Things found on land

By virtue of the prerogative, which in this respect is now obsolete, the Crown is entitled to waifs (that is, things stolen and thrown away by a thief in his flight)[84] and estrays (that is, valuable animals of a tame or reclaimable nature which are found wandering in any manor or lordship, and whose owner is unknown).[85] Beyond these contexts, judges have struggled to establish a clear basis on which to adjudicate contests between finders of lost and abandoned property and occupiers of the land where the property is found. With the probable exception of where the finder of a chattel is a thief or trespasser, the key issue is whether the finder or the occupier first had possession of the objects in dispute. Commentators have generally argued that an occupier possesses those things on his land which are not possessed by someone else.[86] However, following the Court of Appeal's decision in *Parker* v. *British Airways Board* (1981),[87] "the position is reversed and it is clear that the finder will succeed against the occupier in a significant, if uncertain, range of circumstances".[88]

There has been no reported litigation over the rights of a trespassing or theftuous finder as against the occupier of the land. Where such a finder of a chattel obtains actual possession of the thing prior to the occupier of the relevant land, this possession could theoretically give the finder a better right to the thing than the landowner. The occupier's claim against a theftuous but non-trespassing finder appears particularly flimsy because the finder's wrongdoing is at the expense of the chattel's original owner rather than the occupier. Nevertheless, on the policy ground that "wrongdoers should not benefit from their wrongdoing", Donaldson L.J., who gave the leading judgment in *Parker,* stated that he had "no doubt" that an occupier of land has a better title to things lost or abandoned on it than a trespassing or theftuous finder.[89]

Where a member of the public without theftuous intent takes a chattel while lawfully on land, he *prima facie* has best claim to it in the absence of the original owner.[90] The onus of proof is on the occupier of the land to show better title, which he may do by showing that it was his manifest intention to exercise control over all things lost on his land.[91] If he had this intention, he will have been in possession of the chattel prior to the finder even though ignorant of the chattel's existence.

An occupier may expressly manifest his intention to control all things on his land, as by erecting appropriate notices. He may also accept or, like an innkeeper or carrier, be obliged to accept liability for chattels lost on his premises in which case the courts will infer that he intends to control these chattels and so has a better right to them than their finder. The courts may draw a similar inference if the occupier or his employees searched regularly for lost property, but they will not draw this inference simply because the occupier established a lost property office and gave his employees instructions as to the collection of lost property.[92]

In the absence of any specific action by the occupier in relation to lost and abandoned property, the determining factors in ascertaining his intention are the circumstances in which members of the public have access to the land in question. Where members of the public enter the land only by special invitation, as in the case of private houses, the occupier almost invariably will have better rights than the finder to property which has been lost or abandoned on the premises.[93] Where, on the other hand, members of the public have access as of right to land such as roads and parks, they will be able to retain the property which they find.[94]

In between these two extremes is a wide variety of "managed" premises to which members of the public habitually have access even though they do not enter as of right and sometimes must pay an admission charge. In relation to these places, it is now clear, as a result of the decision in *Parker* v. *British Airways Board,* that a member of the public who is lawfully on the premises will generally be able to retain what he finds unless the occupier has taken special steps in relation to property lost or abandoned there. The Court of Appeal affirmed the early decision, *Bridges* v. *Hawkesworth* (1851),[95] in which it was held that a commercial traveller who found a parcel containing money on the floor of a shop had a better right to the parcel than the shopkeeper. As a result, the court decided that the finder of a bracelet in the international executive lounge at Terminal One, Heathrow Airport, was entitled to the bracelet as against the British Airways Board which was the lessee of the lounge.[96] The court considered that the Board's restriction on use of the lounge to a particular category of person – first class passengers and some others – did not involve sufficient control of the lounge to give rise to the inference that the Board intended to possess all things in the lounge. Donaldson L.J. manifestly did not want to induce finders to be thieves by giving them no legal prospect of retaining what they found in such places. He rather wanted the law to conform to public practice, stating that "As the true owner has never come forward, it is a case of 'finders keepers'."[97]

II. DUTIES IN RELATION TO LOST AND HIDDEN THINGS

When a member of the public finds lost property in the countryside, he is not obliged to do anything in relation to what he finds.[98] If he chooses to leave the property where he finds it, he incurs no liability to its owner and also acquires no rights with respect to it.[99] If, however, he takes the property into his possession, he incurs a duty to the owner to take care of it. Possibly this duty will be breached only by gross negligence, but more likely it is a duty to take reasonable care.[100]

According to dicta by Donaldson L.J. in *Parker* v. *British Airways Board*[101] as well as by O'Sullivan J.A. in the Manitoba case, *Kowal* v. *Ellis* (1977),[102] the finder of lost property is also under a general duty to take such measures as in all the circumstances are reasonable to acquaint the owner of its finding. Neither judge specified the consequence of breaching this alleged duty; it is difficult to see how breach of it could give rise to a cause of action in either conversion, trespass or even negligence; and the better view probably is that the duty does not exist. An attempt by the finder of lost property to trace its owner appears significant only in relation to the criminal law.

By advertising the find or notifying the police, a finder who keeps the property can show that he is not "dishonestly" appropriating it and hence is not guilty of theft.[103] For the same reason, a finder of treasure who wishes to take the objects away should notify the police, the coroner or local museum if they appear to be treasure trove and should otherwise inform the occupier of the land.[104] If he does not do so, and removes the things, he will be guilty of theft unless he can show, for example, that he believed he had a legal right to take the things or that he did nothing to trace the owner because he believed that the owner could not be discovered by taking reasonable steps.[105]

NOTES TO CHAPTER 10

1. Limitation Act 1980, s. 2.
2. *Ibid.*, s. 4.
3. The one detailed treatment of this subject, relied on at various points below, is A. H. Hudson, "Is Divesting Abandonment Possible at Common Law?", (1984) 100 L.Q.R. 110–19.
4. 2 Justinian, *Institutes,* tit. 1, s. 47. See especially Buckland, p. 206.
5. See Ray Andrews Brown, *The Law of Personal Property,* 2nd ed., Chicago, Callaghan, 1955, pp. 8–10; 1 C.J.S., pp. 4–19.
6. 1 Bl. Comm. 296; 2 Bl. Comm. 9, 402.
7. The law is particularly confused in Australia. In *Johnstone & Wilmot Pty Ltd* v. *Kaine* (1928) 23 Tas. L.R. 43, 58, Clark J. in the Supreme Court of Tasmania held that intentional abandonment of a chattel does not divest ownership. In the Australian High Court decision in *Robinson* v. *Western Australian Museum* (1977) 51 A.L.J.R. 806, Stephen J. (at 820) suggested that abandonment may only divest ownership of sunken ships, whereas Jacobs J. (at 828) clearly accepted that ownership of all chattels could be divested by abandonment. In *Moorhouse* v. *Angus and Robertson (No. 1) Pty Ltd* [1981] N.S.W.L.R. 700, the New South Wales Court of Appeal did not decide the issue. New Zealand authority clearly favours the view that abandonment of a chattel divests ownership. See *Young* v. *Christchurch City Council* (1907) 10 G.L.R. 28, 31 *per* Chapman J.; *McFayden* v. *Wineti* (1909) 11 G.L.R. 345, 348 *per* Chapman J., noted with approval in *Morris* v. *Consolidated Goldfields of New Zealand Ltd* [1932] N.Z.L.R. 1271, 1277.
8. See Sir Frederick Pollock & R.S. Wright, *An Essay on Possession in the Common Law,* Oxford, Oxford University Press, 1888, p. 124; Holdsworth, vol. 7, p. 496; Vaines, p. 11; Roy Goode, *Commercial Law,* Harmondsworth, Penguin Books/Allen Lane, 1982, p. 58, n. 41.
9. Bracton, vol. 2, pp. 41, 129, 339.
10. Fleta, Book III, c. 1; S.S. 89, 1972, p. 2.

11. St German, *Doctor and Student,* Book II, c. 51; S.S. 91, 1974, p. 292.
12. Vol. 22, p. 409.
13. 1 Bl. Comm. 295; 2 Bl. Comm. 9, 402.
14. 1 H. Bl. 51, 59–60; 126 E.R. 32. The one English precedent usually cited against abandonment, *Haynes's Case* (1614) 12 Co. Rep. 113; 77 E.R. 1389, is, in fact, ambiguous on this issue. Instead of being interpreted as meaning that things cannot be abandoned, it may be taken as meaning that abandonment is effective only when a member of the public takes the thing, and that until then property remains in the original owner. See below, pp. 271–2.
15. 1 H. Bl. 51, 60; 126 E.R. 32, 37. Two members of the court, Lord Loughborough and Gould J., did not discuss this issue. Wilson J. discussed, but did not decide, this issue at 1 H. Bl. 51, 63; 126 E.R. 32, 39.
16. *Brown* v. *Mallett* (1848) 5 C.B. 599; 136 E.R. 1013; *White* v. *Crisp* (1854) 10 Ex. 312; 156 E.R. 463; *The Crystal, Arrow Shipping Co.* v. *Tyne Improvement Commissioners* [1894] A.C. 508; *Barraclough* v. *Brown* [1897] A.C. 615; *Boston Corporation* v. *Fenwick & Co.* (1923) 129 L.T. 766.
17. *R.* v. *Reed* (1842) Car. & M. 306; 174 E.R. 519; *R.* v. *Peters* (1843) 1 Car. & K.; 245 E.R. 795; *R.* v. *Edwards and Stacey* (1877) 13 Cox C.C. 384; *R.* v. *White* (1912) 107 L.T. 528; *Ellerman's Wilson Line Ltd* v. *Webster* [1952] 1 Lloyd's Rep. 179; *Williams* v. *Phillips* (1957) 41 C.A.R. 5. See also *Digby* v. *Heelan* (1952) 102 L.J. 287; *Police* v. *Moodley* [1975] 1 N.Z.L.R. 644.
18. (1886) 33 Ch. D. 562, 566, 568–9.
19. [1969] 2 Q.B. 152, 156. See also *Bentinck Ltd* v. *Cromwell Engineering Co.* [1971] 1 Q.B. 324.
20. Most influentially Holdsworth, vol. 7, p. 496, note 2. See also *Robinson* v. *Western Australian Museum* (1977) 51 A.L.J.R. 806, 820 *per* Stephen J.
21. Hudson, *op. cit.,* p. 117.
22. As to the intention not to confer an interest on anyone else, see 1 C.J.S., p. 5. See also Smith, p. 33. Note that the courts have occasionally used "abandonment" loosely – in contexts where the owner intended to transfer his interest to one party, as where the owner of a sunken ship gave up the wreck to his underwriter *(The Crystal, Arrow Shipping Co.* v. *Tyne Improvement Commissioners* [1894] A.C. 508; *Boston Corporation* v. *Fenwick & Co.* (1923) 129 L.T. 766) or where the purchaser of a lorry intended that the vehicle, which was unsatisfactory, would be repossessed by the vendor *(Johnstone and Wilmot Pty Ltd* v. *Kaine* (1923) 23 Tas. L.R. 43, 50).
23. *Steel* v. *Houghton* (1788) 1 H. Bl. 51, 63; 126 E.R. 32, 39 *per* Wilson J.; *Williams* v. *Phillips* (1957) 41 C.A.R. 5, 8 *per* Lord Goddard C.J.
24. *Haynes's Case* (1614) 12 Co. Rep. 113; 77 E.R. 1389 (in relation to a shroud used to bury a corpse); *R.* v. Edwards (1877) 13 Cox. C.C. 384 (in relation to the buried carcases of diseased pigs).
25. See *Hibbert* v. *McKiernan* [1948] 1 All E.R. 860, 861 *per* Lord Goddard C.J.; Smith, p. 33.
26. *Moorhouse* v. *Angus and Robertson (No. 1) Pty Ltd* [1981] 1 N.S.W.L.R. 700, 713 *per* Mahoney J.A.
27. *Ibid.,* pp. 706–7 *per* Samuels J.A.
28. (1843) 1 Car. & K. 245, 247; 174 E.R. 795.

29. (1977) 51 A.L.J.R. 806, 821 citing Annotation 63 A.L.R. 2d, at p. 1372.
30. See *McFadyen* v. *Wineti* (1908) 11 G.L.R. 345, 348 *per* Chapman J.
31. (1957) 41 C.A.R. 5.
32. *Ibid.*, p. 8.
33. *McFadyen* v. *Wineti* (1909) 11 G.L.R. 345, 348 *per* Chapman J.; *Moorhouse* v. *Angus and Robertson (No. 1) Pty Ltd* [1981] 1 N.S.W.L.R. 700, 706 *per* Samuels J.A.
34. See Buckland, pp. 206–7.
35. *Brown* v. *Mallett* (1848) 5 C.B. 599; 136 E.R. 1013; *White* v. *Crisp* (1854) 10 Ex. 312; 156 E.R. 463; *The Crystal, Arrow Shipping Co.* v. *Tyne Improvement Commissioners* [1894] A.C. 508, *Barraclough* v. *Brown* [1897] A.C. 615.
36. 12 Co. Rep. 113; 77 E.R. 1389.
37. *Ibid.*
38. See, in relation to maritime wrecks, *Brown* v. *Mallett* (1848) 5 C.B. 599; 136 E.R. 1013; *White* v. *Crisp* (1854) 10 Ex. 312; 156 E.R. 463. *The Crystal, Arrow Shipping Co.* v. *Tyne Improvement Commissioners* [1894] A.C. 508; *Barraclough* v. *Brown* [1897] A.C. 615. Compare in relation to chattels, *Dee Conservancy* v. *McDonnell* [1928] 2 K.B. 159, 163–4 *per* Scrutton L.J.
39. Ancient Monuments Board for England, *Twenty-Sixth Annual Report 1979*, London, H.M.S.O., 1980, p. 17.
40. Wireless Telegraphy Act 1949, s. 1(1).
41. See H.C. Deb., 5th series, vol. 988, cols 357–8 (written answers), 14 July 1980.
42. Wireless Telegraphy (Exemption) Regulations 1980 (S.I. 1980/1848).
43. *Ibid.*
44. *Treasure Hunting*, February 1978, pp. 5–8; August 1978, p. 35; *Daily Telegraph*, 8 May 1979, p. 3, col. 2.
45. Local Government Act 1972, s. 235(2).
46. See *Treasure Hunting*, April 1978, p. 5; April 1980, p. 5; April 1982, p. 53.
47. Ancient Monuments and Archaeological Areas Act 1979, s. 42(1).
48. *Ibid.*, s. 42(2).
49. *Ibid.*, s. 42(1).
50. *Ibid.*, s. 42(3).
51. Criminal Damage Act 1971, s. 1(1).
52. See Coroners Act 1887, s. 36; *Attorney-General* v. *Moore* [1893] 1 Ch. 676.
53. [1982] Ch. 277, 291 *per* Denning M.R.; 293 *per* Dunn L.J. Oliver L.J. at 294 agreed with both the other judges on the Court. Confusion had arisen because of conflicting definitions of treasure trove in the work of Bracton, Stanford, Coke, Blackstone and Chitty – which are quoted by Denning M.R. at 287–9.
54. [1982] Ch. 277, 292.
55. [1982] Ch. 277, 291–2 *per* Denning M.R.; 294 *per* Dunn L.J.
56. [1982] Ch. 277, 292 *per* Denning M.R.; 294 *per* Dunn L.J.
57. *The Times*, 28 November 1981, p. 7 col. 7 Compare "Treasure Trove", (1985) 82 Law Society Gazette 3092, 3093.
58. [1982] Ch. 277, 293 *per* Dunn L.J.
59. Coke, *Institutes*, Pt. III, c. 58; 1 Bl. Comm. 295.
60. 1963 S.L.T. 361, 366 *per* Lord Mackintosh.
61. Joseph Chitty, *A Treatise on the Law of the Prerogatives of the Crown*,

London, Butterworth, 1820, p. 152, quoted in *Attorney-General* v. *Trustees of the British Museum* [1903] 2 Ch. 598, 608 *per* Farwell J. Note that the concept of "abandonment" has generally been applied very loosely in the context of treasure trove. Goods relinquished as part of a burial process or as a votive offering are commonly said to have been "abandoned". See N.E. Palmer, "Treasure Trove and the Protection of Antiquities", (1981) 44 M.L.R. 178, 182; *Attorney-General* v. *Trustees of the British Museum* [1903] 2 Ch. 598, 609–11 *per* Farwell J. However, it is clear that a person does not abandon a thing if he intends that no-one else should use it. See above, p. 270.

62. *Attorney-General* v. *Trustees of the British Museum* [1903] 2 Ch. 598, 609 *per* Farwell J.

63. *Attorney-General* v. *Trustees of the British Museum* [1903] 2 Ch. 598, 609 *per* Farwell J. See also *Attorney-General of the Duchy of Lancaster* v. *G.E. Overton (Farms) Ltd.* [1981] Ch. 333, 343 *per* Dillon J.

64. *Attorney-General* v. *Trustees of the British Museum* [1903] 2 Ch. 598, 609 *per* Farwell J.

65. *Attorney-General of the Duchy of Lancaster* v. *G.E. Overton (Farms) Ltd* [1981] Ch. 333, 343 *per* Dillon J.

66. *Attorney-General of the Duchy of Lancaster* v. *G.E. Overton (Farms) Ltd.* [1981] Ch. 333, 341.

67. See Palmer, "Treasure Trove and the Protection of Antiquities", (1981) 44 M.L.R. 178, 180–3.

68. [1981] Ch. 333, 341.

69. [1981] Ch. 333, 341; [1982] Ch. 277, 293.

70. See H.L. Deb., 5th series, vol. 427, col. 30–1, 8 February 1982; vol. 429, col. 44, 5 April 1982, Earl of Avon.

71. *Attorney-General of the Duchy of Lancaster* v. *G.E. Overton Farms Ltd.* [1981] Ch. 333, 343 *per* Dillon J. See also *Elwes* v. *Brigg Gas Co.* (1886) 33 Ch. D. 562; *South Staffordshire Water Co.* v. *Sharman* [1896] 2 Q.B. 44; *Parker* v. *British Airways Board* [1982] Q.B. 1004, 1017–18 *per* Donaldson L.J.

72. *Parker* v. *British Airways Board* [1982] Q.B. 1004, 1010 *per* Donaldson L.J. See also *Elwes* v. *Brigg Gas Co.* (1886) 33 Ch. D. 562, 567 *per* Chitty J. However, note the criticisms of Paul Matthews, "Whose Body? People as Property", (1983) 36 Current Legal Problems 193, 203–4.

73. *Elwes* v. *Brigg Gas Co.* (1886) 33 Ch. D. 562, 568 *per* Chitty J. See also *Parker* v. *British Airways Board* [1982] Q.B. 1004, 1010 *per* Donaldson L.J.

74. *Elwes* v. *Brigg Gas Co.* (1886) 33 Ch. D. 562, 568 *per* Chitty J.; *South Staffordshire Water Co.* v. *Sharman* [1896] 2 Q.B. 44, 46–7 *per* Lord Russell C.J.

75. *Attorney-General* v. *Moore* [1893] 1 Ch. 676, 683 *per* Stirling J.; *Attorney-General* v. *Trustees of the British Museum* [1903] 2 Ch. 598, 611–14 *per* Farwell J.

76. See Sir George Hill, *Treasure Trove in Law and Practice,* Oxford, Clarendon Press, 1936, pp. 208–15, 244–51.

77. British Museum, *Treasure Trove,* July 1979. The development of these *ex gratia* payments is traced in Hill, *op. cit.,* p. 235. Note, there is a possibility that the relevant landowner may be able to recover the reward from the finder. See Palmer, *Bailment,* p. 876; Palmer,

"Treasurer Trove and the Protection of Antiquities", (1981) 44 M.L.R. 178, 185.
78. British Museum, *Treasure Trove*, July 1979.
79. *The Sunday Express*, 28 December 1980.
80. *The Times*, 22 October 1982, p. 4.
81. *The Economist*, 18 April 1981, p. 27.
82. *The Times*, 4 July 1980, p. 4, col. 7.
83. *The Guardian*, 4 February 1981, p. 13, cols 2–4; *The Economist*, 18 April 1981, p. 27; 29 August 1981, p. 24; *The Times*, 17 July 1981, p. 2, col. 2.
84. *Foxley's Case* (1600) 5 Co. Rep. 109a; 77 E.R. 224.
85. 1 Bl. Comm. 297.
86. See, especially, A.L. Goodhart, "Three Cases on Possession", (1928) 3 C.L.J. 195, 202–3, 207.
87. [1982] Q.B. 1004.
88. Simon Roberts, "More Lost than Found", (1982) 45 M.L.R. 683, 689.
89. [1982] Q.B. 1004, 1009. Sir David Cairns expressly chose not to comment on this issue. See *ibid.*, p. 1021.
90. *Ibid.*, p. 1018 *per* Donaldson L.J.
91. *Ibid.*, pp. 1018–19 *per* Donaldson L.J.; 1020 *per* Eveleigh L.J.; 1021 *per* Sir David Cairns.
92. *Ibid.*, p. 1018 *per* Donaldson L.J.
93. *Ibid.*, p. 1019 *per* Donaldson L.J.; 1020 *per* Eveleigh L.J.; 1021 *per* Sir David Cairns.
94. *Ibid.*, p. 1019 *per* Donaldson L.J.
95. 21 L.J.Q.B. 75.
96. The Court reached this conclusion without reference to the British Airports Authority (Lost Property) Regulations 1972 which appear to have been critical to the dispute. Regulation 8(4) provides that the sale of unclaimed lost property "shall not prejudice the right of any person whose rights have been divested by the sale to be paid the proportion due to him of the residue of the proceeds of the sale after deduction of the Authority's reasonable costs in connection with the sale". This provision may have been intended to cover only the original owners of the property. However, it appears also to allow the finder to claim the residue of the sale on the basis that he was in possession of the property before handing it over to the Authority and so had rights in it.
97. [1982] Q.B. 1004, 1019. See also at p. 1020 *per* Eveleigh L.J.
98. Note that a member of the public is not under an obligation to take possession of a stray dog but if he chooses to do so, section 4(1) of the Dogs Act 1906–28 requires him to return the dog to its owner or take it to the police station which is nearest to the place where the dog is found.
99. *Kowal* v. *Ellis* (1977) 76 D.L.R. (3d) 546, 547 *per* O'Sullivan J.A.
100. *Newman* v. *Bourne and Hollingsworth Ltd* (1915) 31 T.L.R. 209. See Palmer, *Bailment*, pp. 873–5.
101. [1982] Q.B. 1004, 1017.
102. (1977) 76 D.L.R. (3d) 546, 547.
103. Theft Act 1968, s. 1(1).
104. Note that at common law the taking of treasure trove was not larceny but there was an offence of concealing treasure trove. This offence has been abolished by section 32(1)(a) of the Theft Act 1968 but taking treasure trove may now be theft under section 1(1) of the 1968 Act.
105. Theft Act 1968, s. 2(1)(c).

Chapter 11

WRECK

When "wreck" – that is, ships, aircraft, their apparel and cargo[1] – is found in tidal waters or on the foreshore,[2] its original owner may reclaim his property within one year of it coming into the possession of the receiver of the wreck.[3] If the property is unclaimed within this period, it goes to the Crown by virtue of the prerogative, unless the Crown has granted a franchise of wreck in the place where the things were found. In all three cases a member of the public who finds the wreck is not entitled to keep it. However, he is entitled to a salvage award if he voluntarily performs salvage services in relation to the wreck and then delivers the property as soon as possible to the local receiver of wreck. A member of the public who fails to deliver wreck in this way not only forfeits any right he may have to a salvage award but is also subject to a variety of penalties.

I. THE FINDER OF WRECK

In an attempt to ensure the return of wreck to its original owner or its transfer to the Crown or grantee if unclaimed, the Merchant Shipping Act 1894 requires any person who finds wreck to deliver it to the local receiver.[4] A member of the public who fails to do so without reasonable cause not only commits an offence under the Act and forfeits any claim to salvage but is also liable to make a payment of twice the value of the wreck to the person entitled to it.[5]

II. THE SALVOR OF WRECK

The salvor's right to an award for his services is generally considered as the sole exception to the common law rule that a stranger who voluntarily intervenes to save the property of another is not entitled to remuneration or even reward.[6] The law's reward of the salvor of wreck but not things lost on land is conventionally attributed to "the character of mercantile enterprises, the nature of sea perils, and the fact that the thing saved was saved under great stress and exceptional circumstances".[7] Yet compared to the position of members of the public who find treasure trove, the legal treatment of salvors is neither so exceptional nor so generous. Whereas a mere finder of treasure trove is entitled as a matter of practice either to the treasure or to its full value,[8] the finder of wreck must deliver it to the receiver or face the heavy penalties outlined in the previous sub-section. He is only entitled to a reward if he has performed salvage services by saving at least part of the wreck from a danger which may be either immediate or contingent but must have in fact existed.[9] Even then he can ordinarily expect to receive at most half the value of the property saved.[10]

III. THE TAKING OF WRECK

A member of the public may take possession of wreck in order only to deliver it to the local receiver. If he retains the wreck, he is open to a range of actions and penalties (in addition to forfeiting any claim to salvage).[11] He may be sued for wrongful interference with goods or be liable under the Merchant Shipping Act to pay twice the value of the wreck to the person entitled thereto.[12] He may also commit two offences under the Merchant Shipping Act[13] and may also be guilty of theft since, regardless of whether the property is claimed by its owner, it is never *res nullius* but property "belonging to another" within the meaning of the Theft Act.[14]

NOTES TO CHAPTER 11

1. *The Gas Float Whitton (No. 2)* [1896] P.42: [1897] A.C. 337, criticized by R.G. Marsden, "Admiralty Droits and Salvage – Gas Float Whitton, No. II", (1899) 15 L.Q.R. 353–66; Aircraft (Wreck and Salvage) Order 1938, continued in force by the Civil Aviation Act 1982, s.89(4).
2. In *The Goring* [1986] 2 W.L.R. 219 Sheen J. held that the right to salvage remuneration extended to salvage services performed on inland waters. However, this decision was overturned by the Court of Appeal at [1987] 2 W.L.R. 1151, notwithstanding the vigorous dissent of Donaldson M.R.
3. Merchant Shipping Act 1894, s. 521.
4. *Ibid., s. 518.*
5. *Ibid.*

6. See, for example, *Crossley Vaines' Personal Property*, 5th ed., London, Butterworths, 1973, p. 426, citing *Binstead* v. *Buck* (1776) 2 Wm. Bl. 1117; 96 E.R. 660; *Nicholson* v. *Chapman* (1793) 2 Hy. Bl. 254; 126 E.R. 536. Compare, Robert Goff & Gareth Jones, *The Law of Restitution*, 2nd ed., London, Sweet & Maxwell, 1978, pp. 267–73.

7. *Falcke* v. *Scottish Imperial Insurance Co.* (1886) 34 Ch. D. 234, 248–9 *per* Bowen L.J.

8. See above, pp. 277–8.

9. *The Tojo Maru* [1972] A.C. 242, 293 *per* Lord Diplock; *The Ella Constance* (1864) 33 L.J. Adm. 189, 193 *per* Dr. Lushington; *The British Inventor* (1933) 45 Ll. L.R. 263.

10. *Kennedy's Civil Salvage,* 4th ed., London, Stevens, 1958, chapter 6, esp. at p. 162.

11. Merchant Shipping Act 1894, s. 518.

12. *Ibid.*

13. *Ibid.*, ss. 518, 519(2).

14. Theft Act 1968, s. 1(1).

INDEX